Confederate General of the West

Drawing by José Cisneros

Confederate General of the West

~: HENRY :~ HOPKINS ~: SIBLEY :~

of the West

by Jerry Thompson
Foreword by Frank E. Vandiver
Illustrations by Leonel Garza, Jr.
Maps by Oralia Roach

Texas A&M University Press
College Station

Originally published in 1987 by Northwestern State University Press,
Natchitoches, Louisiana

The paper used in this book meets the minimum requirements
of the American National Standard for Permanence
of Paper for Printed Library Materials, Z39.48-1984.
Binding materials have been chosen for durability.

Library of Congress Cataloging-in-Publication Data

Thompson, Jerry D.
    [Henry Hopkins Sibley]
    Confederate general of the West : Henry Hopkins Sibley / by Jerry
Thompson ; foreword by Frank E. Vandiver ; illustrated by Leonel
Garza, Jr. ; maps by Oralia Roach. — 1st Texas A&M University
Press ed.
       p.   cm.
    Originally published: Henry Hopkins Sibley. Natchitoches, La. :
Northwestern State University Press, 1987.
    Includes bibliographical references and index.
    ISBN 0-89096-705-9 (alk. paper)
    1. Sibley, Henry Hopkins, 1816–1886. 2. Generals—Confederate
States of America—Biography. 3. Confederate States of America. Army—
Biography. 4. New Mexico—History—Civil War, 1861–1865—Campaigns.
5. United States—History—Civil War, 1861–1865—Campaigns I. Title.
[E467.1.S56T48   1996]
973.7'42'092—dc20
[B]   95-50291
                                                                 CIP

For my Father and
the memory of my Mother

The Texas rebels and the Arizona cutthroats, like the ancient Goths and Vandals, are at the very gates, the portals of the Union, ready with batering cannons to demolish the fairest fabric of freedom ever devised by the wit of man.

—W. M. Need to Simon Cameron,
Ft. Fauntleroy, Territory of New Mexico,
September 27, 1861

Contents

Illustrations

Foreword

Biographies of Confederate generals abound; they range from sublime to ridiculous, often reflecting the nature of their subjects. By that analogy, Jerry Thompson's *Henry Hopkins Sibley: Confederate General of the West* ought to be a howler. It is, in fact, a fine book, one that traces the career of one of America's most curious soldiers.

A Louisianian, Sibley attended the U.S. Military Academy and went on to some fame as inventor of the "Sibley Tent," long a mainstay of army campsites. He fought Indians, served in the cavalry, fought in the ill-starred Seminole War and in Mexico, and at last joined the Confederate Army. In 1862 he led an expedition from Texas into New Mexico in the fervent hope that the southwest would be won for Jefferson Davis' new nation. Blunders, errors, ill-fortune, weather, even an unskilled enemy conspired to ruin the New Mexico venture. A retreat to Texas through bleak, barren, cold mountains recalled Napoleon's efforts in Russia to some of his Texas troops. So badly did he bungle that he should have been sacked. But his own relentlessly erroneous reports of brilliant success charmed President Davis and saved Sibley for further disasters.

A wide and skillful selection of sources enables Thompson to overcome the awkward absence of Sibley correspondence and to construct a full portrait of a man riddled by alcohol, by nagging illness and resurgent self-confidence. Often irascible, sometimes charming, never successful in the field. Sibley ranks a model misfit in war.

His ilk exist, do damage beyond common and deserve the attention Thompson offers precisely because the bungler has sometimes undone the work of skill. A career built on appearances, a reputation eluding reality, an impact exceeding achievement are betimes the rewards of mythology. So it was with Sibley until Thompson blew away the cover of time and luck. His Sibley is a sad knave, a man put by fate where he could do his worst.

Jerry Thompson has produced a major Civil War study, one long needed—and he produced it with literary grace, historical insight and considerable sympathy. Historians and general readers will enjoy his work and profit greatly from its lessons.

Frank E. Vandiver

Preface

Many individuals must be thanked for their help in the writing of this biography. Most important was my friend and colleague, Dennis Kriewald of the Laredo Junior College English Department to whom I am sincerely grateful for his grammatical expertise.

Martin H. Hall, late professor of history at the University of Texas at Arlington, read and commented on all except the last two chapters. An authority on Sibley's New Mexico campaign, Martin shared much data and helped to locate material that otherwise might have been overlooked.

Irving H. Bartlett, John F. Kennedy Professor of American History at the University of Massachusetts at Boston and biographer of Daniel Webster and Wendell Phillips, helped in providing what I believe to be a valid interpretation and explanation for Sibley's failures. His constructive criticisms and comments improved the biography. While Professor of History at Carnegie-Mellon University, Pittsburgh, Pennsylvania, Irving was motivational in many other ways.

Margaret Belcher, a great-great-granddaughter of General Sibley, was generous in entrusting family letters, genealogical data, and photographs to the author for his unrestricted use.

To Sylvan Sibley, purchasing agent at Northwestern State University of Louisiana and a great nephew of General Sibley, I am deeply indebted. Sylvan, who owns General Sibley's exquisite Civil War pistol, helped to open many doors in Natchitoches that otherwise might have remained closed. Sylvan also provided a tour of the old Sibley plantation at Grand Ecore.

To write a military biography it is essential to secure the cooperation of the National Archives. Elmer O. Parker, Assistant Chief, Old Military Branch, provided this cooperation. I am also thankful for the assistance of George Chalou and Jack Best of the Old Military Branch. George Chalou went out of his way to locate a consolidated file in the Quartermaster General's records that proved invaluable in exploring the origins of the Sibley tent and stove.

Page Christensen, professor of history, New Mexico Tech at Socorro, helped to nurture my interest in the Civil War in the Southwest as did Donald Cutter, professor of history at the University of New Mexico, under whose guidance I wrote a small biography of John Robert Baylor, Sibley's rival.

To my *Alpanista* friend Carlos Valle, instructor of radiological technology at Laredo Junior College, I am grateful for his comradeship in an exhausting climb of *Volcan Popocatepetl* in search of a better comprehension of Sibley's attempt on the mountain in 1848. Carlos, who previously trekked with me for five weeks in the Andes of Peru, almost lost his life from high altitude pulmonary endema on the mountain.

I must also thank Henry Sibley of Adams Basin, New York, a great-grandson of General Sibley and the closest living relative, for the use of several family documents. His son, Roger Sibley, Interlaken, New York, also went out of his way to be helpful. L. Boyd Finch of Tucson, Arizona, assisted in locating several articles written by General Sibley. Louisiana Congressman Jerry Huckaby helped in cutting through Washington's intolerable bureaucracy.

Rene Izquierdo, Thelma Acosta, Jorge Mendoza, Graciela Moreno, Susan Lyon, and Rodney Webb of the Yeary Library at Laredo Junior College must be thanked for their enthusiastic aid and assistance. My good friend, Harold B. Simpson of the Confederate Research Center, Hillsboro, Texas, provided data which helped in understanding Sibley's heavy drinking. Patricia Flores, Leticia Limon, Sara Pompa, and Berta Nava cheerfully helped in typing portions of the manuscript.

Finally, I would like to thank several others who extended their services: Don E. Carleton and his assistants at the Barker History Center, the University of Texas at Austin; Kenneth W. Rapp, assistant archivist, United States Military Academy at West Point; Shirley Hickman of the Henry E. Huntington Library, San Marino, California; Myra Ellen Jenkins, chief, Historical Services, New Mexico State Records Center and Archives at Santa Fe; Bruce Laverty, manuscript historian, Pennsylvania Historical Society, Philadelphia; John McDonough, manuscript historian at the Library of Congress;

Michael Wilson, assistant archivist, Rosenberg Library, Galveston; Collin B. Hamer, Jr., head, Louisiana Division of the New Orleans Public Library; Elizabeth A. H. John, Austin; Colonel T.V. Malmquist, professor of government, Laredo Junior College, Laredo, Texas; Mary G. Persyn, social science librarian, University of Miami, Oxford, Ohio; Milton C. Russell, Virginia State Library, Richmond; Robert T. Collins, Patent Office, United States Department of Commerce; Jim Dan Hill, Abilene, Texas; Bernard Pyron, Ironton, Missouri; B. D. Patterson, Hillsboro, Texas; Chris Vela, Laredo, Texas; Ralph Happel, park historian, National Park Service of the Department of the Interior, Fredericksburg and Spotsylvania National Military Park; Mrs. F. H. Beale, Museum of the Confederacy, Richmond, Virginia; Mary Elizabeth Amber, librarian, Lindenwood College, St. Charles, Missouri; Mrs. Donald B. Ehrlich, director of archives, Jackson County Historical Society, Independence, Missouri; and Mary Anne Fulton, reference librarian, Alderman Library, University of Virginia, Charlottesville.

Also, Beverly D. Bishop, associate archivist, Missouri Historical Society, St. Louis; Wilbur E. Meneray, manuscript librarian, Howard-Tilton Memorial Library, Tulane University, New Orleans; Sharon C. Davis, American Antiquarian Society, Worchester, Massachusetts; James J. Heslin, director, New York Historical Society; Robert L. Byrd, manuscripts librarian, William R. Perkins Library, Duke University, Durham, North Carolina; Colonel James S. Sibley, United States Air Force (retired); Lewis Leigh, Jr., Fairfax, Virginia; Morris Raphael, New Iberia, Louisiana; Marion C. Grinstead, El Paso; Michael Keleher, Albuquerque; Jo Emma Arechiga, Austin; William S. Wallace, archivist, Donnelly Library, New Mexico Highlands University, Las Vegas; Midan Ahmed Maher, director, Egyptian National Library, Cairo; Sheila W. Austrian, librarian, American University, Cairo; Hassan Nasr Shabaka of the Institute of Arab Research and Studies, Cairo; Mohamed Mahmoud El-Sorougy, professor of modern history, University of Riyadh, Saudi Arabia; Irby L. Knotts, Jr., Clerk of Natchitoches Parish Court, Natchitoches, Louisiana; and the staff of the Texas State Archives, Austin, Texas.

Editor Carol Wells and the publication staff of the press of Northwestern Louisiana State University deserve credit for seeing the manuscript through the difficult stages of publication. For all of his help and patience, I am especially grateful to John Price, Director of the NSU Press.

The author assumes full responsibility for any errors.

JT
Laredo, Texas
Summer, 1986

Introduction

It has often been said that the biographer comes to love his subject. This was difficult with General Henry Hopkins Sibley, possibly because none of his private correspondence has survived. Thus one sees only the cold, military side of the man. Only a portion of a single letter of a private nature was recovered, and even this came from a Texas newspaper. Over four hundred of his letters were found in the National Archives and at various other historical depositories, but none bears the intimate stamp so valuable to the historian. The intimacies that a captain at some scurvy-ridden and isolated post on the desolate southwestern frontier wrote his loved ones in the East and the details he communicated to his commander at departmental headquarters or his superiors in Washington were two separate and very different things.

My initial interest in General Sibley grew out of my fascination with the history of the American Southwest which began while I was a student at a small high school in the mountains of western New Mexico. This interest was enhanced at New Mexico Tech in Socorro, from where frequent visits to Valverde and Fort Craig were possible. My curiosity about the arid and desolate battlefield, the ruins of the old fort, and the men who fought and died there transcended other studies and involvements. Later, at the University of New Mexico, the pinon and ponderosa hillsides of Apache Canyon and Glorieta Pass, along with the rugged mountains of northern New Mexico, offered equal inspiration.

At Limpia Pass and Fort Davis in the Davis Mountains of west Texas the search for a more profound understanding of Sibley continued. In the Louisiana bayous and at the ruins of the old Sibley Plantation on the banks of the Red River, a few miles north of Natchitoches, Louisiana, the inquiry intensified. Even more revealing were the rain forests near the village of Medellín, not far from Vera Cruz, Mexico, and the awesome and frozen windswept 17,887 foot summit of *Volcan Popocatepetl*. In the final analysis such ventures proved almost as valuable as the exhaustive archival searches.

A major obstacle in compiling a biography of Brigadier General Henry Hopkins Sibley was the confusion brought about by a contemporary distant relative of his named Henry Hastings Sibley. General Henry Hastings Sibley was also a brigadier general but in the Union Army. Each man signed his name in the same manner: Henry H. Sibley.

A vivid contrast can be made between the two Sibleys. Henry Hastings Sibley was unique in that he was probably one of the few Union generals never to have seen a Confederate soldier during the entire war, having spent most of his career fighting Sioux Indians in Minnesota before becoming that state's first governor. Much of his correspondence, both official and private, has survived. Time and time again a tantalizing lead or reference in some library or archive promised valuable information on Henry Hopkins Sibley but turned out to be documents relating to his Minnesota relative. Futhermore, many historical dictionaries and encyclopedias have the two men confused, often crediting accomplishments of one to the other.

It became evident that Henry Hopkins Sibley did not fit any convenient historical stereotype. He was a complex individual. He possessed a fine intellect, yet he was often pitiably and embarrassingly vain. He was good natured and kind, yet he could be demanding and uncompromising. He was bold and defiant yet argumentative and unrealistic. Most of the time he was condescending and obstinate and only occasionally flexible and yielding. He was insensitive yet caring. He was loved by those who knew him best but often hated by those he led in battle. He was a schemer and grandiose dreamer yet convincing and professional. He was perhaps more the politician than the general.

Sibley could be vociferously articulate or meek and withdrawn. His inclinations toward military innovation are illustrative of a unique intelligence; on the other hand, he could not manage the simplest monetary matters. He was a cultured, well educated southern gentleman who loved his country but loved Louisiana and the South more. Like Robert E. Lee, he possessed no reverence for human bondage, but he admired and fought for an elitist culture that did. He was more the opportunist than the secessionist. His values were shaped by his native South; yet he was equally at home in the streets or drawing rooms of his Unionist wife's New York.

General Sibley was the kind of individual with whom men loved to talk around some frontier encampment or Civil War bivouac. He was not the type, however, to inspire the enlightened soldier to follow him eagerly into battle—perhaps in Mexico, but not at Valverde, not at Fort Bisland, and certainly not in Egypt.

I do not presume to understand all that is to be known about the man. Only one thing is certain; he possessed an extremely paradoxical character. Perhaps more important for the historian is the fact that he had visions of conquests and campaigns he was incapable of leading.

There is little doubt that General Henry Hopkins Sibley failed as a military leader. Consequently, he must rank as one of the worst generals to serve the southern Confederacy. Heavy drinking and a chronic illness, evident long before the Civil War, were his primary undoing. The drinking brought numerous reprimands, a near court-martial in Mexico, a lengthy personal feud with his superior in Kansas, a court-martial in Utah, and controversy during the Navajo Campaign of 1860. In 1863 his weakness for the bottle caused his court-martial in Louisiana and a decade later, expulsion and disgrace in Egypt.

In the end there was considerable sorrow, not respect, for the old general. He fought the good fight and lost. His cantankerous individualism was unorthodox and contrary to military philosophy. Somehow he always marched to Thoreau's "different drummer." He was a romantic warrior lost and misplaced in the contemporary world. Regardless, he has his place in history.

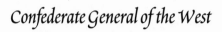

Confederate General of the West

Chapter I

From Natchitoches to West Point

The mood was somber, almost depressing, as the general court-martial convened at Confederate Headquarters, Shreveport, Louisiana, August 15, 1863. The brigadier general stood before his ten fellow officers, accused of deserting his command, refusing to attack the enemy, and allowing Federal prisoners to be overtaken and liberated by advancing Yankees. It was not the general's first court-martial. There had been another, but that had been in another era under different circumstances, and then he had worn a different uniform.[1]

The forty-seven year old windburnt general was fierce looking with beak-like nose, a jutting, pugnacious chin, and a bristling, sweeping, handlebar moustache that grew down past the corners of his mouth.[2] With brooding eyes set under heavy brows, he glared at members of the court. His wizened, fatigued face, his bloodshot eyes, and his al-

[1] General Orders No. 47, 15 September 1863; Special Orders No. 91, 21 July 1863, Letters Received, Trans-Mississippi Department, Confederate War Department, Record Group 109, The National Archives, Washington, D.C.

[2] J.M. Scammell to Charles W. Hackett, 7 October 1948, *Southwestern Historical Quarterly*, 52 (April 1949), 450; Shelby Foote, *The Civil War: Fort Sumter to Perryville* (New York, 1958), 294.

most dejected mood reflected the heavy drinking that had deteriorated and withered his brilliant mind. His once-promising career had at long last entered its final chapter.

At Natchitoches, Louisiana, some seventy miles down the muddy waters of the Red River from Confederate Headquarters, Henry Hopkins Sibley had been born on May 25, 1816, the youngest child of Samuel Hopkins Sibley and Margaret I. McDonald.

Henry was a descendant of one of America's oldest and proudest families—a family with a long record of civil and military distinction. His ancestry can be traced to the Norman conquest of England in 1066 when the Sibley family apparently settled near the Scottish border and became culturally Scottish as well as English.[3]

Henry Hopkins was a seventh-generation descendant of John Sibley, a Puritan layman, who along with his brother Richard, sailed to Salem, Massachusetts, from Dorsetshire, England, with Governor John Winthrop in 1629. From Salem, John Sibley and his wife moved a few miles up the Massachusetts coast to Manchester, acquired land, and reared nine children.

One of John and Sarah Sibley's sons, Joseph, was an original settler of Sutton, a small village a few miles south of Worcester in central Massachusetts. At Sutton, Joseph and his wife Susanna raised six sons and one daughter of whom the second oldest son, John, (Henry's great-great-grandfather) was born in September 1687, and lived to the ripe old age of ninety-five. This John's youngest son, Timothy, Henry's great-grandfather, was born at Sutton in 1727.

Timothy, a large man, was cold, austere, terse, and well-respected for his aristocratic manners and enviable wealth. Described by a grandson as a "gentleman of the old school," Timothy was undeniably one of Sutton's leading political figures, rarely seen without his cocked hat, powdered wig, russet-topped boots, and silver-plated spurs.[4] When the American Revolution swept through the New England countryside in the 1770s, Timothy, without hesitation, joined

---

[3] James Scarborough Sibley, *The Sibley Family in America, 1629–1972* (Honolulu, 1972), 10. Genealogically, an excellent treatment of the Sibley Family in early America can be found in Nathaniel West, *The Ancestry, Life and Times of Hon. Henry Hastings Sibley* (St. Paul, 1889). Also, Christopher Columbus Baldwin to John Sibley, 15 November 1832, George Champlin Sibley Papers, Missouri Historical Society, St. Louis, Missouri; Charles T. Jones, Jr., *George Champlin Sibley: The Prairie Puritan* (Independence, 1970), 1–14. Early spellings of the name were Sybeli, Sibely, and Sibilie.

[4] Sibley, *The Sibley Family in America,* p. 26.

a Committee of Correspondence. Later he rose to the rank of lieutenant-colonel in a regiment commanded by Colonel Ebenezer Learned. Timothy lived to see another war against the British, dying at the age of ninety-one in 1818.

Timothy and his second wife Anna raised nine hardy children, including twins John and Stephen, born some nineteen years before the revolution. John, after studying medicine, also took up arms for the Massachusetts Rebels, serving as a surgeon's mate at Fort Ticonderoga in a regiment commanded by Colonel Ephrain Wheelock and later in the same capacity in a regiment commanded by Colonel Danforth Keyes.[5] Moving to Great Barrington, a village on the Housatonic River in the mountains of western Massachusetts, the ambitious physician resumed his profession and married Elizabeth Hopkins, from whom Henry was to inherit his middle name. Two sons were born to Elizabeth and John Sibley: George Champlin and Samuel Hopkins, Henry's father.

For unknown reasons, John Sibley left his wife in Massachusetts, sailed down the Atlantic coast, and took up residence at Fayetteville, on the Cape Fear River, in south central North Carolina. Here the doctor bought a large farm, acquired town property, established the *Fayetteville Gazette*, and amassed a small fortune. His wife eventually joined him at Fayetteville but died shortly thereafter in 1790. Within one year, the Doctor had remarried; moreover, when his newspaper plant was destroyed by fire he set out again, this time to Louisiana.[6]

In Louisiana, Sibley made friends with William Charles Coe Claiborne, governor of the territory. The doctor, a cultured and refined gentleman, appears to have made a good impression on the governor. Claiborne wrote President Thomas Jefferson, who was always interested in western exploration, suggesting that Dr. Sibley be employed by the government to obtain information on the Indian tribes living in the southwestern part of the territory. Thus, in March 1803, one month before the purchase of Louisiana from the French, the eastern renegade now turned western explorer, sailed up the Red River in an open skiff. As he pushed northward and westward, the doctor filled notebooks with detailed data on the flora and fauna, the topography

[5] Ibid., p. 48.
[6] Julia Kathryn Garrett, "Doctor John Sibley and the Louisiana-Texas Frontier, 1803–1814," *Southwestern Historical Quarterly*, 45 (January 1942), 287.

of the land and the characteristics of its inhabitants, much of which was reported to President Jefferson and Secretary of War Henry Dearborn.[7] Dr. Sibley was in many ways to western Louisiana what Meriweather Lewis and William Clark were to the Oregon country.

At Natchitoches Dr. Sibley found a booming town of forty or fifty families, mostly French, clustered on the west bank of the Red River. Natchitoches was a beautiful place. Fish and fowl were abundant, and great pine and oak forests came to within three hundred yards of the river.[8]

With the purchase of Louisiana, Americans like Dr. John Sibley were now migrating by the thousands to the newly-acquired wilderness. Ever westward they came. From the Carolinas, from Virginia, from Tennessee, and Kentucky they came. Settlers came from Europe. Some came for adventure; others came to get rich. A few came to find something. Others came to get away from something. A handful, like Dr. Sibley, came seeking adventure and fame.

Greatly impressed with Natchitoches, the doctor decided to make his home there. Within months he managed to obtain a job as surgeon to the American soldiers stationed at Fort Claiborne, which occupied about two acres of land on a hill near the river. In 1804 the doctor was appointed Indian Agent for the territory, and he set out to visit the tribes of the area. Making his way up the Red River to its junction with the Ouachita, the doctor was able to visit several Indian tribes in the area, always taking copious notes on the Indians' numbers, dialects, and culture. Much of the information was then reported to Washington.[9]

In 1813, against the wishes of his two oldest sons, Dr. Sibley married again, this time to Eulalie Malige, who at twenty-six was thirty years younger than he. To complicate matters it was widely rumored

[7] Th. Jefferson to J.S. Johnston, 13 February 1825, Josiah Stoddard Johnston Papers, Pennsylvania Historical Society, Philadelphia, Pennsylvania; G.P. Whittington, "Dr. John Sibley of Natchitoches, 1757–1837," *Louisiana Historical Quarterly*, 10 (October 1927), 470; John Sibley, *An Account of Louisiana, 1803* (Boston, n.d.); Thomas Jefferson, *Travels in the Interior Parts of America, Communicating Discoveries Made in Exploring the Missouri, Red River and Washita, by Captains Lewis and Clark, Dr. Sibley, and Mr. Dunbar* (London, 1807).

[8] Milton Dunn, "History of Natchitoches," *Louisiana Historical Quarterly*, 3 (January 1920), 36.

[9] John Sibley, *A Report from Natchitoches in 1807*, intro., Annie Heloise Abel (New York, 1922).

in Natchitoches that Eulalie, who would outlive the doctor by forty years, was mulatto. Four children—Henrietta, Helena, Horatio, and Rufus—were born of this marriage.

At Grand Ecore on the Red River, about five miles north of Natchitoches, the doctor purchased five hundred acres of land. Here, high on the reddish sandstone bluffs, along the west bank of the river, he built a brick manor. The setting was serene and peaceful. Towering pine and oak trees hung with grey Spanish moss dotted the spacious grounds. From the mansion riverboats could be seen going and coming along the murky waters of the Red River. The barges and steamers frequently docked only a few hundred yards downriver from the Sibley mansion. On the east banks of the river, cotton and corn fields, clearly visible from the mansion and encompassing several hundred acres, stretched eastward across the rich Louisiana bottomland to the horizon.[10]

As early as February of 1803 and continuing for several years, Dr. Sibley, who corresponded regularly with his sons in North Carolina, tried in vain to coax Samuel Hopkins westward by referring to Louisiana as the "finest country in the world" and promising a good-paying job working for the government. Calling Samuel "as capable as his brother" George and of "good conduct in every respect," Dr. Sibley was unable, however, to obtain a position for the younger son.[11]

In 1811, with war clouds gathering in the East, Samuel finally decided to join his father in Louisiana.[12] Samuel had married Margaret I. McDonald, a native of Jamaica, at Wilmington, North Carolina, in June of 1809. Their first child, Ann Hopkins, was born the following year, shortly before Samuel moved to Louisiana. At Natchitoches Elizabeth was born a year later, in December 1811, and John George in March 1814.

When Samuel arrived at Natchitoches the western frontier of Louisiana was more agitated by the revolution in Texas than by the war with Great Britain. Samuel saw his father write letters of introduction for the Mexican revolutionary José Bernardo Gutiérrez de Lara

[10] Sibley, *The Sibley Family in America*, p. 49; Dunn, p. 38.

[11] John Sibley to Samuel Hopkins Sibley, 28 February 1803, Johnston Papers; John Sibley to Samuel Hopkins Sibley, 30 June 1807, Johnston Papers; John Sibley to Henry Dearborn, 12 October 1808, Julia Kathryn Garrett, ed., "Dr. John Sibley and the Louisiana Texas Frontier, 1803–1814," *Southwestern Historical Quarterly*, 48 (July 1943).

[12] George Sibley to Saml. H. Sibley, 23 April 1812, Sibley Papers.

and lend Gutierrez two hundred dollars for a trip to Washington. He later observed the preparations in Natchitoches for the Gutiérrez-Magee invasion of Texas.[13] Although the fires of rebellion in Texas were eventually crushed, filibustering expeditions continued long into 1814 with the endeavors of General José Alvarado and Dr. John Hamilton.

Samuel, with the political influence of his father and the help of his brother-in-law Josiah Stoddard Johnston who was parish judge, was appointed the first Parish Clerk of Court in 1815. He remained in that position for the next eight years.[14]

While serving as parish clerk, Samuel set out to create a financial empire at Natchitoches, hoping to follow in the footsteps of his father. He built a large brick mansion, which he called Court Hill, on a rise only a few hundred yards from the banks of the Red River. Another quaint-looking house with a steep French roof at the corner of Second and St. Denis Street near the river banks, coupled with a nearby lot, was purchased for $600. It was thus into moderate wealth that Henry Hopkins Sibley was born on May 25, 1816. To distinguish the boy from his uncle for whom he was named, family members, especially Dr. John, referred to the youngster as Little Henry.

From the time of Little Henry's birth, Samuel, never happy in Louisiana, contemplated joining his brother George in Missouri to engage in commerce. Samuel's displeasure with Louisiana was deepened in 1817 when heavy rains flooded the Red River, washing away bridges, drowning thousands of cattle and horses, and ruining much of Dr. John's crops.[15]

Henry's mother Margaret was an interesting contrast to his father. Margaret was a deeply proud and pious woman with an unlimited amount of patience. In many ways she appears to have been typical of the model southern frontier woman. She supported her husband in whatever business adventures he decided to undertake, even extensive real estate investments, and in whatever hardships the family

[13] Garrett, "Doctor John Sibley and the Louisiana-Texas Frontier, 1803–1814," p. 291.

[14] Succession Records in the Case of Samuel Hopkins Sibley, Clerk of Court Records, Natchitoches Parish Courthouse, Natchitoches, Louisiana.

[15] John Sibley to George C. Sibley, 29 January 1817; George C. Sibley to Saml. H. Sibley, 28 September 1816; George C. Sibley to Saml. H. Sibley, 10 July 1819; Sibley Papers.

might encounter.[16] She was mainly concerned with the ever present duty of bearing and raising children, but with the help of two household servants she did have time for the social life of Natchitoches, however, limited it might be.

Much of Little Henry's childhood was spent amid the tall pines and stately oaks of Natchitoches. It was an exhilarating time for a young boy. Steamboats were now regularly plying their way up the Red River, transporting supplies to the residents of Natchitoches and the settlements which were emerging further westward along the Camino Real in the piney woods of western Louisiana. Many of the riverboats anchored only a few yards from Natchitoches' two-storied businesses on Main Street. The steamers' whistles were easily audible at stately Court Hill behind the town.

Well into Little Henry's youth Natchitoches continued to be a prosperous settlement. In 1821 Dr. John reported the town to be "full of strangers and every place crowded and goods and wagons carrying things out to Sabine and Nacogdoches and droves of horses and mules packing for San Antonio."[17] Caught in the excitement of the times, Samuel bought four slaves and expanded his real estate holdings by purchasing a large tract of land at Laurel Springs some ten miles west of Natchitoches. Here in the piney woods along the Camino Real, five year-old Henry along with Ann, Elizabeth, and John George, came to spend his summers. To avoid the long and unhealthful summers of Natchitoches and Grand Ecore, Dr. John frequently sent his own children, especially Henrietta, a year older than Little Henry, and Helena, a year younger, to Laurel Springs.[18] In 1821 Henry's uncle, Robert McDonald, with the boy's maternal grandmother, joined the family at Laurel Springs. By fall Henry was reported to be at Dr. John's plantation at Grand Ecore, and by November he was back at Court Hill in Natchitoches. Henry would later reflect on his childhood and

[16] Everett Dick, *The Dixie Frontier* (New York, 1964), 274.

[17] John Sibley to Josiah S. Johnston, 26 June 1821; John Sibley to Josiah Johnston, 20 October 1821; John Sibley to Ann Eliza, 24 December 1821; Johnston Papers; Robert Bruce L. Ardoin, comp., *Louisiana Census Records: Iberville, Natchitoches, Pointe Coupée, and Rapides Parishes, 1810 and 1820,* II (Baltimore, 1972), 64–65, Louis Raphael Nardini, Sr., *My Historic Natchitoches, Louisiana and Its Environment* (Natchitoches, 1963), 153.

[18] John Sibley to Josiah S. Johnston, 14 August 1821, Johnston Papers.

refer to himself as being very "precocious," someone who was quite advanced mentally despite his youth.[19]

That year a severe drought and searing heat had scorched the north Louisiana farmland and destroyed much of Dr. John's corn and cotton. The Red River was as low as many old timers could remember. By Christmas the river was frozen, and Dr. John's thermometer had dropped to an unprecedented fourteen degrees.

During this time Henry took what was probably more than just a curious glimpse of the United States Army which was becoming an ever-increasing part of the Louisiana frontier. In 1820 Fort Selden was established by the Seventh United States Infantry on Bayou Pierre, upriver from Grand Ecore. The commanding officer of the post was Colonel Zachary Taylor, with whom young Henry would become familiar in the years to come. Two years later most of the troops were withdrawn, and a new post, Cantonment Jesup, was built on the Camino Real west of Natchitoches.[20] To a young boy the soldiers who came through Grand Ecore and Natchitoches marching ever westward, fulfilling what was conceptualized as Manifest Destiny, would have undoubtedly made a big impression.

Three uncles played prominent roles in Little Henry's early life. First, there was George Champlin Sibley, who, like his brother Samuel, had followed his father westward. Displeased with Louisiana, George had gone north to Missouri. George especially loathed "the great number of slaves in the Red River Country." To be "surrounded by a great majority of miserable wretches who only want a safe opportunity to cut the throats of their masters," was not George's "idea of comfort and worldly happiness."[21] Although a slave owner himself, George greatly preferred Missouri where there were "few slaves," most of whom were "well clothed and kindly treated." This adulation for Missouri led George to attempt for several years unsuccessfully to lure his brother northward.

In 1808 George sailed with an expedition of robust frontiersmen up

---

[19] [Henry H. Sibley], "Recollections of the School for Verdants," *Popular Monthly*, (15 August 1884), 328.

[20] Dunn, p. 41.

[21] George C. Sibley to Saml. H. Sibley, 25 September 1813, Sibley Papers. For George Champlin Sibley see: George Champlin Sibley, *The Road to Santa Fe, the Journal and Diaries of George Champlin Sibley*, ed. Kate L. Gregg, (Albuquerque, 1952); Jones, *George Champlin Sibley: The Prairie Puritan.*

the Missouri River to the site of present Sibley, Jackson County, Missouri, and built Fort Osage. He was determined, as he told his brother Samuel, to "go into Indian Country and live more comfortably than any person who went there before." George became the newly appointed factor at the post and, accompanied by a band of Osage warriors, he explored the area of the Grand Saline River and visited several Indian tribes in the Kansas area. During his tenure at Fort Osage, George accused several fur traders of swindling the Indians, an act for which he was severely criticized. While at the fort in 1825, George was appointed by President John Quincy Adams as a commissioner to survey a road, which was to become the Santa Fe Trail, across the so-called Great American Desert to the Mexican Boundary. Returning to Missouri from Santa Fe, the frontiersman retired from government service to make his home at St. Charles were he built a large mansion. Together with his liberal wife Mary, the Prairie Puritan became a crusader in the fight for women's rights. A school for girls which he established on a nearby tract of land later became Lindenwood College. The high-minded and moral George evidenced much of his father's blood by being an adventurer, an uncompromising Whig, and a profiteer in endless land speculation resulting in burdensome debt.

Another uncle, Robert Henry, a half-brother of George and Samuel, also played a prominent role in the boy's early life. Robert was born in North Carolina but had followed his father and two older brothers westward to Louisiana where he had settled in Rapides Parish, downriver from Natchitoches. A distinguished physician like his father, Robert also served for a period as an assistant surgeon in the United States Army. Robert built a large plantation in the piney woods near Alexandria which he called Mt. Elon.[22]

Another uncle, Josiah Stoddard Johnston, a half-brother of Albert Sidney Johnston, also played an important role in the boy's early years. Married to Dr. John's daughter Eliza, who was said to have been a "renowned beauty," Josiah had settled in Alexandria where he became a distinguished lawyer and statesman. Never one to shy away from a brawl, Josiah nevertheless was well known in Alexandria for his fairness in settling disputes. After serving as parish judge and congressman, Josiah was appointed United States senator in 1823, was

[22] Sibley, *The Sibley Family in America*, p. 48.

elected to the position in 1824, and reelected in 1830, at which time he became a close friend of Henry Clay. Senator Johnston appears to have been attracted to Little Henry largely as a result of the promptings of Dr. John with whom the senator maintained a prolific correspondence. Josiah frequently acted as a legal and personal counselor for the Sibley clan in Louisiana and Missouri, and with his wife Eliza was said to have lived the gracious life which consisted of "dinners, balls, horsemanship, and theatricals."[23]

Many years later, in the twilight of his life, Henry would fondly look back on his childhood, recollecting joyous childhood experiences at Laurel Springs, Mt. Elon, and the Sibley Plantation at Grand Ecore. Henry remembered how many of the wealthy planters in both Rapides and Natchitoches Parish had two residences. One was "somewhat pretentious in its surroundings, on the plantation; the other more simple but quite as convenient, in the pine hills, where water was more abundant, limpid, and pure; and the air, impregnated with the healthful and refreshing odor of the pine, was invigorating and lovely."[24] At both locations the kitchen was invariably located behind the larger manor house. It was here that all the house servants would rendezvous in the evening. "The white children would delight in joining the social circle," Henry nostalgically reminisced, "listening to the ghost-stories, traditions and negro lore, or joining in an impromptu dance to the music of a good banjo, monotonously thrummed by some musical aspirant." Sometimes a plump, fat opossum would be cooked and stuffed with breadcrumbs and pecans, surrounded with sweet potatoes, and accompanied with a pot of hominy. "There's nothing half so delicious within my recollection," Henry recalled. He also remembered how the uninhibited antics of the participants added "a zest to the evening's entertainment."[25]

It was in the fall that "not a breath of air disturbed the foliage; the great pine-trees slept, and dreamed in their majestic splendor; all nature was quiet and in repose and seemed to invite the fairies to their nocturnal sports." With the Louisiana flora turning golden, Henry often assisted the slaves in "corn shucking" and in "coon and possum"

---

[23] Charles P. Roland, *Albert Sidney Johnston: Soldier of Three Republics* (Austin, 1964), 11; Melvin J. White, "Josiah Stoddard Johnston," *Dictionary of American Biography*, ed. Dumas Malone, V (New York, 1961), 147.

[24] [Sibley], "Recollections of the School for Verdants," p. 328.

[25] Ibid., p. 330.

hunts. Mischievously, the white children would dress up in white sheets like ghosts and "frighten the darkies in the kitchen."[26] To say the least, his conception of his early adolescence was highly romantic.

Henry would also remember his fraternization with several of the Indian tribes of the area, especially the Caddo and Choctaw. Frequently the Indians were seen on the streets of Natchitoches or at the Sibley Plantation at Grand Ecore. On one occasion in 1825, when he was only nine, Henry recalled how more than a hundred of the "most stalwart" Caddo and Choctaw gathered on the village common in Natchitoches for a game of "racket" or lacrosse. Hundreds of whites, slaves, freemen, and Indians, "eager and excited," watched as the game was "most violently contested;" the victors stripping their opponents of all their possessions, leaving them to beg in the streets.[27]

By the early 1820s the political fortunes of the Louisiana Sibleys were tottering. Dr. John, the patriarch of the family, was removed as Indian agent in 1815 in what the family called a "pitiful intrigue."[28] Financial difficulties forced the doctor to sell ten of his twenty slaves. There were also fears that the plantation at Grand Ecore, highly cherished by the family, would be lost. The doctor fought back, and went on to become a captain of militia, justice of the peace, parish judge, and state senator.

In 1823, a kidney ailment caused the death of Henry's father. The misfortune would have been as traumatic for Henry as for any other youngster of seven and would have been reinforced by the family disasters which followed. Samuel, who had been "greatly afflicted" and in pain for several months prior to his death had temporarily rallied in early October from one of Dr. John's herbal medicines. By early November the "poor fellow," to use the physician father's words, was in even worse pain and with his grieving family by his bedside, died on November 17 at the age of thirty-nine.[29] Although it is impossible to determine Henry's exact relationship with his father, it is safe to assume that because Henry was the youngest of four children, the two

[26] Ibid.

[27] [Henry H. Sibley], "Indian Gambling," *Frank Leslie's Chimney Corner*, (11 February 1882), 245.

[28] George Champlin Sibley to Saml. H. Sibley, 21 January 1815, Sibley Papers.

[29] John Sibley to Josiah S. Johnston, 15 October 1823, Johnston Papers.

were close.[30] In Henry's eyes his mother was best suited to help him grasp and internalize the tragic event. Margaret did as much as she could to ease the sense of loss and pain, but there were three other children with whom she must share her sympathy. Besides sorrowing, she now was acutely aware of the burden of being financially responsible for her family.

The full repercussions of Samuel's death were yet to be completely felt. During his tenure as clerk of the parish court, Samuel had mortgaged the family property and had run up debts into the thousands of dollars to finance his real estate speculation.[31] Although Samuel had amassed a "considerable estate," Margaret faced an ever-increasing number of creditors demanding their share of the estate.

Margaret pleaded with family members to help her save her property. Uncle George at Fort Osage wrote that he could do little as he too was deeply in debt. Uncle Henry in Rapides Parish was having his share of financial problems, being unable to collect a considerable sum of money owed him, and could do little. He came north in the summer of 1824 to give Margaret his moral support. Margaret also pleaded with Senator Johnston in Washington. Johnston replied that he saw no alternative to selling the family land.[32] Dr. John, always in the middle of family affairs, was in a complicated financial and legal predicament since he had sold a considerable amount of land and property to his son for which he had never been paid.

At a "family meeting" in the Parish Judge's office at which Dr. John, Margaret's brother Robert McDonald, Juan Cortez, Bernard Leonard, and several other friends of the family were present, it was finally decided that Margaret had no choice but to sell the family property at a

---

[30] Erna Furman, *A Child's Parent Dies, Studies in Childhood Bereavement* (New Haven, 1974), 23; Interview, Sara A. Cabello, Psychotherapist, Laredo, Texas, 3 September 1980; Interview, Richard Hughes, Psychologist, Laredo, Texas, 4 September 1980.

[31] Succession Records in the Case of Samuel Hopkins Sibley, Parish Clerk of Court Records, Natchitoches Parish Courthouse, Natchitoches, Louisiana. These records contain a list of individuals who owed Samuel Sibley $16,095.63. The list of debtors is nine pages long with the amounts owed no more than a few dollars. The accounts date as early as 1813 and were evidently for services Samuel Sibley performed while parish clerk. Evidently the executors of the estate did not think the accounts collectable.

[32] M. Sibley to Josiah S. Johnston, 10 August 1824; P.A. Post to J.S. Johnston, 5 December 1824; Johnston Papers.

public auction. Everything was appraised and advertised for sale, including the family clock, harnesses, gigs, trunks, a scythe, and Jenny, a family slave.[33] The day before the auction, the parish judge arrived at Court Hill to inform Margaret that he had been petitioned by Samuel's numerous creditors to stop the auction. Claiming that Samuel owed them thousands of dollars and fearing they would not be able to collect their money, the creditors had asked for an injunction to which the judge had agreed.

Late into 1825 Margaret, obviously disturbed and angry, continued to struggle with the family's financial insecurity. The family problems were especially hard on Henry's older sister Ann, who, Margaret reported, was "mortified" at the idea of losing "house and home." In a rather lengthy battle, Margaret was forced to hire a lawyer to represent herself and the four children. After several months of legal maneuvering, during which time family friends put up $14,000 to save the Sibley property from foreclosure, Dr. John was able to get James P. Harrison, whom Margaret distrusted, disqualified as administrator of the estate and had a friend, Honore F. DeBlieux, appointed. After Margaret swore in court that she would faithfully to the best of her ability provide for the children, she was given custody while Robert Henry Sibley, Henry's uncle, was appointed tutor.[34]

On March 15, 1826, with emotions running high, Margaret and her struggling children watched as some of their most prized family possessions were auctioned off at a public gathering. Margaret, through a few meager savings, was able to salvage a few items. Francis Lee, a young Lieutenant who had only recently married Elizabeth, was able to purchase the servant Jenny for $465.

When the shameful and embarrassing auction was over and all accounts had been settled, the family possessions were gone—house, land, and furniture. Margaret had $482.55 on which to start a new life and rear her growing children. A way of life was ending on that Louisiana day in late March 1826, and another was beginning. A once expanding and promising family fortune had hopelessly and abruptly ended.

For some time Margaret contemplated sending the children to live with Uncle George in Missouri. Although the devout George and his

[33] Succession Records in the Case of Samuel Hopkins Sibley, Parish Clerk of Court Records, Natchitoches, Louisiana.
[34] Ibid.

wife Mary, who were childless, had offered to adopt the children, particularly Henry, Margaret was reluctant, feeling that it was too much of a burden on George, and she vowed to find some means to support her family.[35]

In the summer following his father's death Little Henry had gone with his brother and sisters to spend the summer with Uncle Robert at Alexandria. As usual it was the sickly summers in Natchitoches that drove the family to seek refuge elsewhere. Elizabeth, Henry's older sister, bragged that although Henry had come down with the measles, he had grown an inch or two in the last year.[36] By August of 1824 the family was back at Court Hill, but three months later this property had to be sold. The only good news had come in late November when it was announced in Natchitoches social circles that Elizabeth was betrothed to Lieutenant Francis Lee, a young officer who was stationed at Fort Jesup. The wedding with "everyone invited" was a hurried affair. Lieutenant Lee did not want to wait, for he had orders to make a lengthy exploring expedition up the Red River.[37]

Perhaps the most powerful force in the shaping of young Sibley's mind was the ever present influence of the American frontier, first in Louisiana and later in Missouri. Although the frontier in theory was thought to be a place of equal opportunity, in reality it was the lucky or the industrious, or in some instances the unscrupulous and cunning, who became economically successful.[38] Consequently, they were the ones who dominated southern society. Young Sibley had learned this first from the failure of his father and secondly from the entrepreneuring successes of his grandfather.

Another powerful influence in the formation of Sibley's values was the plantation system. The plantation, the backbone of the southern economy, was in reality a self-contained, self-sufficient, social, political, and economic unit. Here the southern aristocrat like Dr. John Sibley ruled like a medieval lord. His plantation was his fief. His slaves were his serfs. His white columned mansion, built like a Greek temple, was his castle. To maintain the plantation system the southern

---

[35] M. Sibley to Eliza Johnston, 11 July [1825]; George S. Sibley to Josiah S. Johnston, 4 January 1825; Johnston Papers.

[36] Elizabeth Sibley to Dear Cousin, 8 June 1824, Johnston Papers.

[37] John Sibley to Josiah S. Johnston, 29 November 1825, Johnston Papers.

[38] Dick, pp. 334–35.

aristocrat was a vehement advocator of the military and developed a fondness for military schools. In reality he was a omnipotent autocratic tyrant.[39]

Born into a system that relied upon force and coercion to maintain the status quo, young Sibley developed what might be called the martial spirit. The slave owner was all-powerful, literally in most instances having jurisdiction in life or death decisions concerning his slaves. Sibley's South was a "world in which horses, dogs, guns, not books and ideas and art, were . . . normal and absorbing interests."[40] The southern cult of honor encouraged dueling especially in Louisiana, as a means of settling disputes. The plantation as well as the southern frontier experience tended to foster a strong sense of independence, individualism, and militancy in young Sibley which would dominate the rest of his life.

Shortly after the Sibley property had been disposed of and all debts paid in full, Margaret made the decision to take the family to Missouri. Dr. John's sentiments appear to have been a strong factor in the decision to go north. The doctor had never been amiable with Henry's grandmother, insisting that Mrs. McDonald's influence on the family was anything but stabilizing. "I hope she will be happy there," Dr. John wrote of Margaret, "but never since I have known her has she ceased long in whining about the 'Old Saint,' her mother; blames me for their going to Missouri. Whatever else I have been called, I do not believe I have often been called a fool, but if I had interfered in their going, I think I should have deserved that epithet."[41]

In the cold grey winter of 1828 Uncle George made the long trip down the Missouri and Mississippi and up the Red River to Natchitoches where Margaret, Ann, and twelve-year-old Henry busily packed their bags for the trip to Missouri. On February 21 they left Natchitoches on the steamer *Beaver* and three days later were in New Orleans where passage was booked on the *Liberator* which was scheduled to steam for St. Louis the following day. Finding they would be delayed, George took Margaret, Ann, and Henry to the theatre and to see the New Orleans lighthouse. Perhaps more important for twelve-year-old Henry was a visit to the battleground just below the city near

[39] John Hope Franklin, *The Militant South* (Cambridge, 1956), 69.

[40] Wilbur J. Cash, *The Mind of the South* (New York, 1941), 99.

[41] John Sibley to George C. Sibley, 3 July 1831, Sibley Papers. Dr. John's displeasure is also revealed in John Sibley to Ann Eliza, 24 December 1821, Johnston Papers.

the banks of the Mississippi where thirteen years earlier General Andrew Jackson had defeated the British in the bloody Battle of New Orleans.[42] Such a visit was certain to have had a profound effect on the youngster. Any inclination toward a career in the military would have been reinforced.

On the last day of February the party embarked for St. Louis where they arrived ten days later. George remained in St. Louis for almost a month seeing to business interests and visiting friends. One friend who was in the city was Albert Sidney Johnston who appears to have made a big impression on Henry. Their paths would cross many times in the future, and someday Henry would even name his own son after the manly Albert Sidney. The party left St. Louis on April 5 and arrived a day later at the village of St. Charles on the north bank of the Missouri River approximately thirty miles northwest of St. Louis. Margaret and the children remained here while George made his way to Fort Osage.

George had great hope for Henry and Ann and was already planning to give up his valuable land near Fort Osage to build a large home on a tract of land he had acquired near St. Charles as he put it "partly because it will be of advantage to Ann and Henry." George was sure Margaret and the children would become "more and more pleased" with their new home "as they become acquainted with the country."[43] George wrote his brother-in-law, Senator Johnston, in 1828: "It is my purpose to do the best I am able for them all. Ann is a very fine girl and Henry is [a] promising boy for his age. After I return from Ft. Osage I shall put Henry to a school in St. Louis."[44] Margaret and the children's difficulty in adjusting to a new environment was partly alleviated when Lieutenant Lee was transferred to Cantonment Leavenworth from Fort Jesup later in the year. Traveling north with the lieutenant and Elizabeth, much to Dr. John's delight, was that "Old Saint," Mrs. McDonald. Later in the year, Margaret complained of the Missouri and Mississippi Rivers being blocked by ice and of suffering in a "truly severe winter." "I often wish myself back in our mild climate," she wrote.[45]

Two years after the family arrived at St. Charles it was decided that

[42] George S. Sibley to J.S. Johnston, 6 April 1828, Johnston Papers.
[43] Ibid.
[44] Ibid.
[45] Margaret Sibley to Josiah S. Johnston, 17 January 1831, Johnston Papers.

more thought should be given to Henry's education. In 1827, while
the family was still at Natchitoches, Henry's older brother John
George had attended the Grammar School of Miami University at
Oxford, Ohio. By the fall of 1830 Henry was fourteen. Margaret although displeased with John's education and lack of maturity at Oxford, at the urgings of Senator Johnston and Uncle George, decided
that Henry should also attend Miami Grammar School. Thus, in late
October 1830 Margaret helped her youngest child pack his clothing
for the two week trip across the broad Mississippi through southern
Illinois to Vincennes, Indiana, and Cincinnati, Ohio. On Christmas
Day, 1830, Henry excitedly wrote his mother of his arrival in Cincinnati and his expected departure for Oxford.[46]

Oxford, about thirty miles north of Cincinnati, was a bustling town
of five hundred when the Louisiana boy of fourteen arrived in November 1830.[47] The town boasted of "six stores, three taverns, a har-
ness shop, a tanyard, a livery stable and several log and frame
houses."[48]

Westward migration and the era of the common man were now a
way of life. Migrant families, many of them English, Irish, and Scottish, were passing through towns like Oxford daily, their heavily
loaded wagons carrying them westward to a new life in the wilderness. Many were settling in the Oxford area, building homes in the
new land and clearing the wilderness for the spring planting. Smoke
from the clearings often darkened the sun, and the Miami students at
Oxford were forced to light candles, even at high noon.

Little more than a muddy path separated the small town from the
college. The campus consisted of four or five acres enclosed by a neatly
whitewashed fence. All the trees had been cut from the campus, but
the stumps were still visible on a bleak and uninspiring landscape. A
large, imposing building which had been erected in 1824 at a cost of
fifteen thousand dollars, a sizeable sum of money for the period, stood
in the midst of the campus. Center Building, as it was called, was three
storied with several large rooms and topped by an impressive cupola.
One year before the Louisiana lad arrived a drab three storied brick

[46] Ibid.

[47] Mary G. Persyn, Assistant Social Sciences Librarian, Miami University, Oxford,
Ohio, to Jerry Thompson, 17 December 1971.

[48] Walter Havinghurst, *The Miami Years: 1809–1969* (New York, 1958), 43.

dormitory, named Washington and Clinton Hall, had been completed.[49]

Dormitory rooms were heated with iron stoves. Students could either buy firewood from the citizens of Oxford for a minimal fee or cut their own in the nearby forests. Often in the winter when snow lay upon the Ohio countryside, the students, desperate for kindling of any kind to start their fires, hacked away at the doors and stair railings of the dormitory. A surprise inspection of the buildings once revealed that a good one-half of the exposed wood had been neatly whittled away. Although rooms were rent-free, Henry was responsible for furnishing his own bed, a chair, a table, cooking utensils, a box of provisions, and whatever else was necessary.

Grammar school pupils were not segregated from the college students, and Henry often mingled with small boys of ten or men of thirty. All, regardless of age, were subject to the same rules. Henry, like everyone else, arose at five A.M., took his morning meal, and went to an exercise period, after which he was assigned to study and recitation until noon.[50] Classes were summoned by a trumpet as the president thought a bell too extravagant. After lunch, as the trumpet echoed across the campus again, Henry returned to class until the evening meal and prayers. Pupils in the grammar school, like the older college students, were subject to a list of seventeen rigid rules. Morning prayer and all other Presbyterian religious services including Sunday worship were compulsory. Drunkenness or the frequenting of any local tavery was strictly prohibited as were gambling and making unnecessary noise.[51]

The academic year was divided into five-month sessions. The winter session always commenced on the first Monday in November and ended on the last Wednesday of March. The summer session commenced on the first Monday in May and ended on the last Wednesday of September. The year was so arranged to allow the students to return home to assist in the spring planting, usually in April, and the fall harvest in October. Semester tuition in the grammar school was five dollars with a student's yearly expenses amounting to ninety-three dollars, a considerable strain on Margaret's scanty savings.[52] In

---

[49] Ibid., p. 29.
[50] Ibid., p. 39.
[51] Ibid., p. 29.
[52] Mary G. Persyn to Jerry Thompson, 17 December 1971.

fact, Henry was not able to pay his tuition until the closing weeks of the semester.

Although Henry's older brother had not done well at Miami, Henry appears to have performed well. In his first year at the grammar school, Henry was required to take English and Latin grammar, Biblical history, Roman history, Caesar, arithmetic, geography, and English composition.[53] At the end of the first year, he was examined by a committee of the Board of Trustees, who attested to his scholarship and intellectual progress. Second-year courses consisted of Greek grammar, Virgil, Greek history, Euler's Algebra, and English composition. Henry appears to have excelled in languages, writing his mother of his interest in French, Spanish, and Latin.[54]

Other students from Natchitoches journeyed north to attend the grammar school of the university. Several of the youngsters were Indians who had taken white men's names and had been brought to Oxford by the president of the college. The Natchitoches lads included Adolphus, Charles, and Ambrose Sompayrac, Joseph and John Carr, as well as James and William Harrison. Henry's fraternizing with the Indian students may help to explain his later empathy for the Indians while serving in the military on the western frontier.

Henry's loneliness at Oxford was partly relieved when his older brother John George came to live with the William Flint family in Cincinnati to learn the mercantile business. Henry was not only able to visit with his brother but also appeared excited when Senator Johnston stopped at Oxford on his way back to Washington from Louisiana.

Margaret's letters reveal her disappointment in John George, and her satisfaction in Henry. "I am truly grieved to hear that John has not been what you wished," she had written Senator Johnston. Again some eight months later in reference to John George she wrote: "His departure from St. Charles has been a very great relief in my mind."[55]

Miami was an intellectual oasis in the wilderness. The president of the college was Robert Hamilton Bishop, a rugged Scot from Edinburg, who insisted on high academic standards and refused to tolerate any foolishness. Even while praying in the school chapel, he al-

[53] Ibid.

[54] M. Sibley to Eliza Johnston, 11 August 1831, Johnston Papers.

[55] Margaret Sibley to Josiah S. Johnston, 17 January 1831; M. Sibley to Eliza Johnston, 11 August 1831, Johnston Papers.

ways kept one eye open to look for any student who might be causing a disturbance. If he spotted such an offender, the president would make a flying leap from the pulpit, grab the young man by the collar, administer the necessary punishment, and stride back to the pulpit with great Calvinistic pride and dignity, knowing full well that God was overseeing and overwhelmingly approving his actions at all times.[56] A splendid educator, President Bishop was referred to by one of his previous students, Jefferson Davis, as "a man of large attainments and very varied knowledge."[57]

President Bishop brought to Miami some of the best-educated men of the time, many of whom were Presbyterian clergymen like himself. To Oxford in 1826, with "Latin, Greek and Hebrew texts bulging under his saddle bags," came William Holmes McGuffey, a recent graduate of Washington College in Pennsylvania.

McGuffy, who was paid five hundred dollars a year for his teaching abilities, built a brick home near the college and began work on his famous texts, of which 122 million copies would eventually be sold, all containing moral and patriotic lessons for America's youngsters. The conservative and traditional *McGuffey's Readers* would help shape American literacy and moral attitudes for decades to come.[58]

On October 19, 1832, only a few weeks after his graduation from Miami Grammar School, Henry wrote a letter applying for appointment to the United States Military Academy at West Point, New York. The intellectual haven in the wilderness had provided the necessary educational background to launch the military career of Henry Hopkins Sibley—a career that would take him from the burning deserts of New Mexico to the snows of the Wasatch Mountains of the Utah Territory, from the tropical shores of Mexico to the meandering waters of the Nile River.

After two years at Miami Grammar School, Henry returned home. The boy did not go to St. Charles, for Margaret had moved to Fort Leavenworth, Missouri Territory, to live with her daughter Ann, who

[56] Stephen E. Ambrose, *Duty, Honor, Country: A History of West Point* (Baltimore, 1966), 36. For a more recent study of the United States Military Academy see: James L. Morrison, Jr., *The Best School in the World: West Point—The Pre-Civil War Years, 1833–1866* (Kent, Ohio, 1986).

[57] Havinghurst, p. 36.

[58] Howard Zinn, "William Holmes McGuffey," *Encyclopedia of American Biography*, ed. John A. Garraty (New York, 1974), 713.

had married Robert Sevier, a young man from Tennessee and a recent graduate of West Point then serving in the Sixth Infantry. To Henry's dismay Margaret had written that she was partially blind from an inflamation of the eyes and as a partial invalid could do little more than sit in a chair and rock. Henry went instead to Louisiana, back to Natchitoches, to the Sibley plantation at Grand Ecore to live with his grandfather who had become the boy's legal guardian.

Before Henry returned to Natchitoches in the late summer of 1832, he had stopped at Uncle Robert's Mt. Elon Plantation in Rapides Parish. Dr. John in his endless travels through the Louisiana countryside had stopped to visit his son and reported "while I was there little Henry arrived from Cincinnati. I brought him home with me . . . I find him grown tall and slim. He seems to have profited well at school, is handsome and modest . . . I have scarcely ever seen a finer young man. He is now fit to enter West Point."[59] In September 1832, after Henry had visited with Dr. John and with Francis and Elizabeth Lee who were back at Fort Jesup, he went to Mt. Elon Plantation where Dr. John wrote of "finding little Henry and bringing him home with me. He is now here. He perfers staying with me. He has grown in everyway, is a very fine young man, not only as I think but as everybody else thinks."[60] By Christmas Henry was back at Fort Jesup, but Dr. John did not stop bragging on his grandson: "My house is his home and shall be until he is otherwise disposed of. He is a favorite of everybody. He will be at school until we know he can be admitted at West Point."[61]

Ever since the death of Henry's father in 1823, Grandfather John had held a special place in Henry's heart. John, the patriarch of the Sibley clan in Louisiana and one of the most respected men in the state, had done much to help Henry recover from the trauma of his father's death. John had not only become the boy's legal guardian but psychologically a surrogate father. Dr. John, aged seventy-five and still the frontier deist, continued his medical practice and his Whig politics. He cursed "old man" Andrew Jackson in the process, suggesting that anyone believing in nullification should be hanged, and even sent Stephen F. Austin a copy of the *Rights of Man*. Moreover, he walked ten miles a day to retain his physical vigor.

[59] John Sibley to Josiah S. Johnston, 13 August 1832, Johnston Papers.
[60] John Sibley to Josiah S. Johnston, 13 September 1832, Johnston Papers.
[61] John Sibley to Josiah S. Johnston, 11 December 1832, Johnston Papers.

To follow in the footsteps of his grandfather, which young Sibley appears to have aspired to do, was a difficult task. To surpass his grandfather in educational level or professional achievement, besides political influence and wealth, was going to be an extraordinarily challenging endeavor. To lower his expectations would have been to admit defeat. Indeed, the manliness and individualism as dictated by his early life on the frontier would not allow him to do this. The young Sibley was determined to live up to the hopes and aspirations of his grandfather with whom he strongly identified and idolized. Doctor Sibley would be for the remainder of Henry's life a gigantic figure in his memory.

Due to the efforts of Dr. Sibley, still very active in Louisiana politics, Henry did not remain long at the Sibley plantation. Less than one month after his completion of grammar school, Dr. Sibley wrote Secretary of War Lewis Cass, supporting Henry's application to the United States Military Academy at West Point. Dr. Sibley told Secretary Cass that Henry, although only sixteen years of age, was "well grown for his age and a handsome person with perfect organization of constitution."[62] Furthermore, Henry could speak and write French, quote Virgil, write Latin well, and was advanced in mathematics. Dr. Sibley pointed out that Henry's two older sisters were both married to West Point graduates: Ann, married to Lieutenant Sevier, and Elizabeth, to Lieutenant Francis Lee, a native of Pennsylvania and a West Point graduate in the class of 1818. Dr. Sibley emphasized that Henry's aunt was married to United States Senator Josiah S. Johnston. Dr. Sibley had also requested Senator Johnston's support in getting his grandson into West Point.

The doctor also enlisted the support of H.A. Bullard, Edward D. White, and Philemon Thomas, all United States representatives from Louisiana, who wrote a joint letter to Secretary Cass in which they referred to Henry as an orphan boy of great promise.[63] Two months later Congressman Bullard, whose district included Natchitoches, wrote to the Secretary of War again, pointing out that the district which he represented had no cadet at West Point. Bullard was "par-

[62] John Sibley to Lewis Cass, 19 October 1832, Records of the Adjutant General's Office, Application Papers of Cadets, Record Group 94, The National Archives, Washington, D.C.

[63] H.A. Bullard, E.D. White, and Philemon Thomas to Lewis Cass, 26 December 1832, Application Papers, R.G. 94.

ticularly anxious" that young Sibley, "an orphan boy of merit," be admitted to the academy.[64] At Fort Jesup, Henry's brother-in-law Lieutenant Lee enlisted the support of Brigadier General Henry Leavenworth who asked Cass to accept Henry into West Point. General Leavenworth, in a letter to Washington, referred to young Sibley as a young and cultured man and urged Cass to find a place for the lad at the academy.[65]

Henry waited impatiently at Grand Ecore for his expected appointment. For several months no word came. Finally in April, 1833, Dr. Sibley arrived home from New Orleans where he had been serving as state senator, and as Henry later recalled the story, "Grandfather . . . being occupied with his garden, and searching about the house for seeds . . . chanced to open the drawer of the side table, and there he found the missing documents, which had long laid *perdu*." "Tantarabogus!" Dr. Sibley exclaimed, "using the only epithet he was ever known to utter—Tantarabogus!"[66]

One of the plantation slaves had taken the appointment papers from the local post-office, cached the important documents in a side drawer in a table in Dr. Sibley's study, and had forgotten them. Upon discovery, a runner was immediately dispatched to take the exciting news to Henry who was working as a clerk in a small store in Grand Ecore. Hurriedly the boy wrote Secretary Cass: "Having received my appointment as cadet in the service of the United States at West Point and being satisfied with the conditions mentioned I accept it, and do hereby bind myself to serve five years or until such time as the Superintendent at West Point may think fit."[67] Within days, plans were underway for Henry's departure for West Point. Much excited himself, Dr. Sibley went as far as to purchase his grandson a colorful silk umbrella and a black, straight-bodied coat. Dr. Sibley decided that Henry should leave for New York as soon as possible.

Before his departure, news reached Natchitoches of the death of Senator Johnston who had done so much to get Henry into the academy. In May Johnston was on his way to Natchitoches when the

[64] H.A. Bullard to Lewis Cass, 26 February 1833, Application Papers, R.G. 94.

[65] H. Leavenworth to Lewis Cass, 13 December 1832, Application Papers, R.G. 94.

[66] [Henry H. Sibley], "Recollections of Cadet Life Forty Years Ago," *Popular Monthly*, (17 June 1881), 72.

[67] H.H. Sibley to Lewis Cass, 23 April 1833, Application Papers, R.G. 94.

steamboat *Lioness,* on which the senator was traveling, had exploded in Red River above Alexandria.

It was decided that Henry should first go by steamer down the Red River to New Orleans where he could then travel by schooner across the Caribbean and up the East Coast to New York. While traveling overland from Grand Ecore to Natchitoches, Henry recalled how he and his Grandfather happened to stop at an inn near Natchitoches, to see Sam Houston who had recently become a friend of Dr. Sibley. Houston owned 4,000 acres of land along the Red River, and was in Natchitoches busily agitating President Andrew Jackson with news from Texas. The impression that Houston made on the West Point destined lad was profound. "I thought him, at the time," Henry later wrote, "one of the most magnificent specimens of man I had ever seen. He was dressed in Mexican costume, and stood about six-feet-four, with light sandy hair, blue eyes, Roman nose, firm, well-cut mouth, and chin broad and handsomely turned; his face clean shaved; and when he stood up to greet my grandfather, his Mexican *serapi* thrown gracefully over his shoulder, he was every inch a noble Roman—one of those we read of as figures in the Forum."[68] Houston was happy to provide Henry with a letter of introduction to the Superintendent of West Point.

Reaching New Orleans, Henry booked passage on the 600 ton schooner *Niagara* to New York. After several weeks at sea, he docked at Whitehall where he boarded a small steamer for the short trip up the North River. Here another steamer waited to take him up the Hudson River to West Point. Like all other cadets, he was met at the wharf and taken to meet the post adjutant. With silk umbrella in hand and his oversized black coat draped over his shoulders and hanging below his knees, Henry recalled "how the boys laughed at me as we were marched from the wharf at West Point across the plain."[69] After his name was inscribed in a large book by the adjutant, he was then marched across the parade ground to the south barracks where he was issued a pillow, a small table, some blankets, a wash basin, a bucket,

---

[68] [Sibley], "Recollections of Cadet Life Forty Years Ago," p. 12. Llerena B. Friend, *Sam Houston, the Great Designer* (Austin, 1969), 56; Marquis James. *The Raven: A Biography of Sam Houston* (New York, 1929), 190–192. Sibley did not exaggerate Houston's height as various sources list the "Raven" as being anywhere from six-feet-two to six-feet-six. Ibid., p. 68.

[69] Ibid., p. 12.

and a broom. He was then placed in a room with four other much older "plebes" who the youngster from the Louisiana frontier remembered as being almost grown men.

The following evening all five "plebes" were accosted by two senior cadets in the middle of the night and verbally harassed for more than an hour. Cadet Sibley was quick to learn that the "plaguing of Plebes was as old as the institution itself."[70]

For the "plebe" there was much "drudgery and self-imposed hardiness," Henry recalled.[71] Like other cadets, he slept on the floor, always rolling his bed neatly of a morning and storing it orderly in the corner under his bookshelf. The bed was not unrolled until evening tatoo.

Cadet Sibley would never forget the endless marching required of the West Point cadets: "Squads of six and eight were formed for drill, under third[-year] classmen detailed for the purpose. Left foot forward! Left foot rear! Left foot forward! Left foot rear! Ground! Right foot forward! etc., etc. And in the facings and marching and in the goose-step, ah me. How well I remember how assiduous I was in all these teachings."[72]

Sibley found West Point dramatically different from Miami Grammar School. Discipline at Oxford had been demanding, but at West Point it was unconditional. The academy was one of the great military and civil engineering schools of the time. Maintaining high academic standards was expected, and absolute obedience was insisted upon.

Cadet Sibley's stay at West Point was not only a trying time for the young man from Louisiana but also a trying time for the academy. Henry arrived in New York one month before Superintendent Sylvanus Thayer, the man who had made Thomas Jefferson's dream a reality, departed from West Point under political pressure from the Jacksonian Democrats. It was the era of the common man, and Jacksonian Democracy was attempting to sweep the country clean of aristocratic privilege. West Point, like all other institutions of higher learning, had for many years been an enclave for the aristocrats, many of whom used the academy to educate their sons to build bridges, roads, and canals as civil engineers, rather than to serve the country

[70] Ibid., p. 14.
[71] Ibid.
[72] Ibid.

as officers in the United States Army. President Andrew Jackson, ardent foe of West Point, through his self-expanded executive powers, came close to destroying the school during the time Henry was at the academy.[73] Cadets even planted a hickory pole, a symbol of Jacksonian Democracy, in the middle of the parade ground and, when admonished for doing so by the commandant, went so far as to complain to Old Hickory himself, who praised the cadets for their daring. Other cadets, dismissed from the academy for academic or disciplinary reasons, journeyed to Washington to see President Jackson, who demanded that the young men be reinstated.

Fortunately for the school and Cadet Sibley, the curriculum which Sylvanus Thayer had installed remained intact. The core of the curriculum was mathematics and French, two subjects in which Henry took pride. Mathematics was necessary as a prerequisite for civil engineering; French, because most of the advanced texts in military science were written in French.[74]

Henry was required in his first year to enroll in French, algebra, geometry, trigonometry, and mensuration (surveying). The curriculum was demanding, even for Sibley with his excellent preparation at Miami. The mathematics class was divided into three sections with cadets segregated according to their mastery of the subject. Henry found himself in the third section with the least able cadets.[75]

At the completion of the academic year, Cadet Sibley, like all other first-year cadets, was required to attend a summer encampment during which time he lived in a tent, drilled endlessly, and practiced military tactics. Cadets were formed into companies with upperclassmen serving as officers. The young men could thus advance through the ranks much as in the regular army.

It was during this first summer, Cadet Sibley later recalled, that "all our energies were put forth." Particularly distasteful was the ever present duty of making "the rounds of the camp with wheelbarrow, spade, shovel and broom, picking up bits of paper, cigar stumps, etc."[76]

At the end of the first year, Cadet Sibley was promoted from private to corporal and assigned to Company B. At the end of his second

[73] Ambrose, p. 103.

[74] Ibid., p. 71

[75] Post Orders, Volumes VI and VII, The United States Military Academy, 2 October 1833, United States Military Academy Archives, West Point, New York.

[76] [Sibley], "Recollections of Cadet Life Forty Years Ago." p. 14.

year, he was promoted to sergeant and, although later transferred to Company D, was not promoted again until his graduation from the academy.[77]

During his second year at the academy, Henry struggled with much the same subjects as in his first year. Only drawing was added. Mathematics became more advanced as Henry now coped with analytical geometry and fluxions. In his third year at the Point, Henry was required to study topographical drawing and physics, or what the academy called natural philosophy. West Point professors, top men in their fields, many of whom wrote textbooks, were dedicated to learning and teaching and remained at the academy during the tumultuous Jacksonian years.

Because of his previous knowledge of the subject, Henry had an easier time with French which was taught by Claudius Berard, a twenty-year veteran of West Point who had written his own text for the course. Students were also required to read *Histoire de Gil Blas* and Voltaire's *Histoire de Charles XII.*[78]

Henry studied mathematics under Professor Charles Davies, a talented teacher who wrote a series of texts ranging from basic arithmetic to calculus. Davies had made West Point the best mathematical school in the United States. During Henry's third year on the Hudson, Davies was succeeded by his assistant, Albert E. Church, who proved to be a dull, uninspiring, cold, temperamental man who cared little for anything except calculus. The only time his students ever remember his becoming excited happened when a cadet once remarked that the only reason "for + becoming – on passing through zero was that the cross-piece got knocked off in its passage."[79] The uncompromising professor had the cadet arrested. Cadet Sibley continued to struggle with mathematics and at the end of his third year ranked thirty-sixth in a class of forty-six.

For physics the young cadet studied optics, astronomy, pneumatics, dynamics, statics, hydrostatics, hydrodynamics, hydraulics, and things he had never heard of while laboring with Latin and Greek at Miami. William H.C. Bartlett, said to have been the most brilliant

[77] Post Orders, Volumes VI and VII, 13 June 1835, U.S.M.A. Archives, West Point, New York.

[78] Ambrose, p. 92.

[79] Ibid., p. 93.

graduate the academy ever produced and one of America's foremost astronomers, was the physics professor.[80]

Most cadets had their hardest times with Professor Bartlett, who was motivating but extremely demanding. Physics almost ended Sibley's military career. Although Henry ranked thirty-first in a class of forty-six in physics at the end of his third year, he was obliged to take the annual June examination. During this grueling time a Board of Visitors, usually distinguished civilians, meticulously quizzed the cadets. Cadet Sibley was found deficient in "Natural and Experimental Philosophy" and was set back one year and required to repeat his Second Class Year, or his third year at the academy.[81] Henry was therefore not able to graduate with classmates Braxton Bragg, Jubal Anderson Early, John Sedgwick, John Clifford Pemberton, and many others who would blaze their names into history on many a Civil War battlefield. Instead, Henry graduated in 1838 with future greats Pierre Gustave Toutant Beauregard, Thomas Lee Ringgold, Irvin McDowell, and William Joseph Hardee.

Sibley did best in drawing, ranking seventeenth out of forty-six at the end of his third year. His professor was Robert W. Weir, one of America's great nineteenth-century painters, best remembered for his "Landing of the Pilgrims" in the rotunda of the capitol in Washington, D.C.[82] Much of the knowledge Sibley gained in drawing, topography and map-making, was later put to use on the western frontier.

In his third year the young cadet also studied chemistry in which he ranked twenty-ninth out of forty-six.

West Point's most important department and the one on which emphasis was placed during Sibley's last two years, was engineering. Here Henry fell under the tutelage of Dennis Hart Mahan, one of the great military thinkers of the era. Professor Mahan, with his temperamental nervousness and squeaky voice, influenced not only Sibley but also a generation of cadets, most of whom later led armies into battle in the Civil War. Mahan had written pocket-size texts, *Field Fortification* and *Outpost*, with which Cadet Sibley learned how to construct field and permanent fortifications, the basic principles of attack and defense, and the theories of strategy, tactics, and logis-

[80] Ibid., p. 95.

[81] Kenneth W. Rapp, Assistant Archivist, United States Military Academy, to Jerry Thompson, 21 October 1971.

[82] Ambrose, p. 94.

tics.[83] Mahan, like Antoine Henri Jomini, the French-Swiss general of the French Revolution and Napoleonic Wars whom Mahan admired, stressed maneuver, speed, surprise, and the establishment of a strong base of supply.

In his final year on the Hudson, 1837–1838, Sibley was required to take a class in moral philosophy taught by a Presbyterian Minister, Thomas Picot. The class echoed the tedium of Miami Grammar School, for it was boring and dreary, and the cadets cursed it.[84] Fencing exercises were also part of his final year at the academy.

For Cadet Sibley, West Point would also have its nostalgic moments. After the summer encampments, there were semi-weekly dances in which "all the beauties of the land" were invited.[85] The Fourth of July brought a variety of gala festivities. There were speeches, parades, more speeches and more parades, all culminated by a grand ball in the evening. At Christmas the barracks would be turned over to the cadets "and such a jolly time they would have," Henry remembered. Everyone indulged in "singing, dancing, and carousing; awaking in the morning to their recitations with red eyes and haggard faces."[86]

Henry recalled how a few cadets kept wigs stored in hidden "snuggeries" under the barracks floor. The wigs were used at the proper time to make "dummies" in the sly cadet's beds as to deceive the inspectors who, with dark lanterns, would make their nightly rounds after taps. On one particular moonlight night cadets crept silently from their beds to watch a prearranged foot race.[87] On another occasion, Henry remembered, a cadet built six miniature mortars out of the stems of some old brass candlesticks and by using cadet buttons for shells, bombarded a miniature fort near the barracks, all to the amazement of his fellow cadets. Once two cadets stole a six-pounder

---

[83] Thomas E. Griess, "Dennis Hart Mahan: West Point Professor and Advocate of Military Professionalism, 1830–1871," Ph.D. Dissertation, Duke University, 1968; George Peterson Winton, Jr., "Ante-Bellum Military Instruction of West Point Officers and its Influence upon Confederate Military Organizations and Operations," Ph.D. Dissertation, University of South Carolina, 1972, pp. 20–38. The only prominent Confederate Civil War generals who did not fall under Mahan's influence were Robert E. Lee, Joseph E. Johnston, and Albert Sidney Johnston.

[84] Ibid., p. 96.

[85] [Sibley], "Recollections of Cadet Life Forty Years Ago," p. 14

[86] Ibid.

[87] Ibid., p. 15.

cannon used for morning assembly and evening retreat, managed to drag the cannon back to their barracks, somehow got the gun to the second story, and had it loaded, primed, and ready for firing before being discovered.[88]

Sibley, somewhat more than other cadets, had problems with discipline. During his second year he was placed under arrest and confined to his room for making a false report on the state of his company. During his third and fourth years he put in more than his share of guard duty for such infractions as being out of uniform.[89]

Finally, on July 1, 1838, Cadet Henry Hopkins Sibley, who five years before had entered one of the world's great military schools as a frightened seventeen-year-old boy from Louisiana, graduated. Now a young man of twenty-two, he stood thirty-one in a class of forty-five. William Henry Wright, who would soon resign his commission, ranked first in the class, while Zebulon Montgomery Pike Inge, eight years later to die at the Battle of Resaca de la Palma in the Mexican War, ranked last.[90]

It was a major accomplishment to graduate from West Point in 1838 even in the lower half of one's class. More than one-third of the entering cadets failed to complete their studies and were either dismissed or obliged to drop out. Although Cadet Sibley had been set back a year he had completed the rigorous program. A commission as a second lieutenant in the United States Army warranted a measurable amount of prestige. A promising military career loomed on the horizon on that unusually bright graduation day in July 1838. Cadets pledged themselves to duty, honor, and their country. Lieutenant Sibley, however, would have considerable difficulty with all three.

[88] Ibid.

[89] Battalion Orders, United States Military Academy, 1 September 1836, U.S.M.A. Archives, West Point, New York.

[90] Register of Graduates, United States Military Academy Class of 1838, U.S.M.A. Archives, West Point, New York.

Chapter II

In the Land of
Alligators and Watersnakes

Upon graduation from West Point Henry Hopkins Sibley was commissioned a lieutenant in the Second Regiment of Dragoons. The young officer considered himself lucky since the cavalry was more prestigious than the infantry. Only nine cadets were so chosen. Thirteen were assigned to the infantry, and twenty-three to the artillery. No one was given a commission in the engineers.[1]

The Second Regiment of Dragoons, or mounted riflemen, had been created by an act of Congress in May 1836, and was only two years old when Lieutenant Sibley joined its ranks in 1838. The lieutenant was attired in his new uniform, the most colorful in the army. It consisted of blue trousers with yellow stripes and a reinforced seat or "saddlepiece," a short fatigue jacket with yellow braid, and a flat forage cap with a wide yellow band. His dress uniform, worn on parade or festive occasions, consisted of a short yellow-trimmed jacket, a

---

[1] Francis B. Heitman, *Historical Register and Dictionary of the United States Army,* Vol. I, (Urbana, 1965), 144.

heavy tall cap with white horsehair plume, and an "orange silk sword sash."[2]

In 1838 the Second Dragoons were fighting one of the longest and most embarrassing conflicts ever waged by the United States Army, a war against the Florida Seminole. At West Point Sibley had learned that the Seminole, unlike other Indians who had been forced westward, had decided to stand and fight for their homeland, much of which was one of the most uninhabitable regions of the United States—the swamps and bottomland of Florida.

A decade of conflict had not broken the Seminole. In skirmish after skirmish their fewer than five thousand warriors had fought the United States Army to a standstill. The army was learning what many frontiersmen already knew: traditional methods of warfare did not work in the "almost trackless waste of the Everglades."[3] The conflict was further complicated when many blacks who had escaped slavery only to become vassals of the Seminole, also fought the army with guerrilla tactics. The army was slow to adapt to a type of combat for which it was not trained. The war produced little more than a series of confused leaders including Winfield Scott and Zachary Taylor. Such frustrations were to have an influence on others in the army, even lieutenants like Sibley.

Sibley was still a cadet when the Second Seminole War, as it was called, erupted in December 1835, when Major Francis L. Dade with 106 officers and men were ambushed and slaughtered by the wily Seminole in central Florida west of Lake Apopka. Four companies of the Second Dragoons under regimental commander Colonel David Emanuel Twiggs arrived in Florida ten months later, in October 1836, after a march of 1,255 miles from Jefferson Barracks, Missouri. Four other companies of the unit, under the able leadership of Lieutenant Colonel William Selby Harney, reached the scene of action in early January 1837, their ranks filled with eastern recruits. In a series of running skirmishes and firefights, the dragoons learned at a bitter price that the Seminole were formidable opponents. "To say that we can 'perish them out' is nonsense," one dragoon lamented, conceding

[2] John D. Hostetter, "The Second Dragoons and American Expansion: 1836–1861," M.A. Thesis, Florida State University, 1961, p. 5.

[3] Theodore F. Rodenbough, *From Everglade to Canon with the Second Dragoons* (New York. 1875), 2.

that the Indians could elude the dragoons "at any moment."[4] Another horse soldier put his frustrations into poetry.

The Florida war has been raging:
And 'its our expectation
That the last conflagration
Will find us the same contest waging.[5]

Lieutenant Henry Hopkins Sibley was ordered to join his regiment in October 1838, during Colonel Zachary Taylor's tenure as Florida commander. Lieutenant Sibley quickly became part of the fighting colonel's relentless attempt at driving the Seminole from the settlements north of Tampa Bay. The Second Dragoons, in the forefront of his campaign, were helping to divide northern Florida into military districts, each some twenty miles square with a military post in the center. In all, forty-three forts, four thousand bridges, and one thousand miles of new roads, Taylor felt, would be sufficient to subdue the hostiles. The struggle, which had already baffled some of the best officers in the United States Army, had largely become a war of attrition. In fact Taylor was so determined to bring the demoralizing and costly conflict to a conclusion that he considered, and even used to a limited extent, Cuban bloodhounds. The gangly dogs, however, were more interested in chasing the abundant wildlife of the Florida wilderness than the elusive Seminole and thus proved to be of little help.[6]

To join the Second Dragoons, Lieutenant Sibley first traveled to New Orleans and from there to Tampa Bay on the west coast of Florida. He described himself at the time as a "stripling in appearance with scarce the *coupcon* of a mustache," which was considered a distinguishing mark of someone in the Second Dragoons.[7] Arriving in Tampa, Sibley first made a "social" visit to army headquarters as General Taylor had been a friend of his grandfather in Louisiana. The General received Henry with "kindness and affability" and cautioned the young lieutenant to equip himself with a double-barreled shotgun for protection against the Indians while traveling across the peninsula.

[4] Ibid., p. 31.
[5] Ibid., p. 27.
[6] Ibid., p. 44
[7] [Henry H. Sibley], "Military History of a Double-Barreled Shotgun," *Popular Monthly*, (17 May 1883), 440.

From Tampa Bay, Lieutenant Sibley, shotgun in hand, continued inland for five days across what he remembered as "gentle slopes of pine ridges and low-lying swamps . . . bordered with evergreen vines and creepers."[8] He later admitted to being a bit scared at the time as "every nerve" was "strained to the utmost" as he anticipated "a shot from every tree and stump."

At Fort Brooks on the Oklawaha River in north central Florida, Sibley was assigned to Company A commanded by Captain Thomas Bryan. Here Lieutenant Sibley and the men of Company A were employed in scouting the country in the vicinity of the Oklawaha River and Lake George.[9] Few Indians were encountered, and most of the duty proved to be a series of monotonous and seemingly endless marches through countless piney forests, across nameless prairies, and through stifling swamps which served little purpose other than to demoralize the men. During this time three men died of disease and sixteen deserted from Sibley's company, the highest casualty rate in the regiment. Much of what Dennis Hart Mahan had taught him on the banks of the Hudson had to be forgotten in the swamps of Florida. Here Napoleonic tactics were worthless. Army duty was far different from what Sibley had envisioned it to be while still at West Point.

From Fort Brooks, Henry moved his company further into the interior to Fort White on the Santa Fe River. It seemed as if the lieutenant and Company A were constantly on the move. After a few weeks of detached service in December 1838, Lieutenant Sibley rejoined his company on January 10, 1839. By this time the company had been ordered to Fort Gates on the St. John's River about four miles from the river's confluence with the larger Oklawaha. By February Sibley was on the march again. With a detachment from Company A he was now sent to Fort Pierce on Saint Lucie Sound.[10] While Henry was at Fort Pierce, Colonel Taylor negotiated a temporary cessation of hostilities, which although it fell far short of surrender, was welcome.

In the weeks which followed, Lieutenant Sibley appeared more concerned about the revenge-minded whites in Florida, in whose hands the fragile peace rested, than the elusive Seminole. As ex-

[8] Ibid.

[9] Regimental Returns of the Second Dragoons, Adjutant General's Office, Record Group 391, The National Archives, Washington, D.C. Hereafter referred to as R.R., S.D., A.G.O., R.G. 391.

[10] Ibid.

pected, the truce did not last long. In May, while Lieutenant Sibley was on detached service to Black Creek, a detachment of his company which was guarding a trading post, was ambushed by Seminole at Charlotte Harbor on the Caloosahatchie River. The Indians had slipped up on the sleeping dragoons without being detected, and within minutes thirteen Bluecoats were dead or dying.

Fatigued and badly demoralized by the Florida War, Lieutenant Sibley and six companies of the Second Dragoons were ordered to proceed to Garey's Ferry on the east coast of Florida where they were dismounted and embarked for Fort Columbus on Governor's Island in New York Harbor. Here the lieutenant was to await further orders. Some were sent to Trenton, New Jersey, where the dragoons and artillery and infantry regiments underwent training to restore and improve discipline and regimental esprit de corps both of which had been severely tested and found lacking in Florida. Recruiting offices were opened in many eastern cities to help fill the ranks made empty by those who had fallen in Florida, who had deserted, or whose term of enlistment had expired.[11] Since the beginning of the year, thirty-nine Second Dragoons had died in the Seminole War and fifty-five others had deserted.

Lieutenant Sibley remained at Fort Columbus where he assisted in recruiting and training the replacements. On November 29, 1839, he wrote to the adjutant general in Washington bitterly complaining of the nature of this duty. The letter is the earliest hint of Sibley's argumentative and irreconcilable disposition. His work consisted of rearranging post records which were found in total disarray. Regimental papers of the Second Dragoons were also in such disorder that Sibley could find no written record of two soldiers who were confined in the post stockade for desertion.[12]

Henry's social life at Fort Columbus was not so boring. The lieutenant found time to catch the ferry to nearby New York City and to visit places of interest on Long Island. On Governor's Island he met Charlotte Kendall, the eldest daughter of William Kendall, a native of Massachusetts, distinguished gentleman, and veteran of the War

[11] Rodenbough, p. 41.
[12] H.H. Sibley to R. Jones, 28 November 1839, Records of the Adjutant General's Office, Letters Received, Record Group 94, The National Archives, Washington, D.C. Hereafter referred to as A.G.O., L.R.

of 1812.[13] Charlotte was a gentle and cultured young lady who was attracted to the articulate southerner. It is easy to envision romantic scenes of the young lovers strolling hand in hand along sandy Long Island beaches, their blissful quixotic words concealed by a gently rolling surf, or taking moonlit ferry rides across New York Harbor. Only one thing is certain: the young couple met and fell in love.

The army came close to ending the whirlwind courtship when in late December 1839 Sibley was ordered to Carlisle Barracks, Pennsylvania. But Henry's love for Charlotte was deep, and the twenty-four-year old lieutenant remained at New York past his scheduled departure date. He and Charlotte were married at Fort Hamilton on Governor's Island by a Reverend Gorden on January 8, 1840.[14]

It was a good marriage which during the next forty-six years was to endure the most difficult and trying times. Henry could have resigned his commission as many West Pointers did, and found a better-paying job as a civil engineer or gone into business for himself. He chose instead to remain with the Second Dragoons. It was a hard decision, but Charlotte supported her soldier-husband for she too possessed a proud military lineage. During the next twenty years she would regret her decision more than once.

Shortly after his marriage several companies of the Second Dragoons were ordered back to Florida, sailing from Fort Columbus to Savannah, Georgia, but Henry was sent instead to Carlisle Barracks in the Cumberland Valley of southern Pennsylvania. Two months later the army promoted him to first lieutenant.

While at Carlisle Barracks in March 1840, Sibley wrote to the adjutant general asking for more pay on the basis that he commanded enough recruits to comprise a company. The lieutenant was also perturbed that Washington was making a distinction between the First and Second Regiments of Dragoons. Noncommissioned officers of the latter who were mustered into the service as lance sergeants and corporals were receiving the pay of privates which was not the case in the former. The unprecedented procedure was producing "a feeling of

[13] Carrol H. Quenzel, "General Henry Hopkins Sibley: Military Inventor," *Virginia Magazine of History and Biography*, 64 (1956), 168. For a history of Governor's Island see: Edmund Banks Smith, *Governor's Island: Its History Under Three Flags, 1637–1913* (New York, 1913).

[14] Widows' Service Pension Records, Mexican War, Records of the War Department, National Archives, Washinton, D.C.

jealousy" and irritation in the Second Dragoons, the lieutenant claimed.[15]

General Roger J. Jones, adjutant general of the army, refused to take action on the matter and informed Sibley that he could not receive additional pay since "officers in command of detachements of recruits are not nor ever have been entitled to the extra $10."[16]

Sibley watched during the early spring of 1840 as recruits continued to arrive at Carlisle Barracks from eastern recruiting depots for several weeks of drill and intensive training before deployment in Florida. The lieutenant was agitated about the quality of the enlistees, especially those from the New York Depot, many of whom were immigrants just off the boat from various European ports. He was particularly upset with a Private Bernard Mooney, who in six weeks had not performed a single day's duty nor mastered the "first position of a soldier owing to a constant state of drunkenness and confinement." Sibley's insistence brought the private's immediate discharge. Another recruit, John Smith, was found to be even "more worthless," if possible, and was also discharged.[17]

That summer Lieutenant Sibley was granted a week's leave of absence because of illness. Claiming his health to be in a "delicate state," Henry left for Governor's Island to see Charlotte. When his illness continued, he applied for two week's additional leave. Two New York physicians prescribed medicine which had a worsening effect upon his health. For several weeks he remained weak and ill at Governor's Island.[18] With Charlotte by his side, Henry slowly regained his strength and was able to recuperate enough to resume his duties at Carlisle Barracks in late August.

Shortly after arriving back in Pennsylvania, Henry learned from Lieutenant William Nicholson Grier of a vacancy which had developed at West Point. Lieutenant Grier had been unable to fill the assignment because of other commitments. Sibley, preferring duty at West Point to that at some remote and isolated western post, wrote Major General Alexander Macombs, commanding the United States Army, "consenting" to fill the vacancy.[19] It is not known whether

[15] Henry H. Sibley to R. Jones, 13 March 1840, A.G.O., L.R., R.G. 94.
[16] Endorsement on Ibid.
[17] H.H. Sibley to E.V. Sumner, 30 June 1840, A.G.O., L.R., R.G. 94.
[18] H.H. Sibley to R. Jones, July 1840, A.G.O., L.R., R.G. 94.
[19] H.H. Sibley to Alex Macomb, August 1840, A.G.O., L.R., R.G. 94.

Macomb even bothered to reply to the brash lieutenant's hasty request.

After ten months of training recruits at Carlisle, Henry sailed again for Florida in October 1840. The Second Dragoons, now commanded by Colonel William Harney because of Twiggs' lengthy leave of absence, were to experience some of the hardest fighting of the five-year Florida War. Sibley found Colonel Harney, a Louisianan, to be an officer of initiative, bold courage, quick decision, and someone who did not hesitate in challenging higher authorities in Washington. Some of Harney's characteristics, especially the latter, became through the years the military trademark of the young lieutenant. Harney was determined to crush the foxy Seminole. The previous year a band of the evasive hostiles had surprised and ambushed a dragoon detachment commanded by Harney, forcing the embarrassed colonel to flee for his life dressed only in his underdrawers, the ultimate insult. General Walker Keith Armistead, the commander who had succeeded General Taylor, was also anxious for a knock-out blow against the Seminole.

A force of dragoons drove deep into the heart of the Everglades, overtaking and capturing several Seminole warriors whom Harney ruthlessly ordered hanged on the spot. After the skirmish captured Seminole squaws were forced to lead the dragoons, now dressed and painted as Indians, deeper into the swamps. Harney threatened to hang their children if they refused. Additional Seminole warriors were captured, including the great warrior chief Chakaika, a giant of a man, whom Harney mercilessly hanged in plain view of the warrior's wife, mother, sister, and children.[20] Although the more humane element of the Florida command protested the dragoon's treatment of the captives, the Legislative Council of Florida, anxious to rid the territory forever of the Indian menace, voted Harney a commendation and a fine sword.

When Lieutenant Sibley landed in Florida with 145 enlistees from Carlisle in October 1840, he was immediately given temporary command of Company H to which nine of the new recruits were as-

[20] John K. Mahon, *History of the Second Seminole War* (Gainesville, 1967), 283. This is undeniably the best study of the war. For another fine study see: George Walton, *Fearless and Free: The Second Seminole War* (Indianapolis, 1977). Also: Francis Paul Prucha, *The Sword of the Republic* (Toronto, 1969), 269–306. For the naval aspects of the war see: George E. Buker, *Swamp Sailors* (Gainesville, 1975).

signed. Within a few days Harney ordered the lieutenant into the field. Sibley and his company left Camp Fowler on the east coast and proceeded overland to Fort Reid. Remaining there for three months, he set out again for Fort Shannon, near Palatka on the St. John's River about forty miles north of Lake George.[21] While at this post, Sibley assumed command of D Company, since its regular commander, Lieutenant Zebulon Montgomery Pike Inge, was on leave of absence.

On January 1, 1841, Sibley was appointed regimental adjutant and remained at Fort Shannon through the hot and humid summer of 1841 completing the regimental returns and other monthly, weekly, and daily reports required of his new position. By this time both Twiggs and Harney had gone on leave, and Major Thomas T. Fauntleroy now commanded the regiment.

Sibley later wrote of his frustrations at what seemed to be a never ending job of keeping the regimental records: "The young fledgeling, green from the academy, enters the army. . . and finds himself bewildered and involved in an interminable fruitless correspondence, harassed with the persistent returning of them to him for correction, ending with a frightful 'statement of differences'"[22]

In October Sibley helped to move regimental headquarters to Fort Henderson on the north bank of the St. Mary's River near the village of Colerain in extreme southeastern Georgia.[23]

He was shortly ordered to a duty station which, to his delight, was not another isolated, malaria-infested outpost in the swamps or backwoods of Florida. It was Fort Jesup, Louisiana, only a short distance from his childhood home at Natchitoches. Needless to say, he and his dragoons cheered the news of their departure from detested Florida.

Since the Seminole War was not over, five companies of the Second Dragoons were disheartened to learn that they had to remain behind. Soon, President John Tyler, feeling that "the further pursuit of these miserable beings by a large military force seems to be injudicious as it is unavailing" declared the cessation of hostilities in Florida, thus allowing the remaining companies of the Second Dragoons to depart "the land of alligators and watersnakes."[24] Despite Presi-

[21] R.R., S.D., A.G.O., R.G. 391.
[22] [Sibley], "Military History of a Double-Barreled Shotgun," p. 442.
[23] R.R., S.D., A.G.O., R.G. 391.
[24] Rodenbough, p. 74.

dent Tyler's proclamation, the war would drag on for another year and eventually cost more than fifteen hundred lives and twenty million dollars. A handful of Seminole never capitulated and continue to live in the swampy backwoods of the peninsula state. Obviously, the Second Seminole War—the graveyard of military reputations—was something less than a victory.

Ill dragoons too weak to travel overland were transported by water. The others were quickly in the saddle, anxious to depart Florida as soon as possible. Adjutant Sibley rode ahead of the five advance companies. He continued westward across the Chattahoochee, Alabama, Pascagoula, and Pearl Rivers to Baton Rouge where he halted two days before Christmas, 1841, to await the arrival of the command's "heavy baggage."[25] On the second day of the New Year, he boarded a steamer which took him up the Mississippi to the Red River and western Louisiana.

Henry disembarked his horse soldiers at Grand Ecore, four miles from Natchitoches. The Second Dragoons proudly rode down the streets of Natchitoches and on to Fort Jesup where they arrived on January 14. As a lad Henry had watched Zachary Taylor and the United States Army proceed westward from Natchitoches along the Camino Real.

It was a proud and exciting time for the lieutenant. For the first time in several years he was now able to visit with his many aunts, uncles, nieces, and nephews at Natchitoches. Missing from the family was Dr. John Sibley who had died five years earlier while Henry was still at West Point. Although preoccupied with his studies at the Military Academy, the doctor's death had been psychologically tramautizing for Henry who had always had a strong identification with his powerful grandfather.

Fort Jesup, located on high ground in the piney woods of western Louisiana, was one of the better western forts. It contained substantial quarters, some of which were two-storied, a theater, gymnasium, and a spacious parade and drill ground. Adjacent to the post stood a school, a chapel, and a sutler's store filled with "attractive wares" and ardent spirits.[26] After his frustrating Florida experience, Sibley considered Fort Jesup a near paradise.

[25] R.R., S.D., A.G.O., R.G. 391.

[26] Rodenbough, p. 83; Louis R. Nardini, *No Man's Land* (New Orleans, 1961), 103–15.

Supplies came by steamer up the Red River to Grand Ecore and were then freighted overland. Almost no green vegetables were available, and the men subsisted mostly on stew. Frequently pork and wild game shot in the nearby forests augmented the monotonous diet. Despite the post facilities, health conditions were bad, and as many as two-thirds of the dragoons were frequently sick at one time.

Duty for Lieutenant Sibley at Fort Jesup proved to be monotonous, thankless, and less exciting than he had envisioned. Sharing the Lieutenant's sentiments, dragoons deserted in large numbers as was usual during times of peace. Two months after his arrival, Henry was replaced as adjutant by Lieutenant Elias Kent Kane and was ordered to New York on recruiting duty. He left Fort Jesup on Independence Day, 1842, traveling the 1,791 miles by stage to Washington and on to New York.[27] He was anxious to be with Charlotte whom he had not seen since the Florida War. Shortly after his arrival in New York, however, he was directed by army headquarters to report to Carlisle Barracks. Henry, without hesitation, wrote an angry reply requesting that the order be cancelled. Charlotte had been ill, and he was anxious to remain with her at least until late October 1842, when he would "be better prepared to enter more cheerfully upon" a new assignment. While in New York, Henry fortunately met Lieutenant Lawrence P. Graham who was also on leave and who agreed to perform his duty at Carlisle. When this idea failed to excite his commanders, Henry wrote Washington asking to join his regiment directly by sailing from New York to New Orleans, thus giving "Mrs. Sibley the benefit of a sea voyage" which the New York doctors had "recommended for the restoration of her health."[28]

Such an order was never issued and Henry, much to his displeasure, arrived in the Cumberland Valley at Carlisle in October still complaining about his lack of influence in Washington. Within two months after helping to whip two companies of raw recruits into shape, he was ordered to rejoin his regiment in Louisiana.

Charlotte had now sufficiently recovered from her illness and was able to accompany her soldier-husband westward and to see for the first time the bayous and piney woods of Henry's native Louisiana of which he had so fondly spoken during their courtship. In mid-No-

---

[27] R.R., S.D., A.G.O., R.G. 391.

[28] H.H. Sibley to the Adjutant General of the United States, 5 June 1843, A.G.O., L.R., R.G. 94.

vember 1842, and accompanied by a detachment of recruits, the Sibleys sailed from Philadelphia to New Orleans. There they caught a Red River steamer, and soon Henry's wife was meeting her new relatives at Grand Ecore and in Natchitoches.

At Fort Jesup Henry was reappointed adjutant. The couple had no sooner settled into their quarters when one of the coldest winters in memory swept across the southland. With weeks of freezing rain, the dragoons suffered severely in their rock and log quarters. Although other units came and went, the dragoons remained. Some, finding the weather and the fort intolerable, deserted, while others performed their duty without a whimper. A few of the young recruits who had only recently arrived on the western frontier succumbed to the damp Louisiana winter and died. Lieutenant Sibley, as regimental adjutant, held the unenviable job of writing to the parents and loved ones of the deceased soldiers, trying to explain the circumstances of the untimely deaths, and sending their belongings.[29]

Travelers along the Camino Real often stopped at the post for food and lodging. Guests were well received; they usually brought the latest news from New Orleans, the East, or from the interior of the Republic of Texas, all of which was welcomed by Henry and Charlotte.

The continuing desertion problem at Fort Jesup was due to the post's close proximity to the Republic of Texas. In April 1843 a dragoon deserted and fled westward into Texas after stealing $2,000 from the Fort Jesup paymaster. Lieutenant Sibley, at the head of a small detachment of bluecoats, was soon in the saddle. The thief's trail led past Sabine Town on the Sabine River and to Nacogdoches, where Sibley learned that the thief had fled deeper into Texas; so he gave up the chase and returned to Louisiana.[30]

While Sibley was at Fort Jesup the United States Congress was debating the fate of the Second Dragoons. Some Senators, mostly from New England and the Middle Atlantic states, saw no necessity to retain the regiment, especially since the termination of the Florida War. Others, mostly from the South and the West, argued that the dragoons were necessary for protection of the frontier. Winfield Scott, now commanding general of the United States Army, pleaded that the regiment was needed to maintain a chain of forts recently built across

[29] Ibid.
[30] Adolphus Sterne, *Hurrah for Texas*, ed. Archie P. McDonald, (Waco, 1969), 150.

the western frontier. Congress and ex-President John Quincy Adams argued that the unit was too costly and should be abolished. The debate, which Sibley kept abreast of, was often violent in its rhetoric, raging back and forth across Capitol Hill until a compromise was agreed upon: the regiment would be retained, but would be dismounted. Thus, in March 1843, the Second Dragoons became the Second United States Regiment of Riflemen, and the proud cavalrymen, cursing Washington and all politicians, with considerable bitterness and reluctance gave up their horses.[31]

For eight months Lieutenant Sibley continued to serve at Fort Jesup as regimental adjutant. The regiment was next ordered to Fort Washita in the Indian Territory where Sibley arrived on October 24, 1843.[32] Here he was to assist in protecting the peaceful Chickasaw Indians who had been compelled to cede their ancestral lands in Mississippi. Upon settling in the Indian Territory they were raided by wild Texas frontiermen and marauding Comanche alike.

Fort Washita, constructed two years prior to Sibley's arrival, was located just east of the Washita River about thirty miles above its junction with the Red River. It was an isolated place, and Henry, still serving as adjutant, yearned for a return to Fort Jesup. Fortunately orders arrived late in December 1843 directing that regimental headquarters be moved back to Fort Jesup. Sibley and the riflemen arrived back in Louisiana during the first week of January 1844.

Shortly thereafter Lieutenant Sibley and the troopers received news that a bill making the regiment cavalry again had been signed into law by President John Tyler. The post was engulfed in revelry. Guns were fired, duty was suspended, and the post commander ordered distribution of an extra whiskey ration. Considering Sibley's later appetite for "ardent spirits," it is assumed that he must have consumed his share if not more. It was an exciting and happy time.[33]

As winter passed into spring, rumblings were heard from across the Sabine River. Sibley like many dragoon officers, appeared to sense that his future was tied to the political fortunes of the Republic of Texas.

[31] Rodenbough, pp. 81–84.

[32] R.R., S.D., A.G.O., R.G. 391; Post Returns of Fort Washita, Adjutant General's Office, Record Group 94, The National Archives, Washington, D.C. Hereafter referred as Post Returns and by individual post. Also: Herbert M. Hart, *Old Forts of the Southwest*, (New York, 1964), 14–16.

[33] Rodenbough, p. 86.

After ten years of rejection by antislavery forces, Texas was, by a joint resolution signed by President Tyler on March 1, 1845, to be admitted as the twenty-eighth state.

With plans for a military occupation of Texas, Fort Jesup took on added importance. More bluecoats arrived daily. A new commander, Zachary Taylor, also rode into the post, and in June 1845 the War Department ordered the general and his "Army of Observation" to march into the Lone Star State. The force was to concentrate at Corpus Christi on the Nueces River and there await political negotiations then underway with the Republic of Mexico. Lieutenant Sibley and the dragoons, unlike the bulk of the army, were ordered to march overland.

Sibley and the cavalry sallied out of Fort Jesup on July 25, 1845.[34] It was the worst time of the year for a march of 501 miles. Drought plagued the land. The column, slowed by a train of sixty wagons, followed the Camino Real across the Sabine River into the vast expanse that was now the twenty-eighth state. Onward they rode through the piney woods toward San Antonio. Each day was monotonously routine. At three in the morning camp would be broken, and after bedding and cooking utensils had been packed into wagons, the westward trek would be resumed. By noon, as animals began to falter in the heat, the command would halt to seek shade and water. By early afternoon the march would resume and continue until midnight. Usually, the column could cover twenty-five or thirty miles each day. Some mounts floundered and had to be shot or left to die in the blistering Texas sun. Numerous dragoons deserted, and three men died.[35]

Although the Lone Star State was sparsely settled, the dragoons did march through a few towns and villages where they were "greeted by the acclamation of the multitude assembled to welcome them."[36] No recruits came forward to enlist. Manpower potential had already been absorbed by volunteer Texas regiments.

From San Antonio southward the earth became parched and the landscape changed dramatically. Waterholes became fewer, causing the men and their animals to suffer. After a month on the road the regiment forded the Nueces River at San Patricio, with the officers and men swimming their horses to the south bank. The column failed

[34] R.R., S.D., A.G.O., R.G., 391; Post Returns, Fort Jesup, A.G.O., R.G. 393.
[35] Rodenbough, p. 93.
[36] Ibid.

to encounter Taylor's Army as had been planned. Furthermore, thinking that a thunderstorm was a Mexican attack on Corpus Christi, the commander sounded "to horse" and the troopers galloped off to the rescue of the "besieged" village.[37] Three miles south of the Nueces, the regiment ran into General Taylor, who did not appear impressed with the dragoons' inability to distinguish a Texas thunderstorm from gunfire. The general, nevertheless, did seem pleased that the dragoons were in a fighting mood.

Sounds of war echoed over Texas as the "Army of Observation" became the "Army of Occupation." Manifest Destiny was abloom. The American eagle, spreading its wings across the continent, was in a screaming, defiant mood. Lieutenant Henry Hopkins Sibley, caught up in the spirit of the times, was anxious to achieve adventure and glory in the great adventure which lay ahead.

[37] Ibid., p. 94.

"Major Sumner and Lieutenant Sibley, at the head of the first set of fours, had several personal encounters with the enemy, who were, in every instance either killed or dismounted."

> Puente de Moreno near Medellín, Mexico, March 25, 1847, Theophilus Francis Rodenbough, *From Everglade to Canon with the Second Dragoons.*

"For many miles we passed along a ditch, dug from Encera [sic] to the pass of Cerro Gordo, which furnished us excellent water. All along the road were the bodies of Mexican lancers and their horses, cut down by Colonel Harney's dragoons when these fire-eaters chased Santa Anna and his retreating troops beyond Jalapa. Almost every man's skull was literally split open with the sabres of our horsemen, and they lay stretched upon the ground in ghastly groups."

> National Road east of Jalapa, Mexico, April 19, 1847, Theophilus Francis Rodenbough, *From Everglade to Canon with the Second Dragoons.*

"[We charged] through one of the most destructive fires cavalry ever endured, without an immediate and palatable objective. It was at the Battle of Molino del Rey. The Regt. had advanced unflinchingly up to the enemy breastworks, the bullets fairly coming upon us and mowing down our ranks."

> H. H. Sibley to H. S. Scott, November 1, 1847, Cavalry Barracks, Mexico City.

Chapter III

To the Valley of México

Sibley camped on a sandy beach at Corpus Christi from August 1845 until early February of the following year.[1] During this time biting winter storms, known to the Texans as "northers," swept down out of the Rocky Mountains across the Texas Plains, pounding the "Army of Occupation" with cold, drenching rain. When they were not fighting off rattlesnakes during their seven months on the coast, some soldiers found time to race horses while others applied their talents to an amateur theatrical production. Taking advantage of the abundance of game in the brush country and prairies near the American camp, a few bluecoats were able to turn "tours of observation" into hunting safaris.

While in camp at Corpus Christi the Second Dragoons spent most of their time serving as scouts for the army. The regiment not only scouted into the interior but down the coast toward the Rio Grande as far as 150 miles. During the second week in December 1845, Sibley led a scout up the Nueces River by boat. Leaving camp before daylight on December 12, the lieutenant, accompanied by E. Kirby Smith

[1] R.R., S.D., A.G.O., R.G. 391.

and Hamilton W. Merrill, crossed the mouth of Corpus Christi Bay then proceeded up the river before camping. Although the slow-flowing, murky river was lined with live oak trees, vast prairies stretched as far as the eye could see. Huge herds of deer were seen in every direction. Two deer were shot by the explorers which along with twelve turkeys provided a tasty feast. Smith recorded that the whole region was "sandy, unproductive, and unfit for agriculture but admirably suited for grazing."[2] Early the next day the party continued up the river for some eighteen miles. In the afternoon, threatened by an approaching rainstorm, Sibley returned to the American camp at Corpus Christi just in time to avoid a drenching downpour.

War clouds were lowering on the Rio Grande, and attention turned southward. One month before the horse soldiers were ordered to the banks of the muddy Rio Grande, Lieutenant Sibley was sent to New York on recruiting duty. His tour there would last for more than a year, and he would not join his regiment again until February 26, 1847.[3] By this time, México and the United States would be locked in combat for control of a large portion of North America.

Recruiting men in New York was nothing new for the lieutenant. He had been at Fort Columbus on a similar assignment in 1842. The tour of duty was a lucky opportunity to be with Charlotte. She had returned to New York to join her father and two sisters when Henry had left Fort Jesup for Texas in 1845.

Henry's stay in New York proved to be especially pleasant. On October 17, 1845, Charlotte gave birth to a daughter on Governor's Island, whom the couple named Helen Margaret in honor of Henry's mother. She was the Sibley's first child, and her birth helped to make the stay in New York one of the most memorable of their lives.

New York, like Boston where Sibley would go later in search of recruits, was filled with individuals fleeing Ireland's potato famine. The

---

[2] E. Kirby Smith, *To Mexico with Scott: Letters of Captain E. Kirby Smith to His Wife*, ed. Emma Jerome Blackwood (Cambridge, 1917), 22. Smith mistakenly identifies Sibley as a major. Two other Sibleys, both captains, Ebenezer S. of the artillery and Caleb C. of the Fifth Infantry, were in the American army at the time. Smith, however, in his letter of 28 December 1845, makes it clear that he was accompanied by the dragoons. The area Smith described as unproductive and unfit for agriculture is today one of the richest farming areas in Texas. For army life at Corpus Christi see: Darwin Payne, "Camp Life in the Army of Occupation: Corpus Christi, July 1845 to March 1846," *Southwestern Historical Quarterly*, 73 (January 1970), 326–342.

[3] R.R., S.D., A.G.O., R.G. 391.

bustling metropolis was presumed to be a rich ground for enticing destitute men into the American Army. The exodus from the Emerald Isle had brought thousands of debilitated, half-starved Irish peasants to the shores of America. New York Harbor was a forest of masts as thirty to forty ships a day arrived. Many found only continued poverty as, crowded into New York's tenements, they obtained only the most menial employment. New York's wharves were daily crowded with bewildered newcomers from Ireland and the banks of the Rhine.[4] Arriving in New York, Sibley found his duty "exceedingly dull," and he was able to recruit only nine men in two months.[5]

While Sibley struggled to find recruits in New York, a reconnaissance force of two companies of the Second Dragoons, acting as Taylor's "eyes and ears," was surrounded at La Rosia in the lower Rio Grande Valley of Texas by a superior force of sixteen hundred Mexicans. All the Americans were either killed, captured, or wounded. Taylor wrote to Washington that "hostilities may now be considered commenced."[6] Three weeks later President James K. Polk sent a war message to Congress asserting that American blood had been shed "upon American soil" and that a state of war existed, "notwithstanding all our efforts to avoid it."[7]

Sibley found that the commencement of hostilities in Texas and the resulting headlines in the New York newspapers improved his recruiting. Writing from New York, he informed the adjutant general: "Taking advantage of the impetus thus naturally given to the recruiting service, and the consequent excitment in the city, I immediately advertised in several papers for recruits, and had large hand bills printed and profusely distributed throughout the city." Within one month Sibley had recruited over one hundred men, mostly Irish, whom he described as "the very best material."[8] Although he had promised the recruits that they "would be forwarded to Texas in a very short time," the men were confined on Governor's Island for several

---

[4] Edward Wakin, *Enter the Irish-American* (New York, 1976), 38; Bayrd Still, ed., *Mirror for Gotham: New York as Seen by Contemporaries from Dutch Days to the Present* (New York, 1956), 129.

[5] H.H. Sibley to R. Jones, 31 May 1846, A.G.O., L.R., R.G. 94.

[6] James D. Richardson, ed., *A Compilation of the Messages and Papers of the Presidents*, 20 vols. (New York, 1897), VI: 2,292; K. Jack Bauer, *The Mexican War 1846–1848* (New York, 1974), 48.

[7] Ibid.

[8] H.H. Sibley to R. Jones, 31 May 1846, A.G.O., L.R., R.G. 94.

weeks where they became "anxious, most anxious to join their regiment."[9] Sibley felt "the interest of the service would be promoted" as would the continued success of his New York office, if his assurances to the young recruits could be complied with.[10]

In July 1846 Sibley complained of similar problems to his commanding officer: "My experience in the recruiting service, in this city during the past three months, has taught me that the success I have met with, is mainly attributable to the circumstance of having been enabled hitherto give assurances to applicants of a speedy embarkation for the Rio Grande."[11] Week by week the recruits became more anxious and restless. "Nothing seems to deter the intelligent recruits from enlisting more than the prospect of a long continuance at the principle depot on Governor's Island. The confinement here without amusement or relief from the monotonous routine of drill is most irksome and is no doubt regarded by the soldier, whatever toil he may have to endure in after years, as the most unhappy period of his enlistment," Sibley wrote.[12] He hoped to be "informed as early as possible of the intentions to forward recruits to Mexico, and the probable date of the sailing."[13] A few weeks later he received word that as soon as sixty dragoons were enlisted, an officer of the regiment would arrive to supervise their transfer to Taylor's Army which was now in México. A Company of Sibley's recruits sailed to war on October 1, 1846, under the command of Captain Nathaniel Wyche Hunter.[14]

By late October Sibley had enlisted fifty more recruits whom he personally drilled and trained, a task he "modestly" asserted had "heretofore occupied a single officer two years."[15] Sibley even went so far as to propose an alternative to the conditions on Governor's Island. He would march his men to Carlisle Barracks, Pennsylvania, recruit enough men along the way to make a full company, "mount and equip it and march with the least possible delay to the seat of war."[16]

[9] Ibid.
[10] Ibid.
[11] H.H. Sibley to R.B. Mason, 29 July 1846, A.G.O., L.R., R.G. 94.
[12] Ibid.
[13] Ibid.
[14] H.H. Sibley to R. Jones, 1 October 1846, A.G.O., L.R., R.G., 94.
[15] H.H. Sibley to R. Jones, 28 October 1846, A.G.O., L.R., R.G. 94.
[16] Ibid.

Henry was the senior first lieutenant in the Second Dragoons and thus felt fully justified in asking for such orders.

Permission to march to Carlisle Barracks was refused, but Sibley was allowed, at his request, to establish an auxiliary rendezvous in Boston. In June he moved northward leaving his sergeant in charge of the New York recruiting office. Boston, like New York, was full of hungry Irish immigrants, who were flooding into the city at the rate of over twenty thousand a year.[17]

Problems arose in Boston. Sibley complained that he had not received funds for these expenses and that uniforms could not therefore be procured for the recruits. All Sibley had to offer the young men was underwear, which he felt was scant enticement.[18] Disgusted, by late July he was back in New York.

Beginning with the Mexican War, Sibley was to gain a reputation as one of the most stubborn, argumentative, and controversial officers in the United States Army. He was a chronic complainer who did not hesitate to take his faultfinding resentments to the highest authorities in the War Department. His tour of duty in New York is a presentiment of his controversial career which would follow. Henry was informed in January 1847 that bills for advertising could not be paid by the Army and that the auditor had rejected a bill for $6.75. Sibley wrote Adjutant General Roger Jones, complaining: "I knew at the time it was unauthorized but I was confident also that the success that attended it would prove a sufficient reason."[19] Again on January 22, 1847, Sibley wrote Jones informing the adjutant general that since he had commenced advertising for recruits, a total of 420 men had enlisted. When ordered not to advertise, he had recruited only eight men. The lieutenant was hoping the adjutant general would "extend favorable consideration to the amount now suspended."[20] The betterment of the army had been served by the advertising, Sibley argued. After more than two months of wrangling, in a rare turn of events, Washington gave in. "Lieutenant Sibley," the Adjutant General wrote, "has exhibited such zeal in recruiting and has been so successful in training good recruits that I summon the allowance of the suspended vouchers alluded."[21]

[17] Oscar Handlin, *Boston's Immigrants* (Cambridge, 1959), 52.
[18] Endorsement on H.H. Sibley to R.G. Mason, 8 June 1846, A.G.O., L.R., R.G. 94.
[19] H.H. Sibley to R. Jones, 4 January 1847, A.G.O., L.R., R.G. 94.
[20] H.H. Sibley to R. Jones, 22 January 1847, A.G.O., L.R., R.G. 94.
[21] Endorsement on Ibid.

Besides the Irish and German immigrants, many of the New York recruits were social degenerates and refugees from organized society. One such case was that of a young recruit named Edward Henry Keat, alias Edward Henry. Sibley, taking the young man's word of honor that he was unmarried, enlisted him. Shortly thereafter a young lady appeared at the recruiting office claiming to be the recruit's wife. Sibley admitted that he had been deceived: "Yesterday his wife, a very respectable looking woman with a little boy, called upon me in great distress begging and imploring that her husband might be released from his engagement, that he was her only support, that she was in a 'delicate situation' and that separation at this time would kill her. I relieved her distress in a measure by promising to keep her husband here and to intercede for his enlistment, without inconvenience or injury to the service."[22] Sibley's recruiting commander, Lieutenant Colonel Richard Barnes Mason, concurred with the decision and ordered young Keat discharged and a substitute furnished.[23] Washington disagreed, stating that a substitute could not be accepted and that the practice had been discontinued.[24] The recruit had refused to be discharged anyway and on July 13, 1846, had sailed for Texas, leaving a distressed wife in New York without any visible means of support.

Two months after his New York tour of duty had expired and he had sailed for México, Lieutenant Sibley continued to receive letters critical of his recruiting practices. Sibley had remained with Charlotte a few weeks longer than he had anticipated before embarking for Texas. He had hastily compiled his recruiting returns on board ship and forwarded the papers from Brazos Santiago at the mouth of the Rio Grande. The records were in error, and Colonel Ichabod B. Crane complained to Washington of the condition of the returns. Colonel Crane even went so far as to accuse Sibley of "neglect of duty." Sibley, with his fiery temper akindle, wrote the adjutant general from Perote, México, on the last day of April, 1847: "Colonel Crane is the last person in the world to speak of 'neglect of duty' in connection with my name. No one knows better than himself that it was impossible for me to make up my returns and turn over my property in the limited period left us."[25]

[22] H.H. Sibley to R.B. Mason, 8 June 1846, A.G.O., L.R., R.G. 94.
[23] Endorsement on Ibid.
[24] Ibid.
[25] Ibid.

Sailing southward from New York, Sibley, along with a squad of recruits, had arrived at Brazos Santiago on February 26, 1847.[26] Ten days before landing the young officer learned that he had been promoted to captain. To wear the bars of a captain brought a sense of pride and helped to mitigate the embarrassment which resulted from his recruiting reprimands.

Despite his recruiting problems, Captain Sibley was given command of Company I, replacing Captain Benjamin L. Beall. Most of Sibley's fellow combatants had been transferred to General Winfield Scott's command early in January, prior to the battle of Buena Vista, and were now camped at Camp Page at Brazos Santiago near the mouth of the Rio Grande.

After a serious command dispute between "Old Fuss and Feathers" and Colonel William S. Harney, commanding the Second Dragoons, in which President Polk was forced to intervene, Sibley, Company I, and the remainder of Scott's ten thousand men prepared to depart for Vera Cruz. The loading of supplies, equipment, horses, and men took almost a week. The Second Dragoons finally embarked for tropical Vera Cruz on March 5, 1847, in four small transports, the *Eli Whitney*, *Bronson*, *Bangor*, and *Yazoo*. The vessels proceeded down the Mexican coast as far as Lobos Island, fifty miles south of Tampico, where they rendezvoused with Scott's army.

Scott had chosen a beach three miles south of Vera Cruz, beyond the range of the Mexican guns, for the landing. On March 9 in less than four hours, more than ten thousand men went ashore in sixty-five heavy surf boats towed to Vera Cruz especially for this operation. Sibley remained on board ship, watching history in the making. It was the first large-scale amphibious landing in American history. Although Scott's army was unopposed on the beaches, the fortified city of Vera Cruz defied the invaders.

On the 14th of March a severe north wind arose catching the Second Dragoons still at sea near the coastal village of Antón Lizardo, south of Vera Cruz. The storm almost proved fatal to the regiment. The small fleet carrying the dragoons was swept by high winds, battered by heavy waves, and was severely damaged.[27] Hundreds of horses

[26] R.R., S.D., A.G.O., R.G. 391.
[27] Rodenbough, p. 134.

were washed overboard and drowned. Even a part of the regimental records was lost.

Hardest hit was the transport *Yazoo* which was grounded on a reef off Antón Lizardo. On March 21 Sibley's regiment landed safely. Scott reported that the dragoons had landed but were "without effective horses for more than a company, many having been lost at sea, and another large portion rendered unfit for immediate service."[28]

Scott's army was successful in cutting the roads, water supply, and a small railroad leading into Vera Cruz. Scott unleashed his artillery, and for more than a week they bombarded the city with as many as 180 shells an hour, killing enemy troops and civilians alike. Sibley, unmounted since the loss of his horse, took his turn in the trenches with the infantry. More than a week passed before he was able to procure horses for his company. The mounted portion of the dragoons, Sibley's company now included, was deployed in scouting for guerrillas. It was during the seige of Vera Cruz that Sibley was to achieve his brief wartime moment of glory at Medellín, a small village thirteen miles southwest of Vera Cruz. Medellín was the center for guerrillas which were harassing the American deployment before Vera Cruz. Scott ordered Harney to break up the concentration of guerrillas, and Sibley was soon in the saddle.

On March 25 Sibley and several companies of the Second Dragoons, both mounted and on foot, proceeded toward the village but were halted by a large Mexican force at the Puente de Moreno, a stone bridge spanning the Moreno, a small murky tributary of the Medellín River. The bridge was reported to be held by a force of two thousand Mexicans. Artillery was called for, which shelled the bridge. After an initial infantry attack the cavalry was ordered to the assault. Sibley was reported to be "at the head of the first set of fours, which had several personal encounters with the enemy, who were in every instance either killed or dismounted."[29] The Mexican infantry guarding the bridge fled, some to the village of Medellín, some into the tropical underbrush. Sibley, "in the thickest of the melee, several times measured strength with the enemy, killing or dismounting his antagonists."[30] Sibley pursued the enemy six miles to the village of Med-

[28] Ibid. Also, Camdus M. Wilcox, *History of the Mexican War* (Washington, 1892), 249.

[29] Ibid., p. 135.

[30] Ibid.

ellín where he encountered and helped to rout a party of Mexican lancers. Captain Sibley was cited for "gallantry and meritorious conduct," and was breveted a major.[31] His bravery was a highlight of his career. A recognition of his dedication and gallantry seemed to prevail which would partly transcend the trying times in the not-too-distant future. His brevet was much respected by the military as well as by politicians back in the United States. His bravery at Medellín would help to provide opportunities for him in the future that otherwise might not have been possible.

Some felt the Second Dragoons, as a result of its performance at Vera Cruz, were now "the bravest and best disciplined corps in the whole army."[32]

And no company in the Second Dragoons was better known that Company I. Bold, daring and self-reliant, the company had become known throughout the Army of Occupation as the "Forty Thieves." They had first gained a reputation for their toughness in the Second Seminole War while stationed in Northern Florida. On scouting forays into Southern Georgia in the vicinity of Okefenokee Swamp, they had raised the ire of the American settlers in the area because of their petty thievery. Several Georgia "Crackers," in Sibley's words, complained to General Taylor about "them pesky drag-goons. They was wus n' the injuns. They'll steel and pilfer, an' keep a man po' all his life."[33]

Upon the surrender of Vera Cruz, Sibley was one of the first Americans to set foot inside the walls of the city. One day later he was ordered to participate in the combined naval and land attack on Alvarado, a small port some thirty-eight miles south of Vera Cruz. Henry later remembered Alvarado, situated on the left bank of the Alvarado River, some six miles from its confluence with the Gulf of Mexico, as a "quiet, unpretending town, of about a thousand or fifteen hundred inhabitants."[34] The American Army, composed of two regiments of infantry, a battery of artillery, and a squadron of the Second Dragoons, sallied out of Vera Cruz as the American band played "See, the Conquering Hero Comes." Assisted across the Río Jamapa on

---

[31] Heitman, p. 886; Wilcox, p. 257.

[32] Ibid.

[33] [Henry H. Sibley], "How We Took Alvarado," *Frank Leslie's Chimney Corner*, (2 July 1881), 118.

[34] Ibid., p. 117.

small boats provided by the navy, the column continued south down the coast. On March 30, after it was learned that the navy had already taken Alvarado, the infantry and the artillery were countermarched back to Vera Cruz, leaving the Second Dragoons to escort General Quitman, the American Commander, into the town. With Major Benjamin Beall, Captain Seth Thornton, and several naval officers, Henry took up residence in the Mexican customhouse. Years later he fondly recalled his brief stay in the tropical Mexican port. Confiscating the contents of a small Mexican store which contained an ample supply of liquor, Sibley and his comrades-in-arms were content to relax in the courtyard of the customhouse picking limes from the trees which added a delightful taste to their confiscated Mexican whisky.[35]

Two days later Sibley was sent north from Vera Cruz to the village of Antigua to combat Mexican guerrillas who were harassing the American lines and posing a threat to any force desiring to move into the interior. Major Edward V. Sumner, taking two squadrons of dragoons including Sibley's Company I and a section of artillery, advanced up the coast early on the morning of April 2 but progressed slower than anticipated because his Mexican guide proved to be unfamiliar with the area. From local residents it was learned that a force of one hundred lancers were in Antigua. The dragoons were sent at a gallop, but when within site of the Jalcomulco River they were halted by "an almost impenetrable barrier of trees and bushes thrown across the road."[36] With considerable effort the troopers removed the roadblock and continued their advance. With their sabers drawn Sibley and the dragoons raced into the streets of the small village capturing a lieutenant and eight of his men. The remainder of the lancers escaped into the dense tropical undergrowth which surrounded the town. Convinced that the enemy's force was routed, the men returned to the dragoon camp outside Vera Cruz on the afternoon of April 3.

There Sibley learned that "Old Fuss and Feathers" had ordered the Second Dragoons to scout the National Road which lead westward into the Sierra Madre Oriental toward Mexico City. By April 11 Captain Sibley and the regiment had reached the village of Río del Plan,

[35] Ibid.
[36] W.S. Harney to H.L. Scott, 4 April 1847; quoted in Rodenbough, p. 520.

about fifty miles from Vera Cruz, where they halted to await reinforcements. From the 11th to the 17th, Sibley was in the saddle continuously either escorting supply trains from Vera Cruz or reconnoitering the Mexican lines. At the village of Santa Fe, he lost two men, John Moran and Franz Marchinecke, to Mexican guerrillas; their bodies had been left to rot in the stifling heat beside the National Road. Another soldier, Henry Barnes, was killed two days later while carrying dispatches between Río del Plan and Vera Cruz.[37]

Sibley joined the main force in time to encounter the Mexican Army under Antonio López de Santa Anna, estimated at between twelve thousand and eighteen thousand and firmly entrenched on both sides of the National Road. One of their strongest positions was El Telégrafo, a cone-shaped hill which overlooked the surrounding countryside and the village of Cerro Gordo. Harney and the Second Dragoons were placed in position before the seemingly impregnable Mexican position. Several dragoon companies continued to reconnoiter the Mexican lines or to escort supplies from Vera Cruz.[38] On the second day of the Battle of Cerro Gordo, the Americans carried the Mexican positions by storm and Santa Anna's army fled along the National Road. Scott had hoped to use the cavalry to outflank the enemy and force the Mexicans to surrender, but this did not prove possible. Sibley was now sent in pursuit of the fleeing Mexicans. Hundreds of prisoners were taken as the dragoons overtook the retreating Mexicans all the way to Encero, a large hacienda owned by Santa Anna. A reporter who passed over the National Road a few days later wrote: "Colonel Harney's Dragoons chased Santa Anna and his retreating troops beyond Jalapa. Almost every man's skull was literally split open with the sabres of our horsemen, and they lay stretched upon the ground in ghastly groups."[39] Three privates from Sibley's Company I were later decorated for their bravery during the engagement.

Reaching the outskirts of Jalapa the dragoons were met by the town's leading citizens who offered to cooperate with the Americans providing the army agreed not to harm the residents. Within minutes Sibley and the horsemen were in the rocky streets of the hillside town. At more than four thousand feet, Jalapa, which was noted for its flowers and a climate of perpetual spring, was a welcome resting place for

[37] Ibid.
[38] Ibid.
[39] Rodenbough, p. 140.

the captain and the dragoons. From Jalapa the road led upward into the Sierra Madre, past deep gorges, through groves of ponderosa pines, and across beds of red volcanic cinders. To the south stood the 14,049-foot peak of El Cofre de Perote, its green slopes mystically shrouded in clouds and glaring down on the Americans much as it had on Spanish conquerors centuries before. Safely across the rugged eight thousand foot pass Sibley reached the fortress of Perote by April 22. Two days after reaching the colonial outpost, Sibley reported himself ill.[40]

On the 8th of May after preliminary negotiations with the Mexican Government had broken down, Scott ordered the dragoons to move out toward Mexico City again. With Sibley and Company I as the advance guard, the army rode across a lava-strewn bleak and arid landscape towards Puebla. To the southeast loomed the glacial slopes and eternal snows of El Pico de Orizaba. At 18,740 feet, the mountain, known to the Indians as Citlaltepetl, was the third highest in North America.

Crossing El Paso de Penal, which one soldier described as "wild beyond description," Sibley reached the town of Amozoc, twelve miles from Puebla, without incident.[41] Here he encountered a sizable Mexican force. Artillery was ordered forward, and the Mexican squadron was soon in flight. Santa Anna withdrew, and the Americans made elaborate preparations for their entrance into Puebla. With the army in their dress uniforms, the entrance would certainly have been a most grand occasion except for a downpour which ruined the event. The rain even caused the dragoons' "martial plumes to droop." Nevertheless, most of Puebla's eighty thousand inhabitants crowded every street and plaza and occupied every roof and window to gaze at the Americans.

Puebla became the major American supply base, and Sibley remained here throughout the summer of 1847. The American ranks, Company I of the Second Dragoons included, were seriously reduced by disease and desertion. Having just marched through the yellow fever belt, hundreds came down with the dreaded fever and died. Sibley lost five men from Company I.[42] Escorting supply trains arriving from Vera Cruz required occasional duty. Otherwise, Sibley found Pueb-

[40] R.R., S.D., A.G.O., R.G. 391.

[41] John James Peck, *The Sign of the Eagle: A View of Mexico—1830 to 1845* (San Diego, 1970), 87.

[42] R.R., S.D., A.G.O., R.G 391.

la's well-paved streets, orange trees, elaborate cathedrals, and gentle breezes a pleasant distraction from the grim realities of war. There was time to attend the theatre and eat ice cream made by the Mexicans from the icy slopes of the volcano Popocatepetl which "reared its head of purest white" above the city.

One reason for Scott's delay at Puebla was that most of the volunteers were returning home, their terms of enlistment having expired. Although Scott had no doubt that his "Army of Invasion" could take the Mexican capital, he preferred not to risk such a potentially bloody encounter. On July 12, 1847, he sent a flag of truce along the National Road to the capital. Captain Sibley was one of those chosen to carry the dispatches, which called for an exchange of prisoners.[43]

An interpreter, in advance of the cavalry, was dispatched to inform the Mexican Army that the two companies came under the flag of truce, not to do battle. From Puebla, Sibley, accompanied by Captain Philip Kearny, rode across a fertile plateau past large cultivated haciendas. Here, poor peons, bound to the land by a harsh system of serfdom little short of slavery, glared at the Americans. At San Martín, about twenty miles from Puebla, Sibley and Kearny encountered a large troop of Mexican cavalry under Major General Valentín Canalizo. The Mexican force refused to honor the flag of truce and fled along the National Road instead. Sibley and Kearny had advanced about forty-three miles from Puebla, a few miles beyond the village of Río Frío, before they encountered another enemy force. The Mexicans refused to allow the Americans to continue any further but agreed to "deliver their dispatches."[44] Defying the Mexicans, the party continued toward the city of México. Ever since leaving San Martín Sibley and Kearny had ascended through dense pine forests until they were now at a 10,500 foot pass beneath the snowy northern summit of Iztaccihuatl. As the Americans continued to wind along the road toward the capital the country became wild and rugged. Here and there a cross marked the spot where some poor and unfortunate traveler had been waylaid by bandits.

Just west of the pass Sibley and the advance guard came down through the clouds, much as Hernando Cortés had some three cen-

[43] Puebla American Star, 15 July 1847; "Diary of Colonel Benjamin Huger," 14 July 1847. Diary in private possession. Colonel Huger was Chief of Ordnance in Scott's Army.
[44] Ibid.

turies earlier, to see the great valley of México stretching before them. In the distance stood the "Halls of Montezuma," beckoning the Americans onward toward an uncertain destiny. There appears little doubt that Sibley, Kearny, and their men, were the first of Scott's army to see the great valley.

By late summer, with peace overtures failing and reinforcements arriving almost daily, Scott gave orders to move toward the Mexican capital. On the 7th of August the "Army of Invasion" marched from Puebla. As usual, Captain Sibley and the dragoons were the advance guard. Although Mexican cavalry hovered on the army's wings and flanks, the dragoons met no resistance until the column reached the village of Buena Vista four days later. A reporter wrote of the encounter: "Here a body of cavalry of the guerrilla breed made their appearance in the road, brandished their lances, and waved their hats, apparently challenging a fight. Colonel Harney watched their movements for a short time with a spy-glass, in order to ascertain their numbers and position. They figured, or rather ciphered, about in the road, as though they were ready to eat up everything alive that might come in their way. Thereupon Colonel Harney sent Major Sumner down the road with three companies, Captain Ker, Hardee, and Blake, with orders, 'to teach them a lesson,' and soon after followed with the balance of his command present, consisting of Sibley's, Thornton's, Ruff's, and Wheat's companies."[45] The Mexican force, "brandishing their lances and yelling," waited until the dragoons were within six hundred yards of their position and then fled in several directions.[46]

On the 11th of August Sibley led the advance guard through heavy rain to the village of Ayotla, some fifteen miles from México City, where Scott set up headquarters. Just north of Ayotla lay El Peñón, a fortress on a small mountain guarding the city. For three days Sibley and Thornton escorted a squad of engineers, commanded by Captain Robert E. Lee, in a thorough reconnaissance of El Peñón.[47] Although the scouts estimated the fortress to have thirty guns protected and manned by a force of seven thousand, they were able to advance close enough to hear conversation by the Mexican garrison. One Mexican "even jumped upon the parapets and shouted to the observers that all

[45] Rodenbough, p. 150.
[46] Ibid.
[47] Ibid.

was ready for their reception."[48] It was estimated that casualties would run as high as three thousand before the fortress could be seized. Scott had other plans and decided instead to move on México City by marching south of Lakes Chalco and Xochimilco. By the 17th of August Sibley had reached the village of San Agustín, south of México City.[49] Here he was ordered to reconnoiter the area toward Mexicalcingo, a fortified village surrounded by a marsh and approached only by a paved causeway a mile long. General Scott would later refer to the dragoon movements before the capital as "the most daring reconnaissance of the whole war."[50]

On the 19th the Americans clashed with the Mexican Army at the village of Contreras. Here the Second Dragoons came under fire several times, but were held in reserve during most the battle which lasted for only seventeen minutes.

The following day the Americans and Mexicans clashed again, this time for the village of Churubusco. Sibley found himself deployed in the center of the American line to the southwest of the village and on the main causeway leading into the village. The regiment successfully drove the Mexican infantry into the town. It was reported that the dragoons rode at full gallop into the Mexican Army, which was "cut down, ridden over, or dispersed through the ditches into the fields on either side."[51] Mexican artillerists commanding a battery on the causeway were placed in such panic that they "opened fire on friend and foe, causing serious loss and injuring both."[52] Santa Anna and his army fled across the Churubusco River to the safety of México City. By the 21st Sibley was in the picturesque village of Tacubaya, only three miles from the heart of the capital city. At the end of August, he was in camp at Hacienda Jalpén.[53]

Scott, still hoping for a peace treaty without a costly assault on the capital, agreed to an armistice which lasted until September 7. On the 8th of September when negotiations broke down, Scott ordered an attack on Molino del Rey, a strongly fortified village. Scott had re-

[48] Ibid.
[49] R.R., S.D., A.G.O., R.G. 391.
[50] Rodenbough, p. 151.
[51] Ibid., p. 151.
[52] Ibid.
[53] R.R., S.D., A.G.O., R.G. 391.

ceived intelligence reports, which later proved to be false, that the village was being used by Santa Anna as a foundry for cannon balls.

Molino del Rey was also important because of its proximity to the Castle of Chapultepec, another strongly fortified position guarding the capital. The attack against the village ran counter to Scott's usual battle plan. The general, who usually depended on maneuver, decided on a frontal assault. The decision was to cost the Americans heavily. With the infantry carrying the frontal attack, the Second Dragoons, under the command of Major Edwin V. Sumner, were deployed on the American left flank. Here was the Casa Mata, an old Spanish citadel surrounded by bastioned entrenchments and open ravines.

Due to the unfavorable terrain and the fortified proximity of the enemy, Sibley found himself and his men in imminent peril. Sumner reported: "In taking up my position I was compelled to pass within pistol shot of a large body of the enemy, who were protected by a ditch and breastwork. This exposure of my command was entirely unavoidable, in consequence of a deep ditch on my left, which was impossible to cross until I got very close to their line, and I could not pause at that moment, as a very large body of the enemy's cavalry was advancing towards the left of our line." [54] Santa Anna's decision to order Major General Juan Alvarez to turn the American left was to almost cost Sibley his life. Before they could move to meet the attempted Mexican envelopment, the dragoons "advanced unflinchingly up to the enemy breastworks" through what Sibley called "one of the most destructive fires cavalry ever endured." [55]

Moving to meet the Mexican cavalry, the men had to cross a deep ravine, and two of the squadrons in their haste became panicky and confused. Sibley claimed that Major Sumner rode forward and remarked that he "was disappointed in the officers" of the regiment for not preserving "order in their squadrons or platoons." [56] Sibley later wrote that Sumner's tongue-lashing was "harshly and publicly pronounced upon us on the field of battle." Yet "not a voice was raised to express indignation." [57] The major's wrath was not easily forgotten

[54] Rodenbough, p. 156.

[55] H.H. Sibley to H.L. Scott, 1 November 1847, A.G.O., L.R., Army of Occupation, R.G. 94.

[56] Ibid.

[57] Ibid.

and would later cause both Sibley and Sumner considerable embarrassment.

With Mexican "bullets mowing down our ranks," as Sibley later recalled, the Second Dragoons suffered more casualties at Molino del Rey than in all other battles fought under Scott combined.[58] Thirteen out of fifteen officers of the Second Dragoons had their horses either killed or wounded. Sibley, besides having one man killed and five wounded, had his horse shot from under him early in the fray.[59] The captain's brother-in-law, Major Francis Lee, had also come under heavy fire at Molino del Rey and was later cited for bravery. Although the battle was an American victory, Sibley felt that if there were many more triumphs like it there would be little of the American Army left to take México City.

Within a week following the battle of Molino del Rey, the full brunt of the American assault on the Mexican capital was thrust at the fortified Gibraltar-like Castle of Chapultepec. Set upon a lofty hill overlooking the city, Chapultepec, with its white embattlements defying the invaders, presented a formidable obstacle to the invaders. In this battle, Sibley and Company I, although dangerously exposed to the Mexican artillery, were held in reserve until the infantry had carried the heights and then turned loose on the retreating Mexicans. Most of the pursuit was along La Veronica causeway and aqueduct leading to the village of San Cosme Garita. Upon reaching the outskirts of the capital city, Sibley was ordered back to the village of Tacubaya, where he remained during the night. The captain was in the village when word arrived late in the evening that Santa Anna had evacuated the capital.

On the following morning General Scott sent word that the Second Dragoons would accompany his entrance into the city. Theodore F. Rodenbough, historian of the Second Dragoons, reported that: "General Scott and staff, in full dress, escorted by Major Sumner and command, entered the city of México amidst the most intense enthusiasm on the part of his troops. As he arrived at the plaza, the band of the Second Dragoons played with much spirit the appropriate air of

[58] Ibid.

[59] H.H. Sibley to George W. Cullum, 23 October 1859, Archives of the United States Military Academy. Photostatic copy courtesy of James S. Sibley. For a detailed account of the battle see: "Battle of Molino del Rey," *Southern Quarterly Review*, 6 (October 1852), 281–315.

'Hail Columbia,' and while the escort was coming into line discursed with much effect upon the susceptible soldiery the patriotic strains of 'Yankee Doodle.' The gallant bearing of the dragoons—who wore their best clothes in honor of the proud occasion—and the splendor of the staff was strongly contrasted with the immense crowd . . . of the capital who surrounded them."[60] Thousands of the curious Mexicans pressed around the "conquering Gringos," so many in fact, that Scott ordered Sibley to help clear the plaza.

Contrary to what Captain Sibley thought, the fighting was not over. Before Santa Anna had evacuated the city, he had opened the doors of the city's prison releasing two thousand criminals. To cause as much damage as possible to the invading army, the convicts had been armed. Once the "Army of Invasion" had entered the city, the convicts began to snipe at Scott's Army from rooftops. Sibley and the Second Dragoons as well as other cavalry regiments were soon engaged in desperate street fighting that did not subside until late the following evening.[61]

Another unpleasant feature of the final hours of victory for Sibley was the execution by hanging of a number of the Second Dragoons who had deserted to fight for México in the infamous Battalion of San Patricio. Five of those executed were from the Second Dragoons; two, Henry Venalor and Francis Rhode, were from Sibley's Company I. Captured at the Tete-de-Pont near Churubusco, on August 20, 1847, Venalor and Rhode had been found guilty of desertion and treason by a general court martial held at Mixcoac on September 11.[62]

In the weeks and months following the occupation of the capital, Sibley frequently escorted General Scott about the Valley of México. On one occasion Scott was invited to an elaborate feast hosted by the Ayuntamiento of México City. Riding through pine and fur trees to a small village on the western rim of the great valley of México, Sibley recalled watching a "circle of beautiful maidens dance the fandango to the music of their timbrels and castanets."[63] Later he examined an ancient decaying monastery in the small village and climbed to the belfry for a view of the valley: "In the center of the

[60] Rodenbough, p. 158.

[61] R.R., S.D., A.G.O., R.G. 391.

[62] Ibid.

[63] [Henry H. Sibley], "Scott in Mexico," *Frank Leslie's Chimney Corner*, (July 16, 1881), 149.

surrounding lakes, the City of México sat like some imperial moni-
tress at the termination of five distinct causeways. The outline of the
silver aspen trees, the enameled domes and spires of the churches
glistening in the sunlight—all presented a fairy-like view. Interven-
ing and beyond, innumerable villages dotted the plain, lending life and
reality to the enchanting scene."[64]

While he was able to avoid the barracks-room disputes of the generals, Sibley had his share of Mexican War controversy. On October
17, 1847, his daughter's second birthday, Sibley received orders to
preside over a garrison court martial. Because of a large backlog of
cases, Sumner urged the captain to expedite the proceedings. On the
morning of the first day, the court hastily disposed of twelve cases
but adjourned after one of the soldiers scheduled for trial could not
be located. Reconvening the following morning, Sibley was able to
dispose of the remaining case and adjourn. Lieutenant William D.
Smith, the court reporter, was excused for the afternoon, and Sibley
left for an afternoon of drinking at a nearby officer's club.[65]

At evening retreat Major Sumner asked that the findings of the court
martial be read. Due to the October darkness, the adjutant was unable to finish the task. Sumner, observing the adjutant's difficulty,
turned to Sibley and remarked, "This is the consequence of officers
attending to their private business instead of their public duties. If you
had not given Lt. Smith permission to be absent this record would
have been completed."[66]

Captain Sibley snapped back at Major Sumner that he did have "the
right to give Lt. Smith permission to be absent" and that the reporter
had left early in the day giving "assurances that his work would be
completed on schedule."[67]

"The court has not done its duty sir; you should not have taken the
word of the orderly. The court has not done its duty," the major replied.

"The court has done its duty, sir, and has done it well," the captain
angrily shot back.

After a disturbance in the guard house temporarily quelled the fiery

[64] Ibid.
[65] H.H. Sibley to H.L. Scott, 1 November 1847, A.G.O., L.R., Army of Occupation,
R.G. 94.
[66] Ibid.
[67] Ibid.

tempers, the verbal sparring continued. "I will see if I cannot make officers attend to their public business instead of their private affairs," Sumner stated.

Sibley, insulted and angry, wrote that at this point in the heated exchange "endurance ceased to be a virtue." "You have nothing to do with the proceedings of the court," the captain told the major.

Sumner countered by warning Sibley not to address a superior officer in such a manner.

"I will speak to you in that way or in any other way I please," the captain shouted back at the major. Sibley, whose antipathy toward Sumner had not subsided since the incident between the two during the assault on Casa Mata during the battle of Molino del Rey, later admitted that the remark was "altogether impulsive and induced by his own excited manner."[68] On October 19, one day after the verbal encounter, Major Sumner preferred charges against Captain Sibley, accusing the captain of "conduct highly disrespectful towards his commanding officer."[69]

General Winfield Scott, upon hearing of the charges, ordered Sibley to make "amends" to Sumner or face a court martial. The captain, whose pride and ego were badly bruised, apologized instead to Colonel Harney. General Scott, still not satisfied, demanded that the "same amends" be made to Sumner.[70] The captain, realizing that his military career might be seriously damaged by a further pursuit of the feud, with considerable reluctance and hesitation, finally apologized to Sumner. On October 30, Sumner, believing that Sibley "had done what was useful and proper in the matter," asked "permission to withdraw the charges."[71] The feud and resulting consequences had settled very little and had served only to embarrass both men.

Attempts at negotiating a treaty with the chaotic Mexican Government failed, and the war with Mexico was technically still a reality. Sibley was helping to keep the lines of communication open to Vera Cruz. Most of his duty consisted of guarding supply trains which

[68] Ibid.

[69] Charges and Specifications Preferred Against Captain Henry H. Sibley, 19 October 1847, A.G.O., L.R., Army of Occupation, R.G. 94.

[70] H.H. Sibley to H.L. Scott, 1 November 1847, A.G.O., L.R., Army of Occupation, R.G. 94.

[71] E.V. Sumner to H.L. Scott, 30 October 1847, and E.V. Sumner to H.L. Scott, 4 November 1847, both in A.G.O., L.R., Army of Occupation, R.G. 94.

arrived in the capital weekly. Even after the completion of the Treaty of Guadalupe-Hidalgo on February 2, 1848, he remained in México with a portion of the American Army until Congress ratified the treaty.

November of 1847 found Sibley sick in the City of México. By December 9 he was in command of an escort accompanying General Twiggs' division and a large supply train to Vera Cruz. The slow trek from the central valley over the Sierra Madre Oriental to Vera Cruz took until December 22. Spending Christmas in Vera Cruz, Sibley left the coast on January 2, 1848, arriving back in México City three weeks later.[72] In February the captain was dispatched from Mexico City to Puebla to escort supplies and mail back to the capital. He left México City on the 14th, arriving in Puebla on the 17th and returned to the capital on the 26th.[73]

In México City several American officers founded an officer's club in October 1847 which they christened the Aztec Club. Franklin Pierce was elected the first president. The club was really a chance for more relaxed fraternization, gambling, drinking, and merrymaking. Many of Captain Sibley's colleagues in the club would later command major armies in the American Civil War. In fact the roster of the 160 officers in the club, ranging in rank from major-general to lieutenant, read like a who's who of the Civil War. They included P.G.T. Beauregard, Barnard E. Bee, Richard S. Ewell, Thomas T. Fauntleroy, Ulysses S. Grant, William J. Hardee, Joseph Hooker, Joseph E. Johnston, Robert E. Lee, Mansfield Lovell, John B. Magruder, George B. McClellan, Andrew Porter, Charles P. Stone, and Earl Van Dorn.[74]

Although escort duty to the coast took much of his time, Sibley was able to attend bullfights and to drink and play monte at the Aztec Club. Two of his gambling colleagues were future President Pierce and Colonel Magruder.[75]

While at the Aztec Club several of the officers made plans for an expedition to climb the volcano Popocatepetl, which the men mis-

[72] R.R., S.D., A.G.O., R.G. 391.
[73] Huger Diary, 26 February 1848.
[74] Wilcox, pp. 710–11.
[75] *Texas State Gazette*, 2 October 1852; Roy Franklin Nichols, *Franklin Pierce: Young Hickory of the Granite Hills* (Philadelphia, 1958), 167.

takenly thought to be the highest mountain in North America.[76] Officers in the expedition, besides Sibley, included Ulysses S. Grant, James Voty Bomford, Zealous Bates Tower, Andrew Porter, Ralph Wilson Kirkham, Richard Anderson, Charles Pomeroy Stone, Mansfield Lovell, Simon Bolivar Buckner, and George Bibb Crittenden.

Sibley, who was to take Company I of the Second Dragoons as an escort, was appointed "commandante" of the expedition. Lieutenant Grant was chosen as the quartermaster. Jokingly, Henry referred to the other officers in the group as mere "amateur tourists."[77] Leaving México City on April 3, 1848, the expedition proceeded along the main road to Vera Cruz, past Mexicalzingo and Lake Xochimilco to Chalco where the party turned south to Miraflores. Here the officers spent the night in an elaborate hacienda which Henry felt had to be one of the most elegant private residences in all of México. It was also here that Henry recalled "broad and endless fields of corn and wheat, which extended beyond the vision, and the gardens and plantations of tropical fruits nearer the house, lent a full realization to its name, and presented a scene romantic as beautiful."[78]

Early the next morning the explorers rode on to the village of Amecameca where they took time to visit the hill-top shrine of El Sacromonte. Next to the shrine of Guadalupe, El Sacromonte was thought to be the most sacred site in México. Climbing the sacred hill, Henry watched as devout pilgrims knelt at the various stations to deposit small coins and miniature religious figurines. Built around a small cave, the shrine contained a full size image of Santo Entierro. Unimpressed, Henry wrote that the church was "a very ordinary one."[79] After leaving a few coins in the hands of the priest, the adventurers descended to the small village for the night.

The next day the amateur alpinist rode on to the village of Ozumba, at the base of Popocatepetl. Here the northwest face of the mountain

[76] Ulysses to Julia, 7 May 1848, *The Papers of Ulysses S. Grant* (Carbondale, 1967), I: 156; Mexico City *American Star*, 12 April 1848; [S. B. Buckner], "A Visit to Popocatepetl," *Putnam's Monthly*, (1 April 1853), 408–16; Arndt M. Stickles, *Simon Bolivar Buckner: Borderland Knight* (Chapel Hill, 1940), 18–19. Cornelius Irvine Walker in *The Life of Lieutenant-General Richard Heron Anderson of the Confederate States Army* (Charleston, 1917), makes no mention of that officer's ascent of Popocatepetl.

[77] [Henry H. Sibley], "Ascending the Popocatepetl," *Frank Leslie's Chimney Corner*, (25 June 1881), 103.

[78] Ibid.

[79] Ibid.

rose more than two vertical miles above the floor of the valley, and Captain Buckner recalled later that the mountain "presented an appearance of grandeur seldom equalled even in the wildest forms of nature.[80] In the shadows of the spire of a late sixteenth century Franciscan Church, they hired two Indian guides with mules to carry forage for their horses. Grant wrote of the ascent many years later in his memoirs: "It was possible to go on horseback as far as [the] Vaqueria, though the road was somewhat hazardous in places. Sometimes it was very narrow with a yawning precipice on one side, hundreds of feet down to a roaring mountain torrent below and almost perpendicular walls on the other side."[81] One of the mules loaded with sacks of barley, after striking its load against the mountainside, fell hundreds of feet to the bottom of the canyon. To the men's amazement, the animal survived and, with its owner, continued the journey.

Although several of the officers decided to spend the night in the Vaqueria, a cowshed less than twelve feet square, Sibley, along with Anderson, Porter, and Tower, climbed higher up the mountain where they pitched a tent near a deep, dark ravine. Early in the evening a terrible storm arose, and snow fell heavily. Henry recalled the terrifying lightning and thunder more than the snow since the lightning and thunder "came in such successive flashes as to fill us with dread and consternation."[82] The next morning the climbers were astounded to discover that many of the trees in the vicinity had been shattered by the lightning.

Grant, who spent the night in the Vaqueria, reported: "It was very cold and the rain fell in torrents. A little higher up the rain ceased and snow began. The wind blew with great velocity. The log cabin we were in had lost the roof entirely on one side, and on the other it was hardly better than a sieve. There was little or no sleep that night."[83]

At daylight the next morning Sibley, Grant, and the others began

---

[80] [Buckner], p. 410. The author made ascents of Popocatepetl in December 1979, and again in December 1980. The mountain, by Alpine standards, is not technically difficult, requiring only a minimum of mountaineering equipment such as crampons, goggles, ice axe, etc. It would present, however, a formidable challenge to anyone as poorly equipped as the Americans in 1848, despite their youth and excellent physical condition. The ascent, even today, would be especially difficult in bad weather similar to that encountered by the Americans in 1848.

[81] U. S. Grant, *Personal Memoirs of U. S. Grant* (New York, 1885), I: 181.

[82] [Sibley], "Ascending the Popocatepetl," p. 103.

[83] Grant, p. 182.

their ascent. Henry equipped himself well for the climb wearing "thick woolen trousers and socks, a red flannel shirt and cap of the same material, and thick, heavy, long boots."[84] The two guides refused to go much beyond base camp, arguing that the Americans were now in the forbidden region and to ascend further would cause certain blindness or even death. Following the footprints of the more energetic climbers, Sibley, accompanied by Stone, climbed high on the mountain. They continued through the clouds, and on a few occasions, caught glimpses of the countryside below. As they continued up the ever steepening slope, Henry recalled how the violent gusts of icy wind swept the ever deepening snow around the mountain like an alpine hurricane. Grant wrote: "We labored on and on, until it became evident that the top could not be reached before night, if at all in such a storm, and we concluded to return. The descent was easy and rapid, though dangerous, until we got below the snow line. At the cabin we mounted our horses, and by night were at Ozumba."[85]

Sibley and Stone did not give up as easily. They climbed to the base of the Pico del Fraile, a northern spur of the volcano, at an altitude of over 15,000 feet. Here Stone collapsed in the deep snow. Having lost his cap in the high wind, Stone complained of the terrible cold and of "great fatigue" and refused to continue. The two climbers, who had been climbing for over five hours, found shelter under a rocky crag. Henry, lighting a cigar, produced a pint of champagne, hoping the alcohol would help rejuvenate his companion. After a brief rest, Henry prodded Stone to continue the climb. "Go on yourself; let me sleep awhile," Stone replied, obviously suffering from altitude sickness.[86]

Sibley proceeded up the steep snow slope for a hundred feet before coming to the realization that to leave his friend this high on the mountain in the terrible cold might well mean death. Returning to find Stone immobile, Henry massaged his comrade's hands and then assisted him down the mountain. Besides preventing probable frostbite, Sibley may well have saved his friend's life by his decision to descend.

Safely back at base camp, Henry was joined by Bomford, Anderson, and Buckner, who had been in the forward assault. They too had failed in their assault on the towering volcano, climbing to within two

[84] [Sibley], "Ascending the Popocatepetl," p. 103.
[85] Grant, p. 183.
[86] [Sibley], "Ascending the Popocatepetl," p. 103.

thousand feet of the summit. Due to the approaching darkness, it was obvious the men would have to spend the night at the Vaqueria and could not descend to Ozumba as the majority of the party had. The Vaqueria was too small to house all the climbers; thus, Sibley, accompanied by Anderson, Stone, and Tower, spent the night wrapped in their blankets under a wagon cover.[87]

Not long after dark one and then another of the amateur climbers began to complain of a terrible burning sensation in the eyes. As the night progressed the pain worsened. "The agony became so intensified," Henry wrote, "that we arose from our blankets and wandered about on the mountainside."[88] Buckner also recalled his agony: "Never did I pass a night in such agony; and when I made an effort in the morning to open my eyes and look around me, it seemed as if a thousand pointed arrows, instead of rays of light, had pierced to the retina of my eyes."[89] Grant, who was safely back in Ozumba, also experienced much the same pain: "Long before morning first one and then another of our party began to cry out with excruciating pain in the eyes. Not one escaped it."[90]

When they had landed at warm and sunny Vera Cruz some twelve months earlier, snow blindness was the last thing Sibley and the West Pointers expected to encounter in México. The Indian peasants were correct after all. The mountain did cause blindness.

Sibley, like most of the men, was forced to descend from the mountain blindfolded. The men's horses were led by the few in the party who were able to see. Back in Ozumba the men bathed their eyes in cold water, and by late afternoon most were able to see again.

The next morning the clouds were gone from Popocatepetl, and the lure of the mountain peak was too much for some of the men who decided to attempt the mountain a second time. Lieutenants Stone, Buckner, and Anderson, along with several other officers successfully reached not only the rim of the crater, but at twenty minutes past ten o'clock on the morning of April 11, 1848, planted the "stars and stripes" on the summit of the smoking mountain.[91]

[87] Ibid.
[88] Ibid.
[89] [Buckner], p. 413; México City American Star, 12 April 1848.
[90] Grant, p. 183.
[91] México City American Star, 16 April 1848; [Buckner], p. 415. Popocatepetl was not the highest mountain in North America. Mt. McKinley at 20,320, Mt. Logan at 19,850, Orizaba (Citlaltepetl) at 18,855, and St. Elias at 18,008, are higher.

Sibley, Grant, Porter, and several others decided instead to visit the great caves of México, some ninety miles from Amecameca on the road to Acapulco. The party, leaving the others to ascend the 17,887 foot wind-swept summit of Popocatepetl, rode down a beautiful flower filled valley to Cuautla, a picturesque town built near a thermal spring. The future Union general and president reported of the journey: "In the morning we left a temperate climate where the cereals and fruits are those common to the United States; we halted in the evening in a tropical climate where the orange and banana, the coffee and the sugarcane were flourishing."[92]

As Sibley, Grant, and Porter approached Cuautla, they heard bugles and saw soldiers rushing from a guardhouse in their direction. Grant hastily tied a white handkerchief on a stick and began waving it as a flag of truce, still proceeding toward the town with Sibley and Porter following. Grant sent a message to the commanding general in the town and was soon escorted to the general's headquarters where he was told that the Americans were in violation of the truce which had ended the war. The men were allowed to spend the night in a shack adjacent to the guardhouse and the next morning were even given a guide to put them on the right road to Cuernavaca.[93]

On the way from Cuautla to Cuernavaca, the travelers stopped at Yautepec, an Indian village, where they ascended a hill overlooking the town to inspect "the tomb of an ancient king."[94] Pulling a cart behind them, the party reached semitropical Cuernavaca on the evening of the following day where they rested. Striking out again, the explorers traveled south through the colorful countryside. After a few miles they were stopped by armed guards and notified again that they were in violation of the armistice and should travel no further. The Americans attempted to convince the guard that they were "a mere party of pleasure seekers desirous of visiting the great natural curiosities of the country."[95]

The officers were directed to a large hacienda and told to remain there until the commanding general of the area could be notified of their presence. The guard absolutely refused to allow the party to travel farther without directions from his commander. The follow-

[92] Grant, p. 185.
[93] Ibid., p. 186.
[94] Ibid.
[95] Ibid.

ing morning the guard refused to allow the Americans to continue, arguing that he had not received any instructions. Sibley and Grant concluded that the guard had never sent any message. Grant wrote that they "were determined therefore to go on unless stopped by a force sufficient to compel obedience."[96]

The party had traveled but a few miles when once again armed guards ordered them to stop. The commander of the village was hospitable, guiding the Americans around the town and directing them to the proper road leading to the great caves. That night the party rested at a large coffee plantation about eight miles from the caves. It was Saturday night at the hacienda, and "the peons had been paid off, and spent part of the night in gambling away their scanty week's earnings."[97] Grant estimated the poor campesinos had received no more than twenty-five cents in copper for their week's labor.

Early the following morning the explorers were at the mouth of the great caves of Cacahuamilpa. They were well prepared with guides, candles, and even rockets. Grant reported: "We explored to a distance of about three miles from the entrance, and found a succession of chambers of great dimensions and of great beauty when lit up with our rockets. Stalactites and stalagmites of all sizes were discovered. Some of the former were many feet in diameter and extended from ceiling to floor."[98] All were impressed with the enormous chambers, grottos, and limestone deposits which were in fantastic shapes. Grant compared the caves to the Mammoth Caves in Kentucky which he had visited as a youth. Leaving Cacahuamilpa, the officers were in Mexico City within a few days and back on escort duty by April 19.

April regimental records listed Sibley at Hacienda Encero. Late in the month he was reported as sick at México City, having relinquished command of Company I. In May he was ordered on escort duty to Vera Cruz, arriving there on May 6 and returning to México City on May 18 along with fourteen recruits recently arrived from the United States.[99]

In late May, it was announced in México City that the Treaty of Guadalupe-Hidalgo had at last been ratified by the United States Congress and that the war was officially over. On June 4 Sibley said

[96] Ibid., p. 187.
[97] Ibid., p. 188.
[98] Ibid.
[99] México City American Star, 19 May 1848; R.R., S.D., A.G.O., R.G. 391.

goodbye to México City and was already on his way to Vera Cruz when eight days later the Stars and Stripes were lowered from the National Palace as both Mexican and American batteries fired salutes. Sibley reached Puebla on July 11, Perote on the 15th, and Jalapa on the 21st. He was in Vera Cruz on the 22nd and boarded a steamer for New Orleans the same day, arriving in the Louisiana city five days later.[100]

One day after reaching New Orleans, Sibley and his company took passage on the steamer *Galveston* and three days later were in camp on Dog River, six miles east of Pascagoula, Mississippi. For Captain and Brevet Major Sibley, along with Company I, Second Dragoons, the Mexican War was now memories. He had become a combat veteran at age thirty-two.

Chapter IV

The Texas Frontier

Brevet Major Henry Hopkins Sibley remained in camp at Pascagoula, Mississippi, until late September 1848 when he was ordered on another recruiting tour. He received the news with considerable enthusiasm. After several months of monotonous duty in México, Henry was anxious to see American society again and to be with Charlotte and daughter Helen Margaret.

His first assignment was Baltimore. He found Baltimore, nestled against Chesapeake Bay, to be a rich and proud city boasting a population of over 150,000. Merchants and bankers scurried about the bustling city taking advantage of new markets and commerce generated by the Baltimore and Ohio Railroad which was hurriedly building westward across the Cumberlands. Steamers lined the city's bustling wharves bringing hides from Brazil and Argentina to supply the city's growing tanning industry as well as coffee from other Latin American ports. Packets made regular runs to ports north and south.

Most important for Sibley was the large number of immigrants from Germany and Ireland who walked the city's streets. They were mostly

Catholic, usually destitute, and frequently willing to take any job. All were prime recruits for the army.[1]

No sooner had Sibley arrived in the Maryland city than he was reprimanded for allegedly having a bugler from Company I accompany him.[2] Henry was ordered without delay to send the trooper to Carlisle Barracks, Pennsylvania, where the young man was to proceed, along with a company of recruits, to Texas, where the majority of the dragoons were serving on the frontier. It was later learned that Captain Sibley had indeed detached the bugler from his company but that the young man had traveled north with the Fourth Infantry instead. Still, army headquarters felt Henry had "acted without authority" and "regretted that the soldier was separated from his company."[3]

Henry remained at Baltimore in search of recruits from October 1848 until July 1849. While there, Charlotte became pregnant for a second time. A son was born in 1849.

From Baltimore the captain was ordered northward to Boston to find more young men. The Boston of 1849 was much like the city Henry had seen three years before, but now there were more Irish immigrants. As many as forty thousand had arrived in a single year. As the strangers cautiously made their way into the new land, a few young men were attracted to the recruiting office of the brevet major who was more than anxious to enlist them in the United States Army.

Undeniably, Sibley was a tough recruiter whose first impression on interested enlistees was not easily forgotten. Several years later a dragoon, enlisted by Sibley in Boston, recalled the brevet major's stern warnings: "And, mark me, young man, if you take this step you will regret it only once, and that will be from the time you become acquainted with your position until you get out of it; and another thing, a large percentage of men never return to their friends. If you have no friends you ought to have, and if for any reason you want to hide

---

[1] Hamilton Owens, *Baltimore on the Chesapeake* (Garden City, 1941), 260; Robert I. Vexler ed., *Baltimore: A Chronological and Documentary History* (Dobbs Ferry, N.Y. 1975), 43.

[2] L. Thomas to Henry H. Sibley, 6 November 1848, Letters Sent by the Recruiting Service, Vol. V, The National Archives, Washington, D.C. Hereafter referred to as R.S., L.S., R.G. 94.

[3] L. Thomas to Henry H. Sibley, 8 November 1848, R.S., L.S., R.G. 94.

self from the world, try something from which you can free yourself if you so desire."[4]

After a firm caution as to their uncertain and perilous future, the young recruits were told to reappear at the recruiting office the following morning. The moral background of potential recruits was inconsequential as was their degree of inebriation. If a potential recruit arrived at the recruiting office drunk, Sibley simply told him to return when sober. If the individual still expressed a desire to join the dragoons, he was then given a superficial physical examination, ordered to sign the necessary papers, sent to the nearest tailor to be fitted into a uniform, and paid the highly-coveted bounty. When about fifty recruits had been enlisted, they were dispatched as a unit to Carlisle Barracks for training. Brevet Colonel Philip St. George Cooke, a well-known officer who had commanded the Mormon Battalion during the Mexican War, was in charge of the training of recruits for the First and Second Dragoons and a regiment of Mounted Rifles.[5]

While Sibley was on duty in Boston, his distaste for clerical work led to a lengthy dispute with Colonel Cooke. Before it was over the squabble required intervention by the secretary of war. Although dormant for several years thereafter, the feud would later affect Sibley's being court-martialed.

It was most difficult for an officer, especially one with a wife and two children, to survive on the meager salary the army paid its officers. Sibley was frequently penniless. In July 1849 he was forced to admit to Commissary General George Gibson that he could not account for money which had been appropriated for his recruiting expenses. For this General Gibson reported the brevet major to the secretary of war. Henry confessed that he was unable to render his accounts, a mere oversight, he argued, which was due to a "loss of voucher."[6] Sibley assured General Gibson that the money had been "expended in the public service." When pressed on the matter, Henry

[4] Percival G. Lowe, *Five Years a Dragoon and Other Adventures on the Great Plains* (Norman, 1965). 4.

[5] Otis E. Young, *The West of Philip St. George Cooke, 1809–1895* (Glendale, 1955), 241–43.

[6] H.H. Sibley to George Gibson, 24 July 1849, Consolidated Correspondence File on the Sibley Tent, Quartermaster General's Office, Letters Received. Hereafter referred to as C.C.F., Q.G.O., L.R., R.G. 92.

simply stated that he was unable to pay the amount for which he was accountable. Washington took no further action.

So desperate was Sibley for money that he even submitted a voucher to Washington covering all personal losses of property during the Mexican War.[7] When Washington found irregularities in his claim, Sibley asked for permission to go to Washington for a personal interview with the auditor of the treasury, who Henry despondently asserted had not even bothered to reply to his correspondence. Only in this manner could the uniqueness of the voucher be explained, he claimed. Henry asked Roger Jones, adjutant general of the army, for permission to accompany a detachment of new recruits from Boston to Carlisle Barracks, at which time he would have an opportunity to visit Washington.[8] The adjutant general's office, evidently "fed up" with Sibley's constant complaining and inaccurate and seemingly corrupt bookkeeping, informed the brevet major that his presence in Washington was not necessary. A simple "compliance with regulations" was all that was needed.[9]

Henry's continued squabbling with Washington was trivial compared to his growing feud with Colonel Cooke. The dispute started when Cooke accused Sibley of sending to Carlisle Barracks recruits who did not meet the physical standards of the army. The colonel called a Board of Inspection, which rejected two of Sibley's recruits for having stiff fingers. Furthermore, Cooke ordered Sibley to pay out of his own pocket the cost of transporting the recruits to Carlisle and then back to Boston. In a defiantly sarcastic letter Henry assured Cooke that all recruits would thereafter be examined by a physician. Henry, nevertheless, disagreed with the board. Cooke, claiming that he did not know how to reply to Sibley's provocative correspondence, forwarded one of Henry's letters to the adjutant general as proof. Cooke reported that the Board of Inspection was well experienced, having a "united service of 63 years," and that Sibley's criticism was out of line.[10] The board, whose decision on the recruits was unanimous, "could scarcely expect to receive the thanks of a young officer for simply performing their duty," Cooke asserted. The brevet colo-

[7] H.H. Sibley to Roger Jones, 14 September 1849, A.G.O., L.R., R.G. 94.
[8] L. Thomas to H.H. Sibley, 14 September 1849, A.G.O., L.S., R.G. 94.
[9] D. Kayton to L. Thomas, 19 September 1849, A.G.O., L.R., R.G. 94.
[10] P. St. Geo. Cooke to R. Jones, 16 July 1849, A.G.O., L.R., R.G. 94.

nel was angry that Henry was being allowed to "censure" the board.[11]
Cooke's complaints eventually reached Secretary of War George W.
Crawford, who was already angry at Sibley for his poor bookkeeping
practices. Crawford ordered Sibley to "reconsider" the entire matter
and give greater attention to army regulations.[12]

When word reached Boston that both the secretary of war and the
adjutant general had sided against him, Sibley's fiery temper was
ablaze. He furiously argued that his letter to Cooke should never have
been referred to Washington and that it had been sent only because
Cooke hoped to embarrass him. He argued that he had written the
letter in a "half familiar, half official style" which had characterized
his correspondence with Cooke for some time. In no way, Sibley
maintained, was he attempting to be offensive toward his commanding officer.[13]

In the rejection of his recruits, Henry felt the Board of Inspection
had not followed army regulations. He was particularly angered that
Cooke was accusing him of trying to "censure" the board. Sibley boldy
declared that he was not interested in how many years of service the
board could claim: "The most salutary principle of our profession is
that rank and not length of service or length of years gives prece-
dence."[14] Henry was also incensed that Cooke had referred to him as
a "young officer." "I may be young in years compared with himself,
but, the government has thought me not unworthy of the rank of Field
Officer, of which Brevet Colonel Cook can boast no more," Sibley
wrote Washington.[15]

With his feuding and egotistical passions somewhat calmed,
Washington finally agreed that Sibley could hire a physician to examine all recruits. But Henry was unable to find one for the twenty
dollars a month the army was willing to appropriate. "Twenty dollars would secure the services of a physician, but he would not be of
a character I would confide in," Sibley wrote.[16]

In September 1849 fireworks between Sibley and Cooke continued
to explode when Cooke called another Board of Inspection which re-

[11] Ibid.
[12] G.W. Crawford to R. Jones, 24 July 1849, A.G.O., L.R., R.G. 94.
[13] H.H. Sibley to R. Jones, 6 August 1849, A.G.O., L.R., R.G. 94.
[14] Ibid.
[15] Ibid.
[16] H.H. Sibley to R. Jones, 6 September 1849, A.G.O., L.R., R.G. 94.

jected two more of Sibley's recruits. In the case of one, Philip H. Ward, Sibley admitted that "he may have stretched upon me, a trick not uncommon."[17] But after the young recruit had had his first taste of military discipline and was inspected by the Carlisle officers, was it not possible that the recruit had "crouched when measured by the board?" Sibley asked.[18] Further wrath was rained on the Boston recruiter when in October other recruits, while preparing for a march to Carlisle, deserted. Washington demanded to know the exact circumstances of what had happened.

In January 1850 Sibley sent another of his scathing letters to Washington complaining of Cooke's handling of his recruiting returns and asking that his complaint be presented to the secretary of war. Henry was upset that Cooke had for a second time sent back one of his recruiting returns for correction. Henry had corrected the original error but upon folding the large bulky paper had blotted it illegibly. A second error which Cooke overlooked the first time was also pointed out to the brevet major. Sibley assured Washington that he was "entirely blameless." What angered Sibley the most was Cooke's assertion that the recruiting returns "proved themselves untrue," a remark Henry thought derogatory, for which he demanded an apology.[19] Upon examining the case, the secretary of war found that Sibley was indeed responsible for the errors for it was his "duty to be careful and exact in preparation" of all paperwork. The adjutant general further informed Henry that Colonel Cooke was "within military authority to express to you his pointed disappointment."[20] Army regulations specifically stated that all returns were to be "correct in every particular and made in a neat and legible manner." The adjutant general saw nothing "personally offensive" in Cooke's assertion that Sibley's returns "proved themselves untrue" since such had long been the language used by army accountants.[21]

It is impossible to determine at what point alcohol came to affect Sibley's military career. This is primarily because documentation of a nonofficial nature, relative to the captain during this period of his life, is almost nonexistent. It is not known if he was able to keep aloof

[17] H.H. Sibley to R. Jones, 8 September 1849, A.G.O., L.R., R.G. 94.
[18] Ibid.
[19] R. Jones to H.H. Sibley, 10 January 1850, R.S., Vol. VI, L.R., R.G. 94.
[20] Ibid.
[21] Ibid.

from the scenes of drunkenness which were a part of cadet life at West Point. It is equally uncertain to what extent he had relied upon alcohol during the Second Seminole War. It appears that he first began to drink heavily during the war with Mexico. His somewhat erratic behavior and inept bookkeeping while in the recruiting service hints at periods of inebriation.

In late January 1850, after more than six months in Boston, Sibley was told to prepare to move his recruiting office to Pittsburgh. Once again he found time to complain about his orders. Such a move, especially in winter, would cause "serious inconvenience to my family and distress to my young children," the brevet major asserted.[22] Henry was forced to admit, as he should have known from past experience, that family considerations took a low priority when the army was concerned. Still, he found the order to move his office "obnoxious." "It is as much as an officer can do, under the most favorable circumstances, living in a city to keep body and soul together," Henry wrote.[23]

Sibley was not interested in going to Pittsburgh anyway for he felt St. Louis would produce better mounted recruits. Besides, he was anxious to visit his fifty-seven-year-old mother whom he had not seen in more than ten years.

Sibley's hopes of seeing his mother in the West were crushed when he was ordered to Utica, New York. At least there was some consolation since Utica was more acceptable than Pittsburgh. In early February 1850, Henry, Charlotte, and their two small children left Boston by stage, winding their way westward through western Massachusetts across the Connecticut River, the Berkshire foothills to the Hudson River at Albany, and finally by rail to Utica in the Mohawk River Valley of north central New York.

In Utica, Sibley's recruiting misfortunes continued to haunt him. In his haste to leave Boston, he had been faced with a pile of last-minute paperwork besides having to pay several recruiting expenses from his own pocket. In his "neglect, carelessness, or hurry, an incomplete report was sent," Sibley later admitted.[24] He later attempted to justify this by pleading that he was "brooding over the discomfort and distress my family would experience in making the journey to Pittsburgh." When Colonel Cooke returned an incomplete recruiting re-

[22] H.H. Sibley to the Adjutant General, 29 January 1850, A.G.O., L.R., R.G. 94.
[23] Ibid.
[24] H.H. Sibley to R. Jones, 26 February 1850, A.G.O., L.R., R.G. 94.

port for corrections, Sibley confessed that he had given way "to a moment of irritation." In his anger Henry accused Cooke of "an attempt to elicit forgery" and "contemplating a trick" by giving false information on how the blank trimonthly report should be completed. Sibley in his spite either deliberately filled the blank report with ciphers or did not understand Cooke's directions.

Once again the bitter squabbling between the Carlisle colonel and the recruiting captain had to be settled by higher officials and calmer minds in Washington. Henry was bitter toward Cooke, as the terse language in his correspondence to the adjutant general and the secretary of war shows. Sibley accused Cooke of being "most unfortunate and unhappy in the manner of expressing himself to his juniors."[25] In several of his letters Sibley quoted at length from Cooke's correspondence: "I am disappointed at your want of success; I want more men," and "I fear the attractions of your rendezvous are better calculated to swell your numbers than to elevate their character."[26] Sibley considered such phrases disrespectful and degrading, and his impetuous temper was once again ablaze.

The adjutant general, attempting to squelch the growing feud, was highly critical of both officers, especially Sibley. To General Roger Jones, Sibley had committed a "great injustice." Furthermore, Henry's persistent, quarrelsome character was evidence of "a spirit of disrespect, if not of insubordination, hardly excusable in an officer of his rank and experience." If Sibley could not "make out more accurate returns . . . the sooner he applies for orders to join his regiment the better," the general disgustedly wrote.[27] "Henceforth a more friendly and harmonious spirit must prevail," Jones advised in his attempts to halt the feud.

For the third time in less than a year, Washington had sided with Cooke. Sibley was hurt. As Jones had suggested, Henry immediately applied for orders to leave his rendezvous in Utica and join the dragoons in the west. Henry really did not want to go to Texas, where most of the Second Dragoons were then stationed, but was hoping for a transfer to the Sixth Military District where it would be possible to visit his "aged and unfirm mother . . . perhaps for the last time" as

[25] Ibid.

[26] H.H. Sibley to the Adjutant General, 9 March 1850, A.G.O., L.R., R.G. 94.

[27] R. Jones to P. St. G. Cooke, 20 February 1850, A.G.O., R.S., Vol. VI, L.S., R.G. 94.

well as his sister, neither of whom he had "seen for a number of years."[28]

Washington turned a deaf ear, and in July 1850 Sibley was ordered to another recruiting station: Rochester, New York, on the Erie Canal in western New York not far from the shores of Lake Ontario. Henry found the city to be somewhat illogical for recruiting purposes. With a population of slightly more than forty thousand, Rochester in 1850 was experiencing very little growth. Western urban centers like Chicago and Milwaukee were attracting immigrant trains loaded with hungry Irish and disillusioned Germans. Many of the trains hardly paused in the Flower City of Rochester. Declining trade on the Erie Canal did not help the captain's recruiting efforts either.[29] Henry along with his family, was to remain at Rochester into the fall of 1850. The trip from Utica to Rochester had been rigorous for the Sibley family, and the children and Charlotte were taken quite ill. Henry procured the services of a Rochester physician and the family recovered.

Henry, still incensed at Washington's criticism of his actions during the feud with Colonel Cooke, changed his mind about seeing his mother and sisters in Missouri and wrote Washington asking for a recall of his application for duty in the Sixth Military Department. Instead, he was anxious to take "shipping direct from New York to Galveston to join his regiment in Texas."[30]

In late August, Cook ordered Sibley to proceed to Carlisle Barracks where he was to join a detachment of newly-trained recruits and escort them to Texas. Worried about the health of his family, Henry wanted to know how the recruits would be traveling, overland or by sea. He was also concerned about the personal expenses of the trip and appeared to be in the same bad financial predicament that had caused him problems in Boston. In fact he submitted several vouchers to Washington which the adjutant general found unreasonable. Sibley had advertised for recruits which, according to army regulations, was not allowed. This was the same breach of rules for which he had been severely criticized during the War with Mexico. In Rochester and Utica, Henry had spent seventy-two dollars on medicines for his family, an expense which General Jones thought unreasonable

[28] H.H. Sibley to R. Jones, 5 June 1850, A.G.O., L.R., R.G. 94.
[29] Blake McKelvey, *Rochester, the Flower City: 1855–1890* (Cambridge, 1949), 5.
[30] H.H. Sibley to R. Jones, 22 August 1850, A.G.O., L.R., R.G. 94.

and refused to pay. Excessive amounts of money had also been spent for wood and for postage. Washington also rejected Henry's request of fifteen cents per mile in travel expenses from Boston to Utica and from Utica to Rochester, whereas government regulations allowed only for the exact amount of funds expended.[31]

Henry and his family arrived at Carlisle in mid-September 1850, and with ninety-nine recruits took up the line of march for Philadelphia and embarkation for Texas. From the Jones Hotel in Philadelphia, Henry sent a telegraph over the newly-built "Bain's Electro-Chemical Telegraph" to Washington requesting permission to employ a physician named Campbell to accompany the dragoon recruits to Texas. Within hours General Jones wired Sibley that a physician could not be authorized.[32] Dr. Campbell, along with Sibley, his family, and the ninety-nine recruits sailed for Texas, nevertheless. The trip was through a rough and broken sea. For almost a month their small transport was tossed about by the violent waves of the Atlantic. When the party reached the Gulf of Mexico, the storm seemed only to intensify. It was a miserable trip. The Sibley children as well as most of the recruits became seasick. The trip was particularly hard on Charlotte, who was now seven months pregnant. It was not until the middle of October that the dragoons sailed through Cavallo Pass, a sandy break in Matagorda Island, and put in at the bustling Texas port of Indianola.[33] Plans to land at Galveston had been altered since Henry felt Indianola was closer to the Texas frontier where six companies of the Second Dragoons were stationed.

From Indianola the road wound inland along the San Antonio River. The column crossed endless prairies where herds of deer and antelope gazed inquisitively at the bluecoats only to scurry away and disappear in the tall buffalo grass. Not far from the coast three recruits deserted. Henry ordered out a detachment to apprehend the recruits but they returned several hours later having been unable to track the deserters.

The Sibley's young son fell seriously ill and, despite Dr. Campbell's gallant efforts, died from a disease Henry felt had been con-

[31] R. Jones to H.H. Sibley, 12 September 1850, R.S., Vol. VI, L.S., R.G. 94.
[32] H.H. Sibley to R. Jones, 20 September 1850, A.G.O., L.R., R.G.94; R. Jones to H.H. Sibley, 20 September 1850, R.S., Vol. VI, L.S., R.G. 94.
[33] H.H. Sibley to R. Jones, 20 October 1850, A.G.O., L.R., R.G. 94.

tracted at sea.[34] It was especially tragic for Charlotte. Although Henry had been hardened by battle in Florida and Mexico, the untimely death of his son also grieved him deeply. He had not been forced to bear such a burden since the death of his father twenty-seven years earlier. After a hastily organized funeral and quick burial, the column continued its journey.

On October 26, 1850, the party reached San Antonio where Sibley gave the recruits a few days to recuperate from the long sea voyage and tiring overland trek. Henry took time to report to Washington on the progress of the trip. From San Antonio the column turned northward across the Guadalupe and Blanco Rivers through the eastern edge of the Texas Hill Country. As the bluecoats moved north, the land became more broken. Large oak trees dotted the landscape and an occasional tall pine tree was visible on the eastern horizon. At Austin, bustling capital of the Long Star State, the dragoons splashed across the Colorado River. Here the column split with the recruits being sent to various posts on the Texas frontier. The brevet major continued northward across the Brazos where on November 13, 1850, he proudly marched into Fort Graham and assumed command of his old company.[35]

Fort Graham, established by Colonel William S. Harney the previous year, was located on the east bank of the Brazos River near an old Indian village.[36] Sibley found conditions at Fort Graham quite different from his recruiting duty. His quarters, built on the north side of the fort near the road leading to the village of Waco, were crudely constructed of oak logs and a shingle roof. Carpenter, wheelwright, and blacksmith shops of cedar logs were built by hired laborers. The post hospital, made from squared oak logs, included two stone chimneys and an adjacent kitchen. Enlisted men's quarters, which had been built by a company of the Eighth Infantry, were also constructed of logs. The post magazine was the only stone building. Like all frontier posts Fort Graham had a guard house, but it was a peculiar looking roofless structure. The post also included a store house which the

[34] Ibid.

[35] R.R., S.D., A.G.O., R.G. 391.

[36] James Verdo Reese, "A History of Hill County, Texas to 1873," M.A. Thesis, University of Texas, 1961, pp. 50-58; Sandra L. Myres, "Fort Graham: Listening Post on the Texas Frontier," *West Texas Historical Association Year Book*, 59 (1983), 33–51.

dragoons had recently built. Mail at the post arrived from Austin twice a week.

Sibley seemed to like the independence and freedom allowed the post commander but appeared frustrated with all the bureaucratic paperwork required of the position. Although he had all the "responsibilities of [a] commanding officer of an isolated post" he also had "the concomitants of quartermaster, commissary and ordnance office thrust upon him . . . with all the post returns, abstracts and field reports enacted at the end of every month."[37]

On January 8, 1851, less than two months after Henry's arrival at Fort Graham, Charlotte gave birth to a son, Sidney Johnston. Sidney was named after Albert Sidney Johnston, Henry's aunt's brother-in-law, whom Henry admired greatly. Major Johnston was then serving as paymaster for the troops in Texas and was an occasional visitor at Fort Graham. Johnston's affection toward his namesake was illustrated five years later when in 1856 he deeded some 1,150 acres of headright land on the Clear Fork of the Brazos, some 177 miles above its mouth, to Sidney Johnston for a token fee of fifteen dollars.[38] Henry's grief for his first son was lessened by the birth of a second. After finding suitable quarters for Charlotte and the children, the captain did not hesitate in getting to his job.

In April 1851 Henry along with Captain William Chapman of the Fifth Infantry was ordered five hundred miles to the Mexican Border to attend a general court-martial at Ringgold Barracks. While encamped north of Austin one evening, the two officers lost their horses in the darkness and were forced to continue the trip on foot, a disgraceful experience for a dragoon. In Austin, Sibley, although embarrassed, purchased another horse for $132 and continued the trip.[39]

Arriving in San Antonio two days later, the men took up the long march for the Rio Grande. South of the mission town the wagon road wound into a vast desert dotted with thickets of mesquite. For almost a week the men continued on, crossing the Frio River and finally the Nueces River at an old Indian crossing where Fort Ewell was to be built two years later. Always watching the chaparral for a pos-

---

[37] [Sibley], "Military History of a Double-Barreled Shotgun," p. 442.

[38] Deed, Albert Sidney Johnston to Sidney Johnston Sibley, December 8, 1856; document in possession of Henry Sibley, Adams Basin, New York. These papers will hereafter be referred to as Henry Sibley Papers.

[39] H.H. Sibley to Thomas S. Jesup, 1 July 1851, A.G.O., L.R., R.G. 94.

sible Comanche or Lipan Apache ambush, the men reached the Rio Grande at the Mexican-Texan village of Laredo. Here at Fort McIntosh, only a stone's throw from the muddy waters of the Rio Grande, the two were greeted by Captain John H. King and several officers of the Fourth Infantry.[40]

The two did not tarry at Fort McIntosh, one of the most desolate and scurvy-ridden posts on the frontier, but hurried downriver past the small Mexican villages of San Ignacio, Carrizo, and Roma to Ringgold Barracks at Rancho Davis or what some were calling Rio Grande City. The court martial would last for more than two months, well into the hot summer of 1851, and Sibley did not return northward to Fort Graham until June.

Company I of the Second Dragoons had been ordered to Fort Graham to protect the ever-increasing number of settlers from hostile Indians. Bands of Indians visited the vicinity of the post almost weekly, but, contrary to what Sibley and most Americans were led to believe, the Indians proved to be anything but warlike. Frequently the Texas Indians warred among themselves. In April Sibley reported that eight Indians had been killed by a band of Tonkawa north of Fort Graham on the road to Fort Washita. Two weeks later a large party of Indians came to the fort expressing peaceful intentions. Sibley informed the Indians that they were in violation of a treaty that restricted them to an area north of the Red River. Later yet Henry reported to department headquarters that more than two hundred Indians from various tribes were in camp near the fort "on a friendly visit."[41] In June 1851 a Mexican boy, who had been captured from a party of Caddo Indians, was brought into the post. Henry sent the boy to Austin where Governor Peter Bell procured passage for the boy on the next south-bound stage to San Antonio, the Rio Grande, and home.[42]

While at Fort Graham, Sibley was asked to accompany Colonel Samuel Cooper, assistant adjutant general, on an important inspection trip to the Indian villages on the upper Brazos to obtain information for the authorities in Washington. Cooper, a New Yorker married to a Southerner, and Sibley, a Southerner married to a New Yorker, appear to have formed a lasting friendship during the trip.

[40] Jerry Thompson, *Sabers on the Rio Grande* (Austin, 1974), 173.

[41] Register of Letters Received, 1851–1857, Vol. XI, Department of Texas, A.G.O., R.G. 94.

[42] Ibid.

Leaving Fort Graham on the 5th of June, Cooper, Sibley, and a dragoon escort proceeded in a north-northwesterly direction along a route north of the Brazos River.[43] The column passed over a high prairie country, occasionally dotted with post and live oak, to Barnard's Trading Post on the left bank of the Brazos, some thirty-two miles distant from Fort Graham where the men bivouacked for the night. From rough notes taken on the expedition, Henry later drew a detailed map which, along with Colonel Cooper's report, was sent to Washington. The following day the column traveled twenty miles over rolling hills past Comanche Peak, a prairie beacon on the southern horizon, before camping for the evening.

The next day the party crossed to the north bank of the Brazos and continued upriver across rocky ground where they came to the Ioni Indian village nestled in a bend of the Brazos.[44] The Ioni were led by Chief Towysh who was subservient to Chief José María. At the Ioni village the dragoons recrossed the Brazos to the south bank and continued their trek over rolling prairie and through scrawny mesquite thickets. Here the country became more broken as the party again crossed the Brazos at a point where the river wound its way toward the northwest. The landscape, yet unspoiled by civilization, assumed "a more rugged and mountainous aspect," with "beautiful views of high mountain peaks in the distance."[45] One of the "high mountain peaks," which Sibley and Cooper passed within shouting distance of was "Bald-Head," so named because of its timberless summit. Continuing over sparsely-timbered terrain, the men crossed a small tributary of the Brazos which was full of perch and bass. The horsemen named the stream "Fish-Eating Creek"; today it is known as Loving's Creek.

Eight miles farther upstream the column came to the Keechi Village. Situated in a fertile and large valley of the Brazos, opposite a Caddo Indian camp, these Indians were about fifteen miles below the junction of the Clear Fork of the Brazos. At the Keechi Village the men

[43] "Report of Colonel Samuel Cooper, Assistant Adjutant General of the United States, of an Inspection Trip from Fort Graham to the Indian Villages on the Upper Brazos Made in June, 1851," *Southwestern Historical Quarterly*, 41 (April 1939), 330; Kenneth F. Neighbours, *Indian Exodus: Texas Indian Affairs, 1835–1859* (Nortex Publications, 1973), 78–79.

[44] Ibid., p. 328.

[45] Ibid.

were greeted by Chief Chacheruch and across the river by Chief Hadderbar of the Caddo Tribe. The Keechi head chief, however, was Acquash while the leader of the Caddo was José María who also governed the Ioni whom Cooper and Sibley had visited further downstream.[46] Near the Keechi and Caddo villages the party crossed the Comanche Trail, used by the Comanche to drive stolen horses and mules across the Red River to the Washita settlements where the party was told the stolen animals were sold to white traders. No reliable information was gathered about the Comanche except that they frequently passed through the Caddo and Keechi villages on their raids into central Texas and Mexico.[47] The Comanche, led by Buffalo Hump and Yellow Wolf, usually had in their possession horses, mules, and occasional Mexican captives.

After visiting the Caddo village the party commenced their return trek to Fort Graham, descending over broken country across Palo Pinto Creek to Comanche Peak where the men struck their old trail. In all, the expedition had visited four of the six tribes living along the Brazos. The soldiers had also gathered information on the Waco and Tawakoni living further upriver near present Waco Bend in Young County.

The expedition had also encountered a small band of Delaware and Shawnee about thirty-two miles upriver from Fort Graham. They were found to be cultivating corn and were "peaceable and well disposed."

In all the Indians were estimated to number one thousand and in Cooper's words were "perfectly peaceable and in every way disposed to cultivate friendly relations with the whites."[48] According to Colonel Cooper, the Indians desired "the fostering hand of the government to aid and encourage them." The tribes were reported to be raising corn and various vegetables. Their fields were extensive and in a fine state of cultivation. The tribes were anxious to obtain farming implements, especially hoes to "cultivate their crops to better advantage and to greater extent."[49]

Since game was scarce on the Brazos, the Indians asked for a few hogs and some cows from which herds of their own could be started. The Indians also expressed an interest in obtaining the services of a

[46] Ibid., p. 329.
[47] Ibid., p. 331.
[48] Ibid.
[49] Ibid.

blacksmith who could assist them in preparing their implements. Cooper and Sibley felt that the Indian requests were justified and would only "involve a trifling expenditure of money and would greatly contribute to their comfort."[50] In writing his official report of the expedition, Colonel Cooper appeared impressed with José María, head chief of the Anadarko, Towysh, and Ioni bands. The same was true of Acaquash, chief of the Waco, Chacheruch of the Keechi, and Ocherash of the Tawakoni.

In the months to come, Sibley would visit the various tribes on the upper Brazos several times. In Janury 1852 he wrote the editor of the Clarksville *Northern Standard* a lengthy letter explaining some of his feelings toward these Indians. The well-known Indian agent Jesse Stem, who had become a close personal friend of Henry's and who shared similar feelings toward the Indians, delivered the letter to the editor. Sibley reported the Indians hungry, destitute, and without energy to think of resisting his intrusions into their villages. Despite what many frontiersmen thought, the brevet major praised the Indians highly: "You know how often we hear them taxed as a lazy set, unworthy of our sympathy and concern—that they are not to be trusted—that the best of them would shoot you down for your horse, etc. I know of no people whom I would sooner trust with my life and property. I have upon several occasions left in their charge sick men and horses and have invariably found them faithful, and proud of the confidence reposed in them.[51]

Sibley recalled one particular visit to the Caddo Village on the upper Brazos: "At the earliest dawn, as I wandered through the 'patches' pertaining to the various wigwams, toil and industry, hunger and despair . . . were encountered at every turn. It was indeed a pitable sight to meet an occasional object of greater compassion than the rest, in some superan[n]uated old woman, who, as I approached would drop her hoe, and by the unmistakable motion with her hand across her stomach, manifest the cravings of hunger."[52] Since childhood Henry had always had a special place in his heart for the Caddo Indians. As a child he had fraternized with Caddos who had visited his grandfather's plantation at Grand Ecore and had later studied in the same

---

[50] Ibid.
[51] *Northern Standard*, 21 February 1852.
[52] Ibid.

classrooms at Miami Grammar School as young Caddos from Natchitoches.

The brevet major was also interested in the Tonkawa who were accused by many on the Texas frontier of cannibalism. The Tonkawa
had spent the previous summer in camp near Fort Graham. During
this time Henry had visited their village several times and had come
to know the Indians quite well. Sibley, who was inclined to agree that
the Tonkawa were indeed practicing cannibalism, had confronted the
Indian chiefs with the accusations on several occasions but the Indians had always denied it.[53] Sibley was especially interested in seeing
the government set aside land for the Tonkawa. To become agricultural, he felt, would help to cut down on the number of depredations
on the frontier. With the rapid disappearance of the bison in Texas
and in the Indian Territory to the north, Sibley had accurately surmised that it was necessary for the Tonkawa to make a transforma-
tion from their nomadic way of life and give up their dependence on
the buffalo if they were to survive. Sibley confessed to having a "deep
sympathy for these people."[54]

In October a large band of Kickapoo visited Fort Graham. Sibley was
uncompromising with their chief, telling him that he must leave the
area under the jurisdiction of the post commander. He was equally
stern with Creek Indians who passed near Fort Graham late in 1851
and early 1852.[55] Sibley, along with Agent Stem, who had his headquarters at the fort, even tried to pacify the more warlike Comanche
Chiefs Buffalo Hump, Sanaco, and Yellow Wolf. The three had come
into Fort Graham in February 1852 for a general council. Stem, like
Sibley, felt that many reports of depredations on the Texas frontier
were either exaggerated or erroneously blamed on Indians. As far as
Stem was concerned relations with the Indians on the northwestern
frontier of Texas was "entirely satisfactory," especially with the Comanche "who have been conducting themselves well."[56]

[53] Most anthropologists feel that the concept of the Tonkawa as cannibals came from
their ritual eating of flesh from the bodies of their slain enemies. Walter Prescott Webb
and H. Bailey Carroll eds., *The Hanbook of Texas*, (Austin, 1952), II:789.

[54] *Northern Standard*, 21 February 1852.

[55] Register of Letters Received, 1851–1857, Vol. XI, Dept. of Texas, A.G.O., R.G. 94.

[56] Jesse Stem to H.H. Sibley, 18 February 1852, Office of Indian Affairs, Photostatic
copies of originals in Barker Archives, University of Texas, Austin, Texas; Jesse Stem
to P.H. Bell, 20 February 1852, Governor Peter H. Bell Papers, Texas State Archives.

In July 1852, 185 angry residents from the frontier counties of Navarro, McClellan, Ellis, Bell and Williamson, sent a petition to Governor Peter H. Bell in Austin asserting that the Indians on the upper Brazos had killed sixty soldiers and were committing endless depredations. The military, especially Sibley's command at Fort Graham, was providing "no protection to Citizens as they bar[e]ly have a force sufficient for Camp duty and to Guard the Military Stores."[57] Specifically, the petition asserted that Sibley's horses were so broken down that the dragoons could not go in pursuit of the Indians who were constantly stealing horses in the vicinity of the fort. On only one occasion had Sibley sent out a scout and even then the patrol returned after only one day's absence with every man drunk. The incensed frontiersmen demanded that something be done to protect them from the "Savage Enemy."

On August 9 Sibley replied. He bluntly told Governor Bell that the frontiersmen were perpetuating lies. "Your petitioners have, in their enthusiasm, alarm and excitement, done my company an injustice by their departure from the strict truth," he told the governor.[58] To Sibley the petition was "utterly false and without foundation" and he asked Governor Bell to pay it little heed. He was particularly incensed that the drunkenness charge had become such public knowledge on the frontier that his regimental commander had written inquiring into the validity of the assertion. General Persifor F. Smith, commanding the Eight Military Department, was equally perturbed about the petition, feeling that the sole basis of the wild assertions was a vague rumor of an exploring party led by Captain Randolph B. Marcy being attacked north of the Red River by hostile Comanche late in June. To General Smith, there was "no foundation whatever for any of the material assertions in the petition."[59]

In August 1852 Sibley said adieu to Fort Graham. Along with Charlotte, Sidney Johnston and Helen Margaret the captain led his dragoons across rolling prairie some 110 miles to the south-southwest

[57] Petition from Citizens of Navarro, McClellan, and Ellis Counties to P.H. Bell, July 1852, Bell Papers, Texas State Archives.

[58] H.H. Sibley to P.H. Bell, 9 August 1852, Bell Papers, Texas State Archives.

[59] Persifor F. Smith to P.H. Bell, 9 August 1852, Bell Papers, Texas State Archives. Marcy had actually encountered a friendly party of Wichita. W. Eugene Hollon, *Beyond the Cross Timbers, The Travels of Randolph B. March, 1812–1887* (Norman, 1955), 137.

to occupy a post on Hamilton Creek, a tributary of the Colorado, fourteen miles above its junction with the larger river.[60] Fort Croghan, where they arrived on August 29, 1852, was on the edge of the Texas Hill Country, and had been established at the same time as Fort Graham. The forts were similar in appearance. Buildings were made of oak logs with shingle roofs. Officers' quarters consisted of four log houses, each having two rooms separated by a breezeway. For entertainment there was the small community of Hamilton on the opposite bank of Hamilton Creek which boasted of a population of two hundred, a few stores, and a tavern or two. Mail arrived over a rough and rocky road from Austin once a week. Sibley's stay at Fort Croghan, however, was to contrast dramatically with his peaceful tour of duty at Fort Graham.

As Sibley had learned, most Indian depredations came not from some grand design to rob and plunder the Texas frontier but out of desperation. Frequently, the Indians who passed near Fort Croghan were on the verge of starvation.[61]

Indian raids were reported throughout the winter of 1852–1853, many in the vicinity of the post. Matters reached a climax on a rainy night in the spring of 1853 when several Indians stole nine of the dragoons' best horses from the post stables. When the theft was discovered the following morning, Sibley, taking seventeen men, went in pursuit of the Indians.[62] Although heavy rain the previous evening had

[60] R.R., S.D., A.G.O., R.G. 391. Fort Croghan is located at the present town of Burnet.

[61] William Banta and John Wesley Cadwell, "Thirty-Seven Years on the Frontier or Fifty Years in Texas," Typescript, University of Texas Archives, p. 134. Published as *Twenty-Seven Years on the Texas Frontier* (Council Hill, Oklahoma: n.d.). An incident involving Sibley and a Seminole chief named Wild Cat or Coacoochee, as told by Banda and Cadwell, (who falsely identify the chief as Comanche), is no doubt confused since Henry's companion at Fort Croghan is identified as Robert E. Lee. Lee had become superintendent of West Point as of 1 September 1852. Previous to this Lee had been in Baltimore supervising the building of Fort Carroll. Douglass Southall Freeman, *R.E. Lee: A Biography* (New York, 1962), I: 301–19; Carl C. Rister, *Robert E. Lee in Texas* (Norman, 1946). Sibley's alleged cowardice in this incident as well as Lee's bravery, as reported by Banda and Cadwell, was possibly a reflection of the two men's post Civil War reputations. T.R. Fehrenback in his *Comanches: The Destruction of a People* (New York, 1974), makes no mention of any Comanche chief named Wild Cat. Mildren P. Mayhall in her *Indian Wars of Texas* (Waco, 1965), 92, briefly mentions a Seminole chief named Coacoochee who was reported to be camped on the Llano River in 1850 on his way to Mexico.

[62] Rupert Norval Richardson, *The Frontier of Northwest Texas, 1846 to 1876* (Glendale, 1963), 81; *Northern Standard*, 16 April 1853.

obliterated the trail, indications led Sibley to believe that the Indians were making for the villages on the upper Brazos. The column thus struck out for the newly established post on the Clear Fork of the Brazos, commonly known as Phantom Hill, roughly 175 miles distant. Further information caused the brevet major to believe the theft to be the work of the Wichita.

Reaching the Indian Agency on the Clear Fork, Sibley, in a conference with Agent Stem, was able to definitely determine that the horses had been stolen by a party of Wichita. Indian runners were sent to the Wichita village to demand the return of the horses and punishment of the thieves. Sibley waited at the agency for five days, occupying himself in "fishing and in night-shooting of turkeys."[63] On the fifth day, a band of Wichita were reported approaching the agency from the north, driving before them a small herd of run-down horses.

Riding out to meet the Wichita, Sibley was met by Koweaka, one of the principle chiefs of the tribe, who motioned in an "insolent" manner for the brevet major to dismount for a parley. Henry refused but bade the chief to dismount first, which Koweaka willingly did. Henry remembered the chief as "tall, straight, and graceful" and maintaining throughout the discussion a sense of dignity and honor. With Stem acting as interpreter and intermediary, Sibley demanded to know why the horses had been stolen. Koweaka replied that the stock had been "stolen by bad, unruly men; that he had had much difficulty in getting together the remnant he had brought; that he was very sorry, but could not control the bad men of his tribe."[64]

Sibley, unwilling to accept Koweaka's explanation, announced that he was holding the chief and his entire party captive, except for two braves who were to return to the village, until the remainder of the stolen horses were returned. To further intimidate the Indians, Sibley gave the signal for a detachment of dragoons, which had been concealed in a nearby thicket, to advance on the conference grounds. As Sibley later described the dramatic confrontation, Koweaka "arose from the bench upon which he had been seated, and by signs appealed to me not to put the indignity upon him of making him a prisoner. He begged me to dismount and hear him once more."[65] When Stem

[63] [Henry H. Sibley], "A Tragic Story of the Indian Sense of Disgrace," *Frank Leslie's Chimney Corner*, (15 February 1882), 263.

[64] Ibid.

[65] Ibid.

agreed with the Chief, Sibley acquiesced, resuming his previous position on a bear skin rug spread on the bare Texas earth. As a precautionary warning, however, Henry drew a butcher knife and proceeded to cut some tobacco for his pipe.

After sitting on the rug for several minutes, Koweaka suddenly arose and as Sibley recalled "took my hand, and lifting me up from the ground, embraced me twice in succession, then lifting his hand, he pointed to heaven and then to the earth, exclaiming: 'We have the same God in heaven, and the same mother in the earth! The same Great Spirit that watches over my acts watches over yours. Your horses have been stolen by bad men. You have bad men, as well as I. Allow me to return to my village. I will return the balance of the stolen property, and I will punish the criminals. Do not make a prisoner of me!'"[66] Although he was "touched by the conduct and impressive manner of the chief," Sibley persisted in his determination to hold the entire party hostage until the horses were returned. Sentries were doubled to prevent any possible escape.

Early in the evening Koweaka came again to see Sibley and the two sat before a camp fire for more than an hour. Koweaka begged the brevet major to come to his tent and talk with his wife, who had become quite despondent over the circumstances of his being held hostage. Taking some sugar, rice, and coffee as a token gift, Sibley agreed to go to the chief's tent where he remained for more than an hour, finally returning to his own tent about midnight. Years later Sibley could still recall the setting for the dramatic scene that was about to unveil: "The moon was shining as bright as day, and the entire camp, Indians and whites, were in complete repose. The sentries had just been relieved, the new ones were standing examining the Indians at their fires, the corporal of the guard, with his squad of relieved sentinels, was standing on the crest of the plateau looking down on the valley in which the Indian camp was located, when suddenly one of the Indians rose, approached the unsuspecting sentinel, and shot him with a pistol through the heart."[67] In the confusion, Koweaka rushed out of his lodge only to be mortally wounded. All of the Wichita managed to escape in the ensuing melee, except for an elderly squaw who was too feeble to run.

[66] Ibid.
[67] Ibid.

When order was restored, Sibley entered the chief's lodge to find Koweaka's wife and son dead, each stabbed through the heart by the chief. Koweaka's moccasins were at the head of the Indian bed, a practice of the Wichita, Kiowa, and other Indians, signifying that the one who placed the moccasins would never see them again.[68] Sibley wrote a vivid and moving description of the incident to Charlotte: "Nothing in romance or history that I have ever read approximated to his act of devotion and self sacrifice. [James Fenimore] Cooper never would have ventured to paint such a scene. The bright moonlight upon the beautiful countenance of the mother—for she was beautiful and young—with her innocent boy by her side."[69]

Twenty-nine years later the memory of the tragic incident remained deeply inbedded in Sibley's memory: "Alas! Poor Kho-e-wish-ie, how often I have regretted thy death and that of thy wife and child! But a sad fate willed it, and I cannot but die deploring it forever!"[70]

A few days after the dramatic incident at the Clear Fork Crossing, Sibley rode to the Waco village on the Brazos where forty horses thought to have been stolen from the area around San Antonio were found. Taking charge of the animals, the dragoons were in the process of driving the horses from the village when they were set upon by a band of nine arrow-shooting Waco. In the brief skirmish which ensued, one dragoon was wounded in the wrist by an arrow. Leaving the village in haste, Sibley was unable to ascertain the number of Waco casualties but estimated three or four of the Indians to be seriously wounded or killed.[71]

By the fall of 1853, the steadily advancing Texas frontier had all but passed Fort Croghan, moving west and north. Word came from Washington that the post was to be abandoned, and once again Company I of the Dragoons, with Sibley in command, moved out, leaving Lieutenant Newton Curd Givens behind to pack up and make property disposals. Departing Fort Croghan on the 14th of September, the dragoons, accompanied by a train of wagons carrying most of the property from the fort, arrived at the post on the Clear Fork of the Brazos, or Phantom Hill, ten days later.[72] Sibley was not excited about his new

---

[68] Richardson, p. 83; Mayhall, p. 209.
[69] *Northern Standard*, 16 April 1853.
[70] [Sibley], "A Tragic Story of the Indian Sense of Disgrace," p. 263.
[71] Richardson, p. 83.
[72] R.R., S.D., A.G.O., R.G. 391; *Texas State Gazette*, 3 September 1853.

assignment, feeling that the establishment of the fort on the Clear Fork of the Brazos would attract additional settlers and threaten the Indians' lands and peace on the frontier.

Sibley had been in command at Phantom Hill only a few months when word reached him of the death of his friend Jesse Stem. Sibley, Stem, and their wives had become close friends from the time Henry had arrived on the Texas frontier. Stem had resigned as Indian Agent and had purchased a farm on Clear Fork. After returning to his home state of Ohio, where he bought fruit trees, seed, and supplies, Stem had returned to Texas with a friend, William Leppelman, when the two were attacked and killed by a band of Kickapoo four miles outside of Fort Belknap on February 12. Immediately upon hearing the news, Sibley set out after the Indians. With Lieutenant Newton Givens, Arthur Tree, and thirty dragoons, he rode to Fort Belknap where he received reinforcements and on the following morning was able to find the trail of the murderers. Sibley followed their tracks over a rough and broken country but eventually lost them in a rainstorm. The dragoons located several books and Stem's personal belongings which were abandoned by the fleeing Indians near a spring north of the Big Washita where the Indians had camped for the night. A roan mare belonging to Stem was also found in a gully but had been shot by the Indians. After more than ten days in the saddle Henry returned to Phantom Hill. The murderers were later executed by the Kickapoo themselves, rather than turn them over to white authorities.[73]

Two weeks after the death of his good friend Stem, Sibley received word that a party of travelers had been ambushed by Indians about eighty miles west of Phantom Hill on the overland road to California. One of the survivors, a young Mexican teamster, told Sibley of the attack. In early spring a party of five-wagons had started for California. While camped in the desert east of El Paso near the Hueco tanks, the party had lost their horses to a band of raiding Mescalero Apache. Thirteen men pursued the Indians northward past the towering cliffs of El Capitan into the rugged Guadalupe Mountains. There they were ambushed. Only three of the party survived to report their comrades' deaths.

Several of the travelers, after spending the summer at El Paso, lost their enthusiasm for California and decided to return east. Outside

---

[73] *Texas State Gazette*, 6 May 1854; Neighbours, p. 106; Mayhall, p. 95.

Phantom Hill the party was attacked again, this time by Comanche. The surviving Mexican teamster thought the Indians were either Lipan or Mescalero since he had heard shouts of "Nacaye! Nacaye!" Apache for "Mexican! Mexican!"[74] The teamster had grabbed a rifle and attempted to fire on the Indians but was stopped by one of the women. Seeing this, the Indians set upon the party, tied the teamster to the wagon, scalped him and rode off with the woman, Jane Wilson, and her two brothers-in-law, boys seven and twelve years of age, as captives. The teamster, who was shot in the shoulder, was later found by friendly Comanche who sent word to Sibley at Phantom Hill. Henry sent out a relief party who brought the Mexican into the post.

Sibley dispatched a party to pursue the Indians. The sun-baked and drought-seared north Texas earth failed to reveal their trail. Henry did not give up hope of overtaking the Indians and sent out a second patrol. The scouting party, although traveling further west, failed to find any trace of the raiding Comanche. Sibley later wrote Robert S. Neighbors, special agent to the Texas Indians, hoping to procure funds to ransom the captives through friendly Indians.[75]

In October 1853, while Sibley was still at Phantom Hill, Texas Senator Thomas J. Rusk, a proponent of railroad construction in Texas, reached the post from Nacogdoches while searching for a "Pacific Road." Henry provided an escort for the senator who visited several villages of southern Comanche, west and north of the fort. Three of the Comanche Chiefs, Sanaco, Yellow Wolf, and Buffalo Hump were reported to be "perfectly friendly," presenting Sibley and the senator with gifts of beef. The chiefs also promised to secure and bring in the women and her two brothers-in-law, who had been captured earlier by a band of hostile Comanche.[76]

The post at Phantom Hill was not one of the favorites of the Army. Sibley, like his predecessor Caleb C. Sibley, a very distant relative, had problems at the post. In the first few months, seven men deserted from Company I. The captain found that many of the men stationed at the post were raw recruits who were poorly-trained and in need of

[74] H.H. Sibley to Robert S. Neighbors, 8 October 1853, Office of Indian Affairs, Copy of original in Barker Archives, University of Texas. For a thorough biography of Neighbors see: Kenneth Franklin Neighbours, *Robert Simpson Neighbors* (Waco, 1975).

[75] Ibid.

[76] *Texas State Gazette*, 1 November 1853; Mary Whatley Clarke, *Thomas J. Rusk: Soldier, Statesman, Jurist* (Austin, 1971), 190.

additional training. Many were without arms. Health conditions at the fort were terrible. "Scurvy, intermittent fever, dysentery, colds, and pneumonia were common ailments."[77] The post surgeon, who asked for barrels of pickels, argued that the high rate of sickness could be blamed on the fact that there was no variety of food at the fort.

Sibley's quarters—little more than a dilapidated hut constructed of poles—were on the north side of the post near the main road leading northeast to Camp Cooper and Fort Griffin. An inspector visiting the post felt the structure was sure to collapse with the first north wind. Lack of water was a problem. A cistern was dug near the parade ground, but rain was scarce on the Texas prairie. Water could be hauled in wagons from the Clear Fork of the Brazos, but it was often brakish. Sometimes the precious liquid was available from Elm Creek, a small tributary of the Clear Fork, but the water was seasonal and thus unpredictable. An eighty-foot well was dug to the southwest of the fort, but it frequently went dry.

Company quarters were similar to those of the officers: crude jacales walled with upright poles woven with sticks and plastered with mud over which thatched roofs were built. Suitable watertight thatch was difficult to construct and the roofs were like sieves. The guardhouse, one of the better buildings, was constructed of stone. A powder magazine, also built of native stone, was located on the west side of the fort. Sibley's headquarters included a reading room with a few books which had been brought by wagon from Austin. The headquarters and the adjacent adjutant's office, with two large stone chimneys, were often used for reading or during leisure moments for playing cards and drinking. There Henry spent much of his time.

In late March 1854 Sibley left Lieutenant Givens at Phantom Hill to prepare for the abandonment of the fort consequent to orders from the War Department and took a sixty-day leave of absence to visit his sixty year-old mother at Richmond, Missouri.[78] By April 18 Henry had reached Austin where, along with Colonel James Bomford and Captain Robert Granger, he checked into the fashionable Metropolitan Hotel. The captain was to join his company at Fort Belknap in May

[77] C.C. Rister, "The Border Post of Phantom Hill," *The West Texas Historical Association Year Book*, (October 1938), 5; M.L. Crimmins, ed., "W.G. Freeman's Report on the Eighth Military Department," *Southwestern Historical Quarterly*, 53 (April 1950), 448–53.

[78] H.H. Sibley to L. Thomas, 15 May 1854, A.G.O., L.R., R.G. 94.

but was able to get an extended leave for another three months to visit Charlotte and the children who had previously returned to Brooklyn. When his leave was up, Sibley still had not reported for duty and was carried on the regimental returns as "absent without leave" for four months. In fact, Henry did not return to the Texas frontier until March 1855. He found conditions at Belknap almost as bad as those at Phantom Hill: "The whole region for twelve miles around is the most arid and unproductive and the most deficient of building material. The water of the river is salty and the spring, distant more than a mile affords but a limited quantity of water . . . more or less of the same character. Indeed I could discover nothing to recommend the place."[79] Furthermore, Henry found that the location of the post had made the various Indian tribes on the upper Brazos, especially the Caddo, Anadarko, and the Ioni, uneasy and apprehensive.

Less than a month after arriving back on the Texas Frontier, Sibley undertook a scout up the Clear Fork of the Brazos River. The purpose of the excursion was personal in that Henry was interested in locating and surveying the land previously given his son by Albert Sidney Johnston. He had hoped to find the exact location of the land by first finding the spot where Captain Randolph B. Marcy's wagon road, which had been surveyed some six years earlier connecting Fort Smith, Arkansas, with New Mexico, crossed the Clear Fork. Unable to do so, Henry retreated back to Fort Belknap after only one day, having severely burned his hand in a camp accident.[80]

It was while Henry was at Fort Belknap that a rather incidental event was to turn his interests toward military innovation and later place his name on the lips of many a soldier around a frontier encampment or Civil War bivouac. The Sibley tent was to become within a few years a vital part of army military equipment.

With the coming of the winter of 1854–1855, blizzards swept the Texas plains with their usual fury. By early spring when Henry arrived back at Fort Belknap from Missouri, the weather had not changed. With a cold mist hanging over the open prairie, Brevet Major Sibley, accompanied by Surgeon Edward P. Vollum and a detachment of dragoons, rode out of Fort Belknap to one of the Comanche

---

[79] Kenneth F. Neighbours, "Fort Belknap," *Frontier Forts of Texas* (Waco, 1966), 5.

[80] H.H. Sibley to My Dear Colonel, 7 April 1855, Mason Barret Papers, Special Collections, Howard-Tilton Memorial Library, Tulane University, New Orleans, Louisiana.

villages, probably that of Buffalo Hump and Sanaco, not far from the fort. When they arrived at the Indian camp, Sibley and Dr. Vollum were invited into the chief's teepee. The teepee, about fifteen feet high and eighteen feet in diameter, was conical, supported by several poles interlaced at the top, and covered with buffalo hides. In the center of the teepee, a warm fire was burning, the smoke from the blaze making an easy exit through an opening at the top.[81] The men were amazed by the warmth and spaciousness of the dwelling.

On their ride back to Fort Belknap, Sibley and Dr. Vollum commenced a casual conversation on the practicality of the tent, especially in bad weather. Both men commented on the possibility of constructing a similar tent, with one pole in the center instead of several on the inside. The two men felt that such an addition to the Army's meager inventory of tents would be greatly welcomed. A few days later Sibley asked Vollum to supervise the construction of such a tent. The next day Dr. Vollum gathered up the few pieces of canvas that were available at the fort. The post blacksmith was asked to construct a tent pole to which a tripod might be affixed at the lower end, thus permitting a fire to be made with the tripod straddling the fire.

About this time a literary club known as the Brazorian Society met at the fort. The club, comprised of officers serving on military posts not far from the Brazos River, had been organized to help break the bleak monotony of life on the Texas frontier.[82] With Sibley as president and Dr. Vollum as secretary, the society met frequently. Speakers were presented or papers read. At one such meeting the tent became the major topic of discussion. The members decided to call their invention the Brazorian tent in honor of the society.

Sibley, after his lengthy absence in Missouri, had arrived back at Fort Belknap deeply "burdened with debt." Henry was, in the words of one Texas frontiersman, John Salmon Ford, "well charged with a fresh stock of humor and wit." Ford described Sibley as "a man of song and story, and possessed in an eminent degree the qualities constituting a boon companion . . . much loved by the officers and men."[83]

---

[81] "Memories of John Salmon Ford," Typescript, University of Texas Archives, p. 670. This particular data has been edited out of John Salmon Ford, *Rip Ford's Texas*, ed. Stephen B. Oates, (Austin, 1963) and is not mentioned in W.J. Hughes, *Rebellious Ranger: Rip Ford and the Old Southwest* (Norman, 1964).

[82] Ibid.

[83] Ibid., p. 672.

In sympathy with their "genial commander" and his financial problems, the members of the Brazorian Society, with a formal vote,
transferred all rights and title in the tent to Henry. The tent was
thereafter to be known as the Sibley tent.

A few weeks later a board of officers assembled at Fort Belknap for
the purpose of examining and reporting on the new tent. The groups
consisted of Major Hamilton Wilcox Merrill of the Second Dragoons,
Captain Gabriel Rene Paul, Lieutenants James McIntyre and John
Mullins, all of the Seventh Infantry, as well as Dr. Vollum of the
Medical Department.[84] The board met off and on for a period of eleven
days, making numerous experiments on the tent. During this time
the officers were able to witness the effects on the tent of heavy rain,
strong wind, and summer heat. On one occasion with rain pouring
down, a fire was built inside the tent. The officers appeared impressed with the tent's ventilation as well as the number of men it
would accommodate.[85] Recommendations forwarded to the War Department in Washington must have given Sibley reasons to rejoice.
The board found the tent "more comfortable, both in warm and cold
weather than those in use" and especially valuable in "cold weather;
particularly so when fuel is scarce as upon our frontier, where a few
sticks or buffalo chips will keep the tent perfectly comfortable."[86] It
was found that the tent was capable of accommodating twenty-five
men, complete with their arms and equipment. "The board is of the
opinion," the report concluded "that Major Sibley had underrated the
advantages of his improved Conical Tent; and considering its superiority over those now in use, they would recommend its adoption in
the U.S. Army."[87]

Following the meeting of the Board of Officers at Fort Belknap, Sibley wrote Adjutant General Samuel Cooper in Washington forward-
ing a detailed "plan and description" of the tent complete with several sketches. "So well satisfied am I of the superiority of this tent
and the mode of pitching it, over any other ever used and its special
adaptation of foreign services in the winter campaigns, that I have no
doubt of its immediate adoption by any government, to which it shall

---

[84] Report of a Board of Officers, Fort Belknap, Texas, 2 June 1855, Consolidated Correspondence File, Sibley Tent, Q.G.O., R.G. 92.

[85] Ibid.

[86] Ibid.

[87] Ibid.

be properly presented," the brevet major wrote.[88] Sibley told Cooper

[88] H.H. Sibley to Samuel Cooper, 15 June 1855, Q.G.O., L.R., R.G. 92. Sibley's article "Movable Homes and Tent Life," (1881) described his tent in detail: "It consists of a tripod of iron, four and a half feet high, with a socket at the joining of the three legs, into which fits and rests a pole nine feet long, furnished at the upper end with an iron pin. The tent is conical, eighteen feet in diameter at the base, terminating at the top with an iron ring eighteen inches in diameter, over which the canvas is sewed. From this ring spring three chains, meeting in a disk of iron about two inches in diameter. The tent has two doors. When the ground is selected for pitching, the tripod is spread, the pole is then laid down, one end being at the socket, the other end will mark the spot for a pin, which is driven. The measurement is then made in the opposite direction, and a pin driven in. Then the measurement is continued at right angles, and pins driven in. The tent is now spread, two doors attached to their respective pins, as well as the corresponding loops to the opposite pins; a man with the pole now enters under the canvas by one of the doors, inserts the pin into the eyelet of the iron disk, hoists up the fabric, the wind-fly or vane having been, meanwhile, attached to the pin; the tripod is lifted up by a second man, the end of the pole set in the socket, and the whole lifted to the uttermost tension of the canvas. The outer border is then pinned down, and the tent is complete."

"This tent will shelter eighteen or twenty men on a pinch; ordinarily fourteen men may be accommodated, with a fire burning in the centre, or if a stove can be afforded, then a conical stove, eighteen inches diameter at the base, three feet high, and an opening at the top six inches in diameter, with a door at the base, and a single joint of stovepipe twelve inches long, set in the middle of the tent, will afford all the necessary heat, all that is necessary being that the smoke be consumed. The blaze will frequently issue from the pipe two feet high, but it does no harm, and serves to warm and enliven the tent. There being no bottom to the stove, it serves excellently well for an outdoor fire, especially in a dry grassy country, protecting the camp from those frightful accidents which sometimes destroy whole trains. This stove may also, on occasion, serve as a store-chest of cooking equipage for ten or twelve persons. First, the water-bucket is put into the inverted stove; this is then filled with plates, cups, knives and forks, spoons, etc., then a pan for soup, in this a gridiron, the whole topped off with four vessels shaped to fit the space, and to be used for boiling, etc., in spaces cut in the four sides of the stove. These vessels should be made of zinc, and one of them arranged with a door opening outward, and with shelves for baking purposes; or, removing the shelves, for roasting a fowl or game."

"The central pole and tripod may be dispensed with by using three eighteen-foot poles on the outside, tied together at their point of junction, and the apex of the tent made fast to it. By this contrivance the interior space is entirely free, and the tent is more firmly secured from the effect of violent storms. With this arrangement, an excavation three feet deep may be dug, the "Sibley stove" placed in the centre, and quite as much comfort as in a house, and better ventilation, gained. For hospitals this tent, thus arranged, is invaluable, as was attested by all the surgeons on the Utah expedition. With this arrangement, or even with the guy-ropes provided for each tent, the loops may be unloosened, and the canvas stretched to shade four times the ground it occupies. The outside tripod may be made in joints of nine feet each, and transported with the tent, the entire weight not exceeding seventy pounds."

that if England and France had used such a tent during the Crimean War, thousands of lives could have been saved. To further convince the adjutant general of the practicality of the tent, Henry argued that in time of war, packing boxes and broken gun carriages would afford sufficient fuel for warmth and cooking. Sibley notified Cooper in the same letter that he had intention of procuring patents in England and France as well as in the United States. He had already written a friend, Lieutenant William W. Burns of the Fifth Infantry, who was back east, "to take measures to secure a patent."[89]

Despite the optimism of the officers on the Texas frontier toward the Sibley tent, the adjutant general was skeptical. Cooper questioned "whether it would be acceptable to the army for general service," and had doubts about "placing so many soldiers in one tent except in extraordinary occasions." To him the tent appeared to be nothing more than an enlarged French Bell tent with minor changes.[90]

Sibley felt that the tent had been thoroughly tested. In his "plan and description" the tent had been favorably compared to all others. Although the tent weighed six pounds more than the Bell tent, it was fifteen pounds lighter than the Wall tent. The Sibley tent could be pitched faster than the French Bell and Wall tents. Its greatest advantage was that a fire could be built inside even during the most inclement weather. Other advantages were that the fire was concealed and could not be detected by an adversary; and that its conical shape was more wind resistant than the Wall tent, a fact that had been well demonstrated by the Turks during the Crimean War with their conical tents.[91]

Cooper himself, in February of 1856, issued an order for a board of officers in Washington to inspect and examine the tent. General Sylvester Churchill, inspector general, headed the board which after a short delay convened on February 14. The officers concurred with the conclusions of the Fort Belknap report. They were particularly impressed with the use of the tent in cold weather. Like the Fort Belknap officers they concluded that "a few sticks or buffalo chips will keep the tent perfectly comfortable."[92] The tent did produce a slight

[89] Ibid.

[90] Endorsement on Ibid.

[91] Plan and Description of a Tent Constructed by Bvt. Major H.H. Sibley, C.C.F., Q.G.O., R.G. 92.

[92] Proceedings of a Board of Officers Designated to Inspect and Examine Sibley's Improved Conical Tent, n.d., C.C.F., Q.G.O., R.G. 92.

problem for officers for "whose accommodation in writing and other work, a tent with perpendicular walls is essentially necessary."[93] The board, in conclusion, recommended that twenty-five of the tents be made and put into the "hands of marching troops and those in camps, infantry, dragoons, and field artillery, and perhaps the laborers of the Quarter Master's Department, for future trial."[94]

Sibley had been back at Fort Belknap for only a few months when the entire regiment of dragoons was ordered to Fort Riley, Kansas Territory, for the purpose of restoring civil order to that troubled land. He would not return to Texas until June 1861. By then he would be a civilian pledging his allegiance and destiny to the Confederate States of America in what was to be America's most tragic chapter.

[93] Ibid.
[94] Ibid.

"Agreeable to your written instructions of yesterday's date . . . I proceeded to the town of Lawrence."

"Though a stranger in the town, I am satisfied there must be an excess of five or six hundred men over the permanent population. The ruins of a large stone hotel destroyed some months since have been used to construct a rude bastion of four sides, some forty yards in extent, the salients pierced for four guns each. The rubble stone of which this work is constructed would withstand but a shot or two, and the splintered rock would prove more destructive to the occupants than the shot. Besides this, there are two trifling earthworks— one a complete circle, with a shallow ditch—at the head of the main street of the town."

> H. H. Sibley to P. St. George Cooke, August 30, 1856, Dragoon Camp near Lecompton, Kansas.

Chapter V

Bleeding Kansas:
That Turbulent Land

For Sibley, bleeding Kansas beckoned. By late August 1855, six companies of the Second Dragoons had gathered at Fort Belknap for the
long march north. Before daybreak on the morning of August 27 a
column of cavalry and supply wagons wound their way out of the fort.
In command of the caravan was Major Enoch Steen who reported the
strength of his detachment "at 213 men, 228 horses, and 40 mules"
while his transportation consisted of "76 wagons, 428 mules, and 4
horses."[1]

After crossing the Red River the column continued into the Indian
Territory, through the lands of the Chickasaw, Wichita, Osage, and
Cherokee. The route was well chosen. Most of the country was rolling prairie, and rarely were the horse soldiers forced to travel more
than ten miles without finding good grass and water. The river cross-
ings were not difficult and there was "scarcely a stone to be seen until reaching the eastern and northern waters of the Arkansas." Major

[1] Rodenbough, p. 171.

Steen felt the route to be "an easy and perfectly practicable one," especially for the wagons.[2] Most of the animals were in good condition although a few were young Spanish mules that tended to be somewhat wild. Some of the horses developed sore backs caused by the new Grimsly's saddles which had recently been issued to the regiment. Soon the force crossed into the Kansas Territory fording the Arkansas and Kansas Rivers. After thirty-three days and 485 miles Sibley arrived at Fort Riley on September 28, 1855.

The other four companies of the regiment, under the command of Colonel Philip St. George Cooke, were already in Kansas. Since their arrival from New Mexico they had been on the trail of a band of elusive Sioux.

Gone from the regiment were many of Henry's old comrades. Two new regiments, the First and Second Cavalry, had been created, and several dragoon officers had transferred, receiving promotions in the process. Captain William J. Hardee and Lieutenants Nathan G. Evans, Charles W. Field and Davis S. Stanley were in the Second Cavalry. Captain Charles A. May and Lieutenant David Bell found themselves in the First Cavalry. Although the transfers had caused several promotions in the Second Dragoons, Sibley remained a captain and brevet major.[3]

The brevet major found Kansas in 1855 to be a volcano—a disturbed land torn by civil violence and political chaos. The turmoil had come with the passage of the Kansas-Nebraska Act which had repealed the Missouri Compromise. Previous to this the question of slavery in the western territories was considered settled. In May 1854, however, Congress had voted to open the Kansas Territory to settlement, and northerners as well as southerners flocked onto the prairie. The situation was tense as stump orators harangued and petty demagogues prevailed. Although few slaves were brought into Kansas, the issue of slavery tore the territory apart and threatened to plunge the entire nation into civil war.

From the halls of Congress to the sod and log huts of the small Kansas frontier settlements, the issue was argued. Both North and South were determined to have Kansas. In far-off New England Eli Thayer formed the Emigrant Aid Society which raised one hundred thousand

[2] Ibid.
[3] Ibid., p. 170.

dollars to ship arms to Kansas. The Sharp's rifles were dubbed "Beecher's Bibles," named for the abolitionist clergyman Henry Ward Beecher, brother of Harriet Beecher Stowe. Proslavery migrants from Missouri also poured into the territory, many to settle, others only to vote. The Missourians, who expressed a fear of the "foreigners" from New England, were able to gain temporary political control of the territory when in March 1855 an estimated five thousand "Border Ruffians," as abolitionist Horace Greeley called them, invaded Kansas to elect a proslavery territorial legislature. They quickly enacted a strict law prohibiting antislavery agitation and passed an equally harsh slave code. A short time after the Second Dragoons arrived from Texas, abolitionists, refusing to recognize the proslavery legislature, held their own elections. Thus, by January 1856 two governments existed in the territory. Kansas was rehearsing for civil war.

Sibley saw the Kansas winter of 1855–1856 through the frosted windows of the Fort Riley Officers' Barracks. One of the worst blizzards in memory brought life on the Kansas prairies to a halt, killing cattle as far south as Texas. By reading the local papers, however, Sibley came to know Kansas and to realize the immense problem of maintaining law and order in the harrowed territory. Although not yet completed, Fort Riley was one of the better western posts. Most of the fort had been constructed by civilian laborers at a dreadful cost. Three months before Henry's arrival, more than one hundred workers had perished in a cholera epidemic. Built in the shape of a parallelogram, the fort was one of the largest construction projects yet undertaken by the army in the west. The post consisted of several two-storied enlisted men's barracks and officers' quarters, a brick magazine, an ordinance building, a hospital, stables, and a two-storied guardhouse, which were for the most part, only partially completed.[4]

Sibley found that inactivity caused some of the dragoons to grow restless. The enlisted men found time to curse their officers, especially when ordered into a freezing north wind on patrol. Numerous dragoons, regretting the day they had ever heard of the United States Army, deserted. Many voluntarily returned; others were brought back in irons; while some were never seen again. Henry lost several men from Company I, men who were thought to have fled eastward across

[4] Herbert M. Hart, *Old Forts of the Southwest* (New York, 1964), 113.

the Missouri River to civilization.[5] Muster rolls grew short, and Henry was ordered on recruiting duty for a few months. Numerous young men, disgruntled with their hopes of a happier life in Kansas and having little if any knowledge of the military, came to volunteer. Except for a brief two-week, one-hundred-mile trek eastward to Fort Leavenworth, Henry spent the entire winter of 1855–1856 at Fort Riley.

Another acute problem facing the military was alcoholism. The wholesale consumption of ardent spirits in Kansas appears to have been greater than during any period of the dragoons' history. The post sutler at Fort Riley, as well as residents in nearby Riley City, did a thriving business with the military units stationed in Kansas. From past and later reputation it must be assumed that Henry consumed his share of the intoxicants.

The simmering and sporadic violence in Kansas exploded into warfare in the spring of 1856. Two weeks after Henry returned to Fort Riley from Fort Leavenworth, a group of heavy-drinking, hard-riding, proslavery Missourians sacked the antislavery town of Lawrence. The raiders smashed the Free-Soilers' press and burned a local hotel and the homes of several Free-Soilers. Three days later the half-crazed fanatical John Brown and his over-zealous disciples, allegedly acting under God's authority, dragged five men from their homes and brutally hacked them to pieces with broadswords.[6] The Pottawatomie Massacre had inaugurated civil war in Kansas.

One week after Brown's bloody raid, Sibley was ordered from Fort Riley to the Free-Soil stronghold of Topeka to prevent the Free-State Legislature from convening against the desire of Territorial Governor Wilson Shannon. Taking a squadron of dragoons, one platoon of infantry, a squad of artillery and a cannon, Henry rode out of Fort Riley on July 1, 1856, proceeding eastward along the north bank of the Kansas River. At the village of Manhattan, fifteen miles northeast of Fort Riley, he left the infantry under the command of Lieutenant

[5] R.R., S.D., A.G.O., R.G. 391.

[6] Stephen B. Oates, *To Purge This Land With Blood* (New York, 1970), 132–37. Other studies of Brown include: Oswald Garrison Villard, *John Brown: A Biography Fifty Years After* (Glouchester, 1965); Louis Ruchames, ed., *John Brown: The Making of a Revolutionary* (New York, 1971); and James Ford Rhodes, *History of the United States From the Compromise of 1850*, ed. Allan Nevins (Chicago, 1951). Thorough treatments of the Kansas situation are presented in David M. Potter, *The Impending Crisis: 1848–1861* (New York, 1976) and Jay Monaghan, *Civil War on the Western Border, 1854–1865* (New York, 1955).

George B. Anderson with orders to guard the two ferries in the vicinity, one on the Blue River and the other on the Kansas River, and to intercept and disperse any armed bodies of men found "outside the law."[7]

From Manhattan, Sibley continued east along the north bank of the river toward Topeka. At times the dragoons left the main road and scouted north away from the river to cover as much ground as possible in order to apprehend any armed bands. As Sibley rode eastward toward Topeka, a dispatch rider galloped up to inform the brevet major that Topeka was already occupied by several companies of the First Cavalry and that Colonel Edwin V. Sumner was on the march from Fort Leavenworth with the remainder of the regiment.[8] Henry decided accordingly to alter his orders and move downstream to Smith's Ferry. Here he left a platoon and then moved upstream with the remainder of his squadron, crossed to the south bank, and camped. Should trouble develop, he surmised that he would be in easy striking distance of Topeka, Smith's Ferry, or a nearby ford on the Kansas. Henry subsequently sent messengers to Topeka to inform Governor Shannon and Colonel Sumner of his location.

Early on the morning of July 4, Sibley sent out a patrol commanded by Lieutenant Francis C. Armstrong to scout the area around Topeka and arrest anyone suspected of causing trouble. At ten o'clock the same morning a courier hurriedly rode into camp carrying a note from Governor Shannon requesting Sibley to move his force nearer Topeka. Henry hurriedly ordered in several pickets and Lieutenant Armstrong's patrol. By eleven o'clock the dragoons were in the saddle and by late afternoon they had already gone into camp on the Kansas River a short distance above Topeka. With only a small escort Sibley rode into Topeka to find the town filled with three hundred armed and angry Free-State citizens.[9] Continuing through town to the camp of the First Cavalry, Henry hoped to meet Governor Shannon in person. Instead, he was greeted by his Mexican War antagonist "Old Bull" Sumner who informed him that the governor had left for Lecompton only moments earlier and that despite what Henry had seen

[7] H.H. Sibley to Philip St. George Cook, 10 July 1856, A.G.O., L.R., R.G. 94; Marvin Ewy, "The United States Army in the Kansas Border Trouble, 1855–1856," *The Kansas Historical Quarterly*, 32 (1966), 393.

[8] Ibid.

[9] Ibid.

in Topeka the situation was tranquil, the so-called Free-State legislature having already been dispersed.

Feeling that his presence at Topeka was unnecessary, Sibley, on the morning of July 5, led his command westward. Proceeding along the north bank of the Kansas River, he reached Fort Riley on the afternoon of the seventh, after three days of leisurely marches.[10]

A few days after the peaceful dispersal of the Free-State legislature at Topeka, General Persifor F. Smith assumed command of the army in Kansas. Although peace had been restored, it was only temporary. Armed bodies of vigilantes continued to roam the broad Kansas prairies. Henry had been back at Fort Riley less than two weeks when the entire regiment was ordered to Lecompton, a dilapidated collection of shacks and saloons which served as the proslavery capital of the territory. Major John Sedgwick, of the First Cavalry, who was stationed in Lecompton had reported that the town was about to be sacked by eight hundred armed Free-Soilers from the Free-State stronghold of Lawrence. Governor Wilson Shannon, the tactless proslavery partisan governor who had once served as Governor of Ohio and Minister to Mexico, had ridden into Lecompton to inspect the situation himself.[11] The governor found Lecompton just as Major Sedgwick had reported. The town was little more than a "cluster of rude frame and log buildings." All lodging houses were full of angry Free-Soilers. "We are," the governor wrote, "threatened with utter extermination by a large body of Free-State men."[12] General Smith, without hesitation, ordered all available troops to Lecompton including the Second Cavalry from Fort Leavenworth and the dragoons from Fort Riley.

Largely owing to his ineffective and prejudicial handling of the

[10] Ibid.

[11] James A. Rawley, *Race and Politics: "Bleeding Kansas" and the Coming of the Civil War* (New York, 1969), 92.

[12] Wilson Shannon to P.R. Smith, 17 August 1856, *Transactions of the Kansas State Historical Society, Embracing the Fifth and Sixth Biennial Report, 1886–1888; Together with Copies of Official Papers During a Portion of the Administration of Governor Wilson Shannon, 1856, and the Executive Minutes of Governor John W. Geary During His Administration, Beginning September 9, 1856, and Ending March 10, 1857,* F.G. Adams, comp., (Topeka; 1890), IV: 461. These records will hereafter be referred to as *K.S.H.S. Collections.* Many of the letters in this collection may also be found in Letters Sent and Letters Received, Second Dragoons, A.G.O., R.G. 94. Also, Monaghan, p. 48.

critical Kansas situation, Governor Shannon was removed by President Franklin Pierce and replaced by Daniel Woodson who was to serve until a permanent appointment could be made. Woodson immediately issued a proclamation declaring the territory in "open insurrection and rebellion."[13] At high noon on August 20, 1856, Sibley led the dragoons out of Fort Riley past Topeka eastward along the north bank of the Kansas River, the same route he had traveled only weeks earlier. The column was slowed by an incessant late summer rainstorm which poured on the horse soldiers, many of whom were on foot because of a lack of mounts. At 8:30 on the morning of August 24, the column reached Lecompton and went into camp near the town. Although Sibley's dragoons arrived in good order, Colonel Cooke was critical of Henry's neglect in not bringing hospital tents from Fort Riley for the sick at Lecompton who were being kept in ambulances.[14]

Although the contemplated attack on Lecompton never developed, the dragoons were deployed in the vicinity of the town where violence continued to be rampant. Many felt the trouble had been instigated by James H. Lane, leading Free-State agitator and stump orator whose "large prehensile lips denoted fluency and nicotine." Known to his followers as the "Liberator of Kansas," Lane was rumored to be recruiting a large army along the Kansas-Nebraska border to fight the proslavery Missourians who continued to pour into the troubled land. Sibley realized that all-out civil war was still a distinct possibility. "When blood is shed once," General Smith reported, "it will be impossible to say where it is to stop."[15]

Five days after Sibley arrived at Lecompton, Colonel Cooke received an urgent request from Governor Woodson asking that a military force be sent to assist the Kansas Deputy Marshal and Sheriff of Jefferson County in making arrests in Lawrence. One of those to be arrested was James Lane who it was said always loved a fight. An-

[13] Proclamation of Acting Governor Daniel Woodson, n.d., *K.S.H.S. Collections*, IV: 471.

[14] Philip St. George Cooke to George Deas, 29 August 1856, A.G.O., L.S., S.D., R.G. 94.

[15] Persifor S. Smith to S. Cooper, 29 August 1856, *K.S.H.S. Collections*, IV: 469. Monaghan, p. 24. For Lane see: Edgar Langsdorf, "Jim Lane and the Frontier Guard," *Kansas State Historical Quarterly*, 9 (1940), 13–26. For Lane's biography see: John Speer, *Life of Gen. James H. Lane* (Garden City, 1896).

other was the Free-State crusader Captain Samuel Walker. Two other
men unlawfully held by the Lawrence Free-Soilers were to be released. Cooke chose Sibley for the Lawrence detail and ordered him
to proceed immediately. Riding eastward along the Kansas River with
a squadron of seventy-five dragoons, the deputy marshal, and the
sheriff, Sibley reached Lawrence where he halted his men outside of
town. Lieutenant John Green and ten men were ordered to accompany the marshal into town to make the necessary arrests. Lawrence,
founded by the Emigrant Aid Society, was found to be full of Yankee
New Englanders, "their queer houses" and "their books," the focal
point of all antislavery forces in the territory. As the small detachment rode onto Lawrence's muddy streets, they were immediately set
upon by a mob of 350 angry Free-Soilers. Shouts and obscene epithets
were hurled at the besieged bluecoats. The "shouts and groans and
denunciations" were really for the "Marshal and the laws of Kansas"
and not the military, Henry reported.[16] The two men supposedly held
against their will by the Free-Soilers came forward through the hostile crowd to present themselves. They had been set free once the dragoons had appeared on the outskirts of town. A member of the crowd,
who volunteered to find the two men's horses was later discovered to
be Captain Walker, one of the men to be arrested.

It was also Walker who was responsible for calming the angry
crowd. Still not satisfied, the federal marshal asked Sibley to provide
another force of thirty men for a second search of Lawrence, hopefully a more successful and less intimidating experience than the first.
Thirty men under Lieutenant Green were ordered to accompany the
marshal back into Lawrence. The second visit proved to be as fruitless as the first. Walker did not appear in the streets, and the marshal
did not seem interested in pressing the issue as such an arrest would
have required considerable fortitude and might easily have touched
off a riot.

Before departing, Henry paraded his sun-burned troopers down
Lawrence's main street ostensibly to water the men's horses on the
far side of town but also as a show of force to the Free-Soil townsmen.
The streets were still crowded with men, but no threatening innuen-

---

[16] H.H. Sibley to P. St. George Cooke, 30 August 1856, *K.S.H.S. Collections*, IV: 477;
Monaghan, p. 44.

dos rang forth as they had only hours earlier. With Lieutenant Green riding side by side with Marshal Donaldson, the dragoons rode back through Lawrence without being interrupted, then departed for Lecompton. There remained little doubt in Henry's mind that Lawrence was an armed camp: "I am satisfied there must be an excess of five or six hundred men over the permanent population."[17] The Free-Soilers had turned a large hotel previously burned by the proslavery raiders into an armed fortress. Henry was not impressed with the Free-Soilers' attempts at constructing fortifications. "A crude bastion of four sides, some forty yards in extent, the salients pierced for four guns each," had been constructed. "The rubble stone of which this work is constructed would withstand but a shot or two, and the splintered rock would prove more destructive to the occupants than the shot. Besides this there are two trifling earthworks—one a complete circle, with a shallow ditch—at the head of the main street entering town," he wrote.[18]

The next day Sibley was back in Lecompton. Deputy Marshal J.B. Donaldson was still determined to make arrests in Lawrence and asked the governor for help. The governor, as usual, turned to the military. From what Sibley had previously observed in Lawrence the military should take precautions in fulfilling Woodson's request. Cooke agreed with Sibley and refused to enter Lawrence with anything less than a full regiment. Cooke felt that if the dragoons were fired upon, he would have no alternative but to attack the crowd. Such an incident should be avoided if at all possible. For once Henry was pleased with the decision of his commander.

Two days later Woodson again requested the use of the dragoons, this time against the Free-Soilers in Topeka. "Your command," the acting governor wrote, "will therefore proceed at the earliest practicable moment to invest the town of Topeka, and disarm all the insurrectionists or aggressive invaders against the organized government of the territory."[19] All the Free-Soilers' "breastworks, forts, and fortifications" were to be leveled to the ground. Cooke flatly refused. Woodson's request was simply a "call upon me to make war upon the

[17] Ibid.
[18] Ibid.
[19] Daniel Woodson to P. St. Geo. Cooke, 1 September 1856, *K.S.H.S. Collections*, IV: 479.

town of Topeka," Cooke felt. "In my best judgment," he concluded, "I cannot comply with your call."[20]

Further trouble came with the proslavery Territorial Militia in Lecompton with whom the dragoons were under orders not to interfere. A corporal whom Cooke had sent into Lawrence in civilian clothes heard a rumor that the militia was preparing to attack Lawrence and had already driven in the Free-Soil pickets on the outskirts of town.

Just past noon two days later, several excited citizens hurriedly rode into the dragoon camp to report that Lecompton was under attack by the Free-Soilers from Lawrence. Across the Kansas prairie Sibley and the horse soldiers raced. A short distance outside of Lecompton the dragoons ran into about sixty heavily armed Free-Soilers led by Captain Walker. The Lawrence men were all mounted in a line on the crest of a hill overlooking the town. They remained motionless as the dragoons approached. Leaving Sibley in command, Cooke rode forward to confront Walker and demand an explanation for his actions. Walker replied that the Free-Soilers had come to obtain the release of prisoners held by the proslavery Lecompton citizenry and had sent a messenger into town to demand a parley with the governor. Futhermore, Walker informed Cooke, seven hundred more Free-Soilers were within striking distance and could be summoned on a moment's notice. Not intimidated, Cooke warned Walker that if the Free-Soilers attacked Lecompton the dragoons would attack the Free-Soilers.[21] A showdown had developed. Walker asked Cooke to accompany him to meet the other Free-Soilers.

Riding to a wooded area near Lecompton, Cooke found three hundred Free-Soilers poised before the town with two artillery pieces. Cooke asked to address the leaders of the group: "You have made a most unfortunate move for yourself: the Missourians, you know, have gone and the militia here are nearly gone, having commenced crossing the river yesterday morning, to my knowledge. As to the prisoners, whil'st I will make no terms with you, I can inform you that they were promised to be released yesterday."[22] Diplomacy worked. Bloodshed was avoided.

[20] P. St. George Cooke to Daniel Woodson, 2 September 1856, *K.S.H.S. Collections*, IV: 479.

[21] P. St. George Cooke to George Deas, 5 September 1856, A.G.O., L.R., S.D., R.G. 94.

[22] Ibid.

Within an hour Walker and his men were on their way back to Lawrence. Peace reigned temporarily. On that day early in September 1856, "Americans had stood face to face in hostile array and most earnest of purpose," Cooke later wrote. As the horse soldiers rode back to their camp, the colonel felt without doubt that the dragoons had "stayed the madness of the hour."[23] But duty could not be relaxed, for the Kansas peace was fragile. The energies and talents of Colonel Cooke and Brevet Sibley were to be tested further.

Back in camp near Lecompton good news arrived from Washington. The inefficient acting governor, Daniel Woodson, had been removed by President Franklin Pierce and replaced by John White Geary. The new governor, a man of force, character, and integrity, was destined to etch his name into the history of Kansas as a peacemaker. A native of Pennsylvania, he had been a military man himself, serving as a colonel in the Second Regiment of Pennsylvania Infantry during Winfield Scott's campaign against Mexico City in the Mexican War. Standing six-feet-five and a half-inches tall, Geary was an imposing figure who had also served as the first mayor of San Francisco. In the months ahead Geary would distinguish himself as an able politician, skilled orator, and a dedicated diplomat determined to bring peace to the troubled Kansas Territory.[24]

Less than two weeks after the Lecompton confrontation, another crisis developed with Sibley and the Second Dragoons in the forefront of the action. At sundown on the 14th of September an urgent message was received requesting the dragoons to march immediately to Lawrence to prevent bloodshed. The proslavery Kansas militia was threatening to raid the town. Sick as he frequently was, Colonel Cooke placed Colonel Joseph E. Johnston in charge of the dragoons with Sibley as second in command.[25] Five companies from Colonel John-

---

[23] Ibid.

[24] Rawley, p. 159; Heitman, p. 450. Geary compiled a distinguished record in the Civil War, serving in the Union Army as a brigadier general. He was wounded at Harper's Ferry, captured at Leesburg, wounded again at Cedar Mountain, in the forefront of the Battles of Chancellorsville, Gettysburg, Lookout Mountain, and Missionary Ridge, and was with General William T. Sherman in Georgia. Mark M. Boatner, *The Civil War Dictionary* (New York, 1959), III: 327–28; Harry Marlin Tinkcom, *John White Geary: Soldier-Statesman* (Philadelphia, 1940), 61; John H. Gihon, *Geary and Kansas, Governor Geary's Administration in Kansas With a Complete History of the Territory Until July, 1857* (Philadelphia, 1857).

[25] P. St. George Cooke to F.J. Porter, 16 September 1856, *K.S.H.S. Collections*, IV: 500.

ston's First Cavalry, as well as a light battery of the Fourth Artillery, were called out to assist the dragoons. Hurrying along the Kansas River, Johnston and Sibley reached Lawrence on the morning of the 15th to find the town greatly excited by the approach of the proslavery militia. Colonel Johnston and Sibley placed the bluecoats in a strong position two miles outside of town on the Franklin Road to await the militia's arrival. The following morning, just as the governor and the recouperated Cooke arrived from Lecompton, the militiamen approached.

To Sibley the militia was an impressive sight with their flags flying in the cool Kansas breeze. In all they numbered some twenty-five hundred cavalry and infantry besides a six-pounder battery. After consultation with Johnston and Sibley, Cooke rode forward with Governor Geary to meet the militia leaders. Geary asked to address the militia officers, and a meeting was quickly arranged in a nearby farm house. Meanwhile Johnston and Sibley stood by with their men in battle formation anxiously awaiting the outcome. The governor, with his usual eloquence, was able to subdue the passions of the proslavery leaders. Colonel Cooke, too, addressed the group stating that he was "an old resident of Kansas and a friend of the Missourians" but that the militia must submit to the justice of the governor and march off or the army would be forced to sustain the governor at "the cannon's mouth."[26] The militia marched off. As the bluecoats bivouacked on the outskirts of Lawrence, Governor Geary rode into town to calm the excited townsmen and to announce that the militia had left.

Trouble continued, especially in the Topeka area where James Lane remained active. Free-Soilers, dedicated to driving the proslavery element out of the territory, continued to enter Kansas by way of the "Lane Trail" from Iowa through the Nebraska Territory.

In late September 1856 Governor Geary received information that Lane had three cannons and seven hundred men massed at Tabor, Iowa, for an invasion of the territory. Once again Sibley and the dragoons moved out. Taking ten days' rations, they splashed across the Kansas River at Lecompton and rode north for the Nebraska border. Striking the Fort Kearny Road near the northern boundary of the territory, Sibley and Cooke were joined by several companies of the First

[26] Ibid.

Cavalry under Colonel Johnston. For four days they remained in camp astride the "Lane Trail." Rumors of the approach of the large well-equipped army under Lane continued to reach Cooke, Johnston, and Sibley. Another report reached Sibley that the notorious "Osawatomie outlaw" John Brown was on his way out of the territory and had stopped at a house less than six miles from where the dragoons were camped.[27] By midnight Sibley had the house surrounded. Brown was gone and Sibley had lost one of his greatest opportunities to change the course of history. The old man would later shoot his way onto the pages of American history at Harper's Ferry, Virginia.

By October 8 the force from Iowa had still not arrived. Short on rations, Cooke was making preparations to march south with the dragoons, leaving the First Cavalry to protect the northern frontier, when word arrived that a large force was at the village of Archer, twelve miles north of the dragoon camp. Colonel Cooke and Sibley hastily called in all patrols and placed their small army across the Lane Trail.

At nine o'clock on the morning of October 9, 1856, Sibley saw twenty wagons on the horizon. He remained behind to guard the dragoon camp as Colonel Cooke rode forward. Cooke was in the process of negotiating with the leader of the wagon train, when W.J. Preston, the United States Deputy Marshal who had accompanied the bluecoats northward, came forth to read a proclamation from Governor Geary. Preston stated that it was his duty to search the wagons for arms and munitions of war. "There was at first much temper shown at the search," Colonel Cooke recalled, as well as "a disposition to resist."[28]

Although the bluecoats were cursed and threatened—all of which went "unanswered and unnoticed"—the search went on. Cooke reported that the settlers possessed "none of the ordinary baggage of emigrants; not a chair or other furniture; but one tool chest; not agricultural implements." The colonel did find "about 242 percussion muskets, Hall's muskets, and Sharp's carbines; 2 officers' and 61 common sabres; about 50 Colt's revolvers and 4 boxes of ball cartridges."[29] It was obvious to both Cooke and Sibley that the settlers had more in mind than a peaceful occupation of the Kansas Territory. Yet they insisted they were only emigrants who entered Kansas

[27] P. St. George Cooke to F.J. Porter, 7 October 1856, *K.S.H.S. Collections*, IV: 516.

[28] P. St. George Cooke to F.J. Porter, 10 October 1856, *K.S.H.S. Collections*, IV: 516.

[29] Ibid.

through the Nebraska Territory because the Missouri River had been closed by the proslavery "Border Ruffians." The lack of women in the wagon train was explained by the fact that another train with women and children had already left Mount Pleasant, Iowa, and would be arriving in Kansas within three days. The men were all peaceful, legitimate settlers, they argued, and were heavily armed because of the reported lawlessness in the territory. The leaders of the party later told Governor Geary that when their wagons had been searched, the soldiers had broken open trunks and had even thrown "bedding and wearing apparel upon the ground in the rain."[30]

Doubts as to the peaceful intentions of the party prevailed. The deputy marshal insisted that he recognized a number of Lane's men among the leaders. Besides Cooke, Colonel Johnston, Major John Sedgwick, and Sibley all agreed that the party was in violation of the proclamation previously issued by Governor Geary. Whatever their true intentions, the emigrants were arrested and told that they would be escorted south to meet with the governor. Although they insisted that they were innocent and "entirely peaceful," the men were given little alternative but to go peaceably. Early the next morning, October 10, Colonel Cooke issued orders for a military escort: "Brevet Major H.H. Sibley will march tomorrow, in command of the Second Dragoons, for Lecompton, Kansas Territory, and will conduct there and deliver to the Governor of the Territory the prisoners this day arrested as invaders of the Territory, together with the arms and munitions of war found in their possession and seized."[31]

At daybreak on October 11 the wagons, escorted by Sibley's squadron of Dragoons, headed south toward Lecompton. As the long train moved through the cold Kansas autumn, it became evident to Henry that a great deal of confusion existed as to the status of the Free-Soil settlers. The emigrants argued that they were not under arrest and were "merely under military surveillance." Sibley halted the wagon train, gathered the Free-Soil leaders, and read Colonel Cook's orders. The Free-Soilers finally agreed to comply, but argued that if they were under arrest the military "should subsist the whole party

---

[30] S.W. Eldridge, Samuel C. Pomeroy, John A. Perry, Robert Morrow, Edward Daniels, and Richard Realf to John W. Geary, 14 October 1856, *K.S.H.S. Collections*, IV: 610.

[31] Orders No. 14, A.G.O., L.R., S.D., R.G. 391.

and forage their animals."[32] Henry agreed, acknowledging the validity of the Free-Soilers' argument but stating that he did not have the necessary provisions for man or beast. He did agree to purchase at government expense any provisions or forage that could be procured along the march. All that could be found was two days' supply of hay which Henry paid for out of his own pocket since no public funds were available.

As the caravan rolled southward toward the Kansas River, the hostility of the Free-Soilers changed dramatically, a fate which Sibley attributed to the emigrants' realization of the true state of affairs in the territory. Although the party had entered Kansas expecting a violent confrontation with proslavery "Ruffians," they had found instead that "peace and quiet and protection reigned throughout the land."[33]

Henry imposed few restraints on the Kansas travelers. The dragoons even assisted the Free-Soilers in crossing numerous creeks and streams. Several of the alleged settlers, with sore feet and their wagons overcrowded, rode in the military wagons. In the evening they were permitted to choose their own camp site which out of convenience was usually close to that of the dragoons. Henry even returned most of the settlers' personal arms. At Topeka the remainder of the Free-Soilers' arms, which were still unpacked, were turned over to the military commander.

When he arrived in Lecompton, a more important mission awaited the forty-year-old brevet major, for he was ordered to accompany Governor Geary on a tour of the east central part of the territory. The governor was anxious to promote peace and good will and felt he should visit as many of the villages and hamlets in the territory as possible. Only through such a tour could he convince the Kansas settlers of his nonpartisan leadership, and he hoped thus to establish a lasting peace. On October 17, 1856, Sibley, accompanied by Geary, the governor's secretary and orderly, a deputy marshal, and a squadron of dragoons, left Lecompton for the Free-Soil stronghold of Lawrence.[34] By early afternoon the party had reached Lawrence and set up camp on the outskirts of town. Governor Geary and Sibley then rode

[32] H.H. Sibley to John W. Geary, 14 October 1856, *K.S.H.S. Collections*, IV: 610.

[33] Ibid.

[34] Executive Minutes of Governor John W. Geary, *K.S.H.S. Collections*, p. 617. These records may also be found in *House Executive Document No. 10*, 34th Congress, 3rd Session, III: 1–36; Tinkcom, p. 82.

into town to inspect the newly-recruited Territorial Militia. Both were warmly received by the townspeople and invited to dinner by the community's leading citizens.

Early the next morning Sibley and the governor were on the move again, this time southward through the Wakarusa Valley toward the settlement of Hickory Point. This area had been the scene of considerable turmoil and fighting. Rifle pits along the Wakarusa River at Blanton's Bridge were evidence of the prevailing climate in the area. Nevertheless, the governor left Sibley and the main party with his secretary and orderly and rode east along the Wakarusa River to Franklin where he gathered as many of the town's settlers as possible to assure the people of his cooperation in bringing peace to the troubled land. Geary reported the settlers to be "highly intelligent, peaceable, and determined to support" his policies.[35] From Franklin the governor turned west to rejoin Sibley and the dragoons who were camped at Hickory Point.

While Henry and the governor were camped at Hickory Point, word arrived of depredations in the vicinity. The governor quickly dispatched the deputy marshal reinforced by several of Sibley's dragoons to arrest the troublemakers. The mission was accomplished with little effort, and those who had been arrested were sent to Lecompton for trial. From Hickory Point the dragoons rode south to Prairie City. From here the column continued to the Ottawa Indian Reserve and the home of John T. Jones, known throughout the territory as "Ottawa Jones." Acting as intrepreter for the reserve Indians, Jones, a half-breed who had graduated from Hamilton College in New York, was well respected in the territory. While on the Indian Reserve, Geary and Sibley dined with Jones. His wife, a well educated missionary leader from Maine, was very popular with the Ottawa. Jones had at one time run a large hotel in Lawrence, but it had been destroyed in August by about forty proslavery raiders largely because of Jones' free-state convictions. With a population of 325 the Indian reserve along Ottawa Creek encompassed some 120 square miles of the most fertile soil in Kansas. Jones, besides preaching every Sunday at the nearby Baptist Mission, farmed three hundred acres of land and ran one hundred head of cattle and fourteen horses.[36]

[35] Ibid.
[36] Ibid.

Four miles south of the Jones residence Henry and the governor came to the Baptist Mission where about sixty children were in attendance. Resuming their trek, the party crossed the Marais des Cygnes River and continued southward for seven miles where they encamped on a small creek where Sibley's scouts found good grass and water.

On October 29, after riding through a beautiful country, Sibley and Governor Geary reached the settlement of Osawatomie, located on Pottawatomie Creek about one mile above the creek's confluence with the larger Marais des Cygnes. Only months earlier Osawatomie had boasted of a population of two hundred, but in recent weeks many residents had departed for less troubled ground, including the settlement's most noted citizen—John Brown. The remaining villagers, still deeply divided on the issue of slavery, came to see and hear their new governor. A few came to complain and to ask for help while others wished to assure the governor of their cooperation. Sibley stood by as Geary, in one of his lengthy orations, told the settlers "to bury the past and cultivate kind relations for the future."[37] Still the overwhelming majority of the settlers were bitter. Three times their town had been attacked by proslavery Missourians—once in reprisal for John Brown's massacre on the Pottawatomie. In another skirmish, two miles outside of town, one of Brown's sons, Frederick, had been killed.

Leaving Osawatomie, Henry and the governor crossed the Marais des Cygnes River again and rode nine miles north across the short grass country to the town of Paola, county seat of what was then Lykins County. Paola, located on Bull Creek, a small tributary of the Marais des Cygnes, consisted of about thirteen houses and a hotel. The land on which the town was located belonged to a Peoria Indian named Baptiste who in many ways resembled Ottawa Jones; he was well educated and acted as interpreter for his people who lived in the vicinity. Sibley and the governor were able to visit with most of the three hundred Peoria, Kaskaskia, Piankeshaw, and Weas Indians who lived near the town.[38] The party also visited the Baptist Mission outside of town where thirty Indian children were under the tutelage of three missionaries. Before leaving Paola, Governor Geary spoke to many of the town's citizens. Sibley and the dragoons stood by while

[37] Ibid., p. 618.
[38] Ibid., p. 619.

the governor also commissioned a justice of the peace and other local officials.

The party retraced its route to Osawatomie where it proceeded up the valley of the Pottawatomie where the dragoons camped for the night. Although tired and exhausted from the day's march, the governor and Sibley quizzed local residents about the brutal murders which had recently been committed along the banks of the Pottawatomie.[39] Several settlers told of finding the ghastly remains of James P. Doyle and his two sons, Drury and William, all members of the Law and Order Party. The three had been driven from their homes and executed by assailants who hacked them to pieces with broadsword. Although Geary and Sibley were unable to determine who had committed the Doyle and other murders, it was later learned that the crimes were the work of John Brown and his radical abolitionists.

Dawn of the following day brought a pouring rain. There was talk of remaining in camp to wait out the rainstorm, but Governor Geary insisted that the tour continue. Advancing through the drenching rain, the column struck out toward the southeast to Sugar Mound. All day the cold rain continued to fall, and the dragoons as well as the governor and his aids became soaked. The party rode along the brushy creek bottoms of South Middle Creek and Big Sugar Creek. With dusk approaching and the rain still falling in torrents, they decided to camp a few miles south of Big Sugar Creek on the open prairie. Despite the incessant rain, several settlers came to call on the governor. The interested frontiersmen, along with the governor and his secretary, rode to a nearby farmhouse where Geary in his never-ending oratory spoke to the group.[40]

Breaking camp before daylight the next day, October 23, 1856, the party rode on toward Sugar Mound. Along the route the governor stopped to greet several settlers and invite them to ride into Sugar Mound with the party. In town about one hundred citizens had gathered to greet the governor who as usual, spoke at length to the assemblage. Although the townsmen put forth issues which had previously brought bloodshed to the territory, Geary was able to calm the fiery passions of the frontiersmen. Most left the meeting satisfied with the governor's sincerity and determination to bring peace to the terri-

[39] Ibid.
[40] Ibid., p. 620.

tory. Later many of the town's leading citizens invited Geary and Sibley to dinner at which time the political discussions were continued.

Later in the afternoon of the following day, Sibley and Geary departed for Fort Scott. Finding good grass and water, the men decided to camp for the night on little Sugar Creek. Here several settlers who had not met with the governor in Sugar Mound came into camp. The governor welcomed the visitors, continuing to express his hopes and desires for ending the civil strife.

On the following morning, just as Sibley had ordered the Dragoons to break camp for the march to Fort Scott and the Little Osage River, two messengers excitedly spurred their horses into camp, reporting that a robbery had been committed on Big Sugar Creek, north of Sugar Mound, in the direction from which the dragoons had just come. Outraged, Governer Geary ordered an immediate countermarch. At a brisk trot Sibley and the dragoons rode through Sugar Mound to the scene of the crime some seven miles north of town. Finding the thieves gone, Sibley sent out several patrols in hopes of apprehending them. All were under orders to rendezvous later on Pottawatomie Creek near the Oregon Trail. No arrests were made, but enough information was gathered to permit identification of the culprits. Governor Geary issued arrest warrants and offered two hundred dollars reward for the robbers' apprehension.[41]

Plans for the Fort Scott visit were abandoned. Instead the dragoons turned northwest up the Pottawatomie and across the Marais des Cygnes to the Oregon Trail. Although the weather continued bad and the skies poured rain, the column plodded onward. Sibley and the governor, evidently not affected by the rain, stopped at numerous residences along the way to talk with the settlers and press their ideas for restoring peace. Reaching Centropolis at Eight-Mile Creek on the Oregon Trail, the dragoons found good wood and water, so they camped.

The next day, October 26, the column continued westward along the Oregon Trail. All day the party traveled rapidly over a bleak landscape. Not a tree or shrub was visible for miles on the rolling prairie. "No sign of human habitations" was seen until the column reached "110" a famous stopping place on the Oregon Trail.[42] Here Sibley and

[41] Ibid.
[42] Ibid., p. 621.

the dragoons paused while Governor Geary talked to a group of recent emigrants. With the Santa Fe Trail breaking off to the west, the dragoons turned north along the Oregon Trail toward Fort Riley. After a short ride the column reached the headwaters of the Wakarusa River and camped. Half rations were ordered as Henry was becoming concerned about the shortage of food.

Breaking camp at dawn the following morning, Sibley had the blue clad horse soldiers in the saddle by eight o'clock. By evening the party followed the Oregon Trail along a divide between the Neosho and Wakarusa Rivers. They encountered few settlers and the column proceed rapidly over the prairie. Finally on October 28 the fatigued party reached Riley City to find the Kansas River at flood stage from the recent heavy rains. Finally across the river, the governor, Sibley, and the dragoons arrived at Fort Riley to be greeted by the boom of an artillery salute. The brevet major and the governor appear to have gotten along amazingly well during their lengthy trek across the Kansas prairies. Perhaps Geary's military background contributed to the comradeship as did Sibley's realization that the governor's tour was of critical importance. Geary's abilities or inabilities as territorial governor would either bring peace or permit continued bloodshed in the deeply divided territory.

For three days Henry and his dragoons rested at the fort, but the Kansas winter was quickly approaching, and everyone began busily to prepare for cold weather. Governor Geary, frequently accompanied by Sibley, spent much of his time inspecting the post facilities and attending banquets given in his honor.[43]

On November 1, with Sibley still in command of the Governor's escort, the party departed Fort Riley for Lecompton. The column was halted at the village of Pawnee when a ferry across the Kansas River was found to be aground after the recent flooding. Safely on the south bank, a throng of citizens gathered to hear the governor. All day Sibley and Geary rode eastward through a freezing rain. Reaching a spot on the river opposite Manhattan, the men set up camp for the night. Here a delegation from Manhattan led by Reverend Charles Blood came into camp to invite Governor Geary to address the townspeople. Anxious to meet any group, large or small, Governor Geary crossed the swollen Kansas River in a small rowboat to find most of

[43] Ibid.

the community's 150 citizens gathered at the town's largest hotel. After a lengthy speech Governor Geary remained in Manhattan for the night and recrossed the Kansas River early the next morning in a snowstorm. By noon three inches of snow, the first in Kansas that autumn, had fallen. Sibley and the governor, after a brief consultation, decided to remain in camp. Despite the inclement weather numerous settlers came into camp to visit with the governor in the warmth of his Sibley tent.

Breaking camp the next morning, the party continued along the south bank of the Kansas River. Although the snow had stopped, the day was frosty and raw. The bitter Kansas cold did not deter the governor from his duties. All along the route Geary would break off from the dragoons to visit the homes of the settlers along the banks of the Kansas River. In the afternoon at an old Indian camping ground where Mulberry Creek ran into the Kansas River, Sibley's scouts found good grass and wood and the party camped for the evening.

The following day, with the bad weather continuing, the governor and his dragoon escort continued eastward to the Pottawatomie Indian Reserve. The reserve consisted of the village of Uniontown and two missions, St. Mary's on the north side of the river and a Baptist mission on the south bank. Here the men camped. Since it was the last night before reaching Lecompton, Sibley and the governor, both of whom had learned a little Spanish in Mexico, christened the camp "Gracias a Dios," so named because of the prevailing peace throughout the territory. The governor issued a decree proclaiming the twentieth day of November a day of "general thanksgiving."[44]

The next morning Sibley and Geary inspected the Baptist Mission where they were greeted by thirty "bright-eyed, intelligent-looking Indian children." After passing through the villages of Tecumseh, Big Springs, and Washington, the column entered Lecompton late in the evening of November 6, 1856.

For twenty days the governor and the brevet major had been on the road. During this time they had traveled more than 450 miles through a large part of the eastern portion of the territory. To Governor Geary the tour had been a success: "The general peace of the Territory," he

[44] Ibid., p. 623; Thomas P. Barr, "The Pottawatomie Baptist Manual Labor Training School," *The Kansas State Historical Quarterly*, 43 (1977), 420–21.

wrote Secretary of State William L. Marcy, "remains unimpaired."[45]
The commander of the Department of the West, General Persifor F.
Smith, in a letter to adjutant General Samuel Cooper, was highly
complimentary of Sibley and his escort to Governor Geary.[46]

On November 13 Henry was ordered to take thirty-one men and
proceed across the snow-swept plains to Fort Leavenworth where he
was to obtain fresh mounts and ride west to Fort Riley. After reaching Fort Riley, he was to report back to Lecompton to carry dispatches to Washington for Governor Geary.[47] As Henry traveled eastward there was no doubt in his mind that the role of the United States
Army, especially the Second Dragoons, in preventing a full-scale civil
war in Kansas had been vital. Although he was a Southerner and not
totally unaffected by the turmoil in Kansas, he like the other officers
in the army, both North and South, had laid his regional allegiance
aside to rise above the sectional conflict that threatened to tear the
Union apart.

"Bleeding Kansas" had also provided the first lengthy test of the
Sibley tent. Two months after the dragoons arrived in the Territory,
Colonel Joseph K.F. Mansfield, inspector general of the army, asked
the members of a general court-martial which had convened at Fort
Riley to inspect the Sibley tent and make appropriate recommendations to Washington. Besides Colonel Mansfield those inspecting the
tent included Colonels Joseph E. Johnston, Charles Ferguson Smith,
Robert E. Lee, and Major Samuel Peter Heintzelman. The officers were
impressed. Their conclusions were similar to those of a previous board
of inspection which had met at Fort Belknap before the regiment had
been ordered to Kansas. The officers found the tent well ventilated,
spacious, resistant to winds, convenient, comfortable, and the only
tent in which a fire could be made. Colonel Mansfield, speaking for
the board of officers, recommended to Adjutant General Cooper that
a "sufficient number be manufactured for the use of the army to give
it a fair trial."[48]

---

[45] John W. Geary to William L. Marcy, 7 November 1856, *K.S.H.S. Collections*, IV:
626.

[46] Persifor F. Smith to Samuel Cooper, 11 November 1856, A.G.O., Department of
the West, L.S., R.G. 94.

[47] Orders No. 24, A.G.O., L.R., S.D., R.G. 94.

[48] J.K.F. Mansfield to Samuel Cooper, 3 December 1855, Consolidated Correspondence File, Sibley Tent, Q.G.O., R.G. 92.

So popular was "Sibley's Improved Conical Tent" becoming that many officers purchased it at their own expense. Traders at Fort Kearny as well as several citizens of Kansas also bought the tent, "perferring it by far to the Indian lodge."[49]

On April 22, 1856, with the help of First Lieutenant William W. Burns of the Fifth Infantry, Henry was granted patent number 14,740 for his tent. Lieutenant Burns had arranged for the models, drawings, and the technical details necessary for the awarding of the patent. Burns also had twenty-five tents made and shipped to Fort Leavenworth for sale. In return Henry promised Lieutenant Burns one-half interest in all royalties from the tent, a decision he would later regret. The lieutenant asked that the agreement be put in writing, but Henry felt that such a contract was not necessary "between such friends."[50] Sibley was particularly interested in pushing for the acceptance of the tent since he now stood to benefit financially by its use.

In October 1856, shortly before Henry had left on Governor Geary's inspection tour, twenty-two officers of the First and Sixth Infantry gathered at Lecompton to inspect the tent. All tests confirmed what others had already concluded—the Sibley tent was far superior to any the army then used.

Governor Geary was particularly pleased with the use of his Sibley tent and he wrote Henry that during their tour of Kansas he had come to appreciate all its advantages.[51] Colonel Edwin V. Sumner, despite his previous differences with Sibley, confessed that he too found the tent much better than any then in use. Sumner reported that the tent would accommodate only twenty horsemen if their arms and equipment were included and suggested that the tent be made two feet larger in diameter to allow more room for cooking. Still he was anxious to have the tent issued to his First Infantry.[52] Colonel George Andrews, commanding the Sixth Infantry, also praised the tent and ordered one for his own use.

General Smith did not think that the tent should be enlarged since too much weight would be added. The General argued that men do not cook while lying down. He was particularly impressed that a fire

[49] Richard H. Alexander to H.H. Sibley, C.C.F., Q.G.O., R.G. 92.

[50] W.W. Burns, "History of My Connection with [the] Sibley Tent," C.C.F., Q.G.O., R.G. 92.

[51] John W. Geary to H.H. Sibley, n.d., C.C.F., Q.G.O., R.G. 92.

[52] E.V. Sumner to H.H. Sibley, 17 November 1856, C.C.F., Q.G.O., R.G. 92.

could be made safely in the tent.[53] Without reservations, Smith recommended that the army adopt the tent.

Major Lewis A. Armistead, later of Gettysburg fame, wrote Sibley that he had used the tent while on an expedition to the Rocky Mountains in the summer of 1856 and found it much better than any other tent he had seen. "It attracted and won the admiration," he wrote, "of 'mountain,' 'prairiemen,' and Indians alike."[54]

Eight medical officers examined the tent and also praised it highly. Surgeon James Simons thought it would be most valuable, especially in the field and on marches where hospital tents were impractical because of their weight. The light weight Sibley tent, could be carried on pack animals where wagons could not go and was therefore more practical.[55]

Wide-scale acceptance of the Sibley tent continued to be in doubt, primarily because of Quartermaster General Thomas Sidney Jesup and Secretary of War Jefferson Davis. Jesup could not "perceive how sick or wounded men could be well accomodated in it by being placed on the ground."[56] Furthermore, Jesup complained of the manner in which the tent was patented. In particular he objected that the owner of the patent was an army officer. He found "great impropriety in contracting for any military supplies with officers of the Army." Such a conflict of interest was not in the interest of the army, Jesup argued. Secretary Davis agreed. Testimonials in favor of the tent were so numerous, however, that Jesup felt that it would only be fair to continue the testing. Davis concurred, but only if Sibley would grant the government the right to construct fifty tents for further scrutiny.[57]

It was at this time that Sibley was given a chance to lobby in person for the acceptance of his tent. A week after arriving back at Lecompton he learned of the death of Charlotte Kendall, his mother-in-law, who had died in July 1855 at the age of fifty-six; a few days later Henry was granted leave to visit his wife in New York.

On Governor's Island, Sibley continued to press for the use of his tent by the army. Adjutant General Samuel Cooper wrote Sibley that Jefferson Davis was willing to continue its further testing providing

[53] Persifor F. Smith to H.H. Sibley, 20 November 1856, C.C.F., Q.G.O., R.G. 92.
[54] L.A. Armistead to H.H. Sibley, 9 November 1856, C.C.F., Q.G.O., R.G. 92.
[55] J. Simons to H.H. Sibley, n.d., C.C.F., Q.G.O., R.G. 92.
[56] T.S. Jesup to Jefferson Davis, 18 March 1856, C.C.F., Q.G.O., R.G. 92.
[57] Jefferson Davis to T.S. Jesup, 17 December 1856, C.C.F., Q.G.O., R.G. 92.

Henry grant permission for the manufacture of fifty of the tents. On Christmas Eve, 1856, he wrote the adjutant a terse letter: "Such authority is freely given, not only for the manufacture of fifty, but for two hundred and fifty if you like."[58] Sibley told Cooper, probably falsely, that he never contemplated making a contract with the government. In another similar letter to General Jesup, Henry was equally blunt: "The view you have taken is in effect nothing more than a prescription of myself on the one side, and the government on the other; the one because of a prohibitory law, the other because he has had the misfortune to receive a military education, and in consequence, to hold a commission in the Army. The alternative of quitting the service is held out to him."[59]

From early December 1856, until March 1857, Henry remained in New York with Charlotte and the children. He was scheduled to report back to his regiment on January 15, 1857, but was able to obtain an additional sixty days' leave. By March he still had not reported for duty. Finally leaving New York, Henry first went to Baltimore. Here he learned that the position of commandant of the cavalry school at Carlisle, Pennsylvania, was vacant. Always scheming to avoid duty in the West, Henry hastily scribbled a note to Adjutant General Cooper asking that he be considered for the position.[60] It is not known if Cooper bothered to reply to the request.

On his way back to Kansas to rejoin his regiment, Henry stopped at Lindenwood, Missouri, near St. Charles, to visit his aunt and uncle. Ever since Margaret had taken the family to St. Charles after the death of Henry's father, Henry had felt a special kinship toward his uncle. George Champlin Sibley was seventy-five years old in 1857 and Henry remembered him as being quite decrepit.[61] Although Uncle George lived until January 31, 1863, it was the last time Henry would see him.

After being carried on regimental records as absent without leave for a month, Henry finally arrived back in Kansas and reported for duty at Fort Riley on April 16, 1857.[62] He was somewhat embittered at

[58] H.H. Sibley to Samuel Cooper, 24 December 1856, C.C.F., Q.G.O., R.G. 92.

[59] H.H. Sibley to T.S. Jesup, 24 December 1856, C.C.F., Q.G.O., R.G. 92.

[60] H.H. Sibley to S. Cooper, 15 March 1857, A.G.O., L.R., R.G. 94.

[61] H.H. Sibley to John McRae, 12 May 1862, John McRae Papers, Southern Historical Collection, University of North Carolina Library, Chapel Hill, North Carolina.

[62] R.R., S.D., A.G.O., R.G. 391.

being ordered West again and undoubtedly frustrated at the bureaucratic delays in the acceptance of his tent. This, along with Colonel
Cooke's ill health, combined to produce another explosive and embarrassing incident between the two. Their previous differences while
Henry was in the recruiting service had never been forgotten and
probably helped to produce the confrontation. The dispute revolved
around one of Sibley's muster rolls with which Cooke found fault.
When Henry questioned his commander, Cooke replied in "an angry
and disrespectful tone of voice," which caused obscenities and words
of mutual disrespect to be exchanged between the two.

The confrontation was not concluded until the moody and temperamental colonel informed the stubborn and egotistical brevet major that he was under arrest and that charges would be preferred against
him. Henry, his temper ablaze and ego damaged, retaliated by preferring charges against Cooke. To Sibley, Colonel Cooke was clearly in
violation of Article One of the *General Regulations of Military Discipline* by displaying "conduct unbecoming an officer and a gentleman."[63] Henry was relieved of his command the same day, May 8,
1857, and placed under arrest. For one month he awaited his fate at
Fort Leavenworth while higher authorities in Washington decided the
merits of the charges against him. After weeks of pondering, Assistant Adjutant General Fitz-John Porter decided that it would not be
in the interest of the army to pursue either case. He therefore ordered
Henry released from arrest.[64] The bitter feelings between the two officers were not easily forgotten, as future events would reveal.

Shortly after Cooke had Sibley arrested, the entire regiment was
ordered from Fort Riley to Fort Leavenworth to prepare for a long, exhausting march to Utah. At Fort Leavenworth it was decided to retain a portion of the regiment in Kansas. The new territorial governor, Robert J. Walker, who had replaced Geary, was doubtful that the
fragile peace in the territory could be maintained. The regiment was
called out only once by the governor, and this was to oversee a local
election in Lawrence.[65] Otherwise Sibley spent the hot and muggy
summer of 1857 at Fort Leavenworth with little to do. Although a
large part of the army was already marching westward to quell the so-

[63] F.J. Porter to Wm. S. Harney, 29 May 1857, A.G.O., Department of the West, L.S.,
R.G. 94.
[64] Ibid.
[65] Young, p. 288.

called Mormon threat, most of the Second Dragoons remained behind.

Some excitement came in late July when the too-prudent commander of Fort Riley, Major Lewis A. Armistead, reported that a large party of Cheyenne was about to attack the post. With only an infantry company to protect the fort, Armistead was panic stricken, envisioning a terrible massacre. Despite his ill health, Colonel Cooke, with one hundred dragoons, raced west along the Kansas River. Under a blistering July sun and with only meager rations, the bluecoats made the ninety-eight-mile ride to Fort Riley in less than twenty-eight hours.[66] Although the dragoons were prepared for battle, the Cheyenne attack never developed. The post commander's fears had been based on false information. When the Dragoons found that the Cheyenne were more than two hundred miles to the west, their anger fell heavily on Armistead.

It was not Indians but Mormons who would occupy the attention of the Second Dragoons for the next two years. The "Mormon War" was on. Another episode in the life of Henry Hopkins Sibley loomed on the western horizon, this time in the distant Valley of the Saints.

---

[66] Rodenbough, p. 185.

"About five o'clock this evening we were ordered to strike our tents and turn them in to the Quartermaster, and draw a new pattern got up by Major H. H. Sibley. These new-fangled things are very good for what they are intended—that is to say, for an officer or about eight or ten men . . . but when they come to cram eighteen soldiers into them, as they have us to-night, I would prefer, except in stormy weather, to make my bunk out of doors."

William Drown, Camp on Black's Fork near Fort Bridger, November 5, 1857, Theophilus Francis Rodenbough, *From Everglade to Canon with the Second Dragoons.*

Chapter VI

To the Valley of the Saints

In 1857 Henry Hopkins Sibley was forty-one years old. His career in the Second Dragoons had taken him from the mosquito infested swamps of Florida to the rain forests of Mexico and the snow-swept plains of Kansas. Duty now called him toward the western horizon and the Valley of the Saints.

While Sibley was helping to quell the civil disturbances in Kansas, plans were underway for an expedition against the defiant Mormons. In early 1857 President James Buchanan and Secretary of War John B. Floyd had named new territorial officials for Utah whom Brigham Young, leader of the Mormons, had refused to accept. The Latter Day Saints, who through the years had survived a series of persecutions in Ohio, Missouri, and Illinois, were at last, under Young's zealous leadership, determined to make a stand. They had found a haven, their Zion, in the wilds of Utah. Here through ingenious irrigation methods they had turned the desert of the Great Salt Lake Valley into a prosperous community. Misunderstanding and ignorance led to an explosive situation. Congress and the president did not understand the intentions of Brigham Young and his theocratic followers just as the Mormons misinterpreted the intentions of the federal government.

Most Americans like Sibley saw the Mormon leader, known as the Lion of the Lord, as the most despotic of the despots. Young, who had only eleven days of formal education, had become a virtual dictator of the Mormon Church after the lynching of Joseph Smith in 1844.[1] To the beleaguered Saints he was a powerful and resourceful leader. Although a man of God, Young was also a pleasure-seeking materialist who preached a holy war against all Gentiles or non-Mormons.

Americans like Sibley condemned Young and his followers for their practice of polygamy. By 1856 many had gone so far as to brand the practice barbaric. Nothing aroused more anti-Mormon hatred than polygamy. Brigham Young himself had as many as two-dozen wives and fifty-six children. The Lion of the Lord married at every opportunity, even enticing other Mormon's wives to join his growing family and using the law of the church to dissolve their marriages. The Lion's Den in the heart of Salt Lake City, where Young housed his family, looked more like a college dormitory than a family residence. And anyone who questioned Young's motives or actions committed an unpardonable sin.[2]

While Sibley was in Kansas he had read of the origins of the confrontation between Young and the federal government. Most of the trouble in the Utah Territory, or what the Mormons called Deseret, came with the appointment of federal officials by Washington, all of whom were Gentiles. The federal officials, especially the territorial judges, were never welcomed into Young's theocratic haven and often, faced with Mormon bitterness, became hostile in return. Most judges and several Indian agents rarely remained for more than a few years in the contemptuous society of Zion.[3] Most Gentiles were easily ostracized and departed Utah with strong anti-Mormon feelings.

By 1857 President James Buchanan appointed Alfred Cumming of Georgia governor of the remote territory and Delana R. Eckels, Charles

[1] Stanley P. Hirshson, *The Lion of the Lord: A Biography of Brigham Young* (New York, 1969), 184–223. For a more recent biography of Brigham Young see: Leonard J. Arrington, *Brigham Young: American Moses* (Champaign, 1986).

[2] Ibid.

[3] Charles P. Roland, *Albert Sidney Johnston: Soldier of Three Republics* (Austin, 1964), 187.

E. Sinclair, and John Cradlebaugh judges.[4] When Brigham Young rejected the appointees, the president became determined to use the United States Army to install the officials by force if necessary. Young reacted by issuing a proclamation forbidding the United States Army to enter Utah. The Mormon leader next declared martial law and called on his territorial militia known as the Nauvoo Legion estimated to number four thousand. The Congress, President Buchanan, and the American people were outraged.

General Winfield Scott, Mexican War hero and able commander of the army, refused to let the public clamor against the polygamous Mormons dictate army policy. Scott argued that 1857 was already too advanced to facilitate the sending of a large army halfway across the continent. William S. Harney, famous Indian fighter and Sibley's old regimental commander, was placed in charge of the Mormon Expedition but appeared indifferent and like Scott preferred waiting until the spring of 1858 to launch the contemplated expedition. To further complicate matters, Harney's orders differed markedly from those given Territorial Governor Cumming.[5] Still Sibley and the dragoons made preparations for the expedition.

Orders called for the assembly of troops at Fort Leavenworth with the departure of a vanguard force of the Fifth and Tenth Infantry, the Second Dragoons, and two recently arrived artillery batteries, in June 1857. July arrived, and not one soldier had started for Utah. Furthermore, both the Fifth and Tenth Infantry were worn out and disorganized. The Tenth Infantry, which had been chasing Indians in Minnesota, had arrived in Kansas greatly understrength and demoralized. The Fifth Infantry, after an exhausting campaign against the Seminole in Florida, arrived in the territory in need of rest and recuperation. To complicate matters, the Fifth Infantry, after receiving the news of their planned departure for Utah, had suffered two hundred desertions which badly weakened the regiment.

The questioned availability of Sibley's Second Dragoons added to the confusion. Their ranks depleted by scurvy and desertion, the dragoons had gathered at Fort Leavenworth to prepare for the long march westward only to find counter orders directing the regiment to re-

---

[4] Norman F. Furniss, *The Mormon Conflict, 1850–1859* (New Haven, 1960), 98. This study is considered by many to be definitive.

[5] Ibid., p. 98.

main in Kansas.[6] Governor Robert J. Walker with the continued political crisis, remained fearful of wide-scale violence. While Sibley waited out the hot summer of 1857, the Mormon War officially began on July 18, 1857, with the departure for Utah of the Tenth Infantry followed a few days later by the Fifth Infantry and an artillery battery.

Sibley and the dragoons remained at Fort Riley through August when orders recalled them to Fort Leavenworth to make final preparations for the trek westward.[7] The regiment was given only three or four days to prepare for the undertaking.

Horses and equipment had to be inspected. Four company commanders were replaced, and a considerable amount of last-minute paperwork completed. Sibley was busy with recently arrived green recruits who were hurried into the ranks to replace the fifty soldiers who had deserted upon hearing of the orders directing the dragoons to Utah. Late in the afternoon of September 16, 1856, a final inspection of the regiment was completed. Preparations for the thousand-mile march to the valley of the Great Salt Lake had been too hurried, and most companies, Sibley's Company I included, were not ready. Nonetheless, on the morning of September 17, 1857, regimental commander Cooke and squadron and company commander Sibley led their dragoons slowly out of Fort Leavenworth toward the Little Blue River and the road to Utah.[8]

Colonel Albert Sidney Johnston, who had recently replaced Harney as commander of the "Mormon Expedition," left Fort Leavenworth on the afternoon of the same day. Traveling in spring wagons with light baggage and led by the able Mountain Man Jim Bridger, Johnston was able to make as much as forty-two miles a day and race past Sibley and the slower-moving dragoons.[9] Johnston, who had no illusions about the difficulties which lay ahead, was anxious to reach the vanguard of his army already at Fort Laramie some seven hundred miles to the west.

[6] Ibid., p. 101.

[7] Leroy R. Hafer and Ann W. Hafer, eds., *The Utah Expedition, 1857–1858: A Documentary Account of the United States Military Movement Under Colonel Albert Sidney Johnston, and the Resistance by Brigham Young and the Mormon Nauvoo Legion* (Glendale, 1958), 141.

[8] Rodenbough, p. 186.

[9] Roland, p. 191.

The dragoons had proceeded fewer than three miles from Fort Leavenworth when orders arrived directing the regiment to wait for additional supplies and pack animals. On the morning of September 18, 107 mules were driven into camp, almost all of which were broken down, having already traveled the more than two thousand miles to and from South Pass. On the morning of the 19th twenty-seven teamsters, almost all of whom Cooke accused of being utterly ignorant, also joined the column. On the following day Sibley and the dragoons were able to march fifteen miles but were forced to abandon valuable provisions when eleven wagon tongues broke. Three or four "laundresses," who were accompanying each company, also slowed the column.[10] On the 21st a hard rain made the road so slippery that the regiment traveled only six miles.

By September 23 the weather changed for the better and it remained warm for ten days. Many of the dragoons' worst fears, however, were being realized. Trail grass was scarce because a large number of animals had already passed over the route. The dragoon's supply of grain, especially corn for their horses and mules, was reduced. From Fort Riley the column turned up the Little Blue River where they were joined by twenty-five wagons and teams which had recently been used in an expedition against the Cheyenne Indians. Three days later a severe storm with driving winds and rain swept down on the regiment, and orders were given to remain in camp since no fuel was available on the Platte River which the dragoons were scheduled to reach the next day.[11] For two days the horse soldiers moved along the Platte River, or what some jokingly called the Nebraska seacoast. On the morning of October 5, the regiment arrived at Fort Kearny in pouring rain. Although behind schedule, Cooke was happy with the dragoons' progress. The regiment had averaged twenty-one miles a day for two weeks. Desertions had grown to such an extent, however, that by the time the dragoons reached Fort Kearny seventy-seven men had left the horse soldier ranks.

Fort Kearny, once a waystation for thousands of gold-seekers on

[10] Rodenbough's *Everglade to Canon* contains parts of a journal kept by Colonel Philip St. George Cooke during the trek from Fort Leavenworth to Fort Bridger which is the only known source of the near disasterous march of the regiment. Otis E. Young in *The West of Philip St. George Cooke, 1809–1895* (Glendale, 1955), 296, draws the same conclusion.

[11] Rodenbough, p. 186.

their way to California, was crudely built of wood and mud.[12] One of Sibley's comrades remarked that the post reminded him of the abobe villages he had once seen in México. Nevertheless, the fort was a welcome sight. Here the dragoons traded several of their weaker mules for stronger ones. Colonel Cooke had hoped to find enough corn at the post to replenish his dwindling supply of grain, but there was none. On October 7 the men rode out of the post in a drenching rainstorm.[13] For five days the weather remained inclement as the column wound its way along the Platte River.

Each day the temperature dropped. Ice was already forming on the Platte River. With trail grass growing scarce and the decreased store of grain, Sibley realized that great care had to be taken with the horses and mules. For two hours each day when good grass could be found, the horses had to be led and given every opportunity to graze. The hard frosts and the consumption of trail grass by the advance units led to a perilous situation. Still the dragoons plodded onward continuing to average twenty-one miles a day.

By October 15 the column had reached the junction of the South Platte. Here a cold northwesterly wind arose, depressing the men's spirits. The situation had grown worse since the column had left Fort Kearny. The dragoons spent hours searching in vain for sufficient fodder for the hungry animals. No grass could be found along the North Platte, and horses and mules began to die of starvation; their carcasses left along the trail as food for hungry scavengers.

On October 17 the column overtook two wagon trains loaded with corn which had left Fort Kearny twelve days ahead of the dragoons. Cooke announced that he was "relieving the two trains of their precious commodity."[14] That evening, as the bluecoats went into camp on Smith's Fork, a strong northeasterly wind with sleet began to blow. By morning the sleet had turned to snow, and within hours four inches had blanketed the Nebraska prairie. The teams struggled on, but twenty-three mules, all three-year-olds, had to be unharnessed since they were completely exhausted. In late afternoon word arrived that good grass had been found several miles from the river. There the dragoons camped for the evening, allowing the animals to graze.

At Chimney Rock, a picturesque sentinel on the prairie, a private

[12] Herbert M. Hart, *Old Forts of the Northwest* (New York, 1963), 72.
[13] Rodenbough, p. 186.
[14] Ibid., p. 187.

named Whitney succumbed to lockjaw. With the temperature at twenty-three degrees and a fierce north wind blowing, the young dragoon was buried the next morning on a high bluff overlooking the river.[15] By the time the dragoons crossed the river at Scott's Bluff, chunks of ice were floating in the river. Winter was quickly coming on. Trail grass grew even more scarce; yet the regiment was still averaging about twenty miles each day, a feat Cooke bragged of especially since the trail was in as bad a condition as veteran prairie travelers could remember.

On October 22 the column was within sight of Fort Laramie, and on the following day the regiment camped on the Laramie River a half mile below the fort. Cooke called for a board of officers, including Sibley, to report upon the condition of the regiment's horses. Fifty-three were reported to be completely broken down while 278 more were thought unfit to complete the westward trek.[16] Furthermore, the regiment was dangerously short of grain. A small quantity of hay was found at the post, but this was quickly consumed.

Colonel Cooke had previously received orders from Johnston allowing the dragoons to winter near Fort Laramie. Cooke decided instead to continue the march, a gamble considering the lateness of the year.[17] All "laundresses" were left at the post as well as those soldiers reported to be sick. Because of the lack of horses, Sibley and the other company commanders were directed to choose one married man without a horse from each company as well as those thought to be "ineffective afoot," all of whom were to be left at the fort. Much of the dragoons' equipment and baggage was also left behind for the trek westward to join Johnston. Two ambulances, badly needed for the sick, were packed with what grain could be obtained at the post. Once the grain had run out, the ambulances could then be used for the sick.[18] Several of President Buchanan's Utah appointees, including Marshal Peter K. Dotson, Attorney General John Hartnett, and Indian Agent Jacob Forney, joined the dragoons at Fort Laramie.

At one o'clock on the afternoon of October 26, 1857, the "General" was sounded, and the regiment rode west from Fort Laramie. The post was no sooner out of sight on the eastern horizon than a fatigued rider

[15] Ibid.
[16] Ibid.
[17] Ibid., p. 188.
[18] Ibid.

galloped up from the west bearing important dispatches from Johnston. A band of mounted Mormons under the leadership of Lot Smith
had attacked and burned two wagon trains on the Green River and on
the following day surprised and destroyed another on nearby Big Sandy
River. The surprise attack, precisely the kind of tactics Brigham Young
was hoping to employ against the bluecoats, was a severe blow to the
Army of Utah. In all, seventy-two wagons containing three hundred
thousand pounds of food, mostly flour and bacon, enough provisions
to feed Johnston's army for several months, had gone up in smoke.[19]
Besides the prospects of a severe winter, the army now faced the possibilities of starvation. The situation was critical. Without cavalry it
would be difficult for Johnston to stave off Mormon raids. Although
the dragoons were still seven hundred miles to the east, Johnston
urged them to hurry westward. Upon receiving the news of the commencement of hostilities, Colonel Cooke ordered the regiment assembled, and with Sibley and the other company commanders in front
of their respective companies the colonel read a brief message expressing his confidence in the regiment's ability to meet the challenge which lay ahead.

One day out of Fort Laramie, guides found good grass on a cut-off
to the North Platte. Here the regiment went into camp early thus allowing the horses and mules time to graze. For the next three days
the column continued to find good grass as it moved along the North
Platte, still averaging twenty miles a day. Rain was falling heavily on
October 31 as the dragoons reached a trading post on the river where
hay was purchased and a beef slaughtered for food. Here also a hunter
was hired to provide fresh game for the regiment during the final push
through South Pass. Within days the weather had turned even worse.
Rain again turned into sleet, and the dragoons' tents, several of which
were of the Sibley variety, froze during the night. In the higher Laramie Mountains to the south, the sleet had turned to snow, perhaps
an ominous warning that the dragoons were now entering the most
difficult part of their march.

By this time five teams of mules had become so weak that Cooke
ordered them back to Fort Laramie. After a camp on the evening of
November 3 without grass, the regiment reached Independence Rock,
one of the natural beacons along the route, where a camp was made

[19] Furniss, p. 109.

along the Sweetwater River. Here four hundred pounds of good buffalo meat was brought in. Five wagons, their contents consumed by the men and their animals, were sent back to Fort Laramie. The dragoons' problems were complicated by Governor Cumming's wife, who among other things, complained of not being able to wash properly.

On November 5 the regiment passed Devil's Gate on the Sweetwater River and camped in a granite gorge upstream where the troopers awoke the next morning to find the ground covered with a fresh snowfall. Still Cooke ordered the column forward. Not far from the Devil's Gate the regiment reached "four-mile" hill where the men were forced to dismount and lead their horses up a steep slope. Here the cold north wind had drifted the snow to such an extent that it severely retarded the progress of the struggling column. It was here also that the horse soldiers came upon a rare natural phenomenon. "We were struggling through a freezing cloud," Cooke wrote, but despite the frozen fog and the zero visibility, the column blindly pushed on.[20] By evening their chief scout led the column to a large granite outcropping which afforded partial protection from the freezing wind and fog. The regiment, only a portion of which was protected, huddled in the cold through the terrible darkness as a heavy snow continued to fall. All through the night the mules could be heard "crying piteously" from across the Sweetwater where they had gathered en masse. An eerie feeling prevailed among the men when morning brought more driving snow. "It was not time to dwell on the fact that from that mountain desert there was no retreat nor any shelter near, but a time for action," Cooke wrote. "Not a complaint was heard," as the regiment moved out into the blinding snowstorm.[21]

All day the heavy snow continued to fall. A stiff north wind sweeping southward from the eastern slopes of the Wind River Mountains began to drift the snow and further impede the painstakingly slow progress of the column. While attempting to cross the frozen Sweetwater River, several mounted dragoons were plunged into the freezing current when the ice suddenly gave way. That day only ten miles were covered. Along the road the bodies of three less fortunate western travelers were found, their grotesquely frozen remains a startling and grim reminder of the possible fate of the regiment.

[20] Rodenbough, p. 189.
[21] Ibid.

Early on the morning of November 8 the thermometer stood at twelve degrees below zero. Before eight o'clock the Dragoons were already in the saddle and headed westward into the cold northwest wind.[22] What Harney and Scott had feared had come true. It was one of the coldest days in Sibley's memory. Few of the bluecoats could ride for more than a few minutes in the piercing cold, yet all pushed forward. By evening the dragoons had reached Bitter Creek where the men attempted to make camp as the storm continued. Guides brought word that some grass had been found on the hills overlooking the Sweetwater Valley. Here the wind had blown the snow from the higher ridges. The famished animals were driven to the heights, but few could graze for long in the freezing wind. Back in camp twenty-three mules gave out, and five wagons had to be abandoned.

On November 9 the blizzard continued to rage as the regiment pushed westward. Crossing a series of high rolling hills, the men struggled through the storm. Sibley and several other officers rode ahead breaking a trail through the drifting snow for the wagons. That evening the trail descended again into the Sweetwater Valley where camp was made. Only willow sticks and sagebrush could be found for fuel. Trying to keep warm, the men gathered around numerous small fires. At night a high wind came up, and by morning fifteen mules had frozen to death. The next day proved even worse as the regiment pressed toward South Pass. An empty wagon froze so solidly in a small creek that eight mules could not budge it. Nine troopers' horses collapsed and were left dying in the snow. Several soldiers and teamsters were frostbitten. They camped four miles short of the summit of the pass. The temperature continued to drop as the storm swept out of the cloud-shrouded Wind River Mountains. The night was so cold that the regiment's thermometer burst. Cooke estimated that the temperature had dropped to twenty-five degrees below zero.[23] A bottle of sherry wine, although securely packed in a trunk, was found frozen solid. Able Regimental Quartermaster John Buford calculated that fifty mules had been lost in the previous thirty-six hours. So critical was the situation becoming that the regiment was facing the possible fate of the Donner Party, part of which had survived in similar circumstances a decade before by eating the bodies of those who had not.

22 Ibid.
23 Ibid., p. 190.

Seventy-four saddles and bridles as well as part of the regiment's sabers were loaded into a wagon and abandoned.

As the dragoons struggled through South Pass on the morning of November 11, the sun broke through the clouds, heightening the men's spirits. Although the regiment was able to march seventeen miles that day, no grass could be found. During the desperately cold night several mules that were tied to the wagons gnawed four wagon-tongues beyond repair, destroyed several tarps covering the wagons, and after consuming their tie ropes, ate the sagebrush which had been piled near the tents for fuel. A few of the famished animals even began to gnaw at the tents. Nine of the miserable beasts died during the night. Early on the morning of November 12 several men were severely frostbitten, adding more misery to the already beleaguered column.[24]

Besides the mules, fifty horses had been lost since the column left Fort Laramie. Many men were now on foot, slowing the column even further. At last good grass was found on the evening of the 12th along the Big Sandy River, and Cooke ordered a day of rest to enable the starving animals to graze the entire day.

On the 14th the blizzard at last began to break, and by the 15th the dragoons were able to cross the Green River on the ice. Here forty-two mules and nine wagons were abandoned. On the east side of the river the dragoons were depressed to find the charred remnants of the twenty-five wagons which Lot Smith's Mormons had burned. On the opposite bank Sibley was equally dismayed to see the remains of fifty more wagons burned by the Mormons. At the river crossing Cooke met a man named Migette whom he hired to gather and winter any animals that could be found along the road eastward to South Pass.

One day west of Green River near Ham's Fork, the dragoons ran into another storm, and twenty horses died in a twenty-four-hour period. Out of grain and desperate for forage of any kind, guides were sent westward before daybreak on the morning of the 17th. After leading their fatigued and starving horses for miles, the dragoons found some grass on the Little Muddy, a small tributary of Black's Fork. For the next two days the troopers led their horses through mud and snow toward the Army of Utah. Late on the afternoon of November 19, 1857, the dragoons spotted an army camp in the distance. It turned

[24] Ibid.

out to be the Tenth Infantry on Black's Fork near Fort Bridger. Although fatigued and badly demoralized, the regiment had survived. During the march 134 horses had been lost, most of which had starved to death west of South Pass. Only 144 mounts remained.

The Second Dragoons' march westward to join the Army of Utah must rank as one of the epic endeavors of American military history. When Colonel Cooke sat down on November 21, 1857, to write his report of the nearly catastrophic mission, he could not help but think of Napoleon's historic retreat from Moscow: "The earth had a no more lifeless, treeless, grassless desert; it contains scarcely a wolf to glut itself on the hundreds of dead and frozen animals which for thirty miles nearly block the road with abandoned and shattered property; they mark, perhaps beyond example in history, the steps of an advancing army with the horrors of a disastrous retreat."[25] The terrible suffering of man and beast during the march through South Pass to Fort Bridger would also be deeply etched into Henry Hopkins Sibley's memory.

Fort Bridger had been built for protection against the Indians. In 1857 with the approach of the Army of Utah, the post had been burned by the Mormons. Constructed on Black's Fork of the Green River, the fort was so sturdily constructed of stone that although scorched and blackened, the building still stood.[26] Bridger, who hated the Latter-Day Saints almost as badly as the Army did, claimed that he had been driven from the fort by the Mormons who had threatened to kill him. Colonel Johnston had the fort's defenses strengthened by placing cannon on the parapets and constructing a moat and earthwork.

By the time the dragoons arrived at Fort Bridger, the various regimental camps of the Army of Utah stretched for several miles along Black's Fork of the Green River. The entire encampment was named Camp Scott in honor of the army commander and Mexican War hero General Winfield Scott. Civilian territorial officials clustered together in a makeshift camp of tents and huts near Camp Scott named Eckelsville for the territorial chief justice.

Johnston's immediate problem was logistics. With supply trains unable to get through South Pass, a hostile Mormon army to the west, and high mountains to the north and south, the army was isolated in

25 Ibid., p. 191.
26 Furniss, p. 148.

a snowy wilderness, dangerously short of food. A column under the leadership of Captain Randolph Marcy was sent through the Colorado Rockies to Fort Union in the Territory of New Mexico for badly needed horses and mules, but it would take Marcy months to complete the trip.[27]

Sibley found that rations had been reduced to almost starvation level. Oxen were slaughtered for food, but no salt was available for the meat. Brigham Young offered to send Johnston the badly needed salt, but the proud commander flatly refused. Friendly Indians brought small amounts of fruits and vegetables into Camp Scott, but these could be purchased only at exorbitant prices. The Indians, realizing the critical situation of the Army of Utah, even slaughtered their own dogs and attempted to pass the canines off as mountain sheep. Although most of the soldiers were tempted, few paid the dollar the Indians asked for a hind quarter of dog meat.[28] Numerous sutlers, who had followed the army westward, had foodstuffs for sale but charged such high prices that few could afford to purchase even the smallest items. Sibley found that a single biscuit, often rancid, sold for two dollars. Coffee and sugar went for seventy-five cents a pound; tobacco for one dollar and fifty cents a plug; and whiskey, which sold for thirty cents a gallon back East, went for ten dollars. Badly needed boots which sold in the states for three dollars now cost twenty. Furthermore, most of the soldiers' clothing was so worn that many of Sibley's men were in rags. With no alternative but to improvise, soldiers turned coat sleeves into stockings, patched their pants from any available fabric, and made Indian moccasins from the skins of any animal that ventured within shooting range.[29]

Morale became a problem. Johnston, a skilled officer, used everything imaginable to boost the spirits of his army. A small theatre was erected and soon in use. Sibley attended band concerts regularly. Some soldiers established a small library. Weather permitting, drill and training sessions were held daily. Officers conducted a tactical school for their subordinates. Regimental maneuvers were common. Most of the soldiers' leisure moments were spent playing poker and monte. Gambling was especially prevalent on paydays. One of Sibley's men

[27] W. Eugene Hollon, *Beyond the Cross Timbers: The Travels of Randolph B. Marcy, 1812–1887* (Norman, 1955), p. 216.

[28] Rodenbough, p. 217.

[29] Furniss, p. 150.

recalled that in mid-December, when the men received their pay for September and October, all the tents in the regiment could not house the gamblers. Blankets had to be spread on the prairie near the dragoon camp to accommodate all the poker-playing horse soldiers. Others passed their time in small talk, singing, cursing the Mormons, or getting inebriated. Drunken parties at Camp Scott, Eckelsville, and in the dragoon camp were common. In early December a drunken brawl at one of the infantry camps resulted in the death of three soldiers. In January 1858 several soldiers who had been allowed to hold a party at the camp theatre began drinking and then commenced fighting. One sergeant was killed in the melee while several others were severely beaten. Johnston ordered a court-martial for those involved. Several were found guilty and sentenced to hard labor for the remainder of their enlistment. Others were branded over the left hip with the letter M and, with their heads shaven, drummed out of the service.[30]

Only a few days after Sibley and the Second Dragoons arrived at Fort Bridger, they were ordered into the field. Although at one-half strength after the almost catastrophic march through South Pass, the troopers were ordered to protect the mules, horses, and other animals of the Army of Utah that were being grazed on the various streams away from Camp Scott.

On November 26, 1857, the regiment took camp on Smith's Fork. Sibley's squadron, consisting of Companies B and I, remained behind at Camp Scott.[31] Sibley possibly owed his preferential treatment to his distant kinship with Johnston, although the able commander of the Army of Utah does not appear to have been one to play favorites. Sibley was a capable commander, Johnston felt, and his squadron was needed to scout the area around Camp Scott. Another successful Mormon raid on Johnston's meager supplies could easily spell disaster for the Army of Utah.

After less than a week's rest Sibley was ordered by Johnston to prepare a detail of seven men for a patrol around the camp.[32] During November and the first part of December 1857, Sibley, acting as the eyes of the Army of Utah, commanded the patrols that rode forth from

[30] Roland, p. 200.

[31] Rodenbough, p. 218.

[32] F.J. Porter to H.H. Sibley, 28 November 1857, A.G.O., Dept. of Utah, Register of Letters Sent, R.G. 391.

Camp Scott almost daily. Mounted on mules because of the loss of their horses on the march from Kansas, Sibley's men performed ably. Sibley thus played an important role in the Mormon War. Johnston was taking few chances; some of Sibley's reconnaissances were at night.

Frequently the soldiers in the Army of Utah found time for more festive occasions than midnight patrols. Several of the officers, including Sibley, Captains Barnard E. Bee, Jesse L. Reno, John Dunovant, Jesse A. Gove, Dr. Madison Mills, and Colonel Charles F. Smith, would gather for an evening of dining and cards. During one such party held at Captain Gove's tent the men partook of "meatballs, boiled tongue, splendid oyster soup, cookies, rice croquettes and coffee," a radical departure from their usual meager diet.[33] Sibley and Captain Gove, judging from the latter's correspondence to his wife, appear to have formed a close comradeship while at Camp Scott. Weekly parties, usually held in Gove's tent, became the social highlight of the otherwise dreary military routine of the army. Unable to return to the dragoon camp after such parties, Henry would remain in Gove's tent to sleep off the effects of the evening's festivities.

In late February 1858, with the environs at Camp Scott thought to be relatively safe, Sibley was ordered into camp on Black's Fork about five miles below Bridger's Fort and Camp Scott. Black's Fork was a picturesque valley running south from Camp Scott toward the towering Uinta Mountains. The valley was surrounded by high sandstone bluffs dotted with juniper trees where sentinels or mounted pickets were to be placed. Lieutenant Thomas Hight, commanding Company B, was ordered to join Sibley in the new camp, called Camp Quitman in honor of Major General John A. Quitman, a Mexican War hero.[34]

On February 26 Sibley was ordered into the saddle along with fifteen of his men in hopes of overtaking a herd of horses which the Mormons had stampeded from the vicinity of Camp Scott.[35] One day

[33] Jesse A. Gove, *The Utah Expedition, 1857–1858: Letters of Captain Jesse A. Gove,* Otis G. Hammons, ed. (New Hampshire Historical Society, 1928), pp. 123–24, 127–28.

[34] F.J. Porter to Thomas High[t], 25 February 1858, A.G.O., Dept. of Utah, R. of L.S., R.G. 391.

[35] F.J. Porter to H.H. Sibley, 26 February 1858, A.G.O., Dept. of Utah, R. of L.S., R.G. 391.

later he escorted an ambulance eastward to Smith's Fork to recover the body of a dragoon who had died and had been buried in a shallow grave by Lieutenant Hight. The ambulance was escorted back to Sibley's camp and then upstream to Camp Scott the following day.[36]

Furthermore, Sibley was to "prevent all improper persons from entering or leaving camp or hovering in the vicinity."[37] He was to watch the Fort Laramie Road closely, apprehend any travelers who looked suspicious, and make them account for their actions. Those leaving Camp Scott were to be given a passport, especially expressmen, but even then Sibley was to check their dispatches closely. He was also to keep an eye out for deserters, teamsters, and any unemployed individual who might be traveling eastward with the approach of better weather, and to scrutinize their animals to see that none had been stolen from Camp Scott. Any animal branded "U.S." was to be seized, and the thief sent to Camp Scott for punishment. "It is very desirable that the first offenders of this kind be apprehended as tending to deter others from similar attempts and insuring confidence in the watchfulness of our guards," Fitz-John Porter, Johnston's adjutant, wrote Sibley.[38]

From Camp Quitman, Sibley was also to watch the Salt Lake City road closely. On March 1 a man who had recently left Salt Lake City brought word into Camp Scott that three companies of Mormons, reported to number over three hundred, were moving eastward to harass and raid as many army camps as possible.[39] As a result Johnston ordered Cooke to put into the field a squadron of dragoons to patrol the area north of Henry's Fork in the direction of the road leading to South Pass. By moving eastward up Henry's Fork, Cooke could also keep an eye out for good grass. Cooke could thus protect the rear of the army while Sibley was to post a guard of fifteen men at a spot overlooking the Salt Lake City road, while also searching for suitable watering and grazing places.

---

[36] F.J. Porter to H.H. Sibley, 27 February 1858, A.G.O., Dept. of Utah, R. of L.S., R.G. 391.

[37] Headquarters to H.H. Sibley, 27 February 1858, A.G.O., Dept. of Utah, R. of L.S., R.G. 391.

[38] Ibid.

[39] F.J. Porter to H.H. Sibley, 2 March 1858, A.G.O., Dept. of Utah, R. of L.S., R.G. 391.

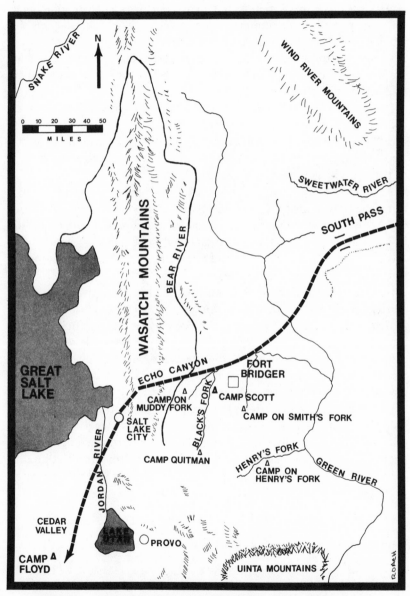

SIBLEY'S MARCH FROM SOUTH PASS TO CAMP FLOYD SHOWING DRAGOON CAMPS PROTECTING CAMP SCOTT

Any small group of men moving eastward was to be apprehended. If a large party was encountered, Henry was to "withdraw keeping the party in sight" until reinforcements could arrive from Camp Scott.[40] A smaller patrol which had been keeping a vigil along the Oregon Trail leading north out of Camp Scott was placed on alert to prevent an attack from that direction.

In another order Johnston instructed Sibley to establish an advance picket on the Muddy Fork of the Green River, to detect any attempted raid from the northeast. Henry sent out Lieutenant Hight but upon inspection found that his location did not overlook the valley of the Muddy as Johnston had ordered.[41]

At Camp Quitman and in the nearby herding camps problems of a different nature arose. On March 6 Sibley reported to headquarters that a group of defiant teamsters had revolted, were refusing to follow orders, and were heavily armed, but that he had successfully disarmed the troublemakers and had run them out of camp the same afternoon.[42]

In early March Colonel Cooke moved the Dragoon Camp from Henry's Fork to Smith's Fork. Sibley was to proceed from Camp Quitman on Black's Fork to Henry's Fork before moving upstream to join Cooke. A severe storm arose, and Henry was unable to move for several days. Finally after making the desired juncture with Cooke, Henry was ordered to continue moving his camp every two or three days for a period of two weeks in hopes of finding better grass.[43]

Less than two weeks later, after Sibley's squadron had moved their camp to Smith's Fork, a squabble developed between Cooke and Johnston. Cooke, who had never been popular with the dragoons, especially Sibley, had become angered at Porter, Johnston's adjutant. The feuding, with Johnston and Porter on one side and the tempera-

[40] Ibid.

[41] H.H. Sibley to Headquarters, 5 March 1858, A.G.O., Dept. of Utah, Register of Letters Received, R.G. 391.

[42] H.H. Sibley to Headquarters, 12 March 1858, A.G.O., Dept. of Utah, R. of L.R., R.G. 391.

[43] F.J. Porter to H.H. Sibley, 6 March 1858, A.G.O., Dept. of Utah, R. of L.S., R.G. 391; H.H. Sibley to Headquarters. 16 March 1858, A.G.O., Dept of Utah, R. of L.R., R.G. 391.

mental Cooke on the other, had to be settled by Washington when Cooke appealed to higher authorities.[44]

While in camp on Smith's Fork, Sibley became angered at Major Marshall Saxe Howe of the dragoons whom he accused of selling various commodities at exhorbitant prices. Sibley preferred charges. Johnston, although refusing to condone the practice, informed Sibley that the major's actions "can reflect no scandal on the Army; nor has the tendency of the transactions charged been, as it is believed, to the prejudice of good order and military discipline."[45] Howe's actions did "not constitute a crime" and were not covered by the statute under which Sibley had preferred charges. Sibley dropped the charges.

While Henry's squadron was camped on Smith's Fork, word arrived that Captain Randolph B. Marcy had reached Fort Union and was returning with badly needed horses and livestock. Marcy had succeeded only with the greatest of difficulty. With forty enlisted men he had followed the Gunnison River into the high mountains of what is now southern Colorado where the party had become lost and almost perished in a snowstorm near Cochetopa Pass. After eating their mules, the men had survived only by crawling through the deep snow on their hands and knees. A relief party had found the frozen men in early January 1858, and by March, after reaching Fort Union, Marcy had begun the return trek to Camp Scott.[46]

On March 19 a severe storm struck Sibley's squadron on Smith's Fork. Snow blasted up the valley in such gusts that the men could scarcely set foot outside their tents. For several hours the wind blew so hard that many tents, mostly of the Sibley type, would not emit smoke properly, and most men could not sleep because of the dense smoke. One of the dragoon cooks became blinded. Yet it was so cold that fires had to be kept burning. Sibley changed guards every hour to prevent the men from freezing.

Finally in late April the weather broke. The terrible winter of 1857–58 was finally over. Still numerous problems faced Sibley and the dragoons on Smith's Fork as well as the infantry at Camp Scott. Many

---

[44] H.H. Sibley to Headquarters, 14 March 1858, A.G.O., Dept. of Utah, R. of L.R., R.G. 391; F.J. Porter to H.H. Sibley, 16 March 1858, A.G.O., Dept. of Utah, R. of L.S., R.G. 391.

[45] F.J. Porter to H.H. Sibley, 1 May 1858, A.G.O., Dept. of Utah, R. of L.S., R.G. 391.

[46] Hollon, p. 226.

relief trains from Forts Laramie, Kearny, and Leavenworth were late in arriving, and the army's food supply was precarious. Colonel Johnston gave orders for another reduction in rations. The men were so short of food that one soldier admitted that he had already "commenced selecting the horses and mules to be first killed."[47] The poor condition of the regiment's animals forced the men to pull their wood wagons by hand, often for distances of up to seven or eight miles. On May 27 Companies C and H of the dragoons arrived from Fort Laramie, driving before them seventy-five head of beef cattle. The men's spirits heightened.

Good news had also reached the dragoons from the Valley of the Saints. The Mormons had decided to submit to the authority of the federal government. Still the army prepared to fight a war if necessary. The War Department created the Department of Utah commanded by General Persifor F. Smith and commenced sending massive amounts of supplies to Camp Scott. The government hired the firm of Russell, Majors, and Wadell to supply the Army of Utah and one hundred wagon trains comprised of forty thousand oxen, one thousand mules, and four thousand teamsters were already headed westward.[48]

Word reached Camp Scott of the exodus of thirty thousand Mormons from the northern part of the Utah Territory to Provo and points south. Brigham Young was hoping to buy time and, if possible, avoid a military confrontation. Young also hoped to win sympathy for the Mormons by creating a picture of the Saints as an oppressed people being driven from their homes. The scene was reminiscent of the Saints' heartbreaking evacuation of Nauvoo, Illinois, little more than a decade before.

Sibley remained in camp on Smith's Fork while Governor Cumming rode into the Valley of the Great Salt Lake in early April 1858. The governor had come to arrange a permanent peace with the Mormons but he found Salt Lake City abandoned. Church leaders, anxious for peace, journeyed northward from Provo to talk with the amiable Cumming. After more than a week of negotiations, the governor reached an agreement with the Mormons in which they agreed to accept the authority of the federal government. Without delay Cum-

---

[47] Rodenbough, p. 228.
[48] Furniss, p. 172.

ming rode eastward through the Wasatch Mountains to inform Johnston, now promoted to general, that peace had come to Utah. General Johnston, who never trusted the governor anyway, was anything but overjoyed and for several days refused even to see Cumming. The governor, who was finally able to communicate with Johnston by letter, found negotiations with the army more difficult than those with Brigham Young. The Mormons were hoping Cumming could stop an invasion of their beloved valley. Johnston, however, was determined to march to Salt Lake City. The impasse between the two led to feelings little short of hatred.

Sibley learned that the Utah political picture was further confused by the arrival at Camp Scott in late May of a peace commission. President Buchanan had appointed Lazarus W. Powell, one-time governor of Kentucky, and Ben McCulloch of Texas Revolution and Mexican War fame, to head the delegation.[49] Four days after arriving at Camp Scott, Powell and McCulloch set out for Salt Lake City where they were joined by Governor Cumming. The envoys informed Brigham Young that the government was willing to pardon him and his followers only if Young would accept the army into the valley and cooperate fully with all civil officials. Young agreed to halt all hostilities and even went so far as to "suggest that Albert Sidney Johnston was probably a fine man."[50]

Even before the conclusion of peace negotiations, Johnston was on the march. By early June, Sibley and the dragoons were at Black's Fork busily preparing for the march to the Valley of the Saints. Everything was hustle and bustle. Enough horses had been brought from New Mexico by the gallant Marcy to mount the entire regiment. It was the first time all the dragoons had been mounted since riding out of Fort Leavenworth in September 1857. Sixty dragoons were on mules, but all agreed that this was better than being on foot.

At eight o'clock in the morning of June 13, 1858, a regimental parade was held, and Sibley's Dragoons, with guidons snapping in the wind and trumpets sounding, marched out from Black's Fork. The regiment was scarcely recognizable as the same unit of motley men who had limped into Camp Scott in November of the previous year.[51] By ten o'clock the regiment was at Camp Scott where Sibley's squad-

[49] Ibid., p. 193.
[50] Ibid., p. 197.
[51] Rodenbough, p. 229.

ron was detached as an escort for General Johnston who would be riding ahead of the army in his carriage to select a suitable camping spot for the army. The rest of the regiment, as the advance guard for the Army of Utah, left shortly thereafter. For the next two days the Army wound its way out of Camp Scott. As the men turned to take one last glimpse of Camp Scott's "chimney-stacks, roof-poles, and other relics and debris," the post resembled the "ruins of an ancient town," but as the army climbed slowly through the juniper-covered hills beyond Camp Scott the ruins of their winter habitation passed from view.[52]

Undoubtedly Sibley was happy to be on the move again. Word had not yet reached the Army of Utah of the successful completion of the peace negotiations, and war was still a reality, at least to the dragoons and the Army of Utah.

As the regiment passed over the rolling hills between Black's Fork and the Muddy Fork of the Green River, they noticed the bright green grass which carpeted the countryside. Spring had come to the Rocky Mountains. Flowers, especially larkspurs, were numerous along the road, and the soldiers stopped to pick a few, many to be dried and sent to loved ones in the east.[53] By early afternoon the Second Dragoons had reached Muddy Fork. After fording the small stream, the horse soldiers bivouacked. Before nightfall Captain John W. Phelps' light battery of artillery and five companies of infantry had joined the dragoons. After leaving camp at sunrise the following day, the regiment reached the Bear River by early afternoon and went into camp on the west bank. The infantry and artillery units joined the dragoons several hours later.

On the third day out of Camp Scott, the dragoons remained in camp on the Bear River to allow other elements of the Army of Utah to join them. At noon the weather turned bad with pouring rain and colder temperatures. During the storm the Tenth Infantry made the mistake of attempting to cross their baggage and supplies over the river on a small bridge. In the heavy rain two wagons loaded with flour slid into the raging waters and were swept downstream. Several mules became tangled in their harnesses and drowned in the torrent. Most of the infantry, already exhausted and soaked from the day's march,

---

[52] Albert Tracy, "Journal of Albert Tracy," *Utah State Historical Quarterly*, 13 (1945), 17.

[53] Ibid.

were helpless. Several of Sibley's dragoons jumped into the swollen river, attached ropes to the wagons and pulled the wagons to dry ground, thus saving the commodities.[54] Other supply trains were ordered to cross the Bear River at a spot where the dragoons had forded the stream the previous day. Most of the Tenth Infantry, including several of the officers' wives, camped on the east bank to await better conditions for crossing.

Across the mountains and into Echo Canyon, Brevet Major Sibley and the horse soldiers led the Army of Utah ever closer to the Valley of the Saints. Upon entering Echo Canyon, Colonel Cooke gave orders for a regimental drill which caused a considerable amount of grumbling since Sibley and most of the dragoons saw little need for such nonsense. Nevertheless, everyone hurried about, officers shouting instructions to their companies and Cooke issuing orders to the officers. One cavalryman asserted that Cooke ordered the drill only to heighten his ego by hearing the reverberations of the bugles off the high basaltic cliffs which towered above the regiment. "Echoes among the rocks surpass anything I ever heard," another officer later recalled.[55]

Back and forth across Echo Creek Sibley and the dragoons rode on. Captain Albert Tracy, an infantry officer who followed the dragoons, recorded his impressions of the picturesque canyon: "Willows spring upon the banks of the stream, and occasionally dwarfed and twisted cedar flaunted its tufts midway or along the brow of the cliffs above."[56] Three miles after entering Echo Canyon, the dragoons came upon a series of fortifications constructed by the Mormons to halt the invaders. Dragoon veterans of the Mexican War laughed at the Mormon's meager defenses. Little did the Saints know of "the modern system of deploying and skirmishing, or the availability of artillery."[57]

From the mouth of Echo Canyon, the trail dropped abruptly to the Weber River and continued westward into the Wasatch Mountains. Climbing past scrubby cedars and into the pines and higher yet through fir and spruce trees, the cavalry found more hastily-constructed Mormon fortifications. Early on the morning of June 25 the

[54] Rodenbough, p. 229.
[55] Ibid., p. 230; Young, p. 308.
[56] Tracy, p. 22.
[57] Ibid., p. 23.

dragoons reached a high pass in the mountains and gazed out to see below them the City of the Saints nestled along the Jordan River. Beyond Salt Lake City the Great Salt Lake was outlined on the western horizon. Many of the dragoons, like Sibley, could not help but compare this magnificent view to their first glimpse of the Great Valley of Mexico which they had seen a decade before. "The view from this point," one soldier observed, "is little less than magnificent."[58] William Drown, chief bugler of the Second Dragoons, also recorded his first impressions of the great valley: "When Brigham Young called this a paradise, I think he did not exaggerate at all; for it is truly the most lovely place I ever saw. If I were situated to do so, I would be almost persuaded to turn Mormon myself, just for the privilage of living here."[59] Within hours Sibley and the dragoons were through Emigration Canyon and in the streets of the city.

Even though the Mormon haven was deserted, the dragoons were impressed. Henry found the city to be laid out in perfect squares with every street straight and fifty yards wide. The Mormon homes were well-constructed of stone or abode. Doors and windows were missing, having been removed during the Mormon hegira. Houses were enclosed by neat picket fences. Yards, some as large as four acres, abounded in flowers and vegetables, all of which were irrigated by a small stream diverted from the Jordan River. Near most of the Saints' homes stood small apple or peach orchards. The dragoons were particularly impressed with Young's mansion which was described as a "magnificent building, being two and a half stories high, with a long range of rooms . . . very tastefully ornamented. In front of the house, on a pillar, lies a large lion cut from stone, and on the very top of the house a large bee-hive, cut from the same material."[60] Captain Tracy, who referred to Young as the "Turk of the Valley," was impressed by the numerous gables on Young's house which Tracy asserted were necessary to shelter the leader's "abundance of wives."[61]

As the dragoons rode into the city, Colonel Cooke, having commanded the Mormon Battalion during the Mexican War, removed his hat in respect for the Saints. All day the Army of Utah marched down the main street of the Salt Lake City, now deserted. It was not until

[58] Ibid., p. 25.
[59] Rodenbough, p. 230.
[60] Ibid.
[61] Tracy, p. 27.

late afternoon that the rear guard made its way through the stately theocratic community. Despite the fact that the army was under strict orders not to stray from the column during the march through the city, all were not as respectful as Colonel Cooke. When Army Adjutant Fitz-John Porter came abrest of Young's mansion, he gave an order to the army's band where upon the musical contigent struck up the popular marching song "One Eye Riley," which was said to have had a thousand verses, most of them obscene.

> As I was strolling round and round,
> A-huntin' fun in every quarter,
> I stopped meself at a little Dutch inn
> And ordered up me Gin and Warter.
>
> One Eye Riley, Two Eye Riley,
> Ho! for the lad with one eye, Riley![62]

From Salt Lake City Sibley and the dragoons led the army across the Jordan River. General Johnston posted guards at the bridge to prevent any possible vandals from returning to loot Mormon property. Johnston wasted little time before seeking a permanent camp because of the lack of forage along the Jordan. After scouting the western slopes of the Oquirrh Mountains, the general decided on a site a few miles from the shores of Lake Utah opposite the Mormon settlement of Provo. On July 7 the army rode south along the west bank of the Jordan River to Cedar Valley. Here the army established Camp Floyd, named in honor of the secretary of war. On the march south the army passed many Mormons returning to their homes in Salt Lake City. Some government officials, including Governor Cumming, feared a confrontation. Although the Mormons mistrusted the soldiers, and the army in its anti-Mormon bitterness despised the settlers, nothing happened.

In Cedar Valley the dormant feud between regimental commander Cooke and squadron commander Sibley erupted anew. The dragoons, as the advance guard of the army, had been the first to leave camp on the Jordan River. On June 29 the regiment made a dusty march of eighteen miles through a blistering desert heat. By evening, with the wind howling and the dust blowing, the regiment had made an uneasy camp. In the morning all dragoon companies were to be mus-

---

[62] Ibid.; Young, p. 309; Furniss, p. 202; Roland, p. 214.

tered so that company and regimental rolls could be completed. The wind and dust were so bad that Sibley's company clerk sought refuge in a wagon to complete the necessary paperwork. By laboring all night he was able to finish.[63]

Despite the bad weather twenty officers, including seven lieutenants from the dragoons, had gathered, as they frequently did in the evening, for a few drinks and a game of cards. The "convivial party," which Sibley later testified he joined only by chance, became boisterous and loud. This, of course, was not uncommon, especially among the dragoon officers who were thought to be the hardest drinking, most arrogant, and most egotistical of any regiment in the Army of Utah. Cooke, who had been in ill health for months and in no mood for any foolishness, did not share the officers' enthusiasm for celebrating. Cooke had the officers arrested and restricted to their tents. The next day Sibley asked Cooke through Regimental Adjutant Pegram for an extension of the limits of his arrest to that of the entire dragoon camp.[64] The colonel, partly acquiescing, agreed that Sibley could visit his squadron. Still not satisfied, Sibley asked for permission to call on his friends in the Tenth Infantry. When Cooke refused, Sibley fired off an angry appeal in which he referred to the colonel as "oppressive and tyrannical."[65]

General Johnston became concerned about the arrest of the officers and the continued Cooke-Sibley feud. The general asked Cooke not to put any "unnecessary restrictions on the social meeting of officers" but at the same time to see that "good behavior and decorum be observed.[66] Johnston did not want the officers treated any differently from those previously arrested. Cooke responded by promising to release all the officers within twenty-four hours. On the following day, however, Johnston intervened in the Cooke-Sibley feud directly by ordering Cooke to extend Sibley's limits of arrest to that of the entire army.[67]

[63] Court Martial Records in the Case of H.H. Sibley, 10 July 1858, Judge Advocate General's Office, R.G. 153, p. 19.

[64] Ibid., p. 22.

[65] Ibid., p. 6.

[66] Henry E. Maynadier to P. St. Geo. Cooke, 1 July 1858, A.G.O., Dept. of Utah, R. of L.S., R.G. 391.

[67] F.J. Porter to Philip St. George Cooke, 2 July 1858, A.G.O., Dept. of Utah, R. of L.R., R.G. 391.

On the morning of Sibley's arrest, Colonel Cooke had discovered that the muster rolls of Sibley's Company I were missing. Cooke gave strict orders for Sibley to supply the rolls without delay. When he finally submitted them, Cooke discovered that none of the records covering May and June had been signed. Further incensed and remembering their previous differences in Kansas and in the recruiting service, Cooke ordered Sibley to report promptly to his tent to explain his negligence. When Sibley appeared at Cooke's tent, the colonel, who prided himself on his literary expertise, gave the brevet major a severe tongue-lashing for not signing the rolls and for several additional errors in the documents.

When Cooke demanded to know why he had failed to sign the rolls, Sibley replied that he had not time to do so since they had been "brought to him just at the time his company was about to be mustered." "You hadn't time to sign it. It would not have required more than a few seconds to have signed your roll," Cooke angrily replied.[68] A bitter argument ensued in which Sibley bluntly told Cooke in a loud and defiant voice that he had no authority to send for the papers in the first place. Furthermore, Sibley continued, Cooke did not have the right to see the rolls until they had been signed and had thus come by the rolls improperly. Shouting at Cooke, Sibley asserted that Company I was his company just as the Second Dragoons was Cooke's regiment. Feeling he was being verbally abused the colonel interrupted. "Major Sibley you appear to be disrespectful. Do you intend to be disrespectful?" The brevet major replied that he respected his commander, "but I have my rights."[69] The heated argument ended when Cooke allowed Sibley to return to his tent, but still under arrest.

Cooke, angered at Sibley and perhaps resenting General Johnston's intervention in the feud, recalled a post order which he had issued at Fort Riley, Kansas Territory, on December 24, 1856, which stated that all muster rolls were to "be completed in all respects and signed" before they were submitted to the commanding officer.[70] Cooke decided to prefer court-martial charges against Sibley.

Sibley was charged with "neglect of duty" and "conduct to the prejudice of good order and military discipline," the all-inclusive pro-

[68] C.M. of H.H. Sibley, 10 July 1858, J.A.G.O., R.G. 153, p. 20.
[69] Ibid., p. 10.
[70] Ibid., p. 8.

visions of the code of military discipline. Under the first charge Cooke specified that Sibley had failed to sign the muster rolls of his company and was thus in violation of the post order previously issued at Fort Riley. Under the second charge Cooke listed two specifications accusing Sibley of using a "very loud and defiant tone and manner" in addressing his commander, and of referring to Cooke as "oppressive and tyrannical."[71]

While Henry was still under arrest, several officers gathered in the dragoon camp on July 4 to celebrate the country's independence. The army had been issued fresh mutton and a ration of whiskey, both of which had raised morale. As the evening progressed, some officers became drunk and commenced shouting and singing. Colonel Cooke, perturbed by the loud festivities, strode onto the scene and had everyone arrested regardless of rank. "The patriotic fervor of said Cooke," one of the officers quipped, "does not appear to lead him to the recognition of too much noise, even upon this, our nation's holiday."[72]

Sibley's court-martial commenced at ten o'clock on the morning of July 10, 1858. Thirteen officers were detailed to hear the case: Colonel Edmund B. Alexander, Lieutenant Colonels Charles F. Smith and Carlos A. Waite, Major William Chapman, Captains Randolph B. Marcy, Charles S. Lovell, Andrew W. Bowman, John C. Robinson, Albert Tracy, Jesse A. Gove, John Dunovant, John Trivitt, and Thomas H. Neill, with Lieutenant John H. Forney as Judge Advocate. When Colonel Alexander, commander of the Tenth Infantry, asked to be excused from the court, he was replaced by Major Edward Richard Sprigg Canby.[73]

Captain Albert Tracy's diary indicates that many of the officers had already determined on Henry's innocence before the trial opened. "But what, now, will a really meritorious officer, and refined writer and gentleman, do next, to make himself absurd?" Tracy queried in reference to Cooke's decision to prefer charges against Sibley.[74] Several officers were also incensed that Cooke, after arresting Sibley and the other officers on the evening of June 30, had done the same to several more on July 4. "Why not, oh, Cooke, the wind itself arrest," Tracy

---

[71] Ibid., pp. 4, 10.
[72] Tracy, p. 29.
[73] C.M. of H.H. Sibley, 10 July 1858, J.A.G.O., R.G. 153, pp. 1–2.
[74] Tracy, p. 29.

wrote in his diary, "for it is upon a most royal blow-out and roaring at the top of its voice?"[75]

On the morning of July 12 the court martial board began hearing evidence. In his defense Henry retained First Lieutenant Grier Tallmadge of the Fourth Artillery and pleaded not guilty to all charges and specifications, and objected particularly to the first charge. He argued that there were discrepancies between army regulations and rulings of the Supreme Court. Consequently, Henry eloquently argued on his own behalf, the post order previously issued at Fort Riley was illegal and therefore, he was not guilty. Furthermore, if he signed the rolls previous to the mustering of his company he would have been attesting to a lie since two soldiers who were listed as present on the roll were absent at the muster.[76] The members of the court retired to deliberate the assertions but returned after a few minutes to announce that Sibley was overruled.

Colonel Cooke, the first witness for the prosecution, testified that Sibley had not signed the muster rolls and that the rolls contained serious errors. He further accused Sibley of shouting at him in a disrespectful and defiant voice. At this point, Henry and his attorney objected to the colonel's testimony on grounds that Cooke's accusations were not covered in the charges. Once again Sibley was overruled, and Cooke went on to recall Henry's various attempts at having the limits of his arrest extended and relating how Sibley had referred to him as "oppressive and tyrannical."[77]

The second witness for the prosecution was Regimental Adjutant John Pegram, who testified that Sibley had not signed the muster rolls and had indeed been disrespectful to his commander. The lieutenant also testified as to the validity of the Fort Riley post orders. Under lengthy cross examination, however, Pegram admitted that the conditions under which the rolls had been completed were extremely bad.

At three o'clock the following afternoon the court recessed to reconvene at ten o'clock the next morning. At this time the order book containing the December 24, 1856, order was admitted as evidence, and the prosecution closed its argument.

Recalled by the defense, Lieutenant Pegram told how Sibley had waved his hand at Cooke but admitted that this was a habit of the

[75] Ibid.
[76] C.M. of H.H. Sibley, 10 July 1858, J.A.G.O., R.G. 153, Document A.
[77] Ibid., Document C.

brevet major and not necessarily disrespectful. Pegram also stated that Sibley's manners were often emphatic and that he frequently spoke in a loud voice even in friendly conversation.[78]

The defense next called First Sergeant M. Holmes of Company I who testified that it had been virtually impossible to complete the rolls on the evening of June 30th prior to the company muster. He went on to state that he had stayed up all night and still could not finish the paperwork. The dust had been so bad in the tents that Holmes had been forced to "get into a wagon" and still could not complete his work because of high winds.[79] Holmes concluded by stating that the rolls had not been completed in time for Sibley's signature.

Corporal William Howard, also of Company I, testified in Sibley's defense that he had carried the written messages to which Colonel Cooke had so strenuously objected. It was Corporal Howard, not Sibley, who had addressed the communication "to the General Commanding."[80]

First Lieutenant William D. Smith was the next witness. He stated that his company had been mustered at the same time as Company I. None of his rolls had been signed, yet Colonel Cooke had said nothing. Second Lieutenant Ebenezer Gay, commanding Company A, told the court that he too had not signed his rolls and that "Col. Cooke made no comment upon it at all."[81]

As the defense rested its case on the afternoon of the third day, Sibley made a most persuasive and emotional appeal to the court. "On the first day of the present month I entered upon my twenty-first year of service in the Army," he told the court. "With what zeal, fidelity, or credit I may claim to have discharged the duties of the various positions in which I have been placed it does not become me to speak. Suffice it to say that this is the first time that I have stood the accused party at the bar of a military tribunal."[82]

"It is with no little mortification that I now find myself arraigned before a court composed of officers with most of whom it has been my pleasure to associate, at different periods, upon terms of agreeable intimacy," he continued.

---

[78] Ibid., p. 24.
[79] Ibid., p. 25.
[80] Ibid., p. 27.
[81] Ibid., p. 29.
[82] Ibid., Document D.

"The consciousness, however, of entire innocence of the charges upon which I am arraigned reconciles me to the novelty of the position in which I now find myself placed," he concluded.[83]

In his lengthy remarks Sibley contradicted much of Cooke's earlier testimony. He admitted that Cooke had issued the post orders of December 1856, but that they had never applied to the entire regiment. Post orders were not regimental orders, he argued. At the time the post orders had been issued, Sibley's company and three other dragoon companies were not at Fort Riley or even under Cooke's command. Sibley stated that once the army had reached Cedar Valley he had done everything possible to see that the rolls were completed on time. With respect to the charge of "conduct to the prejudice of good order and discipline," Sibley admitted that he had been loud but certainly not "very loud." He went on to state that he had not intentionally been disrespectful, that disrespect "implied provoking or threatening gestures" and a "tone of voice . . . which is not habitual."[84]

Sibley's letter of appeal in which he had referred to Cooke as tyrannical was only a rough draft and had never been intended for publication. The company clerk had misunderstood his directions and taken the rough draft, addressed it, and delivered it by mistake. In several biting remarks, in obvious reference to their previous differences in the recruiting service and in Kansas, Sibley argued that Colonel Cooke had a history of spitefulness and had always singled him out for severe criticism. "I disavowed at the moment so I do now most solemnly disavow any intentional disrespect towards my commanding officer," Henry concluded.[85]

After "mature deliberation" the court concluded that Sibley was innocent of all charges except for the first specification of the neglect of duty charge and the second specification of the prejudice of good order and military discipline. In these two instances the court found that the facts were true but did not attach any "criminality." "Brevet Major Sibley is released from arrest and will resume his sword," the forty-two page court-martial proceedings concluded.[86]

Henry's close friend in the Tenth Infantry, Captain Jesse Gove, was bitter at Colonel Cooke for the court-martial of his comrade. Gove

[83] Ibid.
[84] Ibid.
[85] Ibid.
[86] Ibid., p. 31.

took time to write his wife of the "pleasing result of the court's deliberation."[87] To Gove the entire episode had been caused by Cooke's persistent petulance. "It was one of those vindictive annoyances which many of these old fogies inflict on their juniors, but," Gove wrote, "old Cooke got hold of the man of all others he ought to have let alone."[88]

To celebrate the decision of the court, Henry decided to give a party. Captain Tracy, who had served as a member of the court-martial, recalled that he "was invited by the Dragoon people to partake of champagne and sardines."[89] It is assumed that a little whiskey was also present. Colonel Cooke's feelings about the court decision and the subsequent celebration are unknown. Broken in health he left Utah shortly thereafter. Two weeks after his acquittal Sibley applied for a leave of absence but was turned down by General Johnston.[90]

In late July 1859 Johnston decided to regarrison Fort Bridger with several companies of the Tenth Infantry under the command of Major Canby. A volunteer battalion, recruited from civilians and teamsters, was also sent eastward to Fort Bridger and was eventually disbanded. To protect the various wagon trains continuing to arrive with supplies for the Army of Utah, cavalry was badly needed at Fort Bridger. It was thus decided to garrison the post with a squadron of dragoons.

On August 6, 1859, Sibley left Camp Floyd and headed east across the Wasatch Mountains and through Echo Canyon to Fort Bridger where he arrived eight days later.[91] Here Henry continued to press General Johnston for a leave of absence, asserting that he was in ill health and enclosing a medical certificate signed by Assistant Surgeon Robert Bartholow to back up his claim. General Johnston was still reluctant to issue the desired leave. Writing to Major Canby at Fort Bridger, Johnston argued that Surgeon Bartholow had not specifically stated that a change of climate was necessary for the improvement of Sibley's health.[92] Finally after receiving such assur-

[87] Gove, p. 183.

[88] Ibid., p. 184.

[89] Tracy, p. 31.

[90] F.J. Porter to H.H. Sibley, 28 July 1858, A.G.O., Dept of Utah, R. of L.S., R.G. 391.

[91] R.R., S.D., A.G.O., R.G. 391.

[92] H.H. Sibley to Headquarters, 18 August 1858, A.G.O., Dept. of Utah, R. of L.R., R.G. 391.

ances from Bartholow, Johnston authorized Canby to give Henry the leave.

With Lieutenants Charles E. Norris and David Bell of the dragoons and accompanied by a small wagon train, Sibley rode out of Fort Bridger on September 14, 1858. Traveling lightly, the party sped eastward across the plains. By September 20 they were already through South Pass and on the Sweetwater River. Here the party was slowed when a team pulling the party's ambulance became so tenderfooted that Sibley found no alternative to stopping and shoeing the animals. A sergeant rode ahead and was able to locate a forge on the Sweetwater River owned by Percival G. Lowe, who assured the dragoons that he would do everything possible to help them.[93]

Unknown to Sibley was the fact that some ten years earlier while in Boston he had recruited Lowe into the dragoons. Reminiscing years later, the farrier fondly recalled the reunion with Sibley. Lowe invited the three dragoon officers to share his Sibley tent where a hardy meal was prepared. "The Major remarked that he did not remember having met me before, and was pleased with the cordial manner in which I had told the sergeant I would be glad to do anything I could for him," Lowe wrote. "I told him that there was a reason behind all of it, and went on to state that 'once upon a time, etc.,' a young man came to his recruiting office in Boston to enlist. That he, the major had advised the youth against such a step, told him the consequences, the position in which he would place himself, the probable estrangement from family and friends, and finally, after putting him off some days, enlisted the youth against his, the major's protest. That was nearly nine years ago, and this is my first opportunity of showing my gratitude for good advice and the kindly manner in which you treated me; and I never sleep in a Sibley tent without thinking of you." "Are you the young sailor with good clothes and hands so soft that I would not believe him?" Sibley asked. "Well, now, will you please tell me how you got through with your enlistment, and how you happen to be here?" Henry inquired.[94]

The next morning, after the mules had been shod, the party continued eastward along the Sweetwater River. Within days Sibley was at Fort Laramie where he paused briefly before riding on to Fort Kearny

[93] Lowe, p. 253.
[94] Ibid., p. 254.

and then eastward to Fort Leavenworth. Here the officers parted company. From Kansas, Sibley set out on the two week trip to New York to be with Charlotte and the children.

With only a sixty-day leave of absence, Henry wrote Washington in November 1858, asking that it be extended until the spring for the benefit of his health.[95] He also wrote Washington demanding to know why his brevet pay had been stopped. In yet another letter Henry asked that his namesake and nephew, Henry Hopkins Lee, son of Colonel Francis Lee, now deceased, be appointed to West Point.[96]

By April 1859, having succeeded in having his leave extended, Henry was still in New York angrily demanding his brevet pay. He spent May and the first weeks of July on detached service at army headquarters in New York. By late July he was heading west across the Appalachians and the Mississippi to Kansas and the tiring three week trek through South Pass. One August 25 he arrived at Fort Bridger and assumed command of his old company.[97]

As a growing depot for the army in the west, Fort Bridger now boasted of a hospital, barracks, warehouses, and sutlers' shops many of which were the result of a vigorous construction project by post commander Canby.

While at Fort Bridger Henry read shocking news from Virginia. With eighteen raiders John Brown had seized the federal arsenal at Harper's Ferry, and was captured by a detachment of marines under Colonel Robert E. Lee. Brown was later hanged in an open field near Charleston, Virginia. One can only speculate as to Henry's reaction to these emotional issues which were tearing at the conscience of the country.

Although Charlotte and the children had remained in New York, Christmas, 1859, was a festive occasion even at snow-covered and isolated Fort Bridger. Several officers' wives including Louisa Hawkins Canby added a feminine touch to the gaiety.[98] The day was celebrated by Canby's issuing each man a gill of whiskey. Undoubtedly, Henry was in the forefront of the drinking and merrymaking, as long had been his custom.

[95] H.H. Sibley to the Adjutant General, 11 November 1858, A.G.O., L.R., R.G. 94.
[96] H.H. Sibley to the Adjutant General, 24 January 1859, A.G.O., L.R., R.G. 94.
[97] R.R., S.D., A.G.O., R.G. 391.
[98] Max L. Heyman, Jr., *Prudent Soldier: A Biography of Major General E.R.S. Canby, 1817–1873* (Glendale, 1859), 110.

The winter of 1859–1860 proved to be as bad as that of 1857–1858. At snow-swept and frigid Fort Bridger desertions grew, and discipline problems developed. In November, Henry asked for clothing and equipment for his men.[99] In January 1860 he wrote again for badly needed supplies. Several court-martials were convened, in which some of the men were severely punished. As was common in the army, Henry wrote headquarters asking that a few of the sentences be commuted.[100]

In February 1860 Colonel Canby was ordered to Camp Floyd to assume command of the Tenth Infantry. Sibley, as the senior officer at Fort Bridger, took command of the post. Less than two months later Sibley received orders that would take his squadron southward to the Territory of New Mexico to prepare for a campaign against the Navajo Indians.

While on duty in the west, Henry had hired W.E. Jones as his agent to promote the Sibley tent, promising him twenty-five percent of all profits. Henry was hoping for the large-scale adoption of the tent by the army.[101] In March 1857 even before the Second Dragoons had left Kansas, Jones had gone to Washington for a meeting with Secretary of War John B. Floyd to give assurances that the Sibley tent was better than any other then in use. Although the tent cost more than those presently used by the army, the tent would house as many as twenty cavalrymen and was therefore cheaper in the long run.

Quartermaster General Thomas S. Jesup agreed to the manufacture of fifty Sibley tents at the Philadelphia Arsenal on an experimental basis. He was not prepared to enter into any contract with Sibley and Jones until the tent was put through further tests. Jesup argued that the tent would not house twenty cavalrymen as Jones claimed but only thirteen.[102] Furthermore, Sibley had admitted to Jesup that the tent was not yet perfected.

In January 1858 Jones informed Sibley that he was back in Washington pushing for adoption of the tent. He went to see Jesup again but after waiting for two days without seeing the quartermaster gen-

[99] H.H. Sibley to Headquarters, 30 November 1859, A.G.O., R. of L.R., R.G. 391.

[100] H.H. Sibley to Headquarters, 12 December 1859, A.G.O., R. of L.R., R.G. 391.

[101] W.W. Burns, "History of My Connection with [the] Sibley Tent," C.C.F. on the Sibley Tent, Q.G.O., R.G. 92.

[102] Miscellaneous Statement of Thomas S. Jesup, 26 March 1857, C.C.F., Q.G.O., R.G. 92.

eral, he left. Disgustedly, Jones returned to Philadelphia where he contacted Jesup by telegram.[103] The agent agreed to allow the government to manufacture as many as 250 tents which Sibley had earlier authorized as long as Sibley was paid ten dollars royalty for each. Jones further agreed to contact the superintendent of the Philadelphia Arsenal to help make the contemplated changes in the tent, but his request for "speedy action," fell on deaf ears. Jones next turned to Secretary of War Floyd whom he assured the Sibley tent had no equal "against the bitter cold of winter and the burning heat of summer as well as against the drenching rain and sweeping tornadoes of the western prairies."[104] To prove his point he showed the Secretary of War reports from Utah, the Dakotas, and Minnesota, which all expressed high approval of the tent.

To calm Floyd's doubts about the weight of the tents, Jones assured the secretary of war that it weighed only seventy-nine and one-fourth pounds whereas the A-shaped tent, then widely in use, weighed sixty-eight and one-half pounds. Since the Sibley tent would house more men, Jones argued, it was more practical. To convince Washington of his cause, Jones had a pamphlet published which reviewed the history of the tent and presented lengthy testimony by various officers praising it highly.[105]

The Mormon War had indeed provided the first large-scale test of the Sibley tent, for the Quartermaster Department had furnished the Army of Utah with 250 of them which had been used in severe winter weather, in deep snow, and in temperatures as low as thirty degrees below zero.

The tent probably made its greatest impression on the Medical Corps. One surgeon went so far as to state that the Sibley tent and desiccated vegetables would eliminate scurvy from the army. Another officer found the tent responsible for the good health of the Army of Utah and the "greatest blessing the present age had given the soldier."[106] Dr. Madison Mills, Medical Director of the Army of Utah, wrote from Camp Scott that "during the time the tent had been in use the ratio of sickness had been remarkably small." "I have never

[103] W.E. Jones to Thos. S. Jesup, 20 January 1858, C.C.F., Q.G.O., R.G. 92.
[104] W.E. Jones to John B. Floyd, 23 January 1858, C.C.F., Q.G.O., R.G. 92.
[105] "Improved Conical Tent, Invented and Patented by Maj. H.H. Sibley, U.S. Army," (Baltimore, 1860).
[106] E.I. Baily to H.H. Sibley, 14 April 1858, C.C.F., Q.G.O., R.G. 92.

known troops so healthy," he concluded.[107] Among those praising the tent were thirty-four officers of the Fifth and Tenth Infantry including Captain Barnard E. Bee and Major Edward Richard Sprigg Canby. Colonel Cooke, Lieutenants John Pegram and John Buford, and thirteen other officers of the Second Dragoon were also highly pleased with the tent. General Johnston found Sibley's invention "the only tent suitable for a soldier's lodging."[108] The mountain man, Jim Bridger, found it "as comfortable as an Indian Lodge."[109] Chief Justice Eckels, Marshal Dotson, and Attorney General W.J. McCormick also used the tent at Camp Scott and reported it superior to anything then in use by the army. So successful was the Sibley tent that by 1859 guide books were already promoting it for miners and western travelers.[110]

By December 1859 Sibley had grown impatient with Jones' attempts at getting the Sibley tent adopted by the army so he dismissed him. He then completed an agreement with Captain William W. Burns who had helped to secure the patent for the tent in 1856. Burns negotiated a contract with the firm of John H. Landell which agreed to pay five dollars for each tent manufactured and in December 1859 Burns and Sibley received their first royalties. Henry, under pressure from the secretary of war and much against the "solemn protests" of Burns, later reemployed Jones. Captain Burns, who more than once made reference to "Sibley's known carelessness about business matters," was highly critical of the decision.[111]

Still later another agreement was completed in which Burns and Sibley agreed to assume equal shares in the tent while Jones was to receive twenty-five percent. Burns and his descendants would eventually realize more than $100,000 or two dollars and fifty-cents for each tent manufactured. Because of his decision to join the Confederacy in 1861, Henry would receive little more than $8,000. In the meantime the Union Army, with Sibley tents manufactured at the

[107] Madison Mills to H.H. Sibley, 16 April 1858, C.C.F., Q.G.O., R.G. 92.

[108] F.J. Porter to H.H. Sibley, 15 April 1858, C.C.F., Q.G.O., R.G. 92.

[109] Jim Bridger to H.H. Sibley, 15 April 1858, C.C.F., Q.G.O., R.G. 92.

[110] James Redpath and Richard J. Hinton, *Handbook to Kansas Territory and the Rocky Mountains' Gold Region* (New York, 1859), 163. Also of interest is Philadelphia *Daily Evening Bulletin,* 26 October 1858, and *To Utah With the Dagoons and Glimpses of Life in Arizona and California, 1858–1859,* Harold D. Langley, ed. (Salt Lake City, 1974), 69, 110–111.

[111] W.W. Burns to Chas. Thomas, 2 June 1860, C.C.F., Q.G.O., R.G. 92.

Philadelphia Depot, the Schuylkill, Pennsylvania Arsenal, and later yet by private companies in Cincinnati, St. Louis, Boston, and Indianapolis, put to good use 47,541 tents during the Civil War.[112]

By the beginning of the Civil War, Henry was also working on a stove for use in the tent. Three different sizes of the Sibley stove were in use by 1861. All were conical in shape, varying in height from thirty to twenty-four inches, made of wrought iron, with an eight-inch door, three small ventilation and combustion holes, and weighing from eighteen to thirty pounds.[113] The stove was designed to fit in the center of the Sibley tent and with attached stove pipe was a great improvement over anything then in use.

One thousand Sibley stoves costing the Army four dollars and five cents each were manufactured in New York City in August and September 1861, and continued to be used extensively during the Civil War and by the United States Army as late as World War II.

[112] Miscellaneous Data on Number of Sibley Tents Manufactured for the U.S. Army, n.d., C.C.F., Q.G.O., R.G. 92.

[113] Description of Tent Stove, C.C.F. on Sibley Stove, Q.G.O., R.G. 92.

Chapter VII

On the Trail of the Navajo

With the "Mormon War" concluded, Henry Hopkins Sibley, still commanding Company I, Second Dragoons, was ordered southward to the Territory of New Mexico. Washington was hoping to bring an end to the centuries-old and seemingly endless conflict between the Spanish-American population of New Mexico and the Navajo Indians. Such large number of troops were being sent to New Mexico that it was decided that the various companies would have to be divided into two columns due to the lack of grass and water along the route. The first column was led by Colonel Edward R.S. Canby, regimental commander of the Tenth Infantry. The second column, to which Sibley was to be attached, was commanded by Major Isaac Lynde of the Second Infantry.[1]

Complete with civilian guides, teamsters, and six herders, the second column rode out of Camp Floyd on May 15, 1860. Moving eastward through the rugged Wasatch Mountains, across the foothills of the Uinta Mountains, beneath the 13,498-foot summit of King's Peak, and eastward across the Bear River, the bluecoats rode eastward be-

---

[1] Returns of Expeditions, Second Column of Forces for New Mexico, May, June, and July 1860, Records of the Adjutant General's Office, R.G. 94.

fore turning south toward New Mexico. Major Sibley did not join the
column until June 4 when the detachment was already two days east
of Fort Bridger moving along the overland trail. Across the Green River
and the vast Wyoming prairies, the men continued to the North Platte
River. By June 30 the column, now 319 miles out of Camp Floyd, had
reached Cooper's Creek near Fort Laramie.[2] From southern Wyoming, at that time part of the Nebraska Territory, the 364 men turned
southward. On July 29, 1860, Sibley was placed on detached service
and ordered to Fort Garland in what was then the northern part of the
Territory of New Mexico. After two months on the trail, the brevet
major led his men through nine-thousand-foot La Veta Pass in the
Sangre de Cristo Mountains to Fort Garland.

Original plans called for Sibley's Company, along with another
dragoon company and three companies of the Tenth Infantry, to garrison Fort Garland. A few weeks after their arrival at the post on the
eastern slopes of the broad San Luis Valley the dragoons were ordered
to Fort Defiance in the heart of the Navajo Country. By early August
Sibley was at Fort Union with his dragoons and a week later crossed
through Glorieta Pass to Fort Marcy at Santa Fe.[3] The dragoons passed
over the same ground where less than two years later Brigadier General Henry Hopkins Sibley of the Confederate States Army would send
his glory-dreaming Texans into battle.

Fort Marcy was built on a bluff overlooking the narrow streets of
the territorial capital of Santa Fe. The post was a welcome sight to
the weary bluecoats although Colonel Edwin V. Sumner had once referred to the post as a "sink of vice and extravagance." Indeed two men
from Sibley's company became so drunk in Santa Fe that they could
not continue the march. The brevet major, never known for his temperance, was so disgusted that he had the two privates drummed out
of the army.

From Santa Fe the dragoons turned southward to the Rio Grande
River and the sun-battered adobe village of Albuquerque. Situated on
the east bank of the river beneath the rugged west face of the Sandía
Mountains, Albuquerque was to be the launching place for the impending expedition against the Navajo. Here the column secured
supplies and several pack animals for the trek to Fort Defiance.

[2] *Ibid.*
[3] R.R., S.D., A.G.O., R.G. 391.

Ever since the Mexican War more than a decade before, the Spanish-speaking inhabitants of the territory had demanded protection from the raiding Navajo. The ever-increasing and influential Anglo population demanded the same. Governor Abraham Rencher responded by promising to rid the territory of the pesky Indians.

The Santa Fe *Gazette* with its exaggerations of Navajo depredations helped stir the war fever. The *Gazette* estimated that in the first six months of 1860 Navajo raiders had killed three hundred citizens and had stolen livestock and property worth $1.5 million.[4] The *Gazette* did not report that for decades Spanish villagers had raided deep into the heart of the Navajo Country in reprisal for Navajo raids into the Rio Grande Valley. Numerous slaves were taken on such raids. In fact almost all of the three hundred aristocratic leading families in the territory held Navajo slaves. The territorial legislature had even gone so far as to pass a bill legalizing Navajo slavery.

With the coming of Spring 1860, the Navajo commenced raiding into the settlements of the central and upper Rio Grande Valley with greater intensity than ever before. Depredations, although certainly not amounting to $1.5 million, were an almost weekly occurrence. In reprisal, poorly equipped militia units from the various villages rode into Navajo country. In June while Sibley was on his way to the territory from Utah, a militia company from the village of Cebolleta, west of Albuquerque, had straggled into Fort Defiance after having been badly beaten in a desperate fight east of the fort. Thirty Nuevo Mexicanos had died in the fray.[5]

Colonel Thomas T. Fauntleroy, in command of the Department of New Mexico, did not agree with Governor Rencher and the majority of the territorial legislature. Colonel Fauntleroy, nevertheless, felt it was better for the United States Army, rather than the Territorial Militia, to force a peace on the Navajo. The army was compelled to act when the territory's leading citizens met at Santa Fe in August 1860 and with Governor Rencher's blessings called for an all-out war against the Navajo. If Fauntleroy would not order the regular army after the Navajo, the Territorial Militia would be sent out in full force.

Colonel Fauntleroy's Navajo Campaign called for three columns of

[4] Santa Fe *Gazette*, 10 November 1860. Also, Frank McNitt, *Navajo Wars* (Albuquerque, 1972), p. 385. Part of this chapter, especially the portion dealing with the Canby-Sibley Expedition, is drawn heavily from this definitive study.

[5] Ibid.

troops to rendezvous at Fort Defiance. For six weeks the bluecoats would make war on the marauding Navajo. Pueblo and Ute Indians, ancient enemies of the Navajo, would be used as spies and scouts. Colonel Canby was to command the fourteen companies comprising the expedition. Sibley and Canby had come to know one another quite well during the Utah Expedition. Canby had served on Henry's court-martial and had later commanded Fort Bridger.

Sibley was placed in command of the second battalion which left Albuquerque on September 14. His command consisted of his own Company I of the Dragoons, Captain George McLane's Company I of the Mounted Rifles, and Company E of the Mounted Rifles commanded by Lieutenant Joseph G. Tilford. Fifty men of the Seventh Infantry under the direction of Lieutenant Asa B. Carey also accompanied the column. Captain Thomas Claiborne's Company B of the Second Dragoons was scheduled to join Sibley at Albuquerque but did not receive orders in time.[6] Once the column moved westward, Henry decided upon short marches each day, thus enabling Captain Claiborne, by a series of forced marches, to join the battalion as soon as possible. A small, well-equipped squad of Ute scouts moved ahead of the army to guard against a possible ambush.

The route led westward across the dry sands of the Río Puerco to Laguna and Acoma Pueblo and beneath the barren summit of Mount Taylor in the San Mateo Mountains. The column reached Azul Springs, a popular watering spot, five days after leaving the Rio Grande. At Azul Springs, Sibley was joined by Captain Claiborne's Company which had marched through the night. Here the men encountered their first hostiles. Four Indians who had been trailing Claiborne's Company ran into Sibley's pickets. The Navajo were fired on but quickly disappeared into the scrubby piñon and junipers. One of the Indian's leggings was found the next morning "spattered with blood . . . indication that one of the pickets had found his mark," Henry reported.[7]

From Azul Springs, Sibley turned away from the main road to where the Ute scouts said there would be abundant grass and water. The Utes' information proved correct, and Henry wrote department head-

---

[6] H.H. Sibley to D.H. Maury, 21 September 1860, A.G.O., Department of New Mexico, L.R, R.G. 393. Lieutenant Joseph G. Tilford would later be breveted a major for bravery against Sibley's Texans at the Battle of Valverde.

[7] Ibid.

quarters suggesting that route for any future expeditions moving into the Navajo country. At Bacon Springs the column joined the main road again and continued on to Fort Fauntleroy, which was reached two days after leaving the Azul. Fort Fauntleroy, which had been established less than a month before Sibley's arrival, was little more than a temporary camp. Located at Ojo del Oso on the northwest side of the Zuni Range, the post was within easy striking distance of the Navajo country.

With the condition of their animals improved by the leisurely marches and good grass along the route, Henry was now prepared to move northwesterly into the Chuska Valley. Information obtained at Fort Fauntleroy and from the Ute scouts led Sibley to believe that large numbers of Navajo were concentrated in the broad valley. By a night march the column could reach the valley on the following day and strike a surprise blow.[8] For forty miles the invaders rode northward into the broad expanses of Chuska Valley. The southern extremities of the valley revealed colorful sedimentary formations, especially red sandrock outcroppings, jutting into the valley. To the west, Chuska Peak at the southern end of the Chuska Range dominated the landscape. Dry ravines ran from the mountains eastward into the barren valley. A few scrubby junipers dotted the scene.

Major Sibley was sure that sunrise would reveal vast herds of sheep and goats as well as large numbers of Navajo. When dawn came, however, there was only "a single herd of fifteen or twenty horses at a distance of three miles."[9] He immediately ordered Captain Claiborne's Company at full gallop in that direction. Captain McLane's Company of Mounted Rifles was sent in a flanking movement to capture the horses and prevent any Navajo from escaping into the nearby mountains. The frightened horses raced out of sight. All that could be found was a small herd of goats which Captain McLane had shot. A scorched earth policy would probably make the hostile Navajo more likely to submit to peace negotiations and subjugation. A dense smoke soon billowed into the sky from the summit of Chuska Peak, announcing to anyone within fifty miles that the bluecoats had arrived.

[8] Ibid.
[9] H.H. Sibley to D.H. Maury, 29 September 1860, A.G.O., Dept. of N.M., L.R., R.G. 393.

Henry felt the signal fires were proof that his advance into the valley had been "a complete surprise."[10]

Deeper into the Chuska Valley, Sibley's troopers rode. Yet all the Navajo were gone. Several large fields were found, but these had not been cultivated for two years. A few smaller ones were discovered which had been planted the previous summer, but these had been hastily harvested. Perhaps the bluecoats had been under observation for longer than Henry thought. Sibley was bitterly disappointed at not finding any Navajo.

Early the next morning the troopers broke camp and rode westward into the mountains. By a "deeply worn trail" the bluecoats climbed higher into the Chuskas. Upward they went past clusters of piñon trees and stands of ponderosa pine to eighty-five hundred foot Washington Pass. From high in the mountains the men gazed northward across the flat Chuska Valley to the majestic spire of Shiprock jutting forth from the semi-arid plain. North from Shiprock across the San Juan River towered the snow-covered white summits of the La Plata Range indicating that winter had come to the high country.

Sibley's small army was not the first to cross the Chuskas. Lieutenant James H. Simpson had taken a similar route in 1849 during an expedition against the Navajo.[11]

From the fir and spruce trees of Washington Pass, Sibley continued westward to Ciénaga Negra on the western slope of the Chuskas. Here the bluecoats found "extensive fields of corn and wheat" as well as several hogans. The crops had already been harvested, and the hogans had not been lived in for sometime. A few signs of recent activity indicated "evidence of alarm and commotion," Henry thought. All the hogans were ordered burned in hopes of "exciting the rage of the Indians and forcing them into an encounter."[12]

At sunup the next morning the column made a short march southward to Laguna Negra in Cañon Bonito west of Fort Defiance. Here the men found good water and an abundance of grass. While the men were in camp at the waterhole, a Navajo herdsman, Agua Chiquita,

[10] Ibid.

[11] James H. Simpson, *Navajo Expedition*, Frank McNitt, ed. (Norman, 1964). An 1859 expedition through the heart of the Chuskas from south to north is described in J.G. Walker and O.L. Shepherd, *Navajo Reconnaissance*, L.R. Bailey, ed. (Los Angeles, 1964).

[12] H.H. Sibley to D.H. Maury, 29 September 1860, A.G.O., Dept. of N.M., L.R., R.G. 393.

Dr. John Sibley

Frank Leslie's version of Major Sibley assisting General Winfield Scott with his cloak during the Mexican War.

Henry Hopkins Sibley, c. 1850

Daughter Helen, son Albert Sidney and wife Charlotte

Army officers and the Sibley Tent

Sibley's sketch of the Sibley Tent

Brigadier General Henry Hopkins Sibley, 1861 or 1863

General Sibley, c. 1865

General Edward Richard Sprigg Canby

Pasha Sibley, c. 1873

*Helen
Sibley
Stokes*

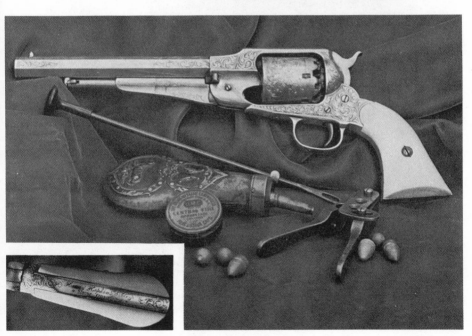

General Sibley's Civil War pistol

Sibley in Alexandria, Egypt, c. 1873

Sibley's tombstone in the City Cemetery, Fredericksburg, Virginia. The date of his death is in error. Sibley died early on the morning of August 23, 1886.

whom Henry referred to as a "considerable character," approached the
camp and in sign language indicated that he wanted to talk. Henry
asked the Ute scouts to communicate with the Navajo and coax him
into camp if possible. As the Navajo neared the camp, several Ute
grabbed at the reins of his horse. Agua Chiquita, obviously frightened, quickly reined his horse away from the Ute and commenced to
gallop away. Every soldier in camp was said to have taken at least one
shot at the fleeing Navajo.[13] For several seconds it appeared as if the
herdsman might manage to escape, but his horse was hit, and he was
thrown to the ground. Unable to escape, the Navajo was hit several
times. Although desperately wounded, the Indian was brought into
camp where Sibley was able to learn through an interpreter that most
of the Navajo were fleeing westward with their herds to Cañon de
Chelly, Pueblo Colorado, and the Hopi villages. So badly wounded was
the Navajo that Henry thought he could not live long. With little hes-
itancy he ordered the Indian shot. The unfortunate Navajo was taken
outside of camp and executed by the Ute scouts.

Refusing to abandon the expedition, Sibley ordered a night march
of twenty miles northwest to Palo Negro, or what the soldiers called
Wheatfield Creek. Still no Indians could be found. Frustrated again,
Sibley ordered Captain Claiborne and Lieutenant Tilford to take their
companies and scout the area thoroughly. Success again eluded the
disappointed brevet major. "The only discoveries made were the evidences of Indians flying in every direction with their herds and flocks
into the inaccessible sierras," Sibley later wrote of his attempt at
catching the elusive Navajo.[14] A number of fields and hogans were
discovered along Wheatfield Creek, but like those at Ciénaga Negra
and in the Chuska Valley they were barren and deserted.

At daybreak the following morning Sibley gave orders for the expedition to march for Fort Defiance and the contemplated rendezvous. Captain Lafayette McLaws would be arriving soon from Fort
Craig, and Colonel Canby was thought to be on his way from Fort
Garland by way of Abiquiu. Several pack mules and a few horses were
so broken down that they had to be shot during the trek into Fort De-

[13] James E. Farmer, *My Life With the Army in the West*, Dale F. Giese, ed. (Sante Fe,
1967), 32; McNitt, p. 392.
[14] H.H. Sibley to D.H. Maury, 29 September 1860, A.G.O., Dept. of N.M., L.R., R.G.
393.

fiance. Henry had hoped to save the pack animals by a series of short, leisurely marches.

Although the expedition had not encountered large numbers of Navajo, Sibley was fearful of an ambush. During the march into Fort Defiance, he placed his own Company I of dragoons in front of the column followed by the mounted rifles, pack animals, infantry, and finally Captain Claiborne's Company of dragoons as a rear guard. Retracing part of their previous route, the column proceeded over rough ground to La Joya, a hay camp some twelve miles north of Fort Defiance. Here the troopers camped along a small creek beneath a high bluff.[15]

At noon the following day while the men were grazing their animals and resting from the tiring night march, a party of Navajo began to fire into the camp from a distance of about one thousand yards. Henry feared the Navajo were encircling the camp, but upon his returning their fire the Indians quickly fled into the nearby hills. Before dusk more shots were fired into camp from the high mesas overlooking the camp. With darkness approaching, the shooting slackened and finally stopped. Early the next morning after the men had broken camp and started for Fort Defiance, Captain Claiborne excitedly rode forward claiming his company was under attack. Henry quickly ordered out the Mounted Rifles to protect the column's supplies while the infantry was sent in a flanking movement to attack the Indians. The attackers proved to be a small band of snipers who were easily driven off. The march continued, and in a short time the column reached open ground, and the sniping stopped.

Several bluecoats, including Captain McLane, were highly critical of Sibley's refusal to order a full-scale attack on the Navajo. After all, the men had traveled day and night in search of a fight. Captain McLane told one of the enlisted men that he thought the troopers "should have run the Indians off."[16] To Sibley, however, the Indians were "utterly inaccessible."

By ten o'clock on the morning of September 28 the column reached Fort Defiance. They had traveled over "150 miles through . . . the heart of the enemy's country" since leaving Fort Fauntleroy. Only one Navajo had been killed. Furthermore, not more than ten of the enemy

[15] Ibid.; Farmer, p. 33.
[16] Farmer, p. 34.

had been seen at any one time. In reality the march had done little more than alert the Navajo to flee to the farthest reaches of their broad and vast land. Consequently Sibley's Chuska reconnaissance had served only to make Colonel Canby's impending campaign more difficult.

Fort Defiance, located at the mouth of picturesque Cañon Bonito, was a welcome sight to the weary soldiers. The post, consisting of flat-roofed rock and adobe buildings, had been founded in September 1851 at an old Navajo camping site. Walls and roofs to protect one from the elements were luxuries on the New Mexico frontier.

On the same afternoon that Sibley's column rode into Fort Defiance, Captain Lafayette McLaws arrived from Fort Craig with two companies of mounted rifles and two of the Seventh Infantry.[17] For six days no word was heard from Canby who was scheduled to arrive at the same time as McLaws. Sibley became apprehensive about the forthcoming expedition when inspection of the post's supplies revealed shortages. Only seventeen days' supply of flour remained; yet none had been requisitioned. Fearful that the campaign might have to be suspended or cancelled unless immediate action was taken to alleviate the critical shortages, and without waiting for Canby's arrival, Sibley sent an express racing eastward requesting the necessary supplies. He was also worried about the shortage of mules at the post since only nineteen beasts were fit for a lengthy march.

Finally on October 4 Canby rode into Fort Defiance with 118 officers and men. The strength of the expedition had now grown to fourteen companies. Furthermore, a battalion of five companies of New Mexico Militia was scheduled to arrive within a few days. The battalion had been recruited in the northern part of the territory and was comprised of Spanish-Americans commanded by Colonel Manuel Cháves.

Canby was determined to take the field immediately. Commanding one column consisting of two companies of dragoons and two of mounted rifles, Sibley would ride westward to Pueblo Colorado near Ganado Mesa and turn northward to the mouth of Cañon de Chelly. Colonel Canby, leaving Fort Defiance the day after Sibley, would march north and turn westward along the north rim of Cañon de Chelly. The two columns would meet at the mouth of the great can-

[17] McNitt, p. 392.

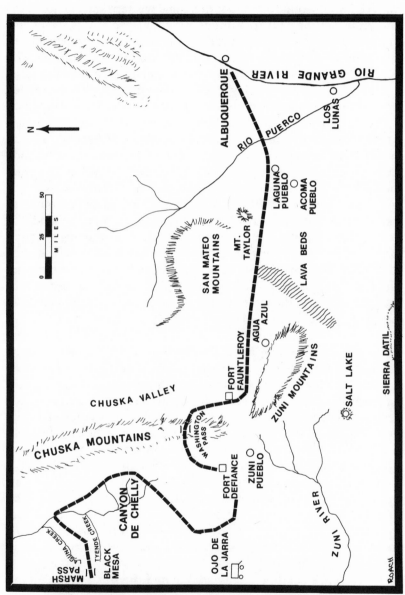

1860 CANBY-SIBLEY NAVAJO EXPEDITION
SHOWING ROUTE TAKEN BY
BREVET MAJOR HENRY HOPKINS SIBLEY

yon. All Navajo found on the southern and western approaches to the canyon would be captured or destroyed. Captain McLaws, commanding a smaller third column, would remain at Fort Defiance to patrol the western slopes of the Chuska Mountains to prevent any Navajo from escaping eastward.[18] If any Indians were able to escape to the west, Canby and Sibley would pursue them. Orders also called for the Ute scouts to patrol the country between the two columns.

Thus on October 10, 1860, Brevet Major Sibley rode westward through forests of ponderosa and piñon pines to the Pueblo Colorado some twenty-seven miles west of Fort Defiance. Just east of Ganado Mesa the column turned northward into Beautiful Valley as Canby had directed. Through the broad valley, known to the Navajo as Nazlini, the column rode. Past colorful shale and sandstone outcroppings, the invaders continued. With drought plaguing the land, the lack of grass and water became critical, further weakening the pack animals that were already in bad shape.

All signs confirmed what Sibley had already suspected from his Chuska reconnaissance. Large numbers of the enemy had fled further west, some toward the Hopi villages, a few to the Little Colorado, and others in the direction of Marsh Pass.

Eight days after leaving Fort Defiance, Sibley was able to rendezvous with Colonel Canby at the western entrance of Cañon de Chelly. Canby brought sad news. Captain George McLane, who had been decorated for bravery at Contreras and Churubusco during the Mexican War and reprimanded in 1858 for attacking a band of Navajo against orders, was dead. McLane, who had shared in Sibley's Chuska reconnaissance, had died at Black Rock north of Wheatfield Creek. The bluecoats had halted to water their horses when several Ute scouts caught sight of ten or eleven Navajo in the distance. McLane, accompanied by scouts on both flanks, had plunged into a thicket after the Indians. Several shots were heard, and within moments the officer's horse raced from the thicket dragging the dead McLane. The brave officer, in front of his scouts, had been caught in a deadly crossfire and killed by the Ute.[19] A travois was constructed, and his body was taken back to Fort Defiance.

The captain's death was only an omen of the frustration that lay

[18] Ibid.
[19] Ibid., p. 400; Farmer, p. 35.

ahead. With the first and second columns now combined, Canby decided to pursue the Navajo by marching north and west toward Marsh Pass and Black Mesa. Canby would either force a battle or drive the Indians dangerously close to the Paiute, their ancient enemies. Northward along Chinle Wash for forty miles the horse soldiers continued. Heavy snow commenced falling and the column began to slow. One soldier later recorded that he would never forget the "intense suffering" of the men during the march. Pack animals had to be driven ahead of the column to make a path for the soldiers through the heavy snow. The going was especially hard for the infantry.

With only blankets for cover the men slept in the snow. Frequently, they would awaken in the morning to find their meager bedding covered with two or three inches of fresh snow. At other times the men slept for hours while sitting on their horses.[20] Most never took off their clothing or boots during the entire campaign. Although subsisting entirely on sowbelly and hardtack, the men did not complain. Sibley could not help recalling the terrible march through South Pass in the winter of 1857.

As the column continued deeper into Navajo land, Canby had to establish a supply base at Ojo de Jarra, a well-known watering place halfway between Fort Defiance and the Hopi villages. The expedition was facing a logistical problem of extended supply lines.

A few miles north of Rock Point, the column turned westward out of Chinle Wash into Tyente Creek. Here for the first time the column found good grass. A halt was called to allow the animals to graze and the men to rest. Colonel Canby still held to the idea that rugged terrain near Black Mesa and Marsh Pass would prevent the Navajo from moving further westward with their flocks. Besides, if the Navajo were able to cross the seemingly inpenetrable series of crags and cliffs to the west, the Paiute would be waiting in the Klethla Valley and beyond. In both assumptions Canby was badly mistaken.[21]

Once again Canby decided to divide his forces. Sibley, taking the dragoons, two companies of mounted rifles, and several Nuevo Mexicano scouts, would continue in a southwesterly direction up Tyente Creek, and would cross Black Mesa to the Long House Ruin on the

---

[20] Farmer, p. 37.
[21] E.R.S. Canby to D.H. Maury, 17 November 1860, A.G.O., Dept. of N.M., L.R., R.G. 393; E.R.S. Canby to D.H. Maury, 21 November 1860, A.G.O., Dept. of N.M., L.R., R.G. 393.

far side of Klethla Valley before pivoting to the northeast to meet Colonel Canby with the infantry at Marsh Pass. As daylight crept across the heights of Black Mesa near present Chilchinbito, on the morning of October 24 Sibley's scouts brought word that a herd of Navajo horses had been spotted several miles in front of the advancing column. Holding two companies of dragoons in reserve, Sibley dispatched the riflemen under command of Captain Claiborne and Lieutenant Pegram at a gallop to surround the horses and capture what Navajo might be in the vicinity. A skirmish quickly ensued in which three women and two children were captured by Blas Lucero's detachment of Spanish American scouts. Two thousand head of sheep and two hundred horses were secured and shot. It was later learned the column had come across a temporary camp of Delgadito, a leading Navajo chieftain. Delgadito was well-known to the bluecoats since he had signed the Treaty of Laguna Negra in 1855.[22] Uncertain as to what lay atop Black Mesa, Sibley, in violation of Canby's orders, turned northwest along the base of the tableland. At Lolami Point near present Kayenta, scouts found the trail of Canby's infantry. Turning abruptly to the southwest, the major followed Canby up Laguna Creek to Marsh Pass where the two forces were united on October 26 three days after having separated.

For several days the expedition remained in camp atop the sixty-seven hundred foot pass. Canby sent several scouting parties out which were able to confirm what Sibley had already told him. Several large bands of Navajo had been able to elude the expedition completely. All indications led Sibley and Canby to believe that the Indians had fled across Black Mesa to the lower Klethla Valley, rugged Tsegi Canyon, and northward toward 10,416-foot Navajo Mountain, a feat which they had thought impossible. Furthermore, the Paiute were not at war with the Navajo as they had previously thought. Delgadito, possibly lured by the captives taken in the skirmish on the 24th, came into camp under a white flag to ask for peace. Canby told him that he would talk terms only with the entire Navajo nation and that he must have an unconditional surrender.

During those cold October days as the two leaders sat atop Marsh Pass, both had time to reflect on the seemingly unsuccessful expedition. Sibley, a forty-four year-old captain from Louisiana, and Canby,

[22] McNitt, p. 401.

a forty-three year-old lieutenant colonel from Kentucky, were both forced to admit that their efforts had been in vain.[23] The Navajo inhabited a land so vast and inaccessible that it would take several expeditions over several years, preferably in the summer, to subdue the Navajo nation.

On November 1 Canby gave orders to retreat from Marsh Pass. It was during the march past Black Mesa, up Chinle Wash, and across the mouth of Cañon de Chelly, to Ewell's Hay camp near Laguna Negra, and to Fort Defiance, that the suffering of men and beasts became acute. Many of the horses and mules, thirsting severely, had to be held back on several occasions to prevent the consumption of alkaline water. Many of the valuable animals sickened and died. Others became so weak that they had to be shot. A large part of the cavalry was without mounts and not only had to walk but also to carry their saddles. The men suffered from scurvy, a dreaded frontier disease caused principally by the lack of vitamin C found in citrus fruits and green vegetables. The men's gums began to swell and bleed and their teeth to fall out.[24]

Bands of Indians continued to harass the expedition's rear guard. Often the Navajo appeared quite bold, deliberately making themselves visible to the bluecoats. In some instances large numbers of the elusive Navajo appeared on the heights overlooking the slow-moving column. Yet the "cowardly tribe," Sibley reported, refused to fight and disappeared into the canyons and crags. The brevet major was excessively frustrated by the Navajo tactics. To Sibley the Indians had won a psychological victory over him and his bluecoats.

Finally on November 8, 1860, a week after leaving Marsh Pass, the column staggered into Ewell's Hay Camp to find good water and grass. The expedition had been defeated, not by the Navajo who chose wisely not to fight, but by the vast expanses of desert, mesa, and mountains they had traversed. The cavalry was in the worst shape. Writing from Ewell's Hay Camp on November 8, Sibley assessed the condition of his squadron. Captain Claiborne's Company B of Mounted Rifles had lost eight mules and horses. Of the remaining animals in the company, "not one can, by any possibility, become serviceable in the next

---

[23] For Canby's biography see: Max L. Heyman, *Prudent Soldier: A Biography of Major General E.R.S. Canby* (Glendale, 1959).

[24] Farmer, p. 37.

twelve days; and of the mules, not one."[25] Lieutenant Pegram's Company of Mounted Rifles was worse, for twenty-three horses and six mules had been shot. Henry reported that the remaining horses in Pegram's Company were so poor that they were "not fit for a hard scout." In Lieutenant Ebenezer Gay's Company of dragoons, not "a single horse could make a march of twenty-five miles." "They are all generally broken down," Sibley reported, "and in my opinion will not be fit for service before the coming spring." Lieutenant Charles Jones Walker, commanding Sibley's old Company I, reported that forty-two of sixty-five horses had been shot. It would be summer before the company would be capable of making a lengthy march. Sibley told Canby that the cavalry could "not be counted upon for any further active service."[26]

Thirty-four Navajo had been killed during the expedition, 960 horses captured or shot, and seven thousand sheep destroyed.[27] There was a sense of defeat as the expedition arrived at Fort Defiance after its brief recuperation at Ewell's Hay Camp. There was little glory for Edward Richard Sprigg Canby or Henry Hopkins Sibley. Glory would have to wait for another day when the two officers would be fighting for control of New Mexico and the Far West. Sibley's promotion to full major would have to wait also.

Canby reported that "physical causes," specifically the lack of grass, water, and the almost impassable terrain over which the expedition had traveled, were to blame for the failure of the expedition.[28] As far as Canby was concerned, there was no hope for a permanent peace until the war party of the Navajo nation, known as the Ladrones, were defeated or destroyed. In 1860 the Ladrones were the dominant faction of the tribe. A much larger force than the one presently deployed would be necessary to force a lasting peace on the Navajo. The establishment of military camps in the Chuskas, near the Hopi villages, on the Little Colorado, and at the mouth of Cañon de Chelly would be necessary, Canby felt. Winter campaigns, contending with snow cover and lack of forage, were ill advised, he concluded. The colonel

[25] Report of H.H. Sibley, 12 November 1860, A.G.O., Dept. of N.M., L.R., R.G. 393.
[26] Ibid.
[27] E.R.S. Canby to D.H. Maury, 21 November 1860, A.G.O., Dept. of N.M., L.R., R.G. 393.
[28] Ibid.

asked for permission to employ fifty of sixty Zuni scouts for any future operation.[29]

The cavalry was in such bad shape that Canby decided to send Major Sibley back to the Rio Grande as soon as possible with the Second Column. Thus on November 23, with a cold wind sweeping out of the Chuskas, Sibley's battalion rode out of Fort Defiance for Albuquerque and the Rio Grande. Slowly, by short daily treks, the brevet major took his men eastward through the Wingate Valley to Fort Fauntleroy. Finally in late November 1860, almost three months after Sibley had ridden west from the Rio Grande, the column arrived back at Albuquerque.

From Albuquerque, Sibley was ordered upriver to take command of Cantonment Burgwin at Taos. On December 3, after a few days' rest on the Rio Grande, the column was able to move up the Rio Grande to Fort Marcy at Santa Fe.[30] With most of their horses still broken down from the Navajo campaign, short marches were required each day. From Santa Fe the road led through the small Spanish American villages of Pojoaque, Luceros, Las Trampas, and Chamisal to the village of Taos, southwest of the snow covered Sangre de Cristo Mountains.

Cantonment Burgwin had been built about ten miles south of Taos near the village of Fernando de Taos. Established to protect the settlers of the Taos Valley from Jicarilla Apache, the post was named after Captain John Henry K. Burgwin, who had been killed at Taos in a violent uprising against American rule in the months following Stephen W. Kearny's occupation of the area during the Mexican War.

Sibley rode into the cottonwood-dotted valley on December 20 and three days later assumed command of the post. Cantonment Burgwin consisted of seven adobe buildings formed in a square. The buildings included a guardhouse, barracks, and commissary warehouse. Sibley took up quarters on the south side of the small fort, only a short distance from the banks of the Rito de la Olla, a small creek which ran into the larger Rio Grande.[31]

A brief inspection revealed that the fort was in terrible condition. It had been poorly constructed eight years earlier and most of the log

[29] Ibid.

[30] Post Returns, Fernando De Taos, A.G.O., R.G. 393.

[31] Ibid. Also, Robert W. Frazer, *Forts of the West* (Norman, 1972), 96; Herbert M. Hart, *Old Forts of the Southwest* (New York, 1964), 23.

walls and ceiling beams were now rotten. The captain had learned in Santa Fe that plans were already underway to close the post but only now did he fully realize the significance of that decision. He was at the post for only a few days when he decided that the buildings were so dilapidated that they were actually dangerous to his small command. He decided to rent quarters in nearby Ranchos de Taos for himself and his men.

Only a few weeks after Sibley arrived at Fernando de Taos, an urgent express arrived from Fort Union. Colonel George Bibb Crittenden was "anxious to make a short scout against the Kiowa and Comanche Indians."[32] Colonel Crittenden, in a previous expedition onto the plains, had destroyed a large Kiowa and Comanche cache. "The Indians," he wrote "are now in a few camps; large numbers are totally unprovided with camp equipage or provisions; all of which were destroyed on our last scout and I believe success to be probable if not certain."[33] The only problem was that Crittenden's command was too weak to attack the Kiowa and Comanche camps alone. It would take the combined efforts of the detachments from Fort Union, Taos, and Hatch's Ranch.

To Sibley, Crittenden's request had placed him in an "embarrassing position" since the "crippled condition" of his squadron precluded his joining Crittenden.[34] Of the squadron of dragoons at Taos only sixty-five or seventy had horses capable of making such a scout. Furthermore, packsaddles, requested when Sibley first assumed command at Taos, had not been received. The brevet major was willing to do what he could. Two officers and fifty men would be furnished if Crittenden would provide transportation and provisions. To further assist Colonel Crittenden, Henry rode into Taos to see Christopher "Kit" Carson, local Indian agent, who agreed to make twenty-five Ute scouts available for the proposed expedition providing the Ute receive a supply of beef.[35]

Sibley, through his post adjutant, Benjamin F. Sloan, pleaded with

[32] G.B. Crittenden to Henry H. Sibley, 13 January 1861, A.G.O., Dept. of N.M., L.R., R.G. 393.
[33] Ibid.
[34] H.H. Sibley to D.H. Maury, 15 January 1861, A.G.O., Dept. of N.M., L.R., R.G. 393; H.H. Sibley to G.B. Crittenden, 14 January 1861, A.G.O., Dept. of N.M., L.R., R.G. 393.
[35] Ibid.

department headquarters in Santa Fe for more horses and men. Twenty-nine recruits were needed to bring the two companies of dragoons to maximum strength. At least ninety-nine horses were needed to replace those lost during the Navajo Campaign. Both the mounted rifles and dragoons were greatly under strength. According to Crittenden's calculations 415 recruits and 293 horses were needed to bring the two regiments to maximum strength.[36]

By late January 1861 the shortage of supplies at Taos had become critical. Lieutenant Gay's Company had not received any clothing in almost a year and the men were performing their duties almost naked. Sibley blamed the lack of clothing on Captain Cuvier Grover, commander at Fort Garland, who had deliberately detained a supply train bound for Taos. Captain Grover, whom Sibley accused of being "ignorant" and causing undue "embarrassment," later admitted that he was unaware of any troops being stationed at Taos.[37]

Besides the shortages of foodstuffs at Taos, morale became a serious problem. Although the post was isolated it was still close enough to the villages of Ranchos de Taos and Taos for the soldiers to get drunk. Drunkenness was a common complaint and evidence indicated that the Cantonment Burgwin officers, Sibley included, indulged in their share of the drinking. Poor morale caused some of Sibley's dragoons to flee into the knee deep snow of the nearby Sangre de Cristo Mountains.

The morale problem was heightened by the men's inactivity since they saw no real reason for their presence in the valley. Sibley found that the Spanish-speaking population of the valley were no longer hostile to American rule and in some instances were even quite friendly. The Pueblo Indians were certainly no threat nor were the Ute or the Apache who had been pushed far to the north and the west. Cantonment Burgwin had simply become a place where soldiers were stationed until they were needed elsewhere.[38]

By late March food supplies were dangerously low. The post's supply of "beans, bacon, rice, salt, and vinegar," was completely depleted and only a week's supply of sugar and coffee remained. Henry

[36] B. Sloan to D.H. Maury, 15 January 1861, A.G.O., Dept. of N.M., L.R., R.G. 393; Statement of G.B. Crittenden, n.d., Enclosure with Ibid.

[37] H.H. Sibley to D.H. Maury, 27 January 1861, A.G.O., Dept. of N.M., L.R., R.G. 393.

[38] Lawrence R. Murphy, "Cantonment Burgwin, New Mexico, 1852–1860," *Arizona and the West* 15 (Spring, 1973), 22.

sent an express to Santa Fe asking for three thousand rations, enough to feed his squadron for a month. Otherwise, there would be no alternative but to vacate the post. Colonel John B. Grayson, in reply to Sibley's request, stated that Sibley had never requested supplies for Taos, and department headquarters was not aware of the shortage.[39]

Several problems of a local nature also plagued Sibley during his stay at Taos. Citizens complained constantly of the mail service between Taos and Denver. To prevent the mail from becoming too bulky, Henry was placed in the unenviable position of deciding what mail could be sent and what could not. To "avoid an ill feeling in the community," he decided to "require a payment of ten cents on each letter carried . . . excepting official letters." The money was to be paid to the express riders in hopes of improving service.[40]

In March 1861 word reached Taos that Colonel Canby had completed a peace treaty with the Navajo Nation. All hostilities against the Navajo, either by the U.S. Army, Territorial Militia, or Nuevo Mexicano slave-raiding parties, were to cease forthwith. Furthermore, all Navajo slaves held by the aristocracy of the territory were to be released. This presented a considerable problem for Sibley since the holding of Navajo slaves by the prominent citizens of the Taos Valley had long been a tradition. To further complicate matters, a company of local militia commanded by Captain Abań Romero had recently returned from an expedition against the Navajo. Captain Romero acknowledged to Sibley that twelve Navajo had been given or sold to various families along the return route, and three had been brought back to Taos.[41] In a meeting between Romero and Judge Pedro Valdez, Romero argued that he had left Taos in February 1861 and did not know of any peace treaty. Romero refused to release the three prisoners until department headquarters in Santa Fe was contacted. In early April, Sibley and Judge Valdez persuaded Romero to free the three Navajo. The Indians were sent to Santa Fe with a government wagon train and were eventually able to return to their homes.

The historically bitter hatred between the local Nuevo Mexicanos and the Navajo Nation had caused the army to station men on the frontier to keep raiding parties from destroying the fragile peace.

[39] John B. Grayson to H.H. Sibley, 26 March 1861, A.G.O., Dept. of N.M., L.R., R.G. 393. Also, endorsement on same.
[40] B. Sloan to D.H. Maury, 13 February 1861, A.G.O., Dept. of N.M., L.R., R.G. 393.
[41] H.H. Sibley to D.H. Maury, 3 April 1861, A.G.O., Dept. of N.M., L.R., R.G. 393.

Brevet Major Sibley was ordered to send a detachment of dragoons to Abiquiu and Jémez to guard one of the major routes into the Navajo Country. The critical shortage of supplies as well as the lack of horses and mules prevented the orders from being carried out immediately. Sibley wrote department headquarters in Santa Fe that his command was "inefficient at the best as a cavalry force, in consequence of the deficiency of horses."[42] Henry was also short of men since thirty troopers had been ordered to Santa Fe and ten more were on express service. With a detachment at Abiquiu and Jémez, Henry would have "scarcely a corporal's guard for duty." Nevertheless, by the second week in April the men had left Taos for Abiquiu and Jémez.[43]

From the moment Sibley arrived at Taos, political rumblings from afar crept into the valley. Express riders who arrived weekly brought newspapers from Santa Fe and the East and letters from Charlotte in Brooklyn.

While Henry was freezing with his men during the painful retreat from Marsh Pass during the Navajo Campaign, a tall man from Illinois had been elected president of the United States. The election, which had been the most traumatic in American history, produced a violent, unprecedented disturbance, even in far off and remote Taos. An ardent Southerner, upon hearing that Lincoln had been elected president, tore down the American flag from the town plaza. Kit Carson, a staunch Unionist, rode to the nearby Sangre de Cristo Mountains, cut down a tall aspen tree for a flagstaff, returned to Taos and raised the Stars and Stripes in the plaza. To ensure the safety of Old Glory, Carson posted a guard day and night to make sure the flag remained atop its lofty perch.[44] Although there is no evidence linking Sibley to the incident, the brevet major was certain to have taken more than just a passing interest in the event.

On the same day Sibley led his column of dragoons into Taos, South Carolina voted to secede from the Union. In early January 1861 Mississippi, Florida, and Alabama quickly followed in the Palmetto State's path. While Henry pleaded for supplies in distant Taos, his native Louisiana became the sixth state to depart from the Federal Union.

---

[42] H.H. Sibley to D.H. Maury, 8 April 1861, A.G.O., Dept. of N.M., L.R., R.G. 393.

[43] Chris Emmett, *Fort Union and the Winning of the Southwest* (Norman, 1965), 232–35.

[44] Edwin L. Sabin, *Kit Carson Days: Adventures in the Path of Empire* (New York, 1953), I: 674–76.

A few days later the Lone Star State of Texas followed Louisiana. Events were moving rapidly. On February 4 the provisional Congress of the Confederate States of America met in Montgomery, Alabama, to adopt a constitution and to elect Jefferson Davis of Mississippi as president. One month after Davis took the oath as president of the Confederate States, Abraham Lincoln was inaugurated in Washington, D.C. On April 12 Confederates fired on Fort Sumter in the harbor of Charleston, South Carolina, commencing the bloodiest war in American history. Bitter political arguments over the issue of secession became common at the various posts in the Territory of New Mexico. A few days after news of the surrender of Fort Sumter reached New Mexico, several officers resigned their commissions, many to become high-ranking officers in the Confederate Army. Among those going South were Lieutenants Joseph Wheeler, Bryan Morel Thomas, Dabney Herndon Maury, James Longstreet, Lucius Loomis Rich, Henry C. McNeill, and Colonel George B. Crittenden.

The secessionist crisis came to Taos when one of Sibley's officers, Second Lieutenant Benjamin F. Sloan, submitted his resignation and asked for a sixty-day leave of absence to proceed to his home in South Carolina. Sibley forwarded the resignation to department headquarters adding that "no objection can be raised against its acceptance."[45] Henry, too, especially after the secession of Louisiana, came to question his future in the army. Rumors of the availability of high-ranking positions in the Confederate Army circulated throughout the territory. Henry, in his letters to Charlotte, expressed a deep desire to go South and join the newly forming Confederate Army, certainly at a higher rank than brevet major. Charlotte, who was still in Brooklyn with the children, pleaded with her husband to remain loyal. Several years later Charlotte told an interviewer that she had been "much opposed" to Henry's "resigning his commission in the United States Army, as were all of my people, for I had been brought up in Army circles, and all of my sympathies were with the Union."[46] Still, the lure of a prestigious Confederate command, far from the cold of the

---

[45] Endorsement on B. Sloan to S. Cooper, 16 January 1861, A.G.O., Dept. of N.M., L.R., R.G. 393.

[46] Seventieth Congress, First Session, "Hearings of Subcommittee No. 2 of the Committee on War Claims on House Report 8749, A Bill for the Relief of the Legal Representatives of the Estate of Henry H. Sibley, Deceased," Washington, 27 January 1928, Library of Congress, Documents Division, p. 29.

Sangre de Cristo Mountains, caused Henry to move closer and closer to resignation. Much of his life had been spent on the western frontier and in the East. He was no planter, no aristocrat, no politician, yet his feet remained firmly planted in the soil of Louisiana and the South.

In late March 1861 with the virtual disintegration of his command at Taos, Sibley was sent to Fort Union. Because supplies were lacking and his troopers were ill, Sibley delayed his march across the frigid Sangre de Cristo Mountains for several weeks.[47] Sibley was greatly perturbed at the inability of the department to supply him. After considerable contemplation and soul-searching and against the wishes of his wife, he submitted his letter of resignation. The possibilities of a high-ranking commission in the Confederate Army and the defense of Southern culture, states' rights, and honor, were overwhelming for the brevet major. On April 28, 1861, Henry, in a few brief sentences made the biggest decision of his military career: "I have the honor to enclose herewith the resignation of my commission in the Army of the United States and request authority to leave this Dept. immediately."[48] As had been his custom in the past, Henry underlined those parts of his letter which he wished to emphasize. In his letter of resignation he underscored the word *immediately*.

Before leaving the department, Sibley took his Taos Command across the mountains to Fort Union. His departure ended the presence of the army in the Taos Valley. Shortly before his departure from Taos, Sibley ordered three privates, whom he accused of being "absolutely valueless," "unfit for duty," and habitual drunkards, drummed out of the service.[49] Sibley arrived at Fort Union four days after leaving Taos and on May 17, 1861, assumed command of the fort.

While Sibley was at Taos and later at Fort Union awaiting approval of his resignation, he entered into a conspiracy with Departmental Commander Colonel William Wing Loring, a prosecessionist North Carolinian, to take his entire command into Texas. The egotistical Loring, who had lost his left arm at Belén Gate on the outskirts of Mexico City during the war with Mexico, had assumed command of the department in March. Loring had resigned his commission on May

[47] H.H. Sibley to D.H. Maury, 25 March 1861, A.G.O., Dept. of N.M., L.R., R.G. 393; H.H. Sibley to D.H. Maury, 3 April 1861, A.G.O., Dept. of N.M., L.R., R.G. 393.

[48] H.H. Sibley to D.H. Maury, 28 April 1861, A.G.O., Dept. of N.M., L.R., R.G. 393.

[49] H.H. Sibley to D.H. Maury, 20 May 1861, A.G.O., Dept. of N.M., L.R., R.G. 393.

13, but like Sibley he had decided to remain in his present position until relieved of command. The specifics of the Loring-Sibley plot are lacking, but the two men's plan to take several companies southward seems almost certain. Henry was partly motivated by the fact that by early April all the military posts in Texas had either been seized or turned over to commissioners of that state. Evidently the seizure of various forts and supplies, especially in the southern part of the territory, was also discussed. Henry later blamed a "sickly sentimentality" for his failure to go through with the plot.[50]

Not hearing any word on his resignation, Sibley on May 31, 1861, issued orders availing "himself of seven days' leave of absence" and relinquished command of Fort Union.[51] Six days after his forty-fifth birthday, he said good-bye to his dragoons and caught the stage southward to Las Vegas. For Henry Hopkins Sibley an era was ending, and another was beginning on that otherwise-tranquil spring morning in 1861 as he rode south from Fort Union past the crumbling adobe ruins of Pecos Pueblo, across Glorieta Pass, and through Apache Canyon to Santa Fe. On the very day he left Fort Union, orders had arrived making him a full major, a rather inadequate attempt at keeping a veteran officer in the Federal Army, after fourteen years at brevet rank. From Santa Fe, Henry continued on to Albuquerque and down the Rio Grande past countless small Spanish-American villages to Fort Craig on the west bank of the river some twenty-five miles south of Socorro. Having never been to the post before, it is impossible to ascertain what observations Henry made of the fort and its environs. It is almost certain that he spent sometime at the fort, perhaps staying overnight. From Fort Craig the sandy road left the Rio Grande and headed across the dreaded sun-baked Jornada del Muerto, a hundred-mile bypass of a big western bend in the Rio Grande. After reaching Fort Fillmore, across the river from the vil-

[50] H.H. Sibley to W.W. Loring, 21 June 1861, *The War of the Rebellion: A Compilation of the Official Records of the Union and Confederate Armies* (Washington, 1889), Series I, Volume IV: 55. These records will hereafter be referred to as *O.R.* Many of these same letters relative to the early part of the Civil War in the Territory of New Mexico are reprinted in: U.S. War Department, *Confederate Victories in the Southwest* and *Union Victories in the Southwest* (Albuquerque, 1961). These two reprints of the *O.R.* will hereafter be referred to as either *Confederate Victories* or *Union Victories*. For a rather superficial biography of Loring see: William L. Wessels, *Born to be a Soldier* (Fort Worth, 1971).

[51] Post Orders No. 30, Fort Union, 30 May 1861, A.G.O., R.G. 391.

lage of Mesilla, Sibley continued downriver. Arriving at Hart's Mill or what would someday become El Paso, Texas, he had time to rest from the long ride and reflect back to the previous few weeks. Never had he been so optimistic. He felt almost grateful that his twenty-three-year career in the United States Army had come to an end.

While at Hart's Mill, Henry wrote a most eloquent and moving letter to his friend and co-conspirator Colonel Loring who, despite his resignation, still retained his departmental command. Henry's personal letter to his friend contrasted vividly with his dreary military dispatches from Taos. Passing into Texas he had been overtaken by "a glorious sensation of protection, hope, and pride" that he was at last "under the glorious banner of the Confederate States of America."[52] As he had ridden southward through the Mesilla Valley into Texas, "southern verdure and familiar foliage" had filled him "with enthusiasm and home feeling." What similarity Henry saw between the dry scrubland of New Mexico or even the Mesilla Valley and the humid bayou and piney woods of his native Louisiana is perhaps a reflection on his illusionary and deep emotional feeling toward the Confederacy.[53] He was, without doubt, a nineteenth-century romantic dreamer.

Safely in Texas, Henry came to regret that he had not brought his command with him. "I am satisfied now of the disaffection of the best of the rank and file in New Mexico," he wrote Loring. Sibley felt that he would be regarded as having betrayed and deserted them. "I wish I had my part to play over again; no such peace scruples should deter me from doing what I considered a bounded duty to my friends and my cause. I do not advocate the meeting of duplicity and dishonesty by the like weapons, but if I capture the treasury buildings I shall certainly not send back to my enemy the golden bricks."[54]

Henry encouraged Loring to hold on to his position as department commander long enough to allow stores and equipment at Fort Bliss to be seized by Confederate forces. Otherwise Henry was afraid the commander of Fort Fillmore, Major Isaac Lynde, might move against Fort Bliss to save the supplies. If Loring was relieved of command too

[52] H.H. Sibley to W.W. Loring, 21 June 1861, O.R., I, IV:55.

[53] Martin H. Hall draws the same conclusion in *Sibley's New Mexico Campaign* (Austin, 1960), 30. This book is undeniably the definitive study of the Confederate Invasion of the Territory of New Mexico.

[54] H.H. Sibley to W.W. Loring, 21 June 1861, O.R., I, IV: 55.

soon to prevent Lynde from seizing the supplies at Fort Bliss, Henry asked him to send an express to Judge Simeon Hart, a well known secessionist of the area. The Fort Bliss supplies could then be seized by local authorities or disposed of through other means.[55]

Henry's zealous letter to Loring did not reach its intended recipient. One day before Henry reached El Paso, Loring placed Colonel Canby in command of the Department of New Mexico and caught the stage for Fort Fillmore, there to await word of his resignation. Henry's letter traveling north thus passed Loring riding south. The letter instead fell into the hands of Canby who became fully aware of the Sibley-Loring plot.

It is probable that Henry's dream of conquering New Mexico and the Far West was conceived at Hart's Mill. While waiting for the twice-a-week stage across the desert to San Antonio, Henry talked at length to James W. Magoffin, Josiah F. Crosby, and Judge Simeon Hart, some of the most influential men in the area.[56] All three were ardently pro-Southern and were desirous of a Confederate conquest of the Mesilla Valley and the Territory of New Mexico. In 1861 Crosby was district judge of that area of Texas west of the Pecos River. Simeon Hart, a veteran of the Mexican War, had settled at El Paso where he built a large flour mill. James W. Magoffin, a Missourian and Santa Fe trader, who as a special agent during the Mexican War arranged the peaceful conquest of Santa Fe, had built a large trading post at Franklin. Magoffin and Hart had married into well-to-do Mexican families, thus increasing their influence in the Franklin-El Paso area.

From El Paso, Sibley caught the stage for San Antonio. The road led down the Rio Grande to Fort Quitman, eastward through the mountains to Fort Davis, through Limpia Canyon and across the burning greasewood-dotted desert to Comanche Springs and the Pecos River near Fort Lancaster. From here the stage route wound overland to the Devil's River and through stifling desert heat to the Rio Grande at San Felipe Springs. After six days on the road, Sibley reached San Antonio early on the morning of June 20, 1861, and after a short rest set out for Louisiana. Traveling by stage through east Texas into southern

---

[55] Ibid.

[56] Rex W. Strickland, *Six Who Came to El Paso: Pioneers of the 1840's* (El Paso, 1963), 26–42; J.F. Crosby to Ed. Clark, 10 May 1861, Governor Clark Papers, Texas State Archives.

Louisiana, Henry reached Berwick's Bay where he caught the Opelousas and Great Western Railroad to New Orleans. A soldier had at last come home to Louisiana. The Civil War had come to America, to Louisiana, and to the grandiose-dreaming Henry Hopkins Sibley.

"An army under my command enters New Mexico, to take possession of it in the name and for the benefit of the Confederate States. By geographical position, by similarity of institutions, by commercial interests, and by future destinies New Mexico pertains to the Confederacy."

> Proclamation of Brigadier General H. H. Sibley, Army of the Confederate States, to the People of New Mexico, Fort Bliss, Texas, December 20, 1861.

". . . except for its political geographical position, the Territory of New Mexico is not worth a quarter of the blood and treasure expended in its conquest."

> H. H. Sibley to S. Cooper, Fort Bliss, Texas, May 4, 1862.

Chapter VIII

Westward the Texans

From the small community of Algiers on the west bank of the Mississippi River, Henry ferried to New Orleans on Saturday, June 29, 1861. The nation's largest cotton port was a bustling metropolis greatly excited by recent news from Richmond and Washington. Flotillas of river boats lined the long, curving waterfront near the city, and many ships crowded against the docks near tree lined Canal Street. Other boats could be seen near the Vieux Carre less than two blocks from the spires of St. Louis Cathedral. A few river steamers were anchored upstream near the American Quarter and the large Greek revival buildings which dominated that portion of the city.

Sibley was joyously welcomed by the citizens of the Crescent City who proclaimed him a hero of the South and cheered him at every opportunity. A veteran warrior gone South was evidence to Southern fire-eaters of the imminent collapse of the Federal Army and the chaotic conditions that were thought to exist in the Territory of New Mexico. The New Orleans *Daily Picayune* reported that a "more gallant and experienced and chivalrous officer could not be obtained."[1]

[1] *Daily Picayune*, 2 July 1861. Also of interest is *Tagliche Deutsche Zeitung*, 8 January 1862.

He was offered command of a volunteer Louisiana regiment which was being hastily recruited. Although the offer must have been tempting, Henry, always the romantic dreamer, had greater aspirations. He did not tarry in the city.

From New Orleans, Sibley took the Jackson and Great Northern Railroad north past Lake Pontchartrain to Jackson, Mississippi, and through the piney woods of northern Alabama to Knoxville, Tennessee, where he arrived on July 4. From Knoxville he caught the East Tennessee and Virginia across the Blue Ridge Mountains to Lynchburg, Virginia, past the peaceful rural village of Appomattox Court House to Richmond.[2]

Sibley found the capital of the Confederacy excited by the approach of war. Even more than New Orleans, Richmond epitomized the floodtide of Southern hopes. News of Lincoln's determination to hold all Federal property in the South and the commencement of fighting in Missouri and western Virginia had reached the tobacco city on the James. Once in Richmond, Henry was able to obtain an appointment with President Jefferson Davis without delay.

The two men had much in common. Both had been educated by Robert Hamilton Bishop who had been president of Miami University. Both had graduated from West Point and had fought in the Mexican War. The two had become well acquainted while Davis was serving as Secretary of War in the Franklin Pierce administration, during which time Sibley had been pushing for the adoption of his tent.

There seems little doubt that Davis gave Sibley his undivided attention. In his general appointments, Davis, who had extensive practical experience at the regimental level and a professional soldier's education, preferred seasoned West Point veterans like Sibley. The president was impressed with Henry's knowledge of the resources of the Territory of New Mexico and the conditions of the Federal forces which continued to garrison the vital frontier forts there. Henry was able to give Davis specifics on the "quantity of government stores, supplies and transportation" in the territory.[3] Sibley also told the president that he could recruit a brigade of Texas troops, equip them

---

[2] Voucher, 4 July 1861, Compiled Military Service Record of Henry Hopkins Sibley, R.G. 109. Hereafter referred to as C.M.S.R.

[3] T.T. Teel, "Sibley's New Mexican Campaign: Its Objects and the Causes of its Failure," *Battles and Leaders of the Civil War*, (New York, 1956), II: 700.

with arms taken from the Federal arsenals and forts in the Lone Star State, and easily overrun the Territory of New Mexico. In fact Colonel John Robert Baylor, with fewer than four hundred men, was already at Fort Bliss ready for a move into the southern part of the territory. Baylor's Second Regiment of Mounted Rifles could be incorporated into Sibley's Army.

The proposed campaign would be self-sustaining. Henry reasoned that enough supplies could be carried until the army reached Fort Bliss. From there he and his men would drive northward into the Mesilla Valley where they could forage from the land. Facing a badly demoralized Federal force, Sibley was certain that he could overrun Fort Craig, Federal bastion in the southern portion of the territory, capture Santa Fe, and then march on Fort Union to the northeast of the capital. With his Army swollen with "Southern men who were anxiously awaiting an opportunity to join the Confederate Army" and with captured foodstuffs, Sibley would then seize the gold and silver fields of Colorado.

One of the major objectives of the campaign, as Henry purportedly relayed it to one of his officers, was the eventual conquest of California. "On to San Francisco" would be the battle cry. California, with its excellent ports and supply of gold, would be a welcome addition to the Confederate States. Furthermore, negotiations would be opened with the governors of Chihuahua and Sonora. In light of chaotic conditions then existing in Mexico, these states would be acquired by negotiations or by conquest.

Doubling the size of the southern republic would have far reaching economic, diplomatic, and military influences on the conduct and progress of the Civil War. Despite the small number of men involved, the campaign promised to be one of the most important of the war, and could go a long way toward making the independence of the Confederacy a reality.

It was easy for Davis to see the importance of the campaign. Military victory in the far West might well bring diplomatic success overseas. One factor which was working against recognition of the Confederacy by England and France was the inability of the South to launch a successful military offensive. The diplomatic dividends from a successful campaign would be far out of proportion to the number of men and sacrifices such an undertaking required. There would be psychological implications on the North and South, as well as the

English and French, from a conquest resulting in a Southern empire stretching from the Atlantic to the Pacific.[4]

Another important aspect of the Sibley Expedition was that it was to be the first test of Davis' little known strategy of the "offensive-defensive" which called for the assembly of Confederate troops at strategic locations on the borders of the Confederacy and an all out attack against any Northern army in that particular theatre of combat.[5] Victory on the battlefield would ultimately lead to Southern independence, Davis hoped. The strategy, which acknowledged the superior resources of the North by emphasizing a quick and decisive war, was also a reflection of the southern social system. In the case of the Sibley Expedition the strategy was also indicative of the aggressive character of both Sibley and Davis. Thus, several months before Albert Sidney Johnston's thrust into the Tennessee-Kentucky middle border and Robert E. Lee's invasion of Maryland, the Sibley Expedition was to be the South's initial step toward achieving independence through what Sibley and Davis both called a Second American Revolution.

With Henry Hopkins Sibley, President Davis was attempting to achieve militarily what the American Colonies had successfully achieved less than a century earlier. In this respect the Sibley Expedition can be compared to the 1775 Richard Montgomery-Benedict Arnold Invasion of Canada.

Davis presented Henry with a commission as brigadier general. The commercially printed document commanded Henry's "Patriotism, Valor, Fidelity, and Abilities."[6] Davis had long been a proponent of Manifest Destiny, and he professed great hope in his newly found general. General Henry Hopkins Sibley, Confederate General of the West, was to actualize a Confederate Manifest Destiny.

With orders signed by his old comrade from the Texas frontier,

[4] Charles S. Walker, "Causes of the Confederate Invasion of New Mexico," *New Mexico Historical Review*, 8 (April 1933), 85; W.H. Watford, "Confederate Western Ambitions," *Southwestern Historical Quarterly*, 46 (October 1940), 162; Duane Allen Smith, "The Confederate Cause in the Colorado Territory, 1861–1865," *Civil War History*, 7 (1961), 32.

[5] Frank E. Vandiver, "Strategy and Tactics of the Confederate Army," Taped Lecture, Michael Glazier, Inc., Wilmington, Delaware.

[6] Commission of Henry Hopkins Sibley as brigadier general in the Confederate States Army, document in private possession. Photostatic copy courtesy of Lewis Leigh, Jr., Fairfax, Virginia.

Samuel Cooper, now adjutant and inspector general of the Confederacy, Brigadier General Sibley was "intrusted with the important duty of driving the Federal troops" from New Mexico.[7] Despite Davis' authoritarianism, an unusually large degree of latitude was given the newly commissioned brigadier general: "It is not deemed necessary to confine you to matters of detail which from time to time may arise. In this respect you will be guided by circumstances and your own good judgement."[8] Henry was to proceed without delay to Texas and, in coordination with General Earl Van Dorn, recruit "in the speediest manner possible" the necessary troops. Henry was entrusted with one of the most ambitious and energetic campaigns of the war and no doubt envisioned himself as a Confederate Napoleon who would plant the Stars and Bars on California's golden shores. The seizure of California was not specifically mentioned in Henry's orders, but there was little doubt that it was the eventual objective of the impending campaign.

Had not the Civil War engulfed the country, Sibley's mediocre career in the Federal Army probably would have continued. Now history thrust him into the forefront of the war in the Southwest. Weeks earlier he had been a forgotten forty-five year old captain in command of a handful of starving and demoralized dragoons at a remote military post of which most clerks in the War Department had never heard. Now he wore the stars of a Confederate brigadier general.

Leaving the Confederate capital shortly after receiving his orders, Sibley returned to Texas by ship. From the James River, Henry went to Havana where he obtained passage to New Orleans on the *Dart*, a well-known blockade runner.[9] The general traveled with his newly completed staff which consisted of Lieutenant Colonel Henry C. McNeill, who was acting assistant adjutant general; Edward N. Covey, surgeon; First Lieutenant Thomas P. Ochiltree, aide-de-camp; and Captain William H. Harrison, quartermaster; all of whom had accompanied him to Richmond. The party arrived in the Crescent City on Monday, July 15, 1861. In a *Daily Picayune* interview the general said his intentions were to proceed "immediately to Texas and to raise a brigade of mounted cavalry for service on the northeastern frontier

[7] S. Cooper to H.H. Sibley, 8 July 1861, *O.R.*, I, IV: 93.
[8] Ibid.
[9] H.N. Cooke to H.H. Sibley, 21 August 1861, Adjutant General's Records, Texas State Archives, Austin, Texas.

of that state." Henry either deliberately misled the *Picayune* or was misquoted for his field of combat would be far from the pines and hardwood thickets of northeastern Texas. The *Picayune* article concluded by congratulating "the country on the appointment of such a gallant and efficient officer."[10]

From New Orleans Henry wrote Confederate Secetary of War Leroy P. Walker that he had decided not to take out a "patent in the Confederate States for the Sibley tent."[11] The decision was a reflection of his Southern patriotism, for Henry had never considered such actions in relation to the Federal Government. He sent Lieutenant Colonel Henry C. McNeill to Texas to meet with Governor Edward Clark and commence the recruiting of troops. The general waited in New Orleans for two weeks until Charlotte and the children could join him from New York. While in the city he was presented with a pistol exquisitely engraved with his name and inlaid with gold and silver. Finally, on August 1, Henry, Charlotte, Helen Margaret, and Sidney Johnston, accompanied by the staff officers left for Texas.[12] The party went by train to Berwick's Bay and overland by stage through New Iberia to Houston.

After spending a few days in Houston, Henry continued by stage to San Antonio where he arrived on August 12. He had little doubt as to the ultimate success of his mission. Texas was preparing for war with vigor and determination. Optimism was reflected in the young Texas recruits. Numerous letters arrived in San Antonio from zealous individuals offering to enlist men for the Sibley Brigade. Henry was certain of being able to obtain the necessary troops. He was to be bitterly disappointed.

After years of isolation on remote frontier posts, the Sibley family felt at home in San Antonio. The city had a population of over eight thousand. Long a predominantly Mexican town, San Antonio had recently experienced a large influx of immigrants, especially Germans. The city was supported by vast cattle and sheep ranches which lined the numerous streams and rivers of the Texas countryside. San Antonio was also a social and fashion Mecca. It was said that the women

[10] *Daily Picayune*, 16 July 1861; *Dallas Herald*, 7, 21 August 1861.

[11] H.H. Sibley to L.P. Walker, *Daily Picayune*, 16 July 1861.

[12] *Daily Picayune*, 2 August 1861; Tom P. Ochiltree to Edward Clark, 15 July 1861, Governor Edward Clark Papers, Texas State Archives.

in San Antonio took greater care with their dress "than they do in New York or in large cities of Europe."[13]

Two of the most magnificent buildings in the town were the French consulate and E.R. Smith's Plaza House Hotel, a two-storied structure on the north side of Main Plaza, where Henry and Charlotte took up residence. It was also here that the newly arriving recruits got their first look at their commander. One of the young recruits wrote home of his first glimpse of the general: "I saw Gen'l Sibley today at the Plaza Hotel. He is a fine looking officer and is said to be a perfect gentleman as well as a fine drill officer. I like the appearance of 'the old rascal' very much. We are bound for Arizona and New Mexico sure enough and I expect as soon as our regiment is filled up and drilled in about 3 weeks they will send us on. Ho for the long march."[14]

Sibley arrived in San Antonio from the East at the same time exciting news came out of the West. Colonel John Robert Baylor, a dashing and daring Texan if there ever was one, had struck north from Fort Bliss into the Mesilla Valley. With four hundred ragged and ill-equipped but determined Texans, Baylor had seized the village of Mesilla, fought off a Federal attempt to drive him out, and although greatly outnumbered by the bulk of the Seventh United States Infantry, had forced by sheer intimidation the evacuation of Fort Fillmore. In an even more incredible maneuver, Baylor captured the entire Fort Fillmore garrison as the soldiers attempted to flee northeastward through the Organ Mountains to the safety of Fort Stanton. Baylor's amazing success was widely reported by the Texas press. The fighting colonel, who was determined to eat his "Christmas dinner in Santa Fe," boasted that two hundred Texans could whip fifteen hundred Yankees anyday.[15] Baylor's achievements in New Mexico served further to convince Sibley of the ultimate success of his mission in the West, but he was disappointed that Baylor had stolen much of his possible thunder and anticipated glory. The general became anxious to get his army into the field and complete the work which Baylor

[13] Charles Ramsdell, *San Antonio: A Historical and Pictorial Guide* (Austin, 1959), 4.

[14] Randolph Howell to Home Folks, September 1861, Howell Papers, University of Texas Archives, Austin, Texas.

[15] *Dallas Herald*, 21 August 1861; 15 January 1862; *Texas State Gazette*, 10 August 1861; Jerry D. Thompson, *Colonel John Robert Baylor: Texas Indian Fighter and Confederate Soldier* (Hillsboro, 1971), 24–48.

had begun. Almost from the beginning serious problems plagued Henry's hopes for an early conquest of New Mexico.

By late August 1861 the first companies which were to comprise the Sibley Brigade had arrived in San Antonio. Like those who would follow, the young men were mustered into the army for the duration of the war, which many of the recruits expected to last no longer than a few weeks.[16] After the soldiers had taken an oath as long as a "fence rail," horses, saddles and arms were appraised, and the men were allowed to parade around town for a couple of hours before the job of soldiering began in earnest.

The first company to arrive in town was from Guadalupe and Caldwell Counties northeast of San Antonio. The unit, commanded by William P. Hardeman, had been recruited from the small farming villages along the Guadalupe and San Marcos rivers.

One day later the "Davis Rifles" arrived in town from the village of Cuero on the lower Guadalupe southeast of San Antonio. Within a month the recruitment and organization of the Fourth Regiment had been completed. The regiment was comprised largely of farm youth from south-central Texas and the piney woods of east-central Texas. Many of the recruits, their egos swollen by Southern patriotism, displayed an almost pitiful naivete toward the bloody conflict which lay ahead. One young private in the Sibley Brigade wrote his family in east Texas of mounting his "noble steed" and riding off to the "glorious struggle" and the "jaws of death." By 1863 that same soldier was writing of the "detestable army" and was praying "to God for the end of this bloody struggle."[17]

Commanding Sibley's Fourth Regiment was Colonel James Reily. Born in Ohio, Reily had gone to Kentucky where he had married a niece of Henry Clay. Later he had moved to Texas, first to Nacogdoches and then Houston. Reily was a seasoned diplomat and had some military experience, having served briefly as aide-de-camp during the Texas Revolution. Reily had also served for a short time as American consul at St. Petersburg, Russia, during the administration

---

[16] H.C. Wright, "Reminiscences of H.C. Wright of Austin," Typescript, University of Texas Archives, Austin, Texas. Texan enthusiasm for the war is also reflected in James Reily to Governor Clark, 27 May 1861, Governor Edward Clark Papers, Texas State Archives.

[17] Diary of Randolph Howell, University of Texas Archives, Austin, Texas. Hereafter referred to as Howell Diary. Typescript in author's possession.

of President James Buchanan. The Fourth Regiment set up camp on Leon Creek but later moved to "Camp Sibley" on the west bank of Salado Creek, outside of San Antonio on the Austin Road.

The next regiment to be organized was that of the Fifth Texas Cavalry, commanded by Colonel Thomas Green which made its camp on Salado Creek two miles above the encampment of the Fourth and was named Camp Manassas. Colonel Green, two years older than Sibley at forty-seven, was as brave and daring an officer as the brigade would see. A Virginian by birth Green had attended both Princeton College in Kentucky as well as Jackson and Nashville Colleges, both in Tennessee, but had gone to Texas where he had arrived in time to help man the "Twin Sisters" as a private during the Battle of San Jacinto. Green had also commanded a company of volunteers during the war with Mexico and had been signaled out for bravery during the American siege of Monterrey.[18]

The last regiment of the Sibley Brigade to be organized was the Seventh Texas Cavalry, commanded by Colonel William Steele. Like Sibley, Colonel Steele was a veteran of the Second Dragoons. Both men had graduated thirty-first in their classes at West Point, Sibley in 1833 and Steele in 1840. As a young lieutenant Steele had been with Sibley during the Mexican War and had later served on the Texas frontier and in Kansas. A native of New York, Steele had resigned from the United States Army the same day as had Sibley.

The Seventh Regiment took camp on Salado Creek above that of the Fifth. Its organization began in earnest in early October with the mustering in of Captain Powhatan Jordan's company from Bexar County. A few days later Company B of the Seventh, consisting of German-Americans and commanded by Captain Gustav Hoffman, the first mayor of New Braunfels, came into San Antonio. By late October the organization and recruitment of the regiment had been completed.

Making soldiers from glory-dreaming plowboys was not easy. Using Winfield Scott's *Infantry-Tactics* and William J. Hardee's *Rifle and Light Infantry Tactics*, Sibley watched as the men were drilled, drilled again, and then drilled some more.[19] With little knowledge of what they were to experience in the months to come, the men constantly

[18] Walter Prescott Webb and H. Bailey Carroll, eds., *The Handbook of Texas* (Austin, 1951), 728.

[19] Hall, *Sibley's New Mexico Campaign*, p. 37.

complained of the quality of food despite an adequate supply of beef. Like most Southerners, Sibley's Texans did not easily take to the discipline and regimentation of army life. One Texan lamented of having to stand guard duty: "We had a camp guard, a picket guard, and everything was so guarded that one had to be on guard when he spoke,"[20] Roll was called both in the morning and in the evening. Daily the sounds of "tattoo" and "reveille" were heard echoing across the Texas prairie. General Sibley in the beginning was pleased with the progress of the brigade writing that "the men and horses cannot be beat, and the progress made in drill evidences a spirit and ambitious determination to excel, which give me entire confidence."[21] Although he had been educated in the North, Sibley somehow seemed to accept the myth of Southern invincibility.

Despite the fact that the Sibley Brigade was becoming a reliable fighting force, General Sibley continued to face serious problems. Weapons were difficult to procure. Sibley and President Davis had originally thought that the brigade could be equipped with the arms which had been seized from the Federal arsenals in Texas, but much of this material had been sent to defend the Texas coast and the Rio Grande Valley. Recruits had been asked to supply their own arms, but several companies arrived in San Antonio without any weapons. To alleviate the problem, Sibley attempted to buy arms on the open market. This proved disadvantageous because the men could not be uniformly equipped. By the time the brigade was ready to leave San Antonio, the men were "armed with squirrel guns, bear guns, sportsman's guns, shotguns, both single and double barrel, in fact, guns of all sorts, even down to guns in the shape of cannons called 'Mountain Howitzers.'"[22] The battery of "Mountain Howitzers" was attached to the Fourth Regiment and was commanded by Lieutenant John Reily, Colonel Reily's son. Another artillery battery was attached to the Fifth Regiment.

Two Companies in Colonel Green's Regiment were equipped with lances and six-shooters. The lances, which Henry had ordered made, were nine feet long and consisted of three-by-twelve-inch blades

[20] Theophilus Noel, *A Campaign From Santa Fe to the Mississippi, Being a History of the Old Sibley Brigade*, Martin Hardwick Hall and Edwin Adams Davis, eds. (Houston, 1961), 13.

[21] *Texas State Gazette*, 9 November 1861.

[22] Hall, *Sibley's New Mexico Campaign*, p. 37.

topped by a large red pennant. General Sibley, always the romantic dreamer, delighted in his lancers. They proved obsolete in combat, relics of a bygone era.

Lack of proper equipment was so bad in San Antonio that the general himself could not even find a saddle. When Major Sacfield Maclin, ordnance officer for the Department of Texas, informed the General that he was not authorized to sell any saddles, Henry angrily appealed to Colonel Ben McCulloch and was finally able to get the desired saddle.[23]

The most acute problem facing the Sibley Brigade was the shortage of men. When Henry arrived in Texas, newspapers in San Antonio and Austin announced his intentions of raising a brigade of troops. Soldiers were asked to "rendezvous at the earliest day possible at San Antonio armed and fully equipped for a Winter campaign." Volunteers in Austin were asked to "furnish themselves with a good horse, saddle, bridle, and blanket; a good double barrel shot gun or rifle, a bowie knife and a six-shooter."[24] Henry was disappointed; progress was slow in completing his brigade. He had hoped to be "able to raise and organize" his force "within a very brief space of time." He was particularly frustrated that Governor Edward Clark had not provided "as efficient a cooperation as was desirable."[25] Clark had ordered the necessary number of companies to report to San Antonio, but Sibley found that "most of these companies had . . . either entirely disbanded, or their numbers had become diminished below the minimum of the Confederate service." Furthermore, many young Texans were far more excited about serving in Virginia or elsewhere in the East rather than in the deserts and mountains of New Mexico. When it appeared that the number of troops ordered out by the governor would not be enough, Henry was forced to appeal "directly to the people."

The general was angry that there was no superior officer in San Antonio who could furnish assistance. General Earl Van Dorn, relieved as commander of the department, had been replaced by Colonel Henry E. McCulloch who had moved his headquarters to Galveston. Henry felt that if he had not taken on the task of equipping the brigade him-

[23] H.H. Sibley to Sacfield Maclin, 28 September 1861, C.M.S.R., R.G. 109.

[24] San Antonio *Daily Ledger and Texan*, 13 August 1861; *Texas State Gazette*, 7 September 1861.

[25] H.H. Sibley to S. Cooper, 16 November 1861, *O.R.*, I, IV: 141.

self it would "have probably paralyzed my command for the winter."[26]

The brigade's uniforms were as diverse as their arms. Most officers were able to afford fancy uniforms, but most enlisted men wore little more than the clothes they had on their backs. Henry was forced to admit that "many of the companies . . . are almost destitute of clothing, and very many men are without arms, and most of those in hand requir[e] extensive repair."[27] With colder weather fast approaching, Sibley became apprehensive about the lack of proper clothing. From experience in New Mexico and Utah, the general knew what a severe winter could do to an army, especially one that was as ill-equipped as his. Pleas went forth to the citizens of Texas to contribute clothing and blankets. The San Antonio Ladies' Southern Aid Society helped by collecting "blankets, comforters, quilts, flannel shirts, socks, drawers, and other items, as well as some cash." Only a few of the recruits were able to obtain a full set of military clothing which included "suits, pants, drawers, pantaloon boots, and coats."[28]

By late October 1861 with the brigade having completed its training, Sibley decided that the long march for New Mexico should begin. Early on the morning of October 21 a grand parade was held through the streets of San Antonio. Many of the town's patriotic citizens came out to see the festive march. For more than an hour the Texans filed down the narrow streets of the town to the cheers of the patriotic townspeople. In an emotional ceremony Helen Margaret, aged fifteen, presented the Seventh Regiment with a battle flag. A reporter for the Houston *Tri-Weekly Telegraph* wrote on viewing the troops: "A finer brigade of men and horses I do not believe can be found in the Confederate Army."[29]

Because of the lack of trail grass and water along the overland route to New Mexico, the general decided that the regiments should depart San Antonio at different dates. Water was so scare that at times the regiments would later be subdivided into squadrons and companies.

[26] Ibid.

[27] *Texas State Gazette*, 9 November 1861.

[28] William Henry Smith, "With Sibley in New Mexico: The Journal of William Henry Smith," *West Texas Historical Association Year Book*, contr. Walter A. Faulkner, XXVII, p. 114.

[29] *Daily Picayune*, 20 October 1861; quoted from the Houston *Tri-Weekly Telegraph*, n.d.

The departure of the Fourth Regiment from San Antonio was much like that of the Seventh. Early in the morning "boots and saddles" was sounded. The men's baggage was weighed (each recruit was allowed fifteen pounds) and was packed into wagons. Each company was alloted three wagons; two for the enlisted men's baggage and the other for the company's officers. Fifteen minutes later "assembly" rang out across and up and down Salado Creek. Everything was "a scene of bustle and confusion."[30] After a few minutes the entire regiment was mounted and formed into a solid square at which time Colonel Reily delivered an inspirational speech telling the men that they "were on the eve of leaving a land that many . . . might never again see." They were departing Texas, Reily said, to "try their fortunes in the field" and to defend Southern honor and states' rights.

Reily went on to say that the citizens of Texas and the Confederacy were expecting great things from the Sibley Brigade.[31] None was more confident of success than the colonel. Many of the young recruits were so moved by Reily's remarks that tears were said to have flowed quite freely. Next, Reily removed his hat and read a prayer which had been written by Alexander Gregg, Episcopal bishop of Texas. Like many other religious leaders in the South, the cleric was sure that God was on the side of the Confederacy. Suddenly the order of "by fours from the right march" sounded across Camp Sibley, and the regiment was on the move.[32]

As the men marched out of Camp Sibley and rode over the rolling countryside between Salado Creek and San Antonio, all remained quiet. The nearer to San Antonio the men got, the heartier their mood became. By the time the regiment reached the outskirts of town, the troops were in a lively and vocal mood and most commenced singing "The Texas Ranger," a favorite marching song.

Arriving at the main plaza in San Antonio, the regiment was again formed into a solid column and a flag presented to Colonel Reily on behalf of the ladies of Nacogdoches. Reily once again addressed the regiment in a most "eloquent manner and style." After Reily had completed his patriotic remarks, General Sibley rode forward. Although the General displayed "a great deal of originality and much determination," one recruit was convinced "that he was no orator."

[30] Noel, p. 14; *Texas State Gazette*, 2 November 1861.
[31] Ibid., p. 15.
[32] Ibid.; *San Antonio Weekly Herald*, 26 October 1861.

To Sibley the recruits were still "green saplings bending to discipline" but would "make the best soldiers in the world."[33] The general went on to say that he was proud of the regiment, that it was an honor to address such a group, and that he, too, would take up the march westward in a few days. Upon bidding the regiment adieu, "three rousing cheers were given for Gen. Sibley." Some felt their general would have been more effective as a speaker had his horse not been prone to prance during the speech.

Early on the morning of November 2, Tom Green's Fifth Regiment rode out of Camp Manassas for San Antonio. Their departure was much like that of the Fourth Regiment. Several of the community's leading ladies lined the streets of the town to wave handkerchiefs at the departing warriors. One young soldier felt the ladies were attempting to say "brave boys, victory awaits you."[34] Colonel Green took time to stop and talk to each company individually, telling the men that he and the Confederacy were counting on them.

The regiment camped for two days on Leon Creek outside of San Antonio and on the morning of November 10 set out on the long march for New Mexico. The general was there to say goodby to the regiment. Henry had ridden in a carriage to the outskirts of town where he reviewed the troops from a hill. He appeared proud as the entire regiment marched by in regular order. One soldier recorded that "The old Gen. pulled off his hat and gave a general salute."[35] The historian is tempted to question why Sibley had chosen to review the regiment from a carriage. Was he in ill health, or was he recovering from the previous night's festivities due to his fondness for alcohol? Perhaps Charlotte and the children accompanied the general for the memorable occasion. There appears little doubt that by 1861 Henry's health was bad. The trip to and from Richmond plus the problem of recruiting and equipping his brigade must have been exhausting. More tragic was the fact that by 1861 Henry had become an excessively heavy drinker.

Before the general could depart with his staff from San Antonio, an urgent plea for help came from the West. Colonel Baylor who had seized the Mesilla Valley in the southern part of New Mexico, which the Confederates were now calling the Territory of Arizona, had given

[33] Ibid., p. 16.
[34] Smith Diary, p. 155.
[35] Ibid.

up the idea of eating his Christmas dinner in Santa Fe and was preparing to fall back to Fort Bliss. Baylor informed Sibley that Colonel Edward R.S. Canby was preparing to invade the lower valley with twenty-five hundred men and a battery of artillery. Baylor, helpless against such a large force, was contemplating a retreat to Fort Quitman below El Paso or even to Fort Davis. Furthermore, Baylor was also convinced that General Edwin V. Sumner, Sibley's Mexican War antagonist, had landed at the port of Guaymas on the west coast of Mexico with two thousand men and would be moving across Mexico to attack him from the west. "Hurry up," Baylor wrote Sibley, "if you want a fight."[36]

The reported landing of a Union Army on the Pacific Coast of Mexico caused Sibley considerable consternation. A few days after the receipt of Baylor's urgent plea, he received another urgent letter from the West. Judge Josiah F. Crosby wrote that most of the merchants sympathetic to the Confederacy in the Franklin area were fleeing to the Mexican side of the river, fearing a Confederate retreat from the Mesilla Valley. Crosby was sure that Canby would be attacking in three columns. One column was reported to be moving downriver from Fort Craig and another across the arid Jornada del Muerto, a route that bypassed a hundred-mile bend in the Rio Grande. A third was reported to be moving westward from Fort Stanton to prevent any retreat by the Confederates. Crosby admitted that his information was based on hearsay. This, the Judge wrote, "seems to be a rather hazardous enterprise for a prudent man like Canby to embark on."[37] Crosby also informed Sibley that he had sent an express to Sonora to ascertain the validity of the debarkation of Union troops at Guaymas.

The urgency of Sibley's hurried arrival in the West was emphasized by a dispatch from Simeon Hart which arrived by the same mail as the letter from Crosby. Hart said that he was in the process of stockpiling ten thousand pounds of corn and three hundred thousand pounds of flour all of which had been purchased in Sonora. Hart was panic-stricken that the vital supplies, which he hoped would be ready for the Sibley Brigade upon its arrival at Fort Bliss, might fall into

[36] John R. Baylor to the Commanding Officer, C.S. Troops en route for Fort Bliss, 24 October 1861, O.R., I, IV: 128; Texas State Gazette, 16 November 1861.

[37] Josiah F. Crosby to H.H. Sibley, 27 October 1861, O.R., I, IV: 133.

Federal hands.[38] Sibley was counting on Hart's foodstuffs and the loss of which might easily mean disaster for his brigade. Sibley also learned that Baylor, from his forward post at Mesilla, was disenchanted with the Confederate high command. "I have petitioned time and again for reinforcements to prevent this disaster, to all of which a deaf ear has been turned," Baylor wrote from his adobe outpost at Doña Ana above Mesilla.[39] To Baylor there was no doubt he would have to "fall back and await the arrival of Brigadier General Sibley." The colonel had gone so far as to direct Hart to remove all commissary goods from Fort Bliss to Fort Quitman or further eastward to Fort Davis if necessary. The quick arrival of the Sibley Brigade thus became vital to continued Confederate successes in New Mexico and the far Southwest.

As Sibley hastened to join Baylor in the West, minor disciplinary problems arose in the brigade. In one case Private Robert Pinkney, a young recruit who, in an argument over some forage, threatened to knock a _____ out of the assistant quartermaster and even went as far as to have a "few rounds" with the officer.[40] Although the private could easily have been court-martialed, he was released without being severely punished.

Not far from San Antonio a recruit named Thomas N. Harvey killed a young private named James Tobin during a heated argument. After the army had reached Fort Bliss, Colonel Green convened a court martial which sentenced Harvey to be "shot to death with musketry." The condemned soldier, evidently unmoved by his fate, placed a small piece of white paper over his heart and asked every man in the firing squad to fire at the target. Harvey said that he did not fear death and did not care to live.[41] He was the only man of the Sibley Brigade to be executed during the entire Civil War.

By the time Sibley was preparing to join Baylor in the West most of the Brigade were well on their way to New Mexico. From San Antonio the overland trail led westward. One of the first settlements the brigade came to on the lower San Antonio Road was Castroville on the west bank of the Medina River. Here many of the soldiers re-

[38] Simeon Hart to H.H. Sibley, 27 October 1861, *O.R.*, I, IV: 134.

[39] John R. Baylor to Commander, Department of Texas, 25 October, 1861, *O.R.*, I, IV: 129. It was later learned that General Sumner had not landed at Guaymas and that Canby had no intentions of moving downriver from Fort Craig.

[40] Noel, p. 16.

[41] Ibid., pp. 16–17.

freshed themselves at the Vance Hotel, some attended church services, and others exchanged some of the commodities they had been issued in San Antonio. Some Alsatian immigrants were eager to trade butter, cheese, and milk for Condederate coffee.[42]

From Castroville the brigade continued westward to the Río Hondo and the small community of D'Hanis on the Río Seco. Here some of the Brigade's supplies began to run out despite the fact that the army was only a few days' march from San Antonio. Several men tried fishing in the muddied Río Seco. One squad feasted on a hawk they shot for breakfast.[43] From D'Hanis the trail led to the Río Frío and the small community of Sabinal. Here many men took time to write letters. A few troopers who had money spent the night at Kennedy's Public House in the village.

Across the Sabinal River the trail turned southwest across the Río Frío to the village of Uvalde. Although residents were mostly Unionists, the brigade was cheered by many townsmen. West of Uvalde the Rebels came to the Nueces River, a clear, appealing stream which drained the western portion of the Texas hill country. Here most of the brigade camped to wash their clothes. For the first time the soldiers were ordered to load their rifles as the brigade was now nearing Indian country. As the army continued westward into a more arid region, the men's inability to forage from the land became a serious problem. Foodstuffs were already scarce although the most difficult part of the overland trek lay ahead.

One day's march west of the Nueces a general court martial was called. Private John Quinn of Green's regiment had made the mistake of striking Captain Ira G. Killough. Quinn was sentenced to wear heavy irons for one month and to be tied to the rear of a baggage wagon.[44] Forty miles west of Uvalde the army came to Fort Clark, a well-built western outpost on Las Moras Creek. Here the brigade was greeted by a company of Baylor's Second Texas Mounted Rifles. Company E of Green's Regiment was temporarily left at the fort because several troopers had contracted measles. Within a month twelve men had died of the "loathsome and painful disease."[45]

---

[42] Julius Giesecke, "The Diary of Julius Giesecke, 1861–1862," *Military History of Texas*, trans. Oscar Haas, 3 (Winter, 1963), 229.

[43] Howell Diary, 12 November 1861.

[44] Smith Diary, p. 116.

[45] Noel, p. 18.

Many of Sibley's soldiers were amazed at the "mountains" and "hills" of southwest Texas. Little did they know that the "mountains" and "hills" were mere mounds compared to what they would painfully encounter in New Mexico.

From Fort Clark the route continued westward to San Felipe Springs near the Rio Grande. Here many of the soldiers were astounded "to see a body of water at least thirty feet deep."[46] A few took time to make the four-mile ride to the larger Rio Grande. At San Felipe Springs the various regiments were split into squadrons in order to better cope with the lack of forage and water on the trail ahead. Beyond the springs the country became more desolate. One soldier lamented that his squadron rode "through a country where mesquite could not grow, cactus were drying up, and grass and such good things were not to be thought of." Many used "weeds and roots for wood."[47] From the Rio Grande the trail turned up the Devil's River to Camp Hudson. Established in 1857 on the right bank of the Devil's River, Camp Hudson had been built to protect travelers along the San Antonio-El Paso road. Passing "high rocky mountains" the army continued to the headwaters on the Devil's River at Beaver Lake. So winding was the trail that the men crossed the Devil's River as many as seven times in eight miles. Now in Indian country a strong guard had to be posted to protect the regiment's small beef herd and their baggage train which the men referred to as "Mexico" since most of the teamsters were Mexican-Texans or Tejanos from San Antonio. While on the Devil's River, several javelina were shot, the meat proving to be a tasteful delight to the men who were now subsisting on meager rations.

From Beaver Lake the Sibley Brigade struck westward toward the Pecos River. For the forty-four miles to Howard Springs, 290 miles from San Antonio, no water could be found. Still fearful of Indian attack many men were now required to guard not only the beef herd but also the horses.

The next rest came at Fort Lancaster just east of the Pecos River on Live Oak Creek. Isolated Fort Lancaster, built like Camp Hudson to guard the San Antonio-El Paso Road, had never been a favorite of the army.

At Fort Lancaster an amusing incident occurred. The commanding

---

[46] Wright, p. 4.
[47] Giesecke Diary, p. 230.

officer of the post had his men appear in dress uniform in honor of the visiting general. The over-zealous Sibley decided to drill the men in person. The general was in the process of marching the company to and fro when he gave the order "file left." The company, unable to hear the command, continued eastward out of the fort and even over a nearby hill. Calmly sitting atop his horse, Sibley, making no effort to stop the confused men but turning instead to an aide, remarked, "Gone to Hell!" and reined his horse toward the west.[48]

Reaching the Pecos River, which one young Rebel described as a "narrow, deep, muddy and a crooked stream," the men of the Sibley Brigade found the red waters to be salty and unfit for drinking.[49] The murky water was good only to make coffee. Proceeding up the Pecos, the men saw their first pronghorn antelope, which stared at the invaders from afar. The army also passed several prairie dog towns. One soldier was amazed at how the strange little creatures "would come to the top of the holes and bark."

Leaving the Pecos River, the brigade turned west to Escondido Springs. Provisions continued to run short, and many were now subsisting entirely on "beef and wormy crackers."[50] Still, morale remained high. They were conquering heroes off to New Mexico to right the wrongs inflicted on their beloved South.

Beyond the Pecos the overland trail became more difficult. A severe drought had turned the west Texas desert to powder and several squadrons almost suffocated in the stifling dust. Freezing temperatures were common in the Trans-Pecos, and each night seemed colder than the preceding one.

Next the army came to Fort Stockton. Located at Comanche Springs on Comanche Creek, Fort Stockton had been established in 1859 to guard commerce along the San Antonio-El Paso road. Owing to the lack of timber and stone in the desert, most of the buildings at the fort were constructed of adobe. Here the men were given time to rest, to wash their clothes, and to write letters to loved ones back home.

Logistics remained Sibley's greatest problem. A few young Confederates were lucky enough to receive presents of clothing and food-

---

[48] W.W. Heartsill, *Fourteen Hundred and 91 Days in the Confederate Army* (Marshall, 1876), 49.

[49] Howell Diary, 3 December 1861.

[50] Ibid.

stuffs from friends, relatives, or Confederate sympathizers.[51] The main
Rebel supply train was either too far ahead or too far behind to supply
most squadrons. Fort Stockton was, nevertheless, a welcome sight.
One soldier wrote that he was impressed with the "articles" of "civilization" he saw at the fort.[52]

Nine miles west of Fort Stockton the men came to Leon Springs.
Although the topsoil was white with alkaline, the water was good and
sweet. The troopers were now in a vast sage and greasewood desert,
and their provisions continued short or non-existent. Still, they did
not complain but continued their march. For two days the men made
a dry camp. Finally they entered the colorful Davis Mountains, which
for days had appeared to the soldiers as only a mirage on the western
horizon. Here the men were impressed to see trees for the first time
since leaving Fort Clark. Many in Sibley's Brigade thought Wild Rose
Pass in Limpia Canyon to be one of the most picturesque spots in all
of Texas. Yuccas and other desert vegetation helped to produce a serene scene. A clear water creek in Limpia Canyon was a pleasing sight.
Groves of live oak trees in the canyon bottoms provided them with
shade and wood. No doubt the mountains gave the army a sense of
relief after the fatiguing march across the desert from Fort Stockton.

Fort Davis had been established in 1854 at the mouth of a small
canyon about one-half mile south of Limpia Creek. Named after Jefferson Davis, the post was one of the most picturesque in the west
and was a favorite resting spot for travelers along the route to El Paso
and California. The Fourth Regiment spent two days at the fort where
many in the regiment, including Colonel Reily, took the opportunity
to get "tight." Others were more interested in purchasing badly
needed clothing from the post sutler. Some were excited by seeing
their first women since leaving Uvalde. Tired and bored of the long
western trek, one soldier wrote: "When I go to another war, I'm goin'
to it in a way I can get to it quicker than I can to this 'ere one."[53] While
at Fort Davis Colonel Reily received alarming rumors that the Federal forces in New Mexico had been reinforced by several thousand.
His enthusiasm for battle was not deterred; the colonel wrote that his
men were fully prepared "to face fire and steel."[54]

[51]*San Antonio Weekly Herald*, 14 December 1861.
[52] Ibid.
[53] Ibid.
[54] *Texas State Gazette*, 14 December 1861.

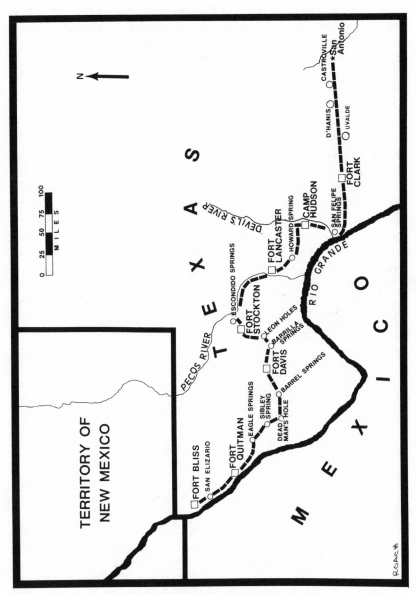

ROUTE OF THE SIBLEY BRIGADE
FROM SAN ANTONIO TO FORT BLISS

From Fort Davis the road led through the mountains to Barrel Springs, a watering spot on the edge of the desert. Even here water was scarce, especially for the late-arriving companies since most of the water had already been consumed. To cross the desert as rapidly as possible, many companies were forced to march until midnight. Despite their fatigue the men stood the ordeal "bravely and cheerfully."[55] One company while making a night march got lost and completely missed the springs and was forced to make a dry camp in the desert. Beyond Barrel Springs the brigade came to Dead Man's Hole, another desert watering spot. From here the Fourth Regiment continued along the main stage route northwest to Van Horn's Wells and Eagle Springs. Sibley instead decided to follow a new route blazed by the Fifth Regiment much farther to the south. The new trail, he reasoned, was not only shorter but provided better grass and ample water. Eight miles from Dead Man's Hole the army came to a watering hole they called Brigade Springs. Forty-five miles to the west the troops came to another small seepage which someone in the brigade named Sibley Springs. The new trail was not only rough, but the men were slowed by having to keep a constant vigil for raiding Mescalero Apache who for decades had made the mountains of west Texas their home. Onward the Sibley Brigade trudged "through heat and cold, wet weather and dry, over mountains and hills, vallies and steril plains, and through a hostile Indian country."[56]

Many men in the army were amazed by the abundance of wild game in the desert, especially deer and antelope. The curious animals stared at the advancing army from afar, but wisely did not advance within shooting range. The troops also noted large numbers of mustangs which roamed the wide-open expanses of west Texas.

The army reached the Rio Grande at Fort Quitman. Located on the left bank of the Rio Grande about seventy miles below El Paso, Fort Quitman was one of the least desirable forts in the entire west. The worst part of the march was now over, and the men once again took time to wash their clothes, write letters home, and attend religious services. At the fort the troops were issued badly needed corn and hay for their hungry horses. Some corn was ground to make bread as most of the army was still without adequate provisions. Here many Tex-

[55] Ibid.
[56] Ibid., 18 January 1862.

ans spent their first wartime Christmas. One soldier wrote his family that December 25 in far west Texas was very different from Christmas back "home in olden days."[57]

From Fort Quitman the army followed the east bank of the Rio Grande to Fort Bliss at Franklin. A strong guard was posted at all times to prevent any of the men from deserting into Mexico. One company, however, was given a chance to visit the village of Guadalupe across the river in Mexico. The Confederates were not impressed since the small village was similar to those on the American side of the river, consisting of little more than mud and brush jacales. All remained quiet as the army continued up the Rio Grande Valley past the crumbling adobe villages of Socorro and Ysleta to Fort Bliss. The only excitement came when Colonel Green's slave fled into Mexico, taking the colonel's horse.

With two regiments on the road the commanding general, accompanied by his staff, had left San Antonio on November 18. Traveling faster than the slower moving regiments, Sibley sped across the deserts and mountains of west Texas. The general passed three squadrons of the Fifth Regiment at San Felipe Springs and the remainder of the regiment on the Devil's River. After giving the men several words of encouragement he continued west to Fort Lancaster. By December 5, he had reached Fort Davis and overtook the Fourth Regiment north of Fort Quitman. By December 14, 1861, he had set up Confederate headquarters at Fort Bliss.

Fort Bliss, built at Magoffinsville near the village of Franklin, was to become the launching place for Sibley's New Mexico campaign. From here the general issued all official orders and consolidated his army of Texans and a few local units into the "Army of New Mexico." It was also at Fort Bliss, five days before Christmas, 1861, that Sibley issued a far-reaching and moving proclamation to the citizens of the Territory of New Mexico. "By geographical position, by similarity of institutions, by commercial interests, and by future destinies New Mexico pertains to the Confederacy," Sibley told the New Mexicans.[58] The general made it clear that the Texans came as friends, not as enemies. The Army of New Mexico had come to liberate the

[57] Howell Diary, 25 December 1861.

[58] Proclamation of Brig. Gen. H.H. Sibley, Army of the Confederate States, to the People of New Mexico, 20 December 1861, *O.R.*, I, IV: 90; *Texas State Gazette*, 16 February 1862.

people "from the yoke of a military despotism erected by usurpers
upon the ruins of the former free institutions of the United States; to
insure and to revere their religion, and to restore their civil and political liberties."[59] To Sibley the present conflict was a wicked war
waged by the Federal Government upon the South. The United States
government was a failure as evidenced by the mere existence of his
Army of New Mexico. "Victory had crowned the arms of the Confederate States wherever an encounter worthy of being called a battle
had been joined." The general bragged of the battles of Bull Run,
Springfield, Lexington, Leesburg, Columbus, and the capture of the
Mesilla Valley.

He assured the New Mexicans that his army was ample to maintain control of the territory against any force the Union might throw
against him. He promised not to harm the natives as long as they followed their peaceful pursuits. "Your persons, your families, and your
property shall be secure and safe," Henry wrote. The general went on
to inform the citizens that "Such forage and supplies as my army shall
require will be purchased in open market and paid for at fair prices."[60]

At the same time Sibley warned the New Mexicans that if anyone
removed any property from the territory, such individuals would be
considered enemies of the Confederate States and would be dealt with
accordingly. The general asked those New Mexicans who has enlisted in the Union Army to throw down their arms and return to their
homes. "But persist in your service and you are lost," he warned.[61]
Sibley promised to respect the natives' religious, civil, and political
rights and to appoint a government for the territory made up of Spanish-Americans. He also made an appeal to any Confederate sympathizer who might still be in the Union Army. "To my old comrades
in arms, still in the ranks of the usurpers of their Government . . . I
appeal in the name of former friendship. Drop at once the arms which
degrade you into the tools of tyrants . . . and array yourself under the
colors of justice and freedom."[62] The Confederates were prepared to
welcome into their ranks anyone deserting the Federal Army.

From Fort Bliss, Sibley sent Confederate sympathizers northward
into the territory to distribute copies of the proclamation. For those

[59] Ibid.
[60] Ibid.
[61] Ibid.
[62] Ibid.

natives who could not read English, proclamations were also printed in Spanish. Few of the documents ever reached their intended recipients, as many fell into the hands of Federal officials.[63] Union commander Colonel Edward R.S. Canby and Territorial Governor Henry Connelly felt the proclamation would have little if any effect on the natives. Although a handful of Nuevo Mexicanos did flee the Union Army, their flight came not from Sibley's proclamation but from the natives' mistrust and lack of confidence in the Federal Army.

From Fort Bliss, Sibley also sent a critical diplomatic mission to the Mexican states of Chihuahua and Sonora. The general chose for this venture Colonel James Reily, commander of the Fourth Regiment. Sibley, aware that Mexico was plagued by French imperialistic intervention and torn by internal strife and anarchy, intended to take advantage of the situation. First, Colonel Reily would ride south to Ciudad Chihuahua to confer with the governor of Chihuahua.[64] From the capital he would return to join the Army of New Mexico before going on to Sonora. Sibley, in sending a diplomatic mission to Chihuahua and Sonora, had neither time nor desire to consult with the Confederate Department of State. His critical and sensitive diplomatic initiatives appear to have been entirely of his own doing. Long had such independence and individualism characterized his military career.

Colonel Reily was to discuss three major points with the Mexican governors. First, he was to obtain permission for the Texans to buy supplies in northern Mexico. Second, Sibley was anxious to find out the truth behind the rumor that the Lincoln government had obtained permission to ship munitions and troops across northern Mexico for an attack on Confederate Arizona. Third, the general was interested in completing an argeement with Chihuahua and Sonora by which troops of the Confederate Army would be permitted to cross the international boundary into Mexico in "hot pursuit" of hostile Indians. Sibley was also interested in persuading the governor of Chihuahua to remit the duties paid by Confederate sympathizers in the Mesilla Valley and Franklin who had taken their goods across the river into Mexico.

Reily, accompanied by Captain Joseph Edward Dwyer and six Mex-

[63] Hall, *Sibley's New Mexico Campaign*, p. 47.
[64] *Texas State Gazette*, 15 February 1862.

icans, left Fort Bliss on January 2, 1862, for the three hundred mile trip to Ciudad Chihuahua. Crossing the Chihuahua Desert in six days, his party arrived in the capital on Janaury 8. Although delayed slightly by Governor Luis Terrazas' insistence that Sibley's requests be translated into Spanish, Reily was finally able to meet with the governor.[65] In regard to the rumored treaty with the Federal government, Terrazas denied that such an agreement existed, and informed Reily that only the Mexican Congress could negotiate such a treaty and that such an arrangement had never been proposed. On another point Reily told the governor that the concept of "hot pursuit" was an accepted legal principle with numerous international precedents. Governor Terrazas refused to accept the idea.

With respect to Confederate agents buying supplies in Chihuahua, the governor gave assurances that he would not interfere with such purchases.[66] In fact, Confederate agents would be welcome. From Ciudad Chihuahua, Reily wrote Sibley that Governor Terrazas and the citizens of the Mexican city had treated his party amicably. He had been well received in Chihuahua not only by "the State officials, both civil and military, but by many leading citizens."[67] Reily told Sibley that Terrazas had even invited him into his private residence where the colonel was introduced to many of Chihuahua's more prominent entrepreneurs.

After a twenty-one day, six hundred mile trip through the heart of Apache country, Reily returned safely to rejoin the Army of New Mexico. The colonel congratulated Sibley on having been instrumental in obtaining the first official recognition of the Confederate States by a foreign government. Reily's enthusiastic assertions were greatly exaggerated and not quite valid, since Governor Terrazas was only governor of Chihuahua and not president of Mexico.[68] Reily, in reality, had only completed an agreement with a foreign agent. Nevertheless, Sibley appeared overjoyed with Reily's apparent success.

Four weeks after Reily had rejoined the Army of New Mexico, Sibley decided to dispatch him to meet with the governor of Sonora, Ig-

[65] James Reily to H.H. Sibley, 20 January 1862, *O.R.*, I, IV: 173.

[66] Louis Terrazas to H.H. Sibley, 11 January 1862, *O.R.*, I, IV: 172.

[67] James Reily to H.H. Sibley, 20 January 1862, *O.R.*, I, IV, p. 171.

[68] Martin Hardwick Hall, "Colonel James Reily's Diplomatic Missions to Chihuahua and Sonora," *New Mexico Historical Review*, 31 (July 1956), 232–45. This article explores in depth the reasons for and the results of Colonel Reily's mission.

nacio Pesqueíra. The colonel's route to the Sonoran capital of Ures took him westward to Tucson in the southern part of Confederate Arizona. Accompanying Reily to Tucson were Captain Sherod Hunter and a company of Confederates which had been recruited in the Mesilla Valley known as the Arizona Rangers. The unit consisted of 105 well-armed men. After a tiring march through several days of pouring wintry rain, the small force arrived in Tucson on February 28, 1862, to be greeted by the Confederate sympathizers of the town. Colonel Reily reached Tucson the following day. Upon his arrival "the Confederate flag was raised in town with some ceremony" at which time the colonel delivered an enthusiastic speech to the citizenry gathered in the village plaza.[69] Colonel Reily was also welcomed to Tucson by Sylvester Mowry, owner of a large silver mine in the area. Mowry had written Sibley giving information on rumored Federal troop movements from Fort Yuma and California and asking for an "efficient exterminating campaign against the Apaches."[70]

For more than two months Captain Hunter continued to occupy Tucson. On April 15, a small Confederate force of eight scouts rode northwest from Tucson to gather information on the reported approach of a Federal force from Fort Yuma. Forty miles out of Tucson in the barren and snake infested desert at Picacho Pass the Rebels met a similar Union reconnaissance. A fierce fire fight ensued. In this, the most western of all Civil War "battles," three Federal soldiers were killed while three Confederates were captured.

While Reily was on his way to Ures, at that time capital of Sonora, he stopped in the town of Hermosillo where he found Governor Pesqueíra. In Ures Reily was given a copy of the San Francisco *Herald and Mirror* which revealed a proposed Federal plan to occupy the Sonoran port of Guaymas. To further complicate his mission, Union men in Hermosillo, whose presence was unknown to Reily, were able to learn not only the intentions of his visit but also, through a friend of Governor Pesqueíra, the specifics of Sibley's letter to the Mexican governor.[71]

The mission to Sonora was similar to the visit to Chihuahua. Reily

[69] Sherod Hunter to John R. Baylor, 5 April 1862, *O.R.*, I, IX: 707.

[70] Constance Wynn Altshuler, "The Case of Sylvester Mowry: The Charge of Treason," *Arizona and the West* 15 (Spring, 1973), 73.

[71] Manuel Escalante to W.G. Moody, 4 April 1862, *O.R.*, I, L, Part I: 909; Hall, "Colonel Reily's Diplomatic Missions to Chihuahua and Sonora," pp. 238–39.

presented Pesqueíra with many of the requests that had been asked
of Governor Terrazas such as the right to purchase supplies and pursue hostile Indians. Reily later wrote John H. Reagan, a friend and
postmaster general of the Confederate States, that although his mission to Sonora had been "difficult and troublesome," he had "obtained the unlimited and unrestricted right to buy supplies in Sonora." Reily maintained that he had also been granted the right "to
establish a Confederate States depot at Guaymas,"[72] In his letter to
Reagan, the colonel reported that Governor Pesqueíra had admitted
negotiating an agreement with the Union Commander of the Department of the Pacific, Brigadier-General George Wright, to occupy
Guaymas with a Union Army. Reily purportedly had persuaded Pesqueíra to negate the agreement. The colonel boasted that his missions to Sonora and Chihuahua, in which he had traveled over fourteen hundred miles in sixty-one days, had been a tremendous success.
In fact he was so proud of his alleged successes in Mexico that he offered his services as Confederate diplomat to either Peru or Chile.
Unknown to Reily, however, Governor Pesqueíra was already telling
Union commander General Wright that any movement of Confederates into Sonora, regardless of motivation, would "be considered as
an invasion by force of arms."[73]

While Reily was in Mexico, Sibley had issued a general order
thanking his Army of New Mexico for its "patience, fortitude, and
good conduct" and congratulating the men on their ability to "make
a successful and rapid march of seven hundred miles in mid-winter
. . . through a country entirely devoid of resources."[74] In reference to
the trek across west Texas, equivalent to a march from Montgomery,
Alabama, to Richmond, Virginia, an army correspondent for the *Picayune* queried: "Is not this enough in itself to make veterans of
men?"[75]

With two regiments at Fort Bliss and a battalion of the Seventh

[72] James Reily to J.H. Reagan, 17 April 1862, John T. Pickett Papers, Domestic Correspondence of the Confederacy, Office of the Secretary of State, Manuscript Division,
Library of Congress.

[73] Ignacio Pesqueíra to George Wright, 29 August 1862, *O.R.*, I, L, Part I: 93. Reily's
report to Sibley of his mission to Sonora has yet to be found. For an overly optimistic
report on Reily's mission see: Houston *Tri-Weekly Telegraph*, 12 May 1862.

[74] *Mesilla Times*, 15 January 1862.

[75] *Daily Picayune*, 27 March 1862.

Regiment only ten days behind, Sibley was now prepared to move into the Mesilla Valley. The stage was set for the conquest of the Territory of New Mexico. Beyond New Mexico's poverty-plagued adobe villages lay the gold and silver mines of Colorado's snow-crowned Rockies. Farther west lay the golden slopes of the Sierra Nevada and California's priceless Pacific ports. The accomplishment of these ambitious objectives could make the New Mexico Campaign one of the most momentous of the war.[76] The author of the grandiose plan to leapfrog the Confederacy into a trans-continental power was the same general who was now preparing to lead his Army of New Mexico northward up the Rio Grande to crush the Federals who were busily preparing to meet his onslaught. Seventeen hundred miles west of Richmond and Washington, far from the blood stained fields of Bull Run, in the deserts and mountains of the American Southwest, the storm was gathering.

---

[76] W.H. Watford, "Confederate Western Ambitions," p. 161.

"At the command to charge, our men leaped over the sand bank, which had served as a good covering to them, and dashed over the open plain, thinly interspersed with cottonwood trees, upon the battery and infantry of the enemy in front, composed of United States Regulars and Denver City Volunteers, and in a most desperate charge and hand-to-hand conflict completely overwhelmed them, killing most of their gunners around their cannon and driving the infantry into the river. Never were doubled-barreled shot-guns and rifles used to better effect."

Thomas Green to A. M. Jackson, Camp Valverde, February 22, 1862.

"Onderdonk was shot through the mouth and his tongue nearly shot out. He pulled out a part of it which was hanging ragged to the edge of the tongue and cut it off with his knife."

Journal of A. B. Peticolas, Friday, February 21, 1862.

"For the first time, perhaps, on record batteries were charged and taken at the muzzle of double-barreled shot-guns, thus illustrating the spirit, valor, and invincible determination of Texas troops. Nobly have they emulated the fame of their San Jacinto ancestors."

H. H. Sibley to S. Cooper, Battleground of Valverde, February 22, 1863.

"Poor John breathed his last at a quarter to two this morning. He spoke not a word but died very easy. Hard indeed to die and be buried in such a country. I am left to bury John Naile. I get a nice black suit for the occasion and a nice coffin is furnished and with the Brass Band to escort his remains out of town, we bury him in the sand hills near Albuquerque."

Diary of William Randolph Howell, Albuquerque, Territory of New Mexico, Thursday, March 20, 1862.

Chapter IX

Bloody Valverde

Considering the vast distances over which they had marched and the shortage of supplies, it was almost a miracle that the Sibley Brigade had arrived at Fort Bliss. In retrospect it is possible to argue that the Army of New Mexico was doomed to failure before it marched north in the Winter of 1862. This was true partially because the Texans' problems were complicated by the fact that Baylor's Second Regiment of Mounted Rifles had consumed much of the forage and foodstuffs at Fort Bliss and in the Mesilla Valley. Furthermore, Crosby and Hart had failed to stockpile the badly needed supplies they had promised Sibley they could purchase in Mexico. Supply houses in Mexico and many of the merchants of the Mesilla Valley were refusing to sell anything for Confederate money. When winter descended on Fort Bliss, the newly arrived Texans found themselves without proper clothing, forage for their animals, or commissary supplies of any kind. The quartermaster of the army was without specie, Confederate credit was nonexistent, and the predicament facing the Rebel Army was indeed perilous.

The key to the success of the campaign lay with the seizure of massive amounts of arms, supplies, and foodstuffs. The capture of Federal supply depots at Albuquerque, Santa Fe, and Fort Union was thus critical. The optimistic Sibley had few qualms about his army's ability to survive with the capture of these posts.

The general spent the last few days of 1861 and the first weeks of 1862 at Fort Bliss preparing for his thrust into the Mesilla Valley and the contemplated attack on Fort Craig. While at Fort Bliss on the evening of January 11, the general personally mustered a portion of the Fifth Regiment after which the Confederates gathered to hear a speech by Lieutenant Thomas P. Ochiltree, the general's aide-de-camp and loyal subordinate. To celebrate the occasion, Sibley treated members of his personal guard to a "basket of champagne."[1]

On January 12 the general and his bodyguard rode nine miles up the Rio Grande Valley from Fort Bliss and camped in a cottonwood grove by the sandy banks of the river. The following day the general, in ill health, remained in camp while his escort continued northward. Later, riding into the heart of the Mesilla Valley, Henry was able to overtake his escort by the 14th.

After the march across the barren wastes of west Texas, the wheat fields of the green valley were a lovely sight. Such greenery was an overwhelming temptation for the horses and mules of the Army of New Mexico. Although Sibley and the officers of his Rebel Army did not condone such actions for fear of alienating the native population of the valley, many a hungry animal somehow strayed into the green fields. The same excuse was always given: "My horse got loose and I could not find him."[2] Usually the men of the Army of New Mexico were reprimanded for their actions and on rare occasions received a few days' extra duty. This did not "cover the damage to the poor Mexican," and such actions went a long way toward antagonizing the Spanish-speaking population of the valley.

Colonel William Steele, with half of his Seventh Regiment, was left behind to occupy and hold the Mesilla Valley while the main force of the Army of New Mexico moved north to conquer New Mexico. As the army pushed upriver, the weather turned cold. Although some Texans had tents, most slept in the open. Many found it more comfortable to sleep in a warm adobe house than under the stars. Frightened by the Confederates, many Mexican-American residents of the

---

[1] Smith Diary, p. 124.
[2] Wright, p. 7; Hall, *Sibley's New Mexico Campaign*, p. 56.

valley were crowded into one room of their houses or driven from their homes. Fearful of retaliation, the Mexican-Americans were unresisting and appeared outwardly "polite and accommodating." Their wrathful revenge, however, would be felt once the Confederates commenced their evacuation of the territory later in the year.

A serious problem facing the Army of New Mexico continued to be the hostility of the Mescalero Apache. Scarcely did a day go by that the raiding Indians did not steal or run off a few of the Confederates' horses. So daring were the Mescalero that they frequently committed depredations within short distances of Confederate camps. At Willow Bar below Fort Fillmore a band of Indians slipped into a Confederate camp and stole eighty mules. Sibley ordered Major Henry W. Raguet with Company A of the Fourth Regiment to pursue the Mescalero. Major Raguet trailed the Apache eastward into the rugged Organ Mountains. Arriving at St. Augustine Springs on the eastern slopes of the mountains, Raguet could find no sign of the hostile Indians, and the party began its retreat back across the desert to the Rio Grande. Out of water, the men suffered intensely. Horses, completely ridden down from the fatiguing march, began to collapse by the roadside. It was daylight of the following morning before the last man of the beleaguered and thirst-crazed party reached the Rio Grande and water. Most were "more dead than alive, more crazed than rational, for the want of both food and water."[3]

On January 15 Sibley and his guard proudly rode into the dusty streets of Mesilla, Baylor's capital of the Confederate Territory of Arizona, where the party remained for the evening. Baylor, having ridden northward with several companies of the Fifth Regiment, was not there to greet General Sibley, but the regimental band of the Second Texas Mounted Rifles was present to serenade the conquering general, his staff, and escort.

With a cold wind sweeping down the Rio Grande Valley, Sibley, still in ill health, rested at Mesilla the following day while his guards were vaccinated against smallpox. On January 17 the general, accompanied by his staff and escort, rode up the Mesilla Valley to the village of Doña Ana where a hospital had been established. Continuing northward the party arrived at Fort Thorn to see its first snowfall crowning the nearby mountains, a sight which served to remind

[3] Noel, p. 21.

General Sibley of difficult times in the not-too-distant past. Fort Thorn, on the right bank of the Rio Grande at the village of Santa Barbara, was to be Sibley's point of departure for his attack on Fort Craig. Fort Thorn, which had been built on the edge of an extensive marsh, had been abandoned in March 1859 because of its unhealthful location. Within the crumbling adobe walls of the post the general set up temporary quarters. Several men, some dying of smallpox and pneumonia, were left at the fort.

On January 14 Sibley ordered Lieutenant Colonel William R. Scurry with two companies to move north up the valley to drive in the Federal outpost at Cañada Alamosa, some thirty-two miles below Fort Craig. Here Captain Bethel Coopwood of Baylor's command had defeated a small Federal force in September 1861. Arriving at Cañada Alamosa, Colonel Scurry found the village occupied by a small contingent of Mexican-Americans, the regular Federal force having retreated northward. Most of the native Nuevo Mexicanos escaped to the secure environs of Fort Craig.

As Sibley planned for his advance against Fort Craig, Colonel Canby busily prepared for the onslaught he knew was imminent. From the beginning Canby had faced numerous problems in organizing an army to meet the Confederate advance. The Union commander's greatest challenge proved to be the apathy of the Spanish-speaking population of the territory. By February 21 Canby had 3,810 men assembled at Fort Craig of which only twelve hundred were regulars. The remainder were hastily recruited volunteers and militia. Most of the Nuevo Mexicanos were poorly trained, ill-equipped, and indifferent toward a war which was not of their making.[4] The natives were more interested in fighting Indians than the "Diablo Tejanos." Canby had attempted to recruit five regiments of volunteers, but only three had been raised by February 1862.

Another problem facing the Federals was the hostility of the Navajo and the Apache and, to a lesser degree, the Kiowa and Comanche. Once the Federals focused their attention on the Confederate advance the Indians appeared to intensify their raids into the Rio Grande and Pecos River valleys. In January 1862 the Territorial Legislature passed a resolution calling on Colonel Canby and Governor Henry

---

[4] Jerry Thompson, "Mexican Americans in the Civil War: The Battle of Valverde," *Texana*, 10 (No. 1, 1972), 1–19; Darlis A. Miller, "Hispanos and the Civil War in New Mexico: A Reconsideration," *New Mexico Historical Review* 54 (April 1979), 105–7.

Connelly to recruit more men including a contingent of Pueblo Indians to combat the growing Indian menace.

Another serious problem facing Canby was the lack of reliable intelligence about the advance of the Confederates. Ever since the Sibley Brigade had left San Antonio, Canby's information led him to believe that the main Confederate attack would be up the Pecos River. By advancing up the Pecos, the Texans could easily move on Fort Union or strike across Glorieta Pass to Santa Fe. To impede the advance of the Confederates, Canby on January 13, 1862, sent the Third Regiment of Volunteers to destroy everything below Hatch's Ranch on the Pecos.[5] Canby had no doubts that a small Rebel force would move up the Rio Grande against Fort Craig. This, he felt, would only be a feint with the real attack coming up the Pecos. As late as January 23, 1862, Canby still thought Sibley would move by the eastern route.[6] On January 24 scouts brought word to the Federal commander, who was then at Belén, that a large force of Confederates was moving north from the Mesilla Valley. Canby hurried south to prepare for the Rebel onslaught. The colonel arrived at Fort Craig on January 31 and was joined five days later by Connelly. The governor had halted for three days at Socorro to await the arrival of a column of militia, which he then accompanied southward.

On the morning after Connelly's arrival at Fort Craig, James "Paddy" Graydon's spy company of volunteers was able to verify that the main body of Sibley's Texans was indeed advancing. A decisive battle to determine the "fate of the territory" was in the making. "I have no fears as to the results here," Connelly confidently wrote Secretary of State William Seward from Fort Craig. "We will conquer the Texan forces, if not in the first battle, it will be done in the second or subsequent battles. We will overcome them."[7]

At Fort Thorn, Sibley eagerly continued to prepare for the attack against Fort Craig. The bad weather grew worse. Daily, more snow could be seen on the distant San Mateo, San Andrés, and Organ

[5] E.R.S. Canby to J.L. Donaldson, 13 January 1862, District of Santa Fe, New Mexico, L.R., R.G. 393.

[6] E.R.S. Canby to J.L. Donaldson, 23 January 1862, District of Santa Fe, New Mexico, L.R., R.G. 393.

[7] Henry Connelly to W.H. Seward, 6 February 1862, O.R., I, IX: 644. Also of interest is B.S. Roberts to E.R.S. Canby, 21 January 1862, Unregistered Letters Received, A.G.O., Dept. of New Mexico, R.G. 393.

Mountains. The cold weather brought intense suffering to the Confederates who were without sufficient blankets. Most of the Texans had never experienced such frigid temperatures.

While at Fort Thorn on January 29, Sibley dispatched two friendly Indians northward as spies. The general was hoping the Indians could reach Santa Fe and return with valuable information.[8]

With the arrival of Lieutenant Colonel John S. Sutton and a battalion of the Seventh Regiment in late January 1862, Sibley was at last prepared to move against Fort Craig. Early on the morning of February 7, Colonel Green's Fifth Regiment and Trevanion T. Teel's artillery set out as the advance guard of the Army of New Mexico.[9] For several days additional units continued to depart Fort Thorn to rendezvous with Green south of Fort Craig.

Reaching a spot some thirty-five miles south of the Union bastion, Green, fearing a Federal ambush, began to advance more cautiously. A strong advance guard was kept out, and the men were warned to keep their weapons loaded at all times. The Fourth Regiment, by slow, cautious marches, moved closer and closer to Fort Craig and an almost certain confrontation.

On February 10 the regiment was able to travel eight miles and camp in a cottonwood grove by the banks of the Rio Grande. Major Samuel A. Lockridge with three companies was sent out as a scout to determine if any Federals were advancing from Fort Craig. On February 11 the regiment moved eight miles closer to Fort Craig and once again camped by the river. Daily, the terrain became more broken and rugged. One soldier felt the area to be "one of the roughest countries" he had ever seen "or ever expected to see." "This territory will be a tax to any government under the shining sun of America," the young private wrote in his diary.[10]

By February 12 Green had advanced to within twenty miles of Fort Craig. That evening the regiment camped in battle formation with the artillery strategically located on a nearby hill overlooking the valley of the Rio Grande. Green expected an attack at any moment. The Federals were still safely behind the walls of Fort Craig. While in camp, Colonel Green was joined by Major Charles L. Pyron with three companies of the Second Regiment and one company of the Fourth.

[8] Smith Diary, p. 127. Also, Peticolas Diary, 27 February 1862, p. 55.
[9] Hall, *Sibley's New Mexico Campaign*, p. 74.
[10] Smith Diary, p. 133.

For the first time in several days, the men were given time to graze their horses and wash their clothes.[11] At eight o'clock on the morning of the thirteenth, the remainder of the Fourth Regiment and part of the Seventh came into camp. The Texans had ridden all night through a piercing hail storm.

As the Texans approached Fort Craig, scouts suddenly brought word that a large Federal force was in battle formation not more than a mile from the Rebel front. Bugles blared, and men raced about as the Confederates prepared for battle. "The men and captains all seemed cool and anxious for a fight," one recruit recalled. "Some were cursing the Yankees, some were careless and unconcerned, while others were almost praying for an attack."[12] The Federal force had been sent out only to ascertain the strength of the Confederates and quickly retreated back to Fort Craig, leaving the field to the Texans.

On the evening of February 12, an advance Rebel reconnaissance ran into a similar Federal force near Fort Craig and captured twenty-one New Mexico Volunteers. The following day the Confederates moved nine miles upriver to a point where the Texans could see for the first time the Stars and Stripes waving over the adobe walls of Fort Craig. Still, the Federals failed to come out and do battle. Canby was content to stay within the strong fortifications of the fort. On February 16 the Confederates remained in camp to await additional units of the Fourth and Seventh Regiments. Despite their lack of supplies, the Texans were in the best of moods and confident of victory. None was cockier than Major Lockridge, who bragged that he would "make his wife a shimmy" from the Federal banner waving over Fort Craig.[13] That same day General Sibley and his staff arrived in the Confederate camp. Sibley was determined to offer battle on the open plain south of the fort. Thus that afternoon a reconnaissance in force was pushed to within a mile of the post. Still, Canby refused to come out and fight. "The force of the enemy were kept well concealed in the bosque above the fort and within the walls," the general later wrote.[14]

Ever since leaving Fort Thorn, General Sibley had been quite ill. On the evening of the sixteenth with a battle appearing likely, Henry became so sick that he was forced to retire to his tent. Dr. Edward N.

[11] Ibid.
[12] Ibid., p. 134; Hall, *Sibley's New Mexico Campaign*, p. 75.
[13] Ibid.
[14] H.H. Sibley to S. Cooper, 4 May 1862, *O.R.*, I, IX: 507.

Covey, medical director for the Army of New Mexico, who had been keeping the general under close observation for sometime, was sent for. Sibley had complained in the morning of his illness, but with a battle appearing imminent he was determined to stay in the saddle. The general was also reported to have been drinking heavily. For several years his custom had been to resort to alcohol during illness. Dr. Covey, upon examining the commanding general, reported the illness to be colic accompanied by acute abdominal pains, causing nausea and vomiting. By the afternoon Henry was suffering "very violent and prolonged attacks."[15]

On the morning of February 17 Henry continued so violently ill that Dr. Covey found him "entirely too unwell for service." At the urging of his general staff, Sibley reluctantly turned command of the Army of New Mexico over to Colonel Green. For the next five days the general remained ill, all the time drinking heavily. Although he remained in his tent or in an ambulance during most of the time, he continued, through his staff, especially his Aide-de-Camp Lieutenant Ochiltree, to direct the general operations of the army. Nevertheless, rumors quickly spread through the Army of New Mexico of General Sibley's inebriation. The rumors, frequently misconstrued, did little to enhance his reputation. Many came to question not only the general's tactics but also his ability to command.

Despite his illness and heavy drinking, General Sibley was determined to force Canby into an open-field fight. Reconnaissances indicated what he had suspected—Fort Craig was too well fortified to be taken by assault.[16] Attack would be suicidal. Although most of his Texans were anxous for battle, Sibley's experiences had taught him a lesson; he did not want to make the same mistake that General Winfield Scott had made at Molino del Rey during the Mexican War, a mistake that had almost cost the brigadier general his life.

Both Sibley and Canby were determined to bring on a fight where they would have the maximum topographical advantage. Sibley was hoping for a fight on the open plain south of the fort where his cavalry could be used effectively. Canby was determined to fight so that his Volunteers and especially his twelve-hundred hastily recruited and ill-equipped militia would not have to maneuver under fire of the

[15] R.T. Brownrigg and Samuel Magoffin to H.H. Sibley, 27 November 1862, A.G.O., L.R. R.G. 109.

[16] H.H. Sibley to S. Cooper, 4 May 1862, O.R., I, IX: 507.

Confederates. Canby felt that Sibley, having spent considerable time in New Mexico, knew too well the inabilities of the Nuevo Mexicanos. But Canby refused to fight on the open plain thus forcing Sibley into a critical decision. He could always assault the fort, but this plan had already been ruled out. He could place cannon on the bluffs opposite Fort Craig and shell the Federals, hoping to force Canby into a fight. As another alternative he could bypass the fort and cut all supply lines to depots in the northern part of the territory.

With supplies running short, a crucial decision had to be made. A council of war was called during which it was decided to bypass the fort and recross the river at a small ford named Valverde some six miles upriver from the fort.[17] Perhaps such a maneuver would provoke Canby into the desired open-field fight.

In bypassing Fort Craig, Sibley was presented with a problem of having to traverse miles of unsuitable terrain. Near Fort Craig the valley of the Rio Grande is bounded on the east by a basaltic mesa, which rises from forty to eighty feet above the river. The pedregal is intersected by ridges of drifting sand and broken in places by protruding beds of lava. The mesa was accessible from Fort Craig in several places by bridle paths and in one place by a road suitable for artillery. Immediately opposite Fort Craig the pedregal projects into the valley, forming a small mesa which from a distance of one thousand yards overlooked the fort. This presented more of a problem to Canby than to Sibley. Two and one-half miles above the fort, the Mesa del Contadero, commonly called Black Mesa, rises to a height of three hundred feet. The mesa, the most distinctive landmark in the area, is about three miles long east and west and two miles in width north and south and protrudes several hundred yards into the valley.

Sibley later admitted that his decision to bypass Fort Craig was a gamble. "To do this involved . . . the hazardous necessity of crossing a treacherous stream in full view of the fort." There appears little doubt that Sibley was indeed undertaking a "hazardous" maneuver. Had Canby been fully aware of the Rebels' plans and courageous enough to throw his regulars against the Texans' rear guard while the Confederates were in the process of crossing the Rio Grande, serious damage could have been dealt the Army of New Mexico.

On February 17th and 18th a severe sandstorm swept into the cen-

[17] Ibid.

tral Rio Grande Valley, rendering both armies immobile, but before daybreak on the morning of February 19, Sibley's plan went into operation. The Texans retreated to the village of Paraje, about seven miles south of Fort Craig, and, without interruption, began crossing to the east bank. By three o'clock in the afternoon the entire command was across the river. The first and perhaps the most dangerous part of the Confederate plan had been completed. By evening the Confederates were safely in camp three miles above the Paraje Ford.

When Canby learned that the Confederates had successfully crossed the river, he conjectured that Sibley was hoping to move upriver to the mesa opposite the fort from which the Confederate light artillery could easily shell the Federals. To counter Sibley's move, Canby decided to send a force of volunteers across the river to occupy the bluff. On February 19th two regiments of Nuevo Mexicanos crossed the icy waters of the river and went into battle formation on the east bank. The volunteers remained in position during the frigid night of the nineteenth.

By sunup on the morning of February 20 the Army of New Mexico was already in the saddle and moving upriver from their camp above Paraje. Sibley calculated that the army should be able to reach the Valverde Ford before nightfall. The progress of the army was slowed by several sizeable arroyos and numerous sand hills. Many of the wagons in the baggage train sank to their axles in the deep sand as they proceeded up a broad ravine more than a mile in length. Many wagons had to be double and triple hitched. By afternoon it was obvious that the Confederates would not reach their goal. After only seven miles the Texans were forced to make a dry camp.

Upon discovering Sibley's plan, Canby moved to contest the Rebels. With his cavalry and Captain Alexander McRae's battery of artillery, Canby crossed the Rio Grande to join the two volunteer regiments who were still holding their position on the east bank. The Rebels had camped in an easily defensible location and were prepared for attack. Canby, intent upon feeling out the Confederates, ordered his army into battle position and threw out skirmishers. The maneuver quickly drew fire from the Rebel artillery. One regiment of volunteers was so panic-stricken by the bombardment that time was wasted restoring order in the Federal ranks.[18] As darkness crept over

[18] Ibid.

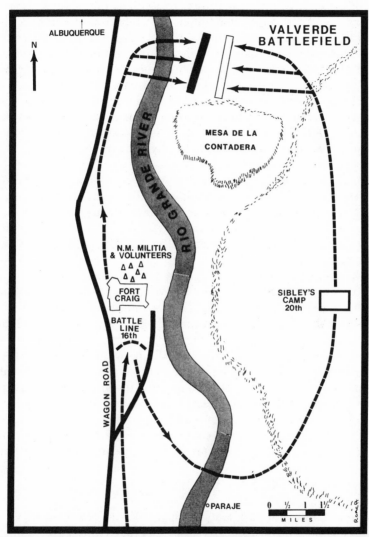

ALBUQUERQUE

N

VALVERDE
BATTLEFIELD

RIO GRANDE RIVER

MESA DE LA
CONTADERA

N.M. MILITIA
& VOLUNTEERS

FORT
CRAIG

SIBLEY'S
CAMP
20th

BATTLE
LINE
16th

WAGON ROAD

PARAJE

0   ½   1   1½
MILES

Romer

OPERATIONS NEAR FT. CRAIG, NEW MEXICO
February, 1862

the valley, Canby ordered a retreat. To cover his withdrawal he sent out a regiment of cavalry to threaten the Confederate right while the Federals withdrew to the security of Fort Craig, leaving a volunteer infantry regiment to hold the strategic bluff opposite the post. Sibley's Rebels spent the night in a dry camp in a mesquite grove less than four miles from the adobe confines of Fort Craig.

During the night the Federal soldiers standing on the walls of Fort Craig could easily count the Rebel campfires to the east across the river. With a stiff east wind blowing, the voices of the Texans could be heard distinctly across the peacefully flowing waters of the Rio Grande.[19]

During that night one of the most mirthful incidents of the entire Civil War occurred. Captain "Paddy" Graydon, who had recruited a spy company of volunteers from the village of Lemitar upriver from Fort Craig, decided to make a surprise raid on the Rebel camp. The daring thirty-one-year-old Graydon had his men fill two wooden boxes with twenty-four pound howitzer shells complete with fuses and attach the boxes to the backs of two aged mules. Graydon, with four of his men, waded the icy waters of the river and approached to within a short distance of Sibley's camp. Graydon assumed that the Union mules would make friends with some Confederate mules which he had observed in the Rebel column the preceding day. Fuses were ignited, and the mules were started at a gallop toward the sleeping Texans. Graydon and his men then took off at top speed toward the river and Fort Craig. The mules, instead of going toward the Rebel camp, headed back toward the fort, close on the conspirators' heels. The silence of the night was soon broken by exploding howitzer shells, which aroused the Confederate camp to possible attack. Graydon and his men entered Fort Craig uninjured but frightened and slightly embarrassed.[20]

---

[19] William A. Keleher, *Turmoil in New Mexico* (Santa Fe, 1952), 168–69; *Las Vegas Gazette*, 1 September 1877.

[20] George H. Pettis, "The Confederate Invasion of New Mexico and Arizona," *Battles and Leaders of the Civil War*, (New York, 1956), II: 110–11; Muster Rolls of James Graydon's Independent Spy Company, Adjutant General's Records, New Mexico State Archives, Santa Fe, New Mexico. The blue-eyed, brown-haired Graydon had been born at Enniskillen, Ireland, but had immigrated to the United States where he had enlisted in the First Dragoons at Baltimore, Maryland, in 1853, listing his age as twenty-two and his occupation as a shoemaker. Graydon was honorably discharged at Fort Buchanan in 1858 and settled in the Sonoita Valley where he ran the U.S. Boundary Hotel

After five days of serious illness, Sibley rose from his bed before daylight, on Friday, February 21, 1862. Although very weak, he was determined to direct the movements of the Army of New Mexico and, much against the advice of Dr. Covey, took to his saddle.

Daylight on the 21st brought some relief from the cold as the sun rose over the central Rio Grande Valley. The sky remained cloudy as the general hastily went over various orders with his aides and regimental commanders. The general became angered when it was reported that during the night more than one hundred of the Fourth Regiment's horses and mules had stampeded to the river in search of water. Most of the valuable animals had been captured by the Federals and taken into Fort Craig. Consequently, more than thirty wagons containing the mess kits, blankets, books, and papers of the Fourth Regiment had to be abandoned.

Sibley's plans called for Green's Fifth Regiment and a battalion of the Seventh under Lieutenant Colonel Sutton, accompanied by Captain Trevanion T. Teel's battery of artillery, to make a strong demonstration against Fort Craig from the east. It was hoped that this manuever would hold the Federals in place at the fort while the bulk of the Army of New Mexico made its way to Valverde Ford and water.

At daybreak Sibley sent Major Pyron with 180 men to reconnoiter a road to Valverde. Pyron rode north across the rough pedregal and sand hills, around the eastern extremities of Black Mesa, before turning west along the north edge of the mesa to the river. Within several hundred yards of the river, Pyron could see the Rio Grande before him. None of the enemy was in sight, and the major immediately sent a message to Sibley telling the general that he was approaching the river.[21] Pyron and his men proceeded leisurely to the river to water their horses. Reaching a small cottonwood grove near the ford, several of the Rebels commenced watering their horses when Pyron suddenly discovered a force of Federal cavalry at his front. Unknown to

---

advertising "a fine assortment of wines, liquors, cigars, and sardines." Graydon's importance to the Federal Army in New Mexico cannot be underestimated. At one time Graydon had ridden a complete circle around Baylor's Second Regiment in the Mesilla Valley. Jerry Thompson, "The Vulture Over the Carrion: Captain James 'Paddy' Graydon and the Civil War in the Territory of New Mexico," *Journal of Arizona History* 24 (Winter 1983).

[21] Charles L. Pyron to A.M. Jackson, 27 February 1862, *O.R.*, I, IX: 512; Houston *Tri-Weekly Telegraph*, 29 March 1862.

Sibley, Canby had dispatched a sizeable force to occupy the Valverde Ford. Without hesitation Major Pyron ordered an attack on the Federals. The Union force fled along the river with Pyron in hot pursuit. The Rebel major now found that he was confronting an even larger Federal force. He ordered the Texans to take cover in the sandy bottomland near a small bosque, which had at one time been the eastern bank of the Rio Grande. A fierce fire-fight erupted. With the sound of musketry echoing across the muddied waters of the Rio Grande, the Battle of Valverde had begun.

Canby, discovering Sibley's advance to the Valverde Ford at an early hour, had sent Colonel Benjamin S. Roberts with regular and volunteer cavalry to occupy that important crossing. Colonel Roberts, who had previously surveyed the Valverde Ford and who was convinced of its strategic importance, was followed by part of Captain Alexander McRae's battery of artillery and two twenty-four pounder howitzers.[22] At the same time Canby also sent Graydon's Independent Spy Company and five hundred mounted militia across the river to watch the movements of the Rebels, threaten Sibley's rear guard, and impede his progress.

On the east bank of the Rio Grande Major Pyron "gallantly held his ground" against overwhelming odds.[23] For two hours he refused to retreat, although the Federal artillery had now begun to shell the outnumbered Rebels.

In the march to Valverde, Major Henry W. Raguet with five companies of the Fourth Regiment had followed Pyron. Raguet, after a march of three miles, however, had been ordered to halt and await the arrival of Lieutenant Colonel William R. Scurry and the remainder of the Fourth Regiment. Scurry, in the confusion, was not aware that Pyron was in the advance and had sent out patrols to his front and flanks. Near Black Mesa Scurry had intercepted Pyron's message to Sibley that the road to Valverde was clear and, after uniting his command, proceeded toward the river at a leisurely pace. Shortly after receiving the first message, a second was received from Pyron that "large masses of the enemy were in his front and threatening an attack."[24] Scurry, feeling that Pyron might easily be overrun, raced for Valverde as fast as his regiment's horses would carry the anxious

[22] Benjamin S. Roberts to William J.L. Nicodemus, 23 February 1862, O.R., I, IX: 494.
[23] H.H. Sibley to S. Cooper, 4 May 1862, O.R., I, IX: 508.
[24] William R. Scurry to A.M. Jackson, 22 February 1862, O.R., I, IX: 513–14.

Texans. As the column approached Valverde, gunfire could easily be heard in the crisp morning air. Scurry quickly ordered his men to dismount and take a position on Pyron's right behind several small sandhills.

Shortly after ten o'clock the roar of cannon from upriver indicated to the intoxicated and ill Sibley that Canby was at last determined to fight. Sibley also realized to his dismay that Canby had anticipated his movements and that the Confederates had been partially outmaneuvered. A furious battle was in the offing.

On the east bank of the river, the arrival of a section of Teel's battery and Lieutenant Reily's howitzer battery helped to bolster the Rebel position. Three times the Rebels stormed the Valverde Ford, and three times they were driven off by the heavier Federal artillery. The sound of cannon and musketry reverberated among the barren cottonwood trees along the east bank of the river.

At nine o'clock, with the arrival of reinforcements, Colonel Roberts began an attempted envelopment of the Rebel right. Although no fords were known to exist for several miles above Valverde, Roberts sent his regulars across the low flowing waters of the Rio Grande. The men searched "step by step their foothold among quicksands and against the strong current of the Rio Grande up to their arms in its water."[25] The Federal maneuver forced Scurry to divide his command and lengthen the Confederate line upriver.

At ten o'clock the heavier Union artillery renewed its deadly bombardment of the Confederate line in the bosque. Within twenty minutes the Confederate batteries were replying with grape and shell. Although the Rebel shots were well directed, the heavier Union guns were getting the better of the duel. For two hours Captain McRae continued to pour a deadly fire into the Rebel positions in the bosque. By eleven o'clock it was evident to Colonel Scurry that the Rebels could no longer hold out against the devastating fire of the Federal guns. There was no alternative but to withdraw. Retreating from the bosque and the eastern bank of the riverbed in considerable disorder, the Texans were able to take refuge behind a low ridge of sandhills which paralleled the east bank of the river. In their flight the Texans almost forgot a valuable artillery piece that had been disabled when

[25] Benjamin S. Roberts to William J.L. Nicodemus, 23 February 1862, *O.R.*, I, IX: 495.

horses pulling the gun were killed. With considerable toil, the Rebels were able to carry the gun off by hand.

During the fierce artillery duel for control of Valverde, Colonel Roberts received a report that five hundred Confederate cavalry had crossed the river higher up and were threatening the Union rear. This report, although later found to be false, forced Roberts to order Colonel Christopher "Kit" Carson's regiment of volunteer cavalry to take a position in a bosque guarding the main road to Valverde on the west bank of the river.[26]

By eleven o'clock both Sibley and Canby were determined to reenforce their army with as many men as possible. Canby withdrew Colonel Miguel Pino's Regiment of Volunteers from the bluff opposite Fort Craig and, after leaving a regiment of militia, two companies of volunteers, and a small detachment of regulars at the ford, raced for Valverde.

Shortly before noon Captain Teel arrived on the river with two guns and immediately went into action. Teel was in a position not only to shell the Federal left but also the Union artillery across the river. In return eight of the heavier Union guns replied with "a furious cannonade."[27] So heavy was the Federal bombardment that several of Teel's men were killed or wounded. The captain was left with only five men to work two pieces. To complicate matters, a shell exploded under one of the Rebel pieces and started a grass fire. Despite the heavy Federal fire Teel continued to hold his position, even seizing a ramrod to assist his men in the furious chaos. Scurry, seeing the captain's predicament, ordered Lieutenant Reily's men to assist Teel. At this same time the remaining two guns of Teel's battery arrived and were placed in position on the Confederate left to assist the hard-pressed Pyron. Shortly before noon Major Lockridge arrived with three companies of the Fifth Regiment and was thrown into battle on the Rebel left.

By noon Sibley, who had remained in the Confederate rear, reported that the action was "becoming warm" and the battle general.[28] Furiously, Sibley's aides, especially Captain Ochiltree raced to and fro across the battlefield carrying the general's orders to the various Rebel commanders. Despite his illness Sibley was determined

[26] Ibid.
[27] William R. Scurry to A.M. Jackson, 22 February 1862, *O.R.*, I, IX: 514.
[28] H.H. Sibley to S. Cooper, 4 May 1862, *O.R.*, I, IX: 508.

to keep the saddle. Suffering from the colic, he continued to drink heavily. His inebriation did not enhance his reputation among those who came in contact with the general.

By midday the tide of battle appeared to be swinging in Canby's favor. Such large numbers of Federal reinforcements were arriving on the battlefield that both Lockridge and Raguet were urgently pleading for reinforcements. By twelve-thirty the Federals were so successful on the east bank that Canby ordered the Union artillery to the river. Safely across, the Federal guns opened an even more effective fire than before, spreading death and destruction among the faltering Rebels. One Confederate recalled how "shell and round shot and minie bullets came whistling in showers over our heads, bombs burst just behind and before, and trees were shattered and limbs began to fall."[29] The same soldier remembered seeing a comrade "shot through the mouth and his tongue nearly shot out." The wounded Texan pulled out a part of his tongue "which was hanging ragged to the edge . . . and cut it off with his knife."[30] The critical situation caused General Sibley to order more men to the front, leaving a token force to guard the Rebel supply train which was stretched out for several miles in the Confederate rear. With as much "speed as practicable," Colonel Green raced forward with eight companies and moved into position between Pyron on the left and Scurry on the right.[31] Three of Green's companies were sent to drive a Federal force from the rocky north face of Black Mesa. The Federals were threatening the Rebel left and the Confederate supply train.

At about one o'clock in the afternoon, Sibley had become so ill, exhausted, and drunk that he could no longer keep the saddle. He was so weakened that he almost fell from his horse several times. Retiring to an ambulance in the Confederate rear, Henry relinquished command of the Army of New Mexico and ordered his aides to report to Colonel Green.[32]

[29] Don E. Alberts, ed., *Rebels on the Rio Grande: The Civil War Journal of A.B. Peticolas* (Albuquerque, 1984), 44.

[30] Ibid. The wounded soldier, Private William H. Onderdonk, Company C of the Fourth Regiment, was taken to the hospital at Socorro where he recovered from his wounds. Martin H. Hall, *The Confederate Army of New Mexico* (Austin, 1978), 79.

[31] Thomas Green to A.M. Jackson, 22 February 1862, *O.R.*, I, IX: 519.

[32] H.H. Sibley to S. Cooper, 22 February 1862, *O.R.*, I, IX: 506; H.H. Sibley to S. Cooper, 4 May 1862, *O.R.*, I, IX: 508; *Texas State Gazette*, 22 March, 5 April 1862.

All along the line the Federals continued to pour a devastating rifle and cannon fire into the Rebel lines. On the Rebel right Captain Willis L. Lang of the Lancers launched a gallant and most courageous attack on the Union line. Scurry and Lang had noticed that the extreme Federal left was composed of individuals in gray uniforms whom the two Rebel officers may have thought were native Nuevo Mexicanos. Knowing the nature and inexperience of the natives, the Texans, with "audacity and desperation," launched a furious attack on the Federal line.[33] With their lances and red pennants gleaming in the wintry air, the Lancers made what Green called "one of the most gallant and furious charges . . . of light troops . . . in the annals of battle."[34] The Texans had charged a company of Colorado Volunteers who had been hastily recruited and hurried south from Denver. The Coloradoans held their fire until the Lancers were within a few yards of the Federal line and then fired a deadly volley into the charging Rebels.

The proud and brave Texans, in Green's words, were "decimated." In the suicidal attack, Captain Lang was so severely wounded that he later committed suicide in a fit of depression at the Confederate hospital at Socorro. Lieutenant Demetrius M. Bass, Lang's second in command, was wounded seven times in the wild charge and also died in the hospital at Socorro. The Lancers, Company B of the Fifth Regiment, suffered a greater loss of life than any other company in the Army of New Mexico. Their courage and sacrifice had not gone for naught, for the Federal left had been lured to within easy firing distance of the Confederate right. A raking Rebel small-arms fire and a devastating bombardment from two of Teel's guns caused the Federal line to break and retreat.

On the Confederate left the Federal artillery continued to pound the Rebel positions with a fulminating cannonade that echoed up and down the valley. With no reinforcements available and the Federal guns continuing to take their toll, Lockridge and Raguet were left little choice but to withdraw. The artillery and the wounded were first taken to the rear and then the retreat was carried out by companies. Safely behind the low ridge of sandhills which ran parallel to the river, about one hundred yards behind their previous position, the Rebels now occupied ground "of great natural strength."[35] The retreat

---

[33] Benjamin S. Roberts to William J.L. Nicodemus, 23 February 1862, *O.R.*, I, IX: 495.
[34] Thomas Green to A.M. Jackson, 22 February 1862, *O.R.*, I, IX: 519.
[35] Ed. R.S. Canby to Adjutant-General of the Army, 1 March 1862, *O.R.*, I, IX: 490.

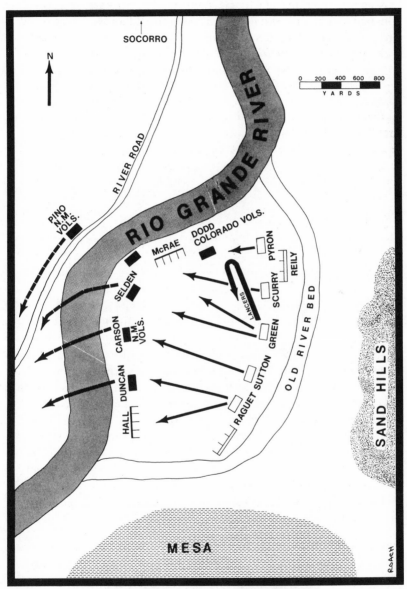

BATTLE OF VALVERDE
February 21, 1862

brought a temporary lull to the Valverde fighting. After five hours of constant combat, the fatigued men, both Federal and Rebel, were given a few precious minutes to rest. In the Union ranks the men ate lunch and replenished their ammunition supply.

A few minutes after three in the afternoon, Colonel Canby arrived on the battlefield to the enthusiastic cheers of his men. Being apprised of the situation, the colonel contemplated a direct frontal attack on the Rebel line but decided such an assault would result in a "great loss" of life and would be of "doubtful results."[36] Canby instead decided to advance his right and center while using his left as a pivot, thus forcing the Rebel left. He hoped that this envelopment would turn the tide of battle. To reinforce his army, Canby ordered Carson's regiment of volunteers across the river.

By mid-afternoon the Union batteries were once again bombarding the Confederate line. The heaviest fire of the day was opened against Lockridge on the Confederate left. With Sutton, who had been guarding the supply train, arriving on the scene with four companies, Green rushed the men to the front to support Lockridge. The Federals opened "upon us a tremendous fire of round shot, grape, and shell," Green later wrote.[37] Sibley, although flat on his back in an ambulance, was appraised of the situation. He concluded that the only way the battle could be won was by a direct and daring frontal attack. The general's orders were hastily relayed by Lieutenant Ochiltree to Green.[38] Colonel Green formulating the particulars of the Rebel plan, decided that the main thrust of the Confederate attack should be against the Federal artillery which was continuing to take a deadly toll in the Rebel ranks. Concealed by the sandhills, Green set about preparing for the crucial attack. "Having the most unbounded confidence in the courage of our troops, I ordered a charge on their battery," Green wrote.[39]

The most critical point in the Battle of Valverde was at hand. One thousand men, with the command of "up boys and at them," jumped over the sandhills and charged the Federal line.[40] "Unmindful of the driving storm of grape and canister and musketry sent hurling around

[36] Ibid.

[37] Thomas Green to A.M. Jackson, 22 February 1862, *O.R.*, I, IX: 519.

[38] W.R. Scurry to A.M. Jackson, 22 February 1862, *O.R.*, I, IX: 515.

[39] Thomas Green to A.M. Jackson, 22 February 1862, *O.R.*, I, IX: 519.

[40] W.R. Scurry to A.M. Jackson, 22 February 1862, *O.R.*, I, IX: 515.

them," the Texans "dashed over the open plain thinly interspersed with cottonwood trees."[41]

On the Confederate left Raguet and his cavalry charged to within one hundred yards of the Federal battery before being driven off by a heavy fire from the enemy guns. With many of their horses killed, the Confederates fell back in confusion to the safety of the sandhills. Although the "gallant charge" had been characterized by "desperate valor" the Rebels paid a terrible price in killed and wounded. In pursuing the Texans, the Federals left a large gap in their center, a mistake that would cost Canby dearly.

At the same time that the Confederate left was in retreat, the Rebel charge on the right was to prove the decisive maneuver of the Battle of Valverde. Although McRae's battery poured a tremendous "fire of round shot, grape, and shell" into the on-rushing Texans, the Rebels fell upon the Union artillery with a hand-to-hand savagery rarely seen in the annals of American military history.[42] Canby and McRae, realizing their critical predicament, pleaded with several companies of the New Mexico Volunteers to save the battery. Many of the volunteers fled, however, as the Texans "with yells and ringing . . . shouts . . . dashed on and on."[43] Within eight minutes the Texans had overrun the Federal battery. McRae and one-half of his men, rather than retreat, died at their guns. Ironically, nine of the regulars who died in defense of McRae's battery were from Company G, Second United States Dragoons, Sibley's old regiment. McRae, bravely defending one of his guns, was said to have coolly emptied his pistol at the charging Texans before falling mortally wounded.

One Federal officer wrote of the Rebel charge: "On they came, without order, each man for himself, and the 'devil for the vanquished,' in true 'Ranger' style down to almost the muzzles of our guns."[44] To another Union officer, McRae's gallant but futile defense "illustrated a courage that will render the battle of Valverde memorable among the glories of American arms."[45] Of all the Federal offi-

[41] Ibid.; Thomas Green to A.M. Jackson, 22 February 1862, *O.R.*, I, IX: 520. Also, David B. Gracy, II, ed., "New Mexico Campaign Letters of Frank Starr, 1861–1862," *Texas Military History*, 3 (Fall, 1964), 173.

[42] Ibid.

[43] Ibid.

[44] Rodenbough, p. 240.

[45] Benjamin S. Roberts to William J.L. Nicodemus, 23 February 1862, *O.R.*, I, IX: 492.

cers who died in the Battle of Valverde, Canby was especially proud of McRae, a North Carolinian. "Pure in character, upright in conduct, devoted to his profession, and of a loyalty that was deaf to the seductions of family and friends, Captain McRae died, as he had lived, an example of the best and highest qualities that man can possess."[46] The furious onslaught had also cost the Rebels dearly. Colonel Sutton, who in Sibley's words "bravely led his men . . . to the cannon's mouth," fell twenty paces in front of the Federal guns.[47] Major Lockridge also fell mortally wounded at the "muzzle of the enemy's guns." Lockridge, "with heart of iron," had placed his hand on one of the captured cannons and proclaimed, "this is mine." He was instantly shot. A sergeant recalled hearing his last words: "Go on my boys, don't stop here."[48]

Although Canby threw a battalion at the Texans in hopes of recapturing the guns, the Rebels regrouped to stop the Federal counter attack. Canby blamed the loss of McRae's battery on the volunteers who refused to obey orders and fled from the field. The Nuevo Mexicanos in their panic had run through a battalion of regulars, causing some of the regulars to flee as well. To heighten the confusion, the Texans turned their captured guns on the retreating Federals.

With the Union line in disarray and snow lightly falling, other Union troops on the right fled for the river, many dropping their guns in their haste. Many of Canby's men were killed while attempting to cross the river. The slaughter was said to have been terrific. "Never were double-barreled shot-guns and rifles used to better effect," Green wrote.[49] In their haste to flee the oncharging Texans, the Federals abandoned a twenty-four pounder cannon in the river. With the Federals in flight Scurry, taking five cavalry companies, went in pursuit of Canby's frightened army. On reaching the west bank, the column was ordered to retreat. Within minutes the terrible sounds of battle had slackened, and all that could be heard was the eerie moans of the wounded easily audible above the smooth, bloodied waters of the Rio Grande. Many of the Nuevo Mexicanos, especially Pino's regiment, of which only one company had been persuaded to cross the river, was

[46] Ed. R.S. Canby to Adjutant-General of the Army, 1 March 1862, *O.R.*, I, IX: 492.

[47] H.H. Sibley to S. Cooper, 4 May 1862, *O.R.*, I, IX: 508.

[48] Peticolas Journal, 21 February 1862, p. 48.

[49] Thomas Green to A.M. Jackson, 22 February 1862, *O.R.*, I, IX: 520; *San Antonio Weekly Herald*, 22 March 1862; *Texas State Gazette*, 22 March 1862.

panic stricken and in total confusion. One group of volunteers even cut the mules from a supply wagon and fled to the mountains. "Our victory was complete," Green wrote. The fighting Colonel wrote the Austin *Texas State Gazette* that he had little doubt that Valverde was "the most brilliant victory that has been won during the war" and would long remain "a brilliant page in history."[50]

Before the Federals could reach the safety of Fort Craig, Canby sent a flag of truce to the Confederates. For two hours Sibley, who had resumed command at seven o'clock, thought the flag was "a proposition to surrender."[51] The general, who blamed his acceptance of the truce flag on an "old association," learned to his dismay that Canby was not offering to surrender but was asking for a cessation of hostilities to remove the Federal dead and wounded. Sibley was especially angry that the Federals used the opportunity to pick up and carry off a large number of small arms and remove the twenty-four pounder howitzer which had been abandoned in the river. Sibley was also angered that Canby's men also carried off a company flag and guidon from the Fifth Regiment which the Federals later claimed as trophies of war.

The Battle of Valverde had been won at a terrible cost. A Rebel private wrote of the scene: "The battlefield was a sad sight after the fighting had ceased—to see so many poor fellows lieing cold in death—horses dead and wounded and the whole seemed to be the abode of death itself."[52] Sibley had lost thirty-six killed and 150 wounded, roughly eight per cent of the Army of New Mexico. Heaviest hit was Green's regiment which had twenty killed and sixty-seven wounded. Federal casualties were even heavier, with sixty-eight men killed and 160 wounded while thirty-five were reported missing.[53] The heaviest Union loss of life was in McRae's Artillery Company. Colonel Canby, who claimed the Rebels outnumbered him three to one, blamed his defeat on the volunteers who refused to cross the river and support the left wing of the army. "Although defeated, my command is not

[50] *Texas State Gazette*, 5 April 1862.
[51] H.H. Sibley to S. Cooper, 4 May 1862, *O.R.*, I, IX: 508.
[52] Randolph Howell to W.S. Howell, 2 May 1862, Howell Papers.
[53] Thomas Green to A.M. Jackson, 22 February 1862, *O.R.*, I, IX: 521; Ed. R.S. Canby to the Adjutant-General of the Army, 1 March 1862, *O.R.*, I, IX: 493. A list of the Union casualties was printed in the *Santa Fe Weekly Gazette*, 10 May 1862. For Confederate losses see Hall, p. 102.

dispirited," Canby wrote.[54] Sibley attributed the Confederate victory to the individual gallantry of his Texans at close quarters: "For the first time, perhaps, on record batteries were charged and taken at the muzzle of double-barreled shot-guns, thus illustrating the spirit, valor, and invincible determination of Texas troops. Nobly have they emulated the fame of their San Jacinto ancestors."[55]

Well into the night of February 21 the grisly task of gathering the dead and wounded continued. In the bitter cold, fires were built at various places on the battlefield, and the wounded were brought to lie near the warmth. Often a wounded Federal soldier lay side by side with a wounded Confederate. The following day the Confederate dead were wrapped in blankets and buried in trenches dug in the bloody soil of Valverde. Gunfire echoing up the river from Fort Craig indicated that the Federals too were "burying many a poor soldier far from his relatives and the home of his youth."[56]

The Battle of Valverde was over. The Army of New Mexico had met the enemy and driven him from the field. Throughout the Lone Star State and across the South, the Confederate presses proudly heralded the glorious news from New Mexico.[57] Sibley, however, had won a battle, not a campaign.

[54] Ed. R.S. Canby to Adjutant-General of the Army, 1 March 1862, *O.R.*, I, IX: 492.

[55] H.H. Sibley to S. Cooper, 22 February 1862, *O.R.*, I, IX: 506.

[56] Howell Diary, 22 February 1862. For a sketch of the Confederate graves see: Peticolas, p. 50. A similar sketch can also be seen at the Daughters of the Confederacy Museum in Austin, Texas.

[57] The farther from the scene of combat the more exaggerated the facts became. For example, the *Charleston Mercury*, in reference to the Battle of Valverde, reported in headlines on 14 April 1862: "Grand Victory—Six Thousand Eight Hundred Prisoners Captured."

Chapter X

Glorieta and Retreat:
Hungry Soldiers in a
Desolate Land

Probably the biggest casualty of the Battle of Valverde was the reputation of General Sibley. By evening of the day of the battle, word had
already spread through the army of the general's drunkenness during
the day. Many of the soldiers, in the Texas tradition, had expected
their commander to lead them into battle; yet few in the Army of New
Mexico besides Sibley's aides had even seen their commander during
the day. This, plus the rumors of his inebriation and possible cowardice, did little to enhance the ability of the general to maintain re-
spectability among the rank and file. Besides the Army of New Mexico many in the Federal ranks had also been exposed to hearsay of
Sibley's heavy drinking. One Union soldier recorded that the Rebel
general was little more than "a walking whiskey keg."[1]

[1] Keleher, p. 201; Ralph E. Twitchell, *Leading Facts of New Mexico History* (Cedar
Rapids, 1912), II: 377; Robert Lee Kerby, *The Confederate Invasion of New Mexico and
Arizona, 1861–1862* (Los Angeles, 1958), 72.

Although the Army of New Mexico was severely crippled by Valverde, Sibley continued to express confidence that the prudent Canby
could be forced or coaxed into surrendering. No one was more confident than Colonel Green who bragged that the Army of New Mexico could "go anywhere and do anything."[2] During the night following the bloodbath the General had sent Captain Shannon and Colonel
Scurry into Fort Craig under a flag of truce to demand the surrender
of the post.[3] When Canby bluntly refused his ultimatum, Sibley was
forced into another critical strategic decision.

The general hastily called a council of war among his regimental
commanders and staff. He could order a full scale attack on Fort Craig
as some had suggested. Based on their observations inside the bastion
Shannon and Scurry cautioned the general that the fort was too well
fortified to be stormed and to do so would result in a disastrous loss
of life. One alternative would be to withdraw to the Mesilla Valley,
there to regroup; however, the Mesilla Valley, after six months of
Confederate occupation, was even more void of supplies than the Rio
Grande Valley above Fort Craig. Besides, a withdrawal down the river
would be interpreted by many in the army as admitting defeat, and
most of the officers, although jolted and battered by Valverde, would
tolerate no talk of retreat. Furthermore, Sibley's rapidly sinking reputation as a military commander would suffer further. A third alternative was to take the army north up the Rio Grande, seize supplies
at Albuquerque and Santa Fe, and mount an all out offensive against
Fort Union. Canby would be left isolated at Fort Craig.[4] Communications between Canby and the Federal outposts in the northern part
of the territory could easily be disrupted or halted. After more than
an hour of debate, the council of war adjourned. Orders went forth for
the Army of New Mexico to prepare immediately for a movement
northward. Sibley had decided not to attack the fort.

To move on Albuquerque and Santa Fe, while leaving a sizeable and
potentially dangerous army in his rear, was another of Sibley's dangerous gambles. In the end it was probably a mistake, but taking into
consideration the strong defenses of Fort Craig, he probably had no

---

[2] *Texas State Gazette,* 5 April 1862.

[3] H.H. Sibley to E.R.S. Canby, 22 February 1862, *O.R.,* I, IX: 632.

[4] H.H. Sibley to S. Cooper, 4 May 1862, *O.R.,* I, IX: 509; Howell Diary, 23 February
1862.

alternative. Yet to advance farther into a hostile land without adequate supplies was greatly limiting his chances for ultimate success.

To spearhead his northern advance Sibley chose Lieutenant-Colonel Henry McNeill, who with five companies of the Fifth Regiment and two pieces of artillery, was to occupy the village of Socorro, about thirty miles up the Rio Grande from Fort Craig.

As the advance guard of the Army of New Mexico moved up-river from Valverde, past several small Spanish American hamlets, one Confederate observed that "every little Mexican house had a white flag sticking upon the top."[5] The natives of the territory were reluctant to become involved in a bloody war which they did not identify with.

Colonel McNeill reached Socorro late in the evening of the 24th only to find the town occupied by three hundred Territorial Militia under the command of Colonel Nicolás Pino. The Federals were hoping to hold Socorro until all property north of the village which might be of any use to Sibley's Rebels could be either removed or destroyed. On the outskirts of town the Texans ran into a militia picket which offered only token resistance. Moving his small army into position on a small sandy mesa southwest of town, McNeill sent a detachment to cut communications upriver and to prevent any militia from escaping. A single cannon shot was enough to coax a large portion of the militia into deserting or going into hiding.

In Socorro, Charles Wesche, a member of Governor Connelly's staff and major in the First Regiment of Militia, raced about town urging the outmanned militia as well as several civilians to take up arms in "defense of their government and their homes." Don Pedro Baca, a local politico, flatly refused, telling Wesche that "the United States Government was a curse to the territory, and if the Texans take and keep possession of New Mexico, the change would only be for the better."[6]

At two o'clock on the morning of February 25 the Federals, realizing their situation to be hopeless, surrendered the town. Eight hours later Pino's Militia, now numbering less than 150, came forth to sur-

[5] Smith Diary, p. 135.
[6] Report of Charles E. Wesche, 24, 25 February 1862, Ritch Papers, Huntington Library, San Marino, California; Report of Charles E. Wesche, 5 May 1862, O.R., I, IX: 605.

render, take the oath of neutrality, and be paroled. Without a single casualty the surrender of Socorro was complete.

With 250 rifles and pistols taken from the militia, Sibley ordered the company of lancers which had fought so bravely at Valverde to be given the arms. Although most of the weapons were antiquated, the men were happy to receive the arms. Valverde had proven the use of lances to be suicidal.

When General Sibley arrived, it was decided to establish a hospital in Socorro for the Confederate sick and wounded. Because of a shortage of wagons and ambulances, it took several painful days for the Valverde casualties to arrive in town.

So critical was the lack of transportation that Sibley had the few tents in the Confederate Army cut up for litters. Many of the wounded were then carried on foot to the hospital at Socorro from the battlefield at Valverde. From four to six men were assigned to each wounded man. Under the guidance of Chief Surgeon E.N. Covey and his staff, over two hundred debilitated Confederates arrived at the Socorro hospital. While in Socorro General Sibley took time to visit the hospital twice a day. Captain Joseph D. Dwyer, inspector general, recalled that Sibley was "exceedingly kind to the sick and wounded soldiers."[7]

With the Army of New Mexico advancing northward up the river, Sibley decided to dismount Colonel Scurry's Fourth Regiment. The regiment, according to Sibley, had become "half foot and half mounted" since many of the men had lost their horses at Valverde. In hopes of making the entire army more efficient, Sibley asked the Fourth Regiment to turn over their mounts to the army quartermaster to be redistributed among the remaining regiments. Sibley wrote Richmond that the entire regiment agreed "without a dissenting voice." One soldier in the Fourth Regiment, on the other hand, confined to his diary that there was "considerable growling."[8]

Although the Rio Grande Valley may have appeared to the Army of New Mexico to be an oasis in a vast wasteland, it did not possess sufficient resources to sustain the Army of New Mexico for any length of time. Many men were already existing on half rations and in some instances, less. "There is great dissatisfaction among the soldiers,"

[7] Memorandum of Jos. E. Dwyer, n.d., L.R., A.G.O., R.G. 109.

[8] H.H. Sibley to S. Cooper, 4 May 1862, O.R., I, IX: 509; Ebenezer Hanna, "Diary of Ebenezer Hanna," Texas State Archives, p. 5.

one Rebel recorded.[9] So profound was the growing anger in the army that several officers in the Fifth Regiment held a parley and came to the conclusion that it would be foolish to continue the invasion. A private perhaps put it best when he wrote: "Starvation seems to stare us in the face. Nothing ahead to eat; an enemy behind and before us."[10] One Confederate remembered his anger at seeing the "officers, every one of them with great sacks of flour and sides of bacon, living high while the men are really suffering for something to eat."[11] The same soldier vividly recalled the lack of food in the army: "I never thought I would ever be so pressed by hunger as to ask for bread when I had no means of paying for it, but I have done it, and without shame too."[12]

The native Spanish-speaking population of the central Rio Grande Valley, probably even more than in any other area of the territory including the lower Mesilla Valley, was forced to suffer a tremendous economic loss as a result of the Confederate occupation. The village of Belén, on the west bank of the river, fifty-five miles north of Socorro, suffered the forceable seizure of thirteen horses, twenty-two mules, eighteen cows and five calves, thirty-six sheep, two bulls, two oxen, two hogs, two heifers, two burros, and forty-two chickens. The foraging and hungry Texans also pilfered three hundred and thirty-eight sacks of corn and one hundred and sixty sacks of flour, while their animals consumed fifty acres of beans and forty-five acres of fodder. The villagers also found themselves to be missing revolvers, carriages, saddles and bridles, brass kettles, blankets, two bundles of carpets, and a cart loaded with firewood. One house was burned to the ground while another home, complete with furniture and bedding, was destroyed.[13]

The Texans stripped the valley clean of anything that could be rid-

---

[9] Smith Diary, 27 February 1862, p. 136.

[10] Ibid., p. 137.

[11] Peticolas Journal, 1 March 1862, p. 56.

[12] Ibid., 5 March 1862, p. 61.

[13] Confederate Depredation Claims, March and April 1862, Adjutant General's Records, New Mexico State Archives, Santa Fe, New Mexico. For monetary gain some claims were exaggerated. Much of what happened to Belén also occurred to other towns and villages in the central valley including Pajarito, Valencia, Peralta, La Joya, Socorro, Sabinal, Lemitar, Bosque, Polvadera, Los Lunas, Los Chávez, Las Nutrias, Los Lentes, Albuquerque, and Santa Fe. The occupation of the valley by the Confederates, along with a series of floods, subsequently helped to produce much starvation in the area, especially in the village of Socorro.

den, harnessed, eaten, worn, or used in any other conceivable manner. Still the valley was so barren that frequently the men could not find sufficient wood for their fires and had to burn dried cow dung. The bone-chilling winter winds swept into the valley from the snow-crowned Magdalena, Manzano, and Sandía Mountains.

The commanding general of the Confederate Army was still optimistic as to the ultimate success of the campaign. No one in the Army of New Mexico knew the Territory of New Mexico as well as he, and Sibley knew that a large government supply depot awaited the Confederates at Albuquerque. Federal Captain Herbert M. Enos, assistant quartermaster who had been placed in charge of the Albuquerque depot, was determined, however, not to let the stores fall into the hands of Sibley's increasingly desperate Confederates. When Enos heard that a Rebel advance guard of two-hundred men was at Belén, thirty-five miles downriver from Albuquerque, and that another fifty Rebels had reached Los Lunas only twenty miles away, he decided to take action.

With only twelve regulars and a few militia and volunteers, Enos ordered all the valuable supplies to be loaded onto wagons and started for Santa Fe. At 6:30 a.m. on the morning of March 2, Enos gave orders to fire the entire depot containing the remaining supplies. "The destruction would have been complete had it not been for the great rush of Mexican men, women, and children, who had been up the whole night, waiting anxiously for an opportunity to gratify their insatiable desire for plunder," Enos later wrote.

When Sibley's Rebels rode into Albuquerque early that afternoon they found the smoldering embers of what had once been one of the largest depots in the territory. The only property that had not been fired or carried off consisted of small quantities of molasses, vinegar, soap, some candles, a few saddles, carpenters' tools, and office equipment.[14] The capture of the Albuquerque depot had been essential to Sibley's plans. The general was bitterly disappointed. The New Mexico campaign appeared to be on the verge of failure.

Shortly after the Confederates entered Albuquerque exciting news reached the general from the west. Richmond Gillespie, a Southern sympathizer, rode into town to report that the military post at Cu-

[14] J.L. Donaldson to G.R. Paul, 10 March 1862, *O.R.*, I, IX: 525–27; Herbert M. Enos to James L. Donaldson, 11 March 1862, *O.R.*, I, IX: 527–28.

bero, a Mexican village about sixty miles west of Albuquerque, had been secured by Confederate partisans. The pro-southerners, especially Dr. F. E. Kavenaugh, had forced Captain Francisco Aragon, commanding a company of New Mexico Volunteers at the post, to surrender without a fight.[15] Cubero was reported to contain valuable Commissary and ordinance stores as well as sixty rifles and three thousand rounds of ammunition. Captain Alfred S. Thurmond with twenty-five men was immediately dispatched to Cubero to transport the supplies to Albuquerque. Sibley's Rebels were also successful in capturing a Federal wagon train bound for Fort Craig at Carnuel Pass in the mountains about fifteen miles east of Albuquerque.

Sibley had been given a reprieve. With the supplies from Cubero arriving on the river and with goods salvaged from the Albuquerque depot, the Confederates now had supplies for three months.

As the general rode north toward Albuquerque, Manuel Armijo, a man of enormous energy but few scruples, who was also a wealthy merchant and influential politician in the territory, along with his brother Rafael, came forth to offer their assistance. In gratitude Sibley invited the brothers to accompany him to Albuquerque. It was agreed that the Otero Brothers' stores, reported to contain $200,000 in valuable merchandise, would be placed at the disposal of the Texan Army.

On the morning of March 8, 1862, Sibley rode triumphantly into Albuquerque to be greeted at the plaza by the roar of thirteen cannons and the raising of the Stars and Bars in the cold March breeze. Here he remained to set up temporary headquarters.

From the beginning one crucial element in the success of the campaign had been the support of a large portion of the Spanish speaking population of the territory. Despite massive desertions from the Federal ranks of large numbers of New Mexico Militia and Volunteers most of the native population remained apathetic or hostile toward the Confederate cause. From his headquarters in Albuquerque, Sibley again appealed to the people of New Mexico for their support. The general offered a general amnesty to all natives who had served in the Federal ranks providing they "lay aside their arms and return to their homes and avocations" within ten days. Sibley spoke of the "honesty and integrity" of his army and their "signal victory" at Valverde.[16]

---

[15] *Texas State Gazette,* 17 May 1862.

[16] Sallta Fe *Gazette,* 26 April 1862.

Despite his continuing effort at enticing the Spanish speaking population to the Southern cause, Sibley's second proclamation was no more effective than his first.

The Armijo Brothers were exceptions. Sibley would later place the blame for many of his misfortunes on the "ricos," or wealthy aristocrats of the territory. To Sibley the "ricos had been completely drained by the Federal powers." They had "become absolute followers" of the Union "for dear life and their invested dollars." "Politically they have no distinct sentiment or opinion," the general would later write.[17]

While in Albuquerque Colonel William R. Scurry, commanding the Fourth Regiment, desiring "to seek service in another and more congenial field," resigned his commission in disgust. Although "Dirty Shirt" Scurry, as his men called him, was adamant about his decision, Sibley did not act upon the resignation until October 1862, long after the conclusion of the campaign. In a letter written from Albuquerque in March Scurry predicted that "the campaign in this territory will be over before this application can be acted upon."[18]

No sooner had the Confederates occupied Albuquerque than Sibley sent an advance guard upriver to capture Santa Fe. Major Pyron, with seventy-five men, the eyes of the Army of New Mexico, accompanied by eleven Arizona Volunteers recruited from the Mesilla Valley, were soon in the saddle racing upriver for the territorial capital. On March 10 the Rebels rode peacefully into Santa Fe to be followed three days later by Major Pyron.

Santa Fe looked like a ghost town. The narrow streets of the once thriving commercial and political capital were deserted. The handful of Union soldiers that had occupied the town had fled through Glorieta Pass toward the safety of Fort Union. Most of the local natives, deathly frightened of the "Diablo Tejanos," were in hiding. Governor Connelly, too, had abandoned the Governor's Palace and fled with the Union troops across the mountains to Las Vegas. A company of brigands called the "Santa Fe Gamblers" did come forth to volunteer their services for the Confederacy.

Rampaging through town the Rebels discovered, much to their dismay, that no supplies were to be found. It was learned that one hun-

[17] H.H. Sibley to S. Cooper, 4 May 1862, *O.R.*, 1, IX: 511.

[18] W.R. Scurry to J.P. Benjamin, 14 March 1862, C.M.S.R. of William R. Scur y, A.G.O, R.G. 109.

dred and twenty wagons, containing $250,000 in supplies escorted by the retreating Santa Fe garrison, had set out for Fort Union only days earlier. Two Santa Fe warehouses containing a large supply of flour had been fired by the retreating Federals. The flagpole in the plaza in front of the Governor's Palace had been cut down to deter the Confederates from raising their banner. Within days a flagpole was erected and the Stars and Bars hoisted over the territorial capital, the second oldest town in the country.

The wives of several Federal officers had remained behind during the evacuation. The women included Louisa Canby, a close friend of General Sibley. Despite the fact that the wives had been provided with adequate food, many of the women feared for their lives. A large part of the native population had run wild through the town following the Federal retreat, plundering the principal commercial establishments. The Rebels were astonished to see the women greet them with an enthusiasm they had not anticipated.

Although the Pro-Union Santa Fe *Gazette* had stopped operations upon learning of the approach of the Confederate Army, the Rebels took control of the press and the following day commenced printing copies of Sibley's Albuquerque proclamation which were distributed to the town's citizenry.

Still at his headquarters in Albuquerque, Sibley continued to gather supplies and prepare for the final push against Fort Union, his major objective in the territory. To save badly needed grain for the army's horses and mules and to give his men time for rest and recuperation, Sibley ordered the bulk of his army eastward into the foothills of the Sandía and Manzano Mountains where good grass was reported to be plentiful. From Carnuel Pass high in the mountains Confederate spies could keep a close scrutiny on the road leading from Fort Craig to Fort Union. Sibley appeared apprehensive about Canby's forming a juncture with Federal forces from Fort Union.

One factor working against Sibley was the severe New Mexico winter which continued to impede the progress of the Army of New Mexico. During the second week of March the weather turned even worse. "The whole face of the earth was covered with snow," a soldier in the Fifth Regiment wrote.[19] Without any tents and little protection from the freezing weather, several soldiers died of pneu-

---

[19] Smith Diary, 12 March 1862, p. 138.

monia. One soldier vividly recorded the death of a comrade: "Poor John breathed his last at a quarter to two this morning. He spoke not a word but died very easy. I am left to bury John Naile. I get a nice black suit for the occasion and a nice coffin is furnished and with the brass band to escort his remains out of town. We bury him in the sand hills near Albuquerque."[20]

As the campaign began to falter, alcohol became a problem. From all indications General Sibley was not the only one in the Army of New Mexico to overindulge in the "ardent spirits." A private in the Fifth Regiment reported that the officers of his regiment were "drunk all the time, unfit for duty and incompetent to attend to their duty."[21]

By mid-March Sibley was at last prepared to move against Fort Union, gateway to the gold and silver laden slopes of Colorado. Four companies of the Fifth Regiment under the command of Major John S. Shropshire would reinforce Pyron in Santa Fe while Colonel Scurry, with the Fourth Regiment and a battalion of the Seventh, would proceed by way of Carnuel Pass and Tijeras Canyon to the village of Galisteo, about twenty miles south of Santa Fe; they would then join Pyron either at Santa Fe or where the Galisteo road met the Santa Fe Trail just west of Glorieta Pass and the entrance to Apache Canyon. "Being somewhat crippled in transportation," Sibley would hold Green's Fifth Regiment in the vicinity of Albuquerque to check any move that Canby might want to make from Fort Craig.[22]

While the general remained at headquarters in Albuquerque, events were rapidly approaching that would hastily bring the campaign to a conclusion. Not long after the Rebel occupation of Santa Fe scouts brought word that a sizeable Federal force was moving southward along the Santa Fe Trail toward the capital. With Sibley far to the rear in Albuquerque, Pyron along with four companies from Shropshire's command and two guns from Teel's artillery company, numbering over three hundred men, decided to move against the enemy. Early on the morning of March 25 the Confederates filed through the narrow and dusty streets of the territorial capital and rode southeast along the Santa Fe Trail toward Glorieta Pass at the southern extremity of the towering and frigid snow-covered Sangre de Cristo. By the eve-

[20] Howell Diary, 20 March 1862.
[21] Smith Diary, 9 March 1862, p. 137.
[22] H.H. Sibley to S. Cooper, 4 May 1862, *O.R.*, I, IX: 509.

ning of the first day they had reached Johnson's Ranch near the mouth of Apache Canyon at the western entrance to Glorieta Pass.

As Pyron prepared to enter the pass from the west, Colonel John P. Slough, with more than thirteen hundred hastily recruited Colorado miners and regulars from Fort Union, was preparing to enter Glorieta Pass from the east. The Coloradoans, or "Pikes Peakers" as the Texans called them, had been rushed south by William Gilpin, territorial governor. Ironically the governor and the Confederate general, now enemies, had been West Point classmates.

In advance of the Federal column rode Major John M. Chivington, a surly and colorful Methodist minister, who had plans of leading a raiding party to Santa Fe. While Pyron's Rebels went into camp at Johnson's Ranch, the hard riding Chivington with his force of 418 regulars and Pikes Peakers was approaching Kozlowski's Ranch at the eastern entrance to Glorieta Pass, about twenty miles from Santa Fe near the adobe ruins of Pecos Pueblo.

Upon reaching Kozlowski's Ranch, Chivington learned that Rebel pickets had already crossed Glorieta Pass and were at Pigeon's Ranch five miles to the west. Chivington, who was determined to take the offensive, decided to send out a detachment of twenty men to capture one of the Confederate pickets in hopes of obtaining information on the exact strength of the Rebel advance. The Federals reached Pigeon's Ranch before sunrise on the morning of March 26 but were unable to find the Rebels who were reported to be in the vicinity. At dawn four Texans calmly rode up to the Federals, mistaking the Union force for one of their own. Without a shot being fired the Confederates were captured and sent to Kozlowski's Ranch where Chivington was able to learn through interrogation the details of the Confederate advance.[23] Unable to raid Santa Fe as he had originally planned Chivington prepared to meet the Rebels head-on. The setting for the Battle of Apache Canyon, the first part of the Battle of Glorieta, was now complete. Among the juniper and ponderosa pines of the foothills of the Sangre de Cristo the Gettysburg of the West was within hours.

On the morning of March 26 Chivington broke camp at Kozlowski's Ranch and set out along the Santa Fe Trail past Pigeon's Ranch for the summit of Glorieta Pass and an almost certain confrontation with Pyron's Rebels. By two o'clock the Pikes Peakers and Regulars

[23] John M. Chivington to E.R.S. Canby, 26 March 1862, *O.R.*, I, IX: 530.

had reached the summit of the pass and were continuing westward into the depths of Apache Canyon. Here in the narrow defiles of the canyon near a grove of piñon pine, gamble oak, and juniper the Federals ran into an advance guard of Rebels, caught completely unaware, and captured without shots being fired. Chivington now had an excellent opportunity to catch the Confederates without warning. Orders were given to move as quickly as possible. "Knapsacks, canteens, overcoats, and clothing of all kinds were flung along the road," as the Federals prepared for battle.[24] Upon turning a sharp bend in Apache Canyon, the Federals spotted the main body of Texans less than two hundred yards down the Santa Fe Trail.

Although totally surprised, the veteran Texans did not panic. Within minutes skirmishers were ordered out and the artillery, consisting of two six-pound howitzers, went into action, hurling grape and shell at the Federals. In support of the artillery a Rebel cavalry company unfurled a large red flag with a white star symbolic of "the glory of that arrogant, impotent state," a Coloradoan recalled.

With the Rebel artillery pounding the Union position the Federals appeared confused and uncertain. Federal officers "plunged wildly here and there, and seemed to have no control of themselves or their men."[25] Finally able to regain control of the situation, Chivington sent two companies scurrying south up the steep slopes of Apache Canyon while another company was sent to the Federal right, up the northern slope of the canyon, all in an attempt to outflank the Rebels. Pyron, seeing that he had been outmaneuvered, was left no choice but to retreat. Chivington had clearly counted on such a move and now ordered one of his cavalry companies to pursue the retreating Rebels. For some unexplained reason the Federal charge never developed and the Rebels withdrew safely.

About a mile and a half down the Santa Fe Trail from the first skirmish Pyron set up defenses for an expected second attack. Topographically, Pyron had chosen an ideal spot, for it was here that Apache Canyon made an abrupt turn to the north leaving a high sandstone bluff squarely in the Federal front. Here also a fifteen feet deep arroyo crossed the canyon diagonally. Below the bluff and behind the arroyo Pyron placed his howitzers. To prevent another pos-

[24] Ovando J. Hollister, *Colorado Volunteers in New Mexico, 1862*, Richard Harwell, ed. (Chicago, 1962), 98.
[25] Ibid., p. 99.

sible envelopment Pyron extended his skirmish lines up the walls of the canyon.

Chivington proceeded down the canyon cautiously to within shouting range of the Rebels where the Federals halted to regroup. Dismounting a company of his cavalry, he decided to employ the tactics that had proven successful in the first skirmish—to strengthen both his flanks and encircle the Rebels.[26] As before, he decided to hold a cavalry company in reserve to charge the Texan center in the event there would be a Rebel retreat.

For more than thirty minutes the battle raged, the Federals attempting to outflank the Rebels as both sides sought shelter behind the numerous trees and large boulders on the steep hillsides. The Rebel artillery continued to fire on the Union line, but most of the shells exploded harmlessly among the rocks and boulders. Suddenly, however, Pyron's left flank on the northern slopes of Apache Canyon began to break and fall back across the broken terrain. With his artillery in peril, Pyron was forced to order a retreat. With sword in hand, Captain Samuel H. Cook launched a furious charge down the canyon. Although hit by a minie ball in the thigh, Cook was able to keep the saddle and continue the charge—an inspiring sight to his men. Before reaching the arroyo that protected the Rebel position, Cook's horse stumbled, throwing the captain to the ground. Temporarily shaken, the captain ran for cover, only to be wounded in the foot.

To secure their position the Rebels had torn up a small bridge that spanned the arroyo in their front. This did not deter the Coloradoans who were able to jump their horses across the arroyo. Wielding their sabers above their heads the Federals charged furiously into the Rebel line, scattering the Texans in all directions. Almost simultaneously a group of Federal infantry was able to gain the Rebel rear and commenced to send a deadly fire into the retreating Texans from the steep hillside. With Pyron's Texans in full retreat the Federals poured down upon the Rebels like "wild Indians" screaming to the top of their lungs.[27]

By late afternoon, as the long shadows from the tall pines on the crest stretched across the canyon floor, it was evident that the Federals had won the day. As the disheartened Confederate prisoners were

---

[26] J.M. Chivington to E.R.S. Canby, 26 March 1862, *O.R.*, I, IX: 530.
[27] Hollister, p. 102.

marched wearily up the trail toward the crest of Glorieta Pass, the real
extent of the day's savagery became evident. Victims of the battle lay
in the canyon bottom in ghastly form, some partially decapitated,
others missing legs or arms. One unfortunate Rebel lay against a tree
with his "brains shot out."[28]

After the bloody encounter Chivington gave the order to retreat, and
the Federals began to file back along the Santa Fe Trail through Glorieta Pass to Pigeon's Ranch where a field hospital for the wounded
had hastily been set up. Almost simultaneously with Chivington's
arrival, reinforcements began to reach the Union camp from the east.
Upon hearing of the Federal victory in Apache Canyon the reinforcements were said to have cheered for more than an hour.

The defeated Pyron retreated to Johnson's Ranch where a flag of
truce was sent to Chivington who agreed upon a cease fire until 8:00
A.M. the following morning for the nursing of the wounded and the
burying of the dead. There was little jubilation in the Confederate
camp that night. Confederate losses were reported at four men killed
and six wounded while Chivington reported the Southern losses at
thirty-two killed, forty-three wounded, and seventy-one taken prisoner.[29] Another Pikes Peaker, Ovando J. Hollister, was probably more
accurate when he reported sixteen Texans killed, thirty to forty
wounded, and seventy-five prisoners.[30] Although both forces had retreated following the battle, there was little doubt that it was the
Rebels who had taken the more severe beating.

While the battle at Apache Canyon was in progress, Sibley remained at Confederate headquarters at Albuquerque. News of the attack on Pyron's advance column was received with astonishment by
the general. He no doubt contemplated a confrontation but was confident the Federals could not defend Fort Union and were not prepared to move south to mount an offensive.

News of the defeat at Apache Canyon reached Scurry's Fourth regiment and a battalion of Steel's Seventh regiment at the village of
Galisteo about twenty-five miles south of Santa Fe. An urgent express from Pyron pleading for reinforcements had reached their camp
on the afternoon of March 26. Colonel Scurry was in the saddle tell-

[28] Ibid., p. 264.

[29] J.M. Chivington to E.R.S. Canby, 26 March 1862, *O.R.*, I, IX: 530; Charles J. Walker
to N.M. Macrae, 20 May 1862, *O.R.*, I, IX: 531.

[30] Hollister, p. 109.

ing his men of the engagement and the critical situation that now beset the Army of New Mexico. Within minutes the Fourth Regiment, with two of Teel's artillery pieces, was on the march across the mountains toward Apache Canyon and the outmanned Pyron. All was in haste. The regiment's supply train was left behind as was the battalion of the Seventh Regiment which had arrived at Galisteo from the south only minutes before Pyron's express had raced into the Confederate camp from the north.

The road through the rugged terrain, which in places was little more than a well beaten trail, was found to be so steep that on more than one occasion the men had to unharness the horses from the artillery and pull the artillery up the steep hillsides by hand. Many of the men who were thinly clad suffered intensely in the cold. Although the march through the darkness turned into a fatiguing ordeal, the men plodded on without a whimper. At three o'clock on the morning of the 27th the Fourth Regiment reached Pyron at Johnson's Ranch.

Just as the first rays of daylight began to stretch westward across Glorieta Pass and down the Santa Fe Trail and into the depths of Apache Canyon, Scurry was in the saddle and making a brief reconnaissance of the area. Scurry found Pyron's position to be strategically secure. By eight o'clock, at which time the cease fire was to expire, Scurry was ready for the Federal advance he felt imminent. Anxiously the already fatigued Rebels awaited the impending attack. The "Pikes Peakers" did not come. Unknown to Scurry, Chivington had retreated following the engagement in Apache Canyon. When it became evident that the Federals were not advancing, Scurry decided to take the offensive.

Taking nine companies of the Fourth Regiment, four companies of the Seventh, three pieces of artillery and the company of brigands, altogether numbering slightly less than six hundred, Scurry struck out along the Santa Fe Trail toward Glorieta Pass. Only a small force remained behind to guard the Confederate supply train. Scurry's decision to deploy a small force to guard the supplies would prove to be one of the worst mistakes of the campaign.

As the sun reached meridian, Scurry, with an advance guard in his front, was already through the pass and down into Glorieta Canyon on the eastern slopes of the Sangre de Cristo Mountains. Shortly thereafter a courier excitedly raced up to the advancing Rebels to report that Scurry's advance guard had made contact with a large body of "Pikes Peakers" a short distance west of Pigeons's Ranch, a well known way-station and watering hole on the Santa Fe Trail. Scurry pushed forward to find the Federals moving westward about one mile west of Pigeon's Ranch under the command of Colonel John P. Slough.[31]

Scurry ordered his cavalry, which had made first contact with the Federals, to withdraw and dismount and then move up as infantry. Three pieces of artillery were hurried forward to a small rise in the canyon bottom and immediately opened fire on the Federals. The Battle of Glorieta was at hand. The infantry, along with the cavalry on foot, formed a long line stretching from a grove of piñon trees on the north side of the canyon of a stand of ponderosa pine on the south side.

Just as Scurry was surging ahead to deploy his men into position, the Federals commenced a rapid advance in columns on the Rebel flanks. With initiative lost, Scurry sent Pyron to reinforce the Confederate right, placed Major Raguet in command of the center, and hastened himself to command the left. The Rebel left was especially vulnerable. Here a large body of "Pikes Peakers" were advancing up a large arroyo which ran through a corn field in the Rebel front. The Federals were within minutes of turning the Rebel flank. With little time to ponder the situation Scurry ordered his men forward. With "pistol and knife" in hand, the Confederates threw themselves into the gulch where Scurry reported "a most desperate and deadly hand-to-hand conflict raged."[32] It was Valverde over again. After several minutes of horrendous fighting the Federals began to break from the gully and retreat to the more secure environs of Pigeon's Ranch.

On the Confederate right Major Pyron's advance had also forced a Federal retreat as had Major Raguet's wild charge against the Federal center. Although their advance had succeeded in forcing the "Pike Peakers" to retreat, the Rebels had become too scattered to follow up their success. While Colonel Scurry scampered about attempting to bring order to the confused Texans, the Federals were able to regroup behind an adobe wall near Pigeon's Ranch. Others found safety near a bluff in back of the ranch house. Hoping to follow up on his advantage, Scurry brought two artillery pieces forward and began firing on

[31] W.R. Scurry to A.M. Jackson, 31 March 1862, O.R., I, IX: 542.

[32] Ibid., p. 543. For an excellent description of the fighting at Glorieta see: Peticolas Journal, 28 March 1862, p. 79.

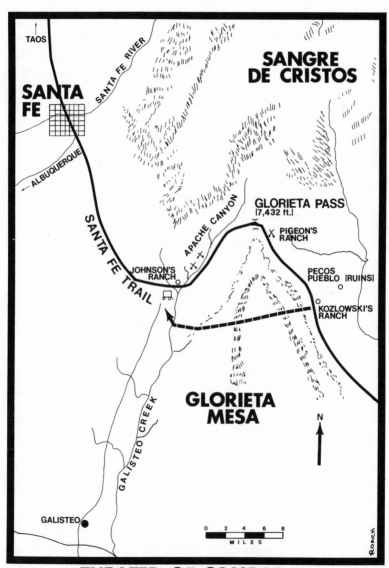

TAOS

SANTA FE RIVER

SANTA FE

SANGRE DE CRISTOS

ALBUQUERQUE

SANTA FE TRAIL

APACHE CANYON

GLORIETA PASS
[7,432 ft.]

X PIGEON'S RANCH

JOHNSON'S RANCH

PECOS PUEBLO (RUINS)

KOZLOWSKI'S RANCH

GLORIETA MESA

N

GALISTEO CREEK

GALISTEO

0 2 4 6 8
MILES

ROACH

THEATER OF COMBAT-
NORTHERN NEW MEXICO-1862

■ ■ ■ ■ ■ ■ ■ CHIVINGTON'S ROUTE

X BATTLES
🚃 SUPPLY TRAINS

the Federal position. The colonel was determined to drive the "Pikes Peakers" from the field. On the Rebel right, Major Shropshire was ordered to attack a group of Federals who had gathered in the grove of tall pines on the south side of the canyon. At the same time Major Raguet was sent to the northside of the canyon in hopes of striking the enemy's right flank. "I informed these gallant officers that as soon as the sound of their guns was heard I would charge in front with the remainder of the command," Scurry later wrote in his official report.[33]

Not hearing any gunfire on his right and detecting only slight movement on the Confederate left, Scurry rode off to find out why Shropshire was not attacking as ordered. Scurry found the Texans in total disarray and Shropshire dead. Scurry took command of the Confederate right and charged the Federals who by this time had gathered at the adobe ranch. The sound of gunfire also brought the columns under Majors Raguet and Pyron into the fray. Once again the Federals were driven back where they made their "final and most desperate stand" along a ledge of large sandstone boulders behind the ranch house.[34] As the Texans charged the Federal position, eight cannon in the Union rear poured a deadly fire of grape and cannister into the charging Rebels, but the Texans pressed on despite heavy casualties. Scurry dramatically recalled the final stages of the battle three days later: "Here the conflict was terrible. Our men and officers, alike inspired with the unalterable determination to overcome every obstacle to the attainment of their object, dashed among them. The right and center had united on the left. The intrepid Raguet and the cool, calm, courageous Pyron had pushed forward among the rocks until the muzzles of the guns of the opposing forces passed each other. Inch by inch was the ground disputed."[35]

Twice the Colorado infantry rushed forward to save the Federal guns. The fighting again became furious. Colonel Slough's decision to counter attack saved the Federal guns as the artillerymen were given time to withdraw eastward along the Santa Fe Trail. Shortly thereafter the Federal infantry also beat a hasty retreat. Many of the Federals were so panic stricken that they cut the horses loose from several supply wagons and then set the wagons on fire before fleeing

[33] Ibid.
[34] Ibid.
[35] Ibid., pp. 543–44.

eastward along the Santa Fe Trail. Scurry's fatigued army attempted a halfhearted pursuit of the fleeing "Pikes Peakers" before returning to Pigeon's Ranch. After six hours of continuous combat the Battle of Glorieta was over. Although the Confederates held the field, an exhorbitant price had been paid for the blood stained soil of the Sangre de Cristo.

The ferocity of the struggle was illustrated by the fact that twice during the battle Colonel Scurry had had his cheek grazed by a Federal minie ball and his clothes torn to shreds by other near fatal Federal bullets. Tragically, both Major Shropshire and Major Raguet had fallen mortally wounded during the last desperate Rebel charge. But the Texans had driven the enemy from the field and had apparently won the day. Many years later Alexander Valle, owner of Pigeon's Ranch, recalled the battle: "Government manns was at my ranch, and fill is cahnteen viz my whisky (and government nevaire pay me for zat vishey); and Texas mahns coom opp, and soorprize zen, and sey fouhgt six hour by my vatch, and my vatch was slow!"[36]

Shortly after the firing ended, Scurry rode up to a squad of his exhausted Texans and asked for a white handkerchief to be sent to the "damned Yankees" as a flag of truce so they could return to gather their dead and wounded. When none of the Rebels came forth with the desired handkerchief, Scurry replied in a loud voice: "God Damn it, tear off your shirt tail, we have got to have a white flag."[37] One soldier finally came forward with a white silk scarf which a Union soldier had lost during the speedy Federal retreat, and a courier with the flag galloped eastward along the Santa Fe Trail.

The Confederate flag bearer had to ride all the way to Kozlowski's Ranch before Colonel Slough, who agreed to a one-day truce, could be found. As nightfall crept across the towering Sangre de Cristo and down into Glorieta Canyon, a Federal detachment returned to Pigeon's Ranch, and Union and Confederate soldiers roamed the battlefield gathering their dead. Even in the remote mountains of New Mexico, far from Richmond and Washington, the Civil War had taken a terrible toll.

The number of Confederate dead was placed at thirty-six with twice as many wounded. Union losses were placed at between forty and

---

[36] Twitchell, p. 384.
[37] Hall, *Sibley's New Mexico Campaign*, p. 153.

fifty.[38] The Confederates were too exhausted to advance or retreat and remained upon the battlefield the following day. No picks or shovels were available to bury their dead, so the necessary tools had to be borrowed from the Federals before the grisly task could proceed. The dead were buried in the corn field in front of Pigeon's Ranch. The wounded were given whatever meager medical assistance was available. It was on the evening of the 28th when the artillery, which only hours before had belched their message of death, was at last silent, that Scurry, who had not slept in three days and could barely hold his eyes open, was able to issue an order congratulating the Confederates for their "daring courage and heroic endurance." "You steadily drove before you a foe of twice your number over a field chosen by themselves and deemed impregnable." Like Sibley after Valverde, Scurry compared his veterans to those of the Texas Revolution: "You have proven your right to stand beside those who fought and conquered on the red field of San Jacinto." Contrary to what he had previously thought in Albuquerque, Scurry now felt that it was only a matter of time before "not a single soldier of the United States will be left upon the soil of New Mexico" and the beautiful valleys of the territory will once again "blossom as the rose."[39]

Scurry and Sibley, in their seemingly eternal optimism, were to be sorely disappointed. Late in the evening following the Battle of Glorieta disastrous news reached the Confederate camp at Pigeon's Ranch. The Rebel supply train, which Scurry had left behind in Apache Canyon and upon which the Confederate Army of New Mexico was largely dependent, had been totally destroyed.

Early on the morning of the 28th, as Colonel Slough pushed his "Pikes Peakers" westward toward Pigeon's Ranch, Major John M. Chivington, the Methodist minister from Denver, with 430 men had broken away from the main Federal column to make his way toward the Rebel rear. Led by Lieutenant-Colonel Manuel Cháves, a daring native New Mexican who knew the Sangre de Cristo Mountains as few others did, Chivington had left the Santa Fe Trail about three miles west of Kozlowski's Ranch, and had ridden west along San Cristóbal Canyon through thickets of piñon and juniper toward the

---

[38] W. R. Scurry to A.M. Jackson, 31 March 1862, *O.R.*, I, IX: 545; H.H. Sibley to S. Cooper, 31 March 1862, *O.R.*, I, IX: 540; John P. Slough to E.R.S. Canby, 29 March 1862, *O.R.*, I, IX: 535; *Dallas Herald*, 10 May 1862.

[39] Santa Fe *Gazette*, 26 April 1862; Giesecke Diary, 28 March, 1862, p. 237.

village of Galisteo. Chivington was hoping to strike the Confederate flank at the same time Slough made contact with the Rebels in Apache Canyon. At nine-thirty in the morning the thunder of artillery to the north announced that the contemplated confrontation had commenced. Swinging away from the San Cristobal Trail, Chivington with Cháves still in the lead, scurried north across the rugged boulder-strewn summit of Glorieta Mesa. By one o'clock in the afternoon the Coloradoans had reached a high ridge overlooking the Rebel camp. More than three hundred feet below lay Johnson's Ranch in Apache Canyon. Cháves turned to Chivington and remarked: "You are right on top of them."[40] Chivington spent an hour carefully observing the scene below to insure that the Federals did not ride into an ambush. Clearly visible was Johnson's Ranch and the main road leading westward toward Santa Fe and eastward to the summit of the pass. A Confederate cannon was spotted on a small knoll near the ranch house as were hundreds of draft animals and cavalry horses. The two hundred man Rebel rear guard, which milled leisurely about, was unaware of its peril.

Quietly the order to attack was given and the descent into Apache Canyon began. So steep was the descent that some of the miners had to lower themselves with ropes over the bluffs. They were not seen by the Rebel camp until they were far down the mountainside. Reaching the bottom of the canyon, the Coloradoans, who had become disorganized during the steep descent, were able to form a skirmish line near the ranch and charge the few Confederates who remained to defend the supply wagons and the artillery piece. Many of the Texans who had been left to guard the supply train were either sick or wounded. Five times the Rebels were able to fire salvos at the charging Federals before the cannon was seized, spiked, and sent crashing down a small hill, ripping the carriage apart. Within moments the Federals were in possession of the entire supply train.[41] Most were not aware of the importance of their victory. Here were Sibley's quartermaster stores, camp and garrison equipage, and ordnance supplies, all of which were critical to the Confederates hopes

[40] A.A. Hayes, Jr., *New Colorado and the Santa Fe Trail* (New York, 1880), 169; Marc Simmons, *Little Lion of the Southwest* (Chicago, 1973), 184.

[41] John M. Chivington to E.R.S. Canby, 28 March 1862, *O.R.*, I, IX: 538. For a favorable biography of Chivington see: Reginald S. Craig, *The Fighting Parson, Biography of Col. John M. Chivington* (Los Angeles, 1959).

of capturing the Territory of New Mexico and Richmond's dream of a western empire.

Unable to transport the valuable supplies through Glorieta Pass which remained in Rebel hands or across the rugged terrain to the south, orders were given to destroy the entire train. Wagons were pulled together, overturned and then set on fire under the supervision of Superintendent of Indian Affairs James L. Collins. Still the destruction was not finished. Some of the five to six hundred horses and mules, which the Texans had been guarding in a ravine near the ranch house, were bayoneted. The Federals made sure the destruction was complete before ascending the perilous precipices of Apache Canyon and making their way through the chilling dark night to the Federal lines.

As the sound of the exploding ammunition echoed from Apache Canyon, soon to be accompanied by a cloud of dark bellowing smoke, Brigadier General Henry Hopkins Sibley's hopes of a Confederate conquest of the Territory of New Mexico vanished. Three Texans died in the raid and seventeen were captured. One of those wounded was the Reverend L.H. Jones, Chaplain of the Fourth Regiment, who the Texans later asserted was shot while holding a white flag.

In the Rebel camp at Pigeon's Ranch word reached Colonel Scurry of the disaster in Apache Canyon. News of the wounding of Jones and rumors that Chivington had decided to shoot the seventeen Rebel prisoners aroused the wrath of Scurry, who proclaimed that the Federals had "lost all sense of humanity in their insane hatred of the Confederacy."[42] Fatigued, low on ammunition, out of food, and with all of his supplies gone, Scurry was left no choice but to retreat through Glorieta Pass to Santa Fe. As soon as the sick and wounded were made as comfortable as possible at the ranch, a bugle called the weary Texans into line. Scurry dejectedly told his men the news from Apache Canyon and his decision to fall back on Santa Fe as soon as possible.

All through the night the Rebels wound their way back through the sandy slopes of Glorieta Pass and down through Apache Canyon past the still warm embers of what remained of their supplies. Although Scurry reached the capital early the next morning, his well-worn men continued to straggle into Santa Fe for several days. Some of the Reb-

[42] W.R. Scurry to A.M. Jackson, 31 March 1862, *O.R.*, I, IX: 545.

els "rode, some walked and some hobbled in," the Santa Fe *Gazette* reported.[43]

One of the ladies in Santa Fe who came to help the Confederate wounded was Louisa Hawkins Canby, General Sibley's friend from Fort Bridger and other frontier encampments. Mrs. Canby converted her home in Santa Fe into a makeshift hospital where she personally nursed many of the Rebel wounded. Daily her carriage could be seen on the road to Glorieta Pass as she helped to transport the wounded. One Rebel later remarked that Mrs. Canby "captured more hearts of Confederate soldiers" than General Canby "ever captured Confederate bodies."[44]

During the battles of Apache Canyon and Pigeon's Ranch General Sibley was sixty miles to the south in Albuquerque. A courier had brought in news of the Battle of Apache Canyon on the night of March 29 and word of the Battle of Pigeon's Ranch the following morning. Evidently misinformed and possibly drunk, the general appeared excited by the news and decided to celebrate the occasion. The Rebel brass band struck up some moving bars of "Dixie" which Sibley's rear guard greeted with loud boisterous cheers. Soon thereafter the general, who it was reported consumed his share of liquor to celebrate the occasion, struck out for Santa Fe.[45] A small guard and a detachment of Reily's artillery remained behind to protect the Albuquerque depot.

[43] Santa Fe *Gazette*, 26 April 1862.

[44] Lansing B. Bloom, ed., "Confederate Reminiscences of 1862," *New Mexico Historical Review*, 5 (July 1930), 320. For the Rebels' respect for Mrs. Canby see: Houston *Tri-Weekly Telegraph*, 28 May, 18 June 1862; Peticolas, 31 March 1862, p. 88.

[45] Theophilus Noel, *Autobiography and Reminiscences* (Chicago, 1904), 61–62, 99. Noel, who also wrote *A Campaign From Santa Fe to the Mississippi*, makes several specific references to Sibley's heavy drinking. Recalling the Confederate occupation of Albuquerque, he wrote: "Our men were getting drunk on whisky and our commander had never been sober." Later he wrote: "The commanding general of our forces was an old army officer, whose love for liquor exceeded that for home, country or God." In another place Noel refers to the Confederate dead at Glorieta as "victims of General John Barleycorn." In recalling the arrival of the Sibley Brigade back in San Antonio after the conclusion of the campaign, he wrote: "What became of General Sibley along about this time no one ever knew, but it was generally supposed that he crawled into a jug hole and pulled the jug and hole in after him." The book, written some thirty-nine years after the war, however, is so severely distorted and faulted by inaccuracies and half-truths that it can not be considered a credible source for the New Mexico Campaign.

On March 31 after learning details of the battle, Sibley realized the extent of what happened in the Sangre de Cristo. He wrote General Sámuel Cooper in Richmond, advising the adjutant general of the battles at Apache Canyon and Pigeon's Ranch and of the destruction of his supply train. In his closing remarks the general was terse: "I must have re-enforcements . . . send me re-enforcements."[46]

Before leaving Albuquerque on the afternoon of April 1, Sibley took time to appeal to Governor Francis R. Lubbock of Texas for supplies and reinforcements. The letter written in his own hand, instead of that of his adjutant which was the custom, was in an almost illegible scrawl. Sibley started by telling the governor of his victories at Valverde and Glorieta and of how the Texans were entitled to the "sympathies . . . of their neighbors and friends at home." But Sibley continued, "I must appeal to you for help. The enemy, not content with destroying their own supplies (drawn from the slim resources of the country) have employed their forces in destroying our train and supplies. There we have been crippled and for this reason ask assistance."[47]

Once in Santa Fe Sibley found the "whole exultant army assembled" and "the sick and wounded," to be "comfortably quartered and attended."[48] Despite the loss of their supplies, a warehouse which had been concealed from the Rebels was found to be full of foodstuffs and blankets, all previously destined for the Navajo Indians but now in the hands of the desperate Confederates.

Several friends were found in the capital including William Pelham, ex-surveyor general of the territory, recently released from the Fort Union stockade and now appointed by Sibley to head the territorial government. Other citizens whom the general had known during his tour of duty at Taos, Fort Union, and during the Navajo Expedition, extended their greetings. Sibley also exchanged pleasantries with Louisa Canby.

While in the capital General Sibley was drunk a large part of the time. A barber who shaved the general one morning in the capital testified that Sibley was drinking heavily but felt his consumption of alcohol was a result of the general's ill health.[49]

[46] H.H. Sibley to S. Cooper, 31 March 1862, O.R., I, IX: 540.
[47] H.H. Sibley to Governor Francis R. Lubbock, 1 April 1862, Francis R. Lubbock Papers, Texas State Archives.
[48] H.H. Sibley to S. Cooper, 4 May 1862, O.R., I, IX: 509.
[49] Twitchell, p. 384.

After assessing the situation and counseling with his general staff, Sibley decided to secure a strategic position at the village of Manzano, on the eastern slopes of the Manzano Mountains, southeast of Albuquerque. From here the consolidated Confederate Army could strike against either Fort Craig, Fort Union, or Albuquerque. From Manzano a vital line of communication could be maintained to Fort Stanton, the Mesilla Valley, and Texas.

Such plans had to be scrapped when rumors were confirmed that General Canby had left Fort Craig with a sizeable army and was pushing rapidly up the Rio Grande Valley. Fearing the loss of what remained of his supplies at Albuquerque, Sibley was left no alternative but to order a series of forced marches to save the depot. The plan to capture Fort Union, gateway to Colorado, which had been one of his major objectives, had to be given up. It seems almost certain that Sibley had learned of the construction of a new fort on the plain east of the original fort where he had been briefly stationed in 1861. Sibley's cannon could easily have reached the new fort from a position on the bluffs to the west, but the Rebel Army now was on the march in the opposite direction.

After only a few days in the capital, Green's Fifth Regiment was the first to leave for Albuquerque early on the morning of April 7. Traveling up to thirty miles a day, the regiment hurried across the arid plains south of town and down the Rio Grande, arriving in Albuquerque three days later. The following day Sibley and the remainder of the army arrived.

The general's "chief regret" in leaving the capital was that approximately one hundred sick and wounded Rebels had to be abandoned. A surgeon and several assistants were left behind to care for the unfortunate Confederates. It is interesting to note that the Santa Fe *Gazette*, in obvious reference to Henry's heavy drinking, remarked that all the Rebels left behind were "some of Sibley's proclamations and empty Champagne bottles."[50]

The day before the Army of New Mexico reached Albuquerque, Canby arrived from Fort Craig with 860 Regulars and 350 New Mexico Volunteers. Canby sent out Graydon's Spy Company to reconnoiter the town and its environs. In the village were two companies, commanded by Captains William P. Hardeman and Bethel Coop-

[50] Santa Fe *Gazette*, 26 April 1862.

wood, which had arrived from the Mesilla Valley. Upon spotting the advancing Union Force, Captain Hardeman sent couriers racing northward to notify Sibley. Although greatly outnumbered, Hardeman was determined to defend the town and the small depot. To deceive the Federals the four Rebel cannon were moved several times to give the appearance of a much larger force. Canby responded by placing his artillery in position about a mile east of the village near a large irrigation ditch.

With Graydon's Spy Company supported by Canby's Regulars making a sortie toward the town, the "Battle of Albuquerque" was underway. Rebel batteries fired on the advancing Federals as Canby replied with a harmless cannonade. In the midst of the Federal bombardment several citizens, including a few of the town's more prominent women, made their way to Canby's position where they complained that the Confederates were not allowing the citizens of the village to take cover and that the Federal guns were damaging their dwellings. Responding to the ladies' complaints, Canby called off the attack and withdrew to a position some three miles southeast of town. During the skirmish, a Union officer, Major Thomas Duncan, fell off his horse and seriously injured himself, thus becoming the only casualty of the battle.[51]

The following day the two forces continued to snipe at one another, but except for an occasional cannon shot, Canby remained content only to harass the besieged Rebels. Outnumbered, Hardeman did not move from the village. As nightfall enveloped the central valley and the adobe jacales of the village, Canby made the decision to withdraw. Campfires were left burning brightly, and buglers remained for the usual evening "tattoo" as Canby struck out eastward for Carnuel Pass. Here at the village of San Antonio on the eastern slopes of the mountains, about twenty miles east of Albuquerque, the Federals would be in a better position to form a junction with the Union force known to be moving south from Fort Union.

On the same night that Canby marched for Carnuel Pass, Green's Fifth Regiment arrived in Albuquerque. Throughout the next day the Army of New Mexico continued to straggle into town. A clash of major significance in which Canby would have been greatly outnumbered had narrowly been avoided.

[51] Ed. R.S. Canby to Adjutant-General of the Army, 11 April 1862, *O.R.*, I, IX: 550.

Once again a decision of critical importance weighed heavily upon the shoulders of Henry Hopkins Sibley. The general, with his army united for the first time since Valverde, contemplated moving against Canby, whom he felt would go north to defend Fort Union, but with only "scant rations" such a move would be a "desperate" gamble. Sibley decided instead to evacuate the territory—a decision which in itself meant the failure of the campaign. Nonetheless, in council with his staff officers and regimental commanders, "the course adopted was deemed the wisest."[52]

Early on the morning of April 12, after burying their "Mountain Howitzers," the Confederates retreated from Albuquerque with Scurry's Fourth Regiment crossing to the west bank of the river. Sibley ordered the Fifth Regiment to act as the army's rear guard, but Green was unable to make the desired crossing and elected to remain on the east bank in hopes of finding a better crossing lower down the river the following day.

The next day the Rebel retreat continued with the two Rebel armies moving downriver parallel to one another. Sibley, with the bulk of the army, moved downriver on the west bank of the Rio Grande while Green and the Fifth Regiment, in a more precarious and vulnerable position, traveled along the east bank. By nightfall Sibley had reached the village of Los Lunas on the west bank whereas Green, still unable to find a suitable crossing, was approaching the small adobe village of Peralta on the opposite shore. That evening both armies settled contently into camp with several officers from Green's Regiment leaving to attend a Mexican fandango in the village of Peralta.

Unknown to Sibley, Canby had made his desired junction with the force from Fort Union in Tijeras Canyon to the west of Carnuel Pass and, with his army swollen to twenty four hundred men, had decided to march for the Rio Grande to confront Sibley and hopefully drive the Rebels from the territory.[53] In the evening Canby's Federals were able to make camp within a short distance of Green's Fourth Regiment. The Union soldiers could even hear the sounds of festive music from the fandango in the village of Peralta as the cool night breeze blew eastward toward their camp. Many in the Federal camp, especially Colonel Chivington, were anxious to attack the Rebels, but the

[52] H.H. Sibley to S. Cooper, 4 May 1862, *O.R.*, I, IX: 510.
[53] Ed. R.S. Canby to Adjutant-General of the Army, 23 April 1862, *O.R.*, I, IX: 551.

prudent Canby felt the Confederates were in too strong a defensive position. Canby was correct. Green had set up his defense around Governor Henry Connelly's large hacienda which afforded excellent protection for the beleaguered Texans. Connelly's residence was surrounded by groves of cottonwoods for at least a half mile in every direction. In addition, several irrigation ditches ran parallel to the Federal lines making any forward advance, especially by artillery, impractical.

Early the next morning the Texans were startled to hear the sound of Union bugles within shouting distance of their lines. Soon, however, the "stirring strains of Dixie" echoed forth from the barren cottonwood trees challenging Canby to combat.

Unmoved by Sibley's Brass Band, Canby sent out a detachment of cavalry supported by two companies of infantry which were able to capture a Rebel supply train of seven wagons which had bogged down in the deep sand north of the village. A sharp skirmish ensued in which four Confederates were killed and the remaining Rebels taken prisoner. More of Sibley's valuable quartermaster and commissary supplies were now gone. A brass howitzer, seventy mules, and about fifteen horses were also lost.

A sharp firefight followed when Canby attempted to drive the Rebels from the bosque in front of the village. Canby was hoping to deploy the major portion of his army in a position from which it would be able to command the river ford; this would prevent Sibley's force on the west bank from reinforcing Green on the east and with two columns, both accompanied by artillery, move against the Rebels.

The Federal attack in Sibley's words, was "a furious, but harmless cannonade."[54] Hearing the rumble of cannonfire across the river and learning of Green's "critical situation," Sibley was forced to cross his army to the east bank. Colonel Scurry instead of General Sibley, however, successfully led the army, complete with a battery of artillery, across the Rio Grande. Sibley with his staff remained behind to arrange for the protection of what remained of the Confederate supplies on the west bank. With the task completed the general accompanied by Major Teel, Captain Willis L. Robards, and Captain Henry E. Loebnitz galloped toward the river and the sounds of battle.

[54] H.H. Sibley to S. Cooper, 4 May 1862, *O.R.*, I, IX: 510. For the Battle of Peralta see: Don E. Alberts, "The Battle of Peralta," *New Mexico Historical Review*, 58 (October, 1983), 369–79.

No sooner was Sibley across the river than several officers raced forward to warn him that the Federals had driven the Texans from the bosque in front of the village and were attempting to gain a position between the ford and Peralta. Finding himself cut off from his troops, Sibley recrossed the Rio Grande. Halfway across the river the Federals opened fire on the general and his party. Several shots splashed harmlessly into the brown muddy waters as the general scurried to gain the safety of the west bank. Besides a brief moment early in the Battle of Valverde, it was the only time during the entire campaign that the Confederate general came under enemy fire. Sibley remained helplessly on the west bank as a battle, one that could easily be the most decisive of the entire campaign, was in the making less than a mile away. Once again the commander of the Army of New Mexico was not at the head of his men when a crucial battle appeared probable.

About two o'clock in the afternoon a stiff wind swept down the valley engulfing both armies in a cloud of suffocating dust. Rebels and Federals alike could see ahead no more than a hundred yards. Canby felt that to order an attack in such weather across difficult terrain and against a strong defensive position would be suicide. Thus the Federals broke off contact with the Texans and retreated to their previous position. A dust storm had ended the skirmish at Peralta.

Sibley, although in command of a badly crippled army, claimed that his plan was to push ahead of Canby along the river route, attack the weakened garrison at Fort Craig and demolish the fort. Colonel Green's inability to find a suitable ford downriver from Albuquerque, the lack of forage and grass, and the slowing of the Confederate artillery by deep sand caused the plan to be abandoned.

Many in the Federal Army surmised that Canby deliberately allowed Sibley's Army to escape downriver. Canby was "castigated unmercifully" for failing to crush the fatigued and starving Rebels who were in full retreat.[55] Untrue rumors were circulated that Sibley and Canby were brothers-in-law. The rumors undoubtedly originated from knowledge in the Federal ranks of the two men's ante-bellum comradeship and Sibley's friendship with Louisa Hawkins Canby. Nevertheless, insinuations of the cowardice, stupidity, and treachery of the Federal Commander were whispered.

[55] Heyman, p. 178.

By ordering a full scale attack Canby probably could have overrun the Confederate Army, but to have done so would have meant appallingly high casualties on both sides. Another factor which must have entered the Federal commander's mind was the fact that he did not have the resources to feed almost fifteen hundred Rebel prisoners. Canby's strategy was probably the wisest.

Taking into consideration the weakened condition of the Texan Army, several officers, including Colonels Green and Scurry, approached Sibley about the possibilities of abandoning the river route. Fort Craig should be avoided at all costs, they argued. Another do-or-die battle with the combined Federal forces might be a disaster. A route west of the river, west of the Magdalena Mountains, and east of the San Mateo would enable the Army of New Mexico safely to reach the river below Fort Craig.

General Sibley appears to have had qualms about abandoning the well-traveled river road. The area west of the Rio Grande was a rugged, virtually unexplored, wilderness inhabited only by roaming bands of Apache and Navajo Indians. His officers assured the general that Major Bethel Coopwood was familiar with the mountain route, having scouted the area two weeks previously on a trek north from the Mesilla Valley. Sibley still seemed doubtful, especially about getting the artillery through. Despite the ruggedness of the terrain, Green and Scurry were determined to "push the artillery through at all hazards" and "at any expenditure of toil and labor."[56] Furthermore, the artillery had become a serious burden on the sandy river road. The mountain route was thought to be much firmer.

At this point in the retreat it appears that the command system in the Army of New Mexico had broken down completely. Regimental commanders and in some instances company commanders were making major decisions without consulting General Sibley or his staff. A strong chain of command, upon which an efficient army must function, had ceased to exist. Anarchy prevailed. It was later rumored that Sibley, realizing the seriousness of the situation, even suggested that the army be surrendered.[57]

Nevertheless, on the afternoon of April 17, orders were issued. Every man was to take with him only his rifle and ammunition and what

[56] H.H. Sibley to S. Cooper, 4 May 1862, *O.R.*, I, IX: 510.
[57] Houston *Tri-Weekly Telegraph*, 6 June 1862.

he could carry on his back. Seven days' rations were packed on mules. Everything that could not be taken was either burned or abandoned. Thirty-eight wagons were left on the sandy west bank of the river. The Confederate sick were left huddled around a fire with a yellow hospital flag flying from the corner of one of the wagons. Accompanying the Rebels in their retreat were several prominent Nuevo Mexicano Confederate sympathizers who, because of their politics or assistance to the Texans during the invasion, thought it best to evacuate the territory. The natives, many with their women and children and carrying their personal property, traveled in light wagons and ambulances.[58]

Led by Major Coopwood and a party of natives called Aragón's men, the Rebels departed in a southwesterly direction toward the Magdalena Mountains. "We struck out for the mountains," a Rebel wrote the Houston *Tri-Weekly Telegraph*, "like so many Bagdad peddlers, everyone was driving a packed mule or broken down horse."[59] The trail, however, proved to be much more difficult than anticipated. Trail grass was plentiful, but the route was "most hazardous," with watering holes few and far between. Sibley would later write that during the mountainous trek "not a murmur escaped the lips of these brave boys."[60] Such was, without a doubt, a misrepresentation of the facts. One young Confederate wrote that the army was "led to bitterly complain against General Sibley for leaving the river."[61] As the army passed the Magdalena Mountains and the extreme southeastern end of the vast St. Augustine Plains, they commenced a traverse of the eastern slopes of the rugged and unexplored San Mateo Mountains, and the going became particularly rough. Here the terrain was extremely broken with hundreds of steep and perilously deep canyons and arroyos running perpendicular to the route. In some instances the artillery and wagons had to be lowered and then pulled out of the deep gorges with ropes and arduous labor.

When the army would break camp in the morning the column would be about a mile long, but by nightfall it would stretch to ten as the sick and weak dragged behind. A private in the Fifth Regiment recorded his thoughts of the terrible retreat: "Surely such a march over

[58] Peticolas Journal, 19 April 1862, p. 112.
[59] Houston *Tri-Weekly Telegraph*, 6 June 1862.
[60] Ibid.
[61] Noel, *A Campaign From Santa Fe to the Mississippi*, p. 44.

such a country and made by men mostly on foot, not accustomed to walking, was never surpassed. It reminds one of reading Bonaparte's celebrated march over the Alps."[62]

The suffering of the Sibley Brigade had become particularly acute. With inadequate clothing some men froze in the higher altitude. Others contracted smallpox and pneumonia. All lived in constant fear of hostile Indians. Hunger intensified.

Many men had to kill their oxen. A few lived on bear and antelope meat. Sibley's men had come to obey a higher authority—near starvation and exhaustion. Yet the army continued to cross a seemingly endless landscape of canyons and rugged mountains. The full effects of the disastrous march were perhaps best recorded by Federal Captain James Graydon, who retraced the route of Sibley's march three weeks later. All along the route Grayson found a trail of devastation. In one place nineteen wagons, ten ambulances, six caissons, and three carriages were found burned. In fact, the Rebels had been forced to bury some of their artillery. Sixty to seventy horses and mules were left dead along the route. Harnesses, medicine and valuable hospital supplies, camp equipment, and all kinds of personal items were found abandoned. In one place Graydon found three of Sibley's dead soldiers half buried and in another, a man's arm half eaten by wolves. Yet the Sibley Brigade made the 109 mile march in seven days, a miraculous feat, considering the ruggedness of the route.[63]

What is so incredible is the fact that Sibley expended so much effort to avoid a pitched battle with the Federal forces at Fort Craig, yet the route along the eastern slopes of the San Mateo Mountains led the Confederates to within fifteen miles of the fort. "Marched about twenty miles without water. To the left we could see Fort Craig," one soldier wrote in his diary.[64] "Pass in view of Craig today," another recorded.[65]

[62] Howell Diary, 21 April 1862.

[63] George H. Pettis, "The Confederate Invasion of New Mexico and Arizona," *Battles and Leaders of the Civil War*, (New York, 1956), II: 104; Jas. Graydon to Colonel Paul, 14 May, 1862, *O.R.*, I, IX: 671; G.K. Paul to Assistant Adjutant General, 6 May 1862, Unregistered L.R., A.G.O., Dept. of New Mexico, R.G. 393. Graydon reported the Confederates completed the route in five days. Most of the Rebels took seven to eight days to make the tortuous trek, however. Howell Diary, 19 April to 25 April 1862; Giesecke Diary, 17 April to 25 April 1862; Peticolas Journal, 17 April to 25 April 1862; Starr Campaign Letters, p. 182.

[64] Giesecke Diary, 21 April 1862, p. 239.

[65] Howell Diary, 22 April 1862.

Sibley undeniably had made another tactical mistake, one that might easily have meant final defeat for his debilitated army. Had Canby, whose army was living on full rations, caught and struck the weakened Rebels at any time during the mountain trek, especially in an area west of Fort Craig, the results could have put an end to Sibley's New Mexico Campaign. The Rebel Army seemed to sense this. "Canby . . . had he been disposed to fight, he surely let his good chances slip him here. Had he moved down the river—which he could have done with ease—to where we struck it thirty-eight miles below Fort Craig, something would have been done, to say the least of it," one soldier wrote.[66] Only Canby's reluctance to shed more blood allowed the Texans to escape safely back into the Mesilla Valley. By the end of April the last of Sibley's Army reached the Rio Grande, there to be supplied by several companies of Colonel William Steel's Seventh Regiment who had remained behind during the fighting in the north.

As Sibley rode southward through the Mesilla Valley to the safety of Fort Bliss, little doubt remained that the bulk of the Army of New Mexico must be evacuated to Texas. The New Mexico Campaign, which was to have secured Colorado and the golden coast of California for the Confederacy, for all practical purposes, was over.

The Sibley Brigade was shattered and defeated, as much or more by the vastness and the sterility of the land and by inadequate and incompetent leadership as by the Union Army. Yet by reading Sibley's final report to Richmond, the opposite impression is given. "I have only to say that we have beaten the enemy in every encounter and against large odds; that from being the worst armed my forces are now the best armed in the country. We reached this point last winter in rags and blanketless. The army is now well clad and well supplied in other respects."[67] So deliberately deceiving was Sibley's report of the campaign that it amounted to little more than deception. The general undoubtedly was fearful of repercussions had he accurately reported the facts to Richmond. Had he done so, he would have risked any hope for a successful future in the Confederate Army. Furthermore, his lack of leadership, which led to tactical errors little short

[66] Noel, *A Campaign From Santa Fe to the Mississippi*, p. 47.
[67] H.H. Sibley to S. Cooper, 4 May 1862, *O.R.*, I, IX: 509.

of blunders, might easily have resulted in a court martial or reduction in rank.

Many survivors of the disastrous campaign viewed their commander with contemptuous disdain. A captain in the Fourth Regiment, in obvious reference to Sibley's heavy drinking, perhaps expressed it best when he wrote a friend back home in Texas: "It is to be hoped that there will be some Courts of Inquiry, and let the people of Texas see whether certain persons can be any longer allowed to play-off when the bullets begin to whistle, and stay in comfortable quarters in town soaking themselves with rum and whisky while others are doing the work."[68] Another Texan, who was taken prisoner during the campaign, bitterly wrote his wife in Texas: "I hope the day is not far distance when Gen. Sibley will be hung."[69] A sergeant in the Fourth Regiment recorded that Sibley was "heartily despised by every man in the brigade for his want of feeling, poor generalship, and cowardice."[70] Another sergeant in the same regiment expressed similar feelings in a letter to his father: "Among the soldiers I hear ridicule and curses heaped upon the head of our gen'l. They call him a coward, which appears very plausible too, for he had never been in an engagement or where there was any appearance of there going to be one."[71]

In a letter to General Hamilton P. Bee, commanding the Western District of the Department of Texas, Sibley described a much more accurate picture of the true state of his army. "Briefly and to the point" Sibley told Bee that his ammunition, forage, and provisions were completely exhausted. The men were in little more than rags. The food situation was especially critical with the entire army subsisting on "poor meat and bread." Vital commodities such as salt, sugar, and coffee were completely gone. Only an adequate supply of flour remained.[72]

Following the Battle of Valverde, Sibley had sent his aide-de-camp, Captain Thomas P. Ochiltree, to Richmond to report personally of the

[68] George H. Brown to Dear Wife, 30 April 1862, in Hollister, p. 260.

[69] W.L. Alexander to Charles S. Taylor, 31 May 1862, in Martin Hardwick Hall, "An Appraisal of the 1862 New Mexico Campaign: A Confederate Officer's Letter to Nacogdoches," *New Mexico Historical Review*, 51 (October 1976), 332.

[70] Peticolas Journal, 27 April 1862, p. 178.

[71] Starr Campaign Letters, p. 182.

[72] H.H. Sibley to H.P. Bee, 27 May 1862, *O.R.*, I, IX: 714.

victory at Valverde and to plead for reinforcements. President Jefferson Davis, still convinced of the far reaching importance of the New Mexico Campaign, asked that two regiments of cavalry, which had previously been ordered to Little Rock, be sent from Texas to reinforce the Army of New Mexico. Realizing "the very destitute and critical condition of General Sibley's command," President Davis also asked that all available supplies be rushed westward.[73]

Almost two weeks after he made the final decision to abandon the campaign, Sibley received a congratulatory letter from President Davis, sent through General Robert E. Lee, praising him for his personal conduct of the campaign which was "recognized as most praiseworthy."[74] With the total collapse of the campaign and his dream of a Confederacy stretching to the shores of the Pacific defunct, probably irrevocably, Sibley felt that Davis' message of congratulations did little more than embarrass him. During the campaign Sibley had sent "report after report to the government" but had not received a "single line of acknowledgement or encouragement." In short, Sibley was depressed and indignant. Despite Richmond's determination that "New Mexico and Arizona be held at all hazards" the area to Sibley was now "not worth a quarter of the blood and treasure expended in its conquest."[75] New Mexico had to be forsaken. Because of the lack of rapid and adequate communications Davis had not been appraised of the current situation in New Mexico.

While still at Fort Bliss, on May 14, 1862, Sibley issued a salutatory proclamation congratulating the Army of New Mexico for the defeat of the enemy "during the short but brilliant campaign." "The boasted valor of Texans has been fully vindicated. Valverde, Glorieta, Albuquerque, Paralto, [sic] and not least, your successful and almost unprecedented evacuation, through mountain passes and over a trackless waste of a hundred miles through a famished country, will be duly

[73] R.E. Lee to Hebert, 31 May 1862, O.R., I, IX: 716.

[74] Ibid. Also, Jefferson Davis to H.H. Sibley, 7 June 1862, O.R., I, IX: 717; Texas State Gazette, 3 May 1862. Davis' praise of Sibley was largely due to the fact that Captain Ochiltree had misled the Confederate president, especially with respect to the Battle of Glorieta. Considering the fact that Ochiltree's report to Davis was sent from San Antonio it is possible that Ochiltree himself was misled. Nevertheless, the captin asserted that seven hundred Federals were either killed or wounded at Glorieta. Ochiltree made no mention of the destruction of the Rebel supply train. Tom P. Ochiltree to President Davis, 27 April 1862, Official Reports of Battles (Richmond, 1862), 186.

[75] H.H. Sibley to S. Cooper, 4 May 1862, O.R., I, IX: 509.

chronicled, and form one of the brightest pages in the history of the
Second American Revolution."[76]

Before leaving Fort Bliss, Sibley took time to write to many of the
parents and spouses of the officers and enlisted men who had lost their
lives during the campaign. One particularly moving letter was addressed to John McRae of Fayetteville, North Carolina, whose son had
died so gallantly while defending the Federal guns at Valverde. Sibley
assured the father that he would do everything possible to recover
McRae's pistol and sabre which were in the possession of two officers
in the Rebel Army. The senior McRae had written Sibley of his past
friendship with the general's father and uncles in North Carolina.
Sibley responded at length by recalling his own memories of his family and thanking McRae for the query. In closing his letter, Sibley
briefly mentioned the New Mexico Campaign and the initial southern victory at Valverde: "You will naturally speculate upon the causes
of my precipitate evacuation of the Territory of N.M. after it had been
virtually conquered. My dear Sir, we beat the enemy whenever we
encountered them. The famished Country beat us."[77] In the latter part
of May the first of Sibley's Army were called into line and sauntered
out of Fort Bliss to take up the long six hundred mile march to San
Antonio. The general himself left El Paso three weeks later.

The march of the Army of New Mexico across the sun-scorched
deserts of west Texas to San Antonio proved to be a monumental ordeal. With a critical shortage of food and inadequate transportation
the men of the Sibley Brigade trod eastward for what seemed like an
eternity—day after day, week after week. Roads were bad. Watering
holes were often dry, and in some instances hostile Mescalero Apache
had filled them with debris and rotting sheep carcasses.[78] The Apache
hovered on the Confederate rear, frequently attacking the weak and
sick stragglers. The men's only consolation was that they had fought
bravely, although for a losing cause, and they were going home.

It was the worst time of year in the west Texas desert. The thermometer soared to over a hundred degrees in the oppressive heat.
Many of the fatigued men, their morale broken, their lips and tongues

[76] Noel, *A Campaign From Santa Fe to the Mississippi*, p. 57.

[77] H.H. Sibley to John McRae, 12 May 1862, John McRae Papers, Southern Historical
Collection, University of North Carolina Library, Chapel Hill, North Carolina. Copy
courtesy of Marion C. Grinstead.

[78] Noel, *A Campaign From Santa Fe to the Mississippi*, p. 53.

swollen from lack of water and terrible heat, simply gave up and laid down by the road to die. A few in their desperation even drank the blood of their dying animals. A woman who passed the retreating Rebels on the San Antonio Overland Stage recorded that "they were suffering terribly from the effects of heat; very many of them are a-foot, and scarcely able to travel from blistered feet. They were subsisting on bread and water, both officers and men; many of them were sick, ragged, and all hungry."[79]

Sibley and numerous other officers, were frequently drunk on the trek back to San Antonio. One soldier sarcastically dubbed the march "the famous whiskey retreat" and remarked that the only reason the Mescalero did not attack the column was that Sibley had drunk all the whiskey and did not have enough to share with the Indians.[80]

Throughout the hot summer of 1862 the men of the Sibley Brigade, their health broken, and looking like scarecrows, wandered back into San Antonio to be given a sixty-day furlough to return home for rest and recuperation.

A resident of San Antonio who had watched the departure of the Sibley Brigade eight months earlier vividly recalled the sad return of what remained of the "Army of New Mexico." "I saw that gallant force march away, with drums beating and flags flying, and every man, from the General downwards, confident of victory. I saw the first detachment of the remnant come straggling back on foot, broken, disorganized, and in an altogether deplorable condition."[81] The general, with a heavy heart, reached town during the second week of July. The New Mexico Campaign had been a total disaster. Casualties were appallingly high. Almost one-third of the general's army had been lost.[82]

The Austin *Texas State Gazette* editorialized that if the Sibley Brigade was part of Davis' defensive strategy, it had "proven to be a grand failure." The newspaper complained that the brigade had been "sent

[79] San Antonio *Herald*, 5 July 1862.

[80] George T. Stansbury to Jennie Gordon, 3 July 1864, George T. Stansbury Papers, Texas State Archives.

[81] R.H. Williams, *With the Border Ruffians: Memories of the Far West, 1852–1868* (London, 1907), 201.

[82] Hall, *The Confederate Army of New Mexico* p. 37. A close examination of the records of the Army of New Mexico lists 119 killed on the battlefield or died of wounds received in combat, sixty-seven died of disease or exposure, and at least 532 taken prisoner. Thus of the 2,515 men who made up the invading army, less than eighteen hundred returned safely to San Antonio.

to conquer a barren wilderness . . . where the soil is sand, the water the essence of bitterness, the towns hovels of mud, the comforts fleas and rattlesnakes, and the people coyotes." Sibley had been "chasing a shadow" while the "flower and strength" of the brigade frittered away.[83]

Much of the blame for the failure of the campaign lay on the shoulders of General Sibley. His biggest mistake was to have underestimated his enemy. He had not only misjudged southern sentiment in the Federal Army but had also miscalculated Union sentiments in California and the mining regions of Colorado. Sibley had moreover shown a great deal of ignorance of the political inclinations of the native Spanish-speaking population of New Mexico who were apathetic toward the South at best and decidedly Unionist at worst. He exhibited considerable ignorance in assessing the political situation in northern Mexico, especially with respect to the willingness of merchants in Sonora and Chihuahua to supply the Rebels.

Other strategic errors can be found in Sibley's inability to prepare adequate logistical support for his army. The general had made a serious mistake in placing blind faith in the ability of his secessionists friends, Josiah F. Crosby and Simeon Hart, to stockpile huge quantities of foodstuffs at Fort Bliss. Sibley had also overestimated his ability to capture badly needed commodities from Federal forces in the territory, especially at Fort Craig and Fort Union.

In addition to the larger more glaring strategic errors, numerous tactical mistakes can be blamed on Sibley. Critical mistakes were made at Valverde and especially at Glorieta by Sibley's regimental commanders, many of which might have been avoided by a dynamic and assertive leader who was on the field of combat. Surely Sibley knew better than to advance deep into a hostile land in the dead of winter without a decisive victory, which Valverde was not, without a strong base of supply. All this had been emphasized time and again at West Point. Few in the Army of New Mexico had more battle experience than Sibley, yet he was absent from the field during most of the Battle of Valverde and sixty miles to the rear during the critical Battle of Glorieta. If Glorieta was the Gettysburg of the West, then Peralta, where he foolishly allowed his army to be divided, might easily have been the Appomattox of the West. Still another glaring error

---

[83] *Texas State Gazette*, 7 June 1862.

had been made by Sibley in his decision to leave the river road for an unfamiliar mountain trek during the retreat—a decision which further demoralized and badly weakened his already defeated army.

Major Trevanion T. Teel, the Rebel artillery commander, accurately summarized General Sibley's lack of leadership when he wrote: "General Sibley was not a good administrative officer. He did not husband his resources, and was too prone to let the morrow take care of itself." This, plus the lack of "supplies, ammunition, discipline, and confidence," left little doubt that "failure was inevitable."[84]

For twenty-three years, ever since he had taken his oath on the plain at West Point in 1838, Sibley had dreamed of commanding a great army in battle. When his one big moment in history arrived, he had failed miserably. All his preconceptions about a conquest of New Mexico and the far West had been shattered; he was a romantic warrior lost in contemporary times. Had the New Mexico Campaign succeeded, Sibley would probably have been hailed as one of the South's greatest military heroes, and the course of the American Civil War might have been radically altered. Instead, he had been badly defeated. As the last of his fatigued and sore-footed soldiers limped into the streets of San Antonio in the summer of 1862, Confederate hopes for the realization of a western Manifest Destiny ceased to exist.

[84] Teel, p. 700.

"It was now about the end of October, 1861, and General Sibley was organising his Texan Brigade of 3,000 mounted men, or three regiments in all, for his expedition to New Mexico. It was a foolhardy scheme to send the flower of our Texan youth on a march like this of 800 miles, into a country where they had no base of operations and could get no reinforcements, and no help, unless they met with complete success. But our leaders were crazy, I think, in those days, and believed they had the game in their own hands; so no enterprise was too rash for them to undertake. I saw that gallant force march away, with drums beating and flags flying, and every man, from the General downwards, confident of victory."

"Alas! A few months after, I saw the first detachment of the remnant come straggling back on foot, broken, disorganised, and in an altogether deplorable condition."

R. H. Williams, *With the Border Ruffians: Memories of the Far West, 1852–1868.*

"In the second week of March a brigade of mounted Texans, with a four-gun battery, reached Opelousas, and was directed to Bisland on the lower Teche. This force numbered thirteen hundred, badly armed; and to equip it exhausted the resources of the little arsenal at New Iberia. The men were hardy and many of the officers brave and zealous, but the value of those qualities was lessened by lack of discipline. Distinctions of rank were unknown. Officers and men addressed each other as Tom, Dick, or Harry, and had no more conception of military gradations than of the celestial hierarchy of the poets."

Richard Taylor, *Destruction and Reconstruction.*

Chapter XI

Failure in the Bayou Country

General Sibley had been in San Antonio only a few weeks when controversy broke out over his leadership of the New Mexico campaign, a controversy which threatened his future in the Southern military. The general had first heard rumors that charges would be filed against him while in the Mesilla Valley in May 1862. At Fort Bliss before the trek back to San Antonio he had seen a copy of the accusations. The culprit, in Sibley's opinion, was a forty-six-year-old captain in the Seventh Regiment, Alfred S. Thurmond. Captain Thurmond was a tough combat veteran of the War for Texas Independence and had spent two years in Mexico's Perote Prison as a result of the Mier Expedition. The outspoken Thurmond had a reputation in the Army of New Mexico for fierce independence and disrespect toward his commanding general. Thurmond, whom Sibley had previously praised for securing the vital supplies at Cubero, had become so disrespectful during the parley on the Rio Grande when it was decided to take the mountainous route to evacuate the territory, that General Sibley had threatened to place him under arrest.

Sibley had attempted to suppress the charges by appealing to Thurmond's regimental commander, Colonel William Steele, a veteran of the Second Dragoons with whom Sibley had served in Florida and

Mexico. The general had every reason to believe that Steele, whom he referred to as "my most intimate friend," would silence the accusations. Shocked by the "scandalous character of the charges" and fearing "the notoriety . . . of being brought before a court," Sibley relied heavily on his personal friendship with Steele.[1] Colonel Steele, who may have encouraged Thurmond to prefer the charges in the first place, refused to cooperate with his commander. Steele, laying aside his personal relationship with Sibley, had sent the charges to Secretary of War George W. Randolph in Richmond. Randolph passed the papers on to President Davis who sent a copy of the charges to General Theophilus H. Holmes, commander of the Trans-Mississippi Department, for investigation. General Holmes, discovering Sibley to be his superior in rank, sent the charges to Major G.M. Bryan, Assistant Adjutant-General of the Trans-Mississippi.[2] More than five months of bureaucratic delays and Bryan's illness with pneumonia caused the investigation of the charges to be delayed, and they were never thoroughly investigated.

Sibley, in the meantime, under orders from General Holmes, had gone to Richmond, where he reported to Adjutant General Cooper on November 25, 1862.[3] Richmond was very different from the city Henry had seen in July 1861. The mood was depressing. Rowdyism, drunkenness, and crime had become a way of life for many. The city was crowded with refugees, many of them women and children. Thousands of slaves also scurried about, carrying their meager belongings tied to their backs. The streets were full of soldiers on leave as well as profiteers and shady characters of all sorts. The glowing optimism Sibley had witnessed in 1861 had turned to pessimism with the repulse at Antietam of Lee's Army of Northern Virginia. After the bloodbath in Maryland on September 17, Lee had escaped back across the Blue Ridge Mountains into Virginia and was preparing defenses along the Rappahannock. Richmond's fifty hospitals were amputat-

[1] H.H. Sibley to S. Cooper, 25 November 1862, Letters Received, Adjutant General's Office, R.G. 109. Captain Thurmond himself in January 1865, would be found guilty in a court-martial of "behaving with contempt toward his commanding officer" and "conduct to the prejudice of good order and military discipline." He was suspended from rank for eight months but remained on duty. General Orders; No. 16, Headquarters, District of Arkansas, 22 January 1865, C.M.S.R. of Alfred S. Thurmond, R.G. 109.

[2] M. Bryan to P.O. Hebert, 21 November 1862, C.M.S.R. of H.H. Sibley, R.G. 109; S.S. Anderson to H.H. Sibley, 24 October 1862, *O.R.*, I, XV: 843.

[3] H.H. Sibley to S. Cooper, 25 November 1862. L.R., A.G.O., R.G. 109.

ing arms and legs at an appalling rate, with doctors working day and night without anesthetics.

The Union Army of the Potomac under its new commander, Ambrose E. Burnside, was slowly moving toward the town of Fredericksburg for a certain confrontation with Lee's determined Rebels. Blankets and overcoats were being impressed from the city's populace to comfort the army in the rapidly approaching winter. To complicate matters, badly needed English and French recognition, which had seemed so close only months before, now appeared distant. On the seas the tightening Union blockade stretching from Chesapeake Bay to the mouth of the Rio Grande was strangling Confederate commerce. But with the tramp of Confederate cavalry and infantry almost daily through the streets, the Rebel government was determined to go down fighting. Plans were even underway to blow up the Capitol if the fall of Richmond seemed likely.[4]

General Sibley, having seen a copy of the accusations against him, had more than adequate time to prepare his defense. He had taken to Richmond several members of his staff, all of whom had remained intensely loyal during the campaign. They included his young aide-de-camp, Thomas P. Ochiltree, whom Sibley had promoted to captain after Valverde and transferred to the Adjutant General's Department; Major Richard T. Brownrigg, Chief of Commissary; Captain Joseph Magoffin, volunteer aide-de-camp who had also served in the Commissary Department; Lieutenant Joseph E. Dwyer who had replaced Ochiltree as aide-de-camp; and Chief of Ordnance Captain Willis L. Robards.

Specifically, Captain Thurmond accused Sibley of being drunk while on duty, of inhumane treatment of sick and wounded soldiers, cowardice, and misappropriation of confiscated goods.

Under the first charge Thurmond claimed that Sibley was drunk at Fort Thorn as the army was preparing to move against Fort Craig, again before and during the Battle of Valverde, and at Albuquerque during the first week of March 1862. Under the second charge Thurmond asserted that Sibley had cruelly abandoned sick and wounded soldiers at Santa Fe and Socorro. Under the third charge Sibley was accused of cowardice, first at Valverde, second in his decision to evacuate the

[4] Virginius Dabney, *Richmond, The Story of a City* (New York, 1976), 173; Alfred Hoyt Bill, *The Beleagured City: Richmond, 1861–1865* (New York, 1946), 152.

territory, and third in the decision to take the mountainous route to avoid the Federals at Fort Craig. Under the peculation or misappropriation charge Sibley was accused of taking items from the Stapleton Ranch, upriver from Fort Craig, for his personal benefit.[5]

Two days after arriving in Richmond, Sibley had Ochiltree, Brownrigg, Magoffin, Dwyer, and Robards write out lengthy affidavits in his defense. Ochiltree in a strong defense of his commander referred to the charges as "fallacious and disgusting" and an example of "slander from beginning to end." No one had been "more cognizant of your actions than myself," Ochiltree wrote Sibley.[6] According to the auburn-haired Ochiltree the general was not drunk at Fort Thorn but under medical treatment. In fact Sibley was so ill, Ochiltree argued, that there was some doubt as to his recovery.

During his time with the Army of New Mexico, Ochiltree had seen Sibley only as "cool, calm, and deliberate." Although the young captain had left the army prior to the evacuation and had not been present when the Confederate sick and wounded were abandoned, "I do know that you visited the soldiers with small pox in the hospital at Doña Ana and remained with them for hours." With reference to the charge of cowardice, Ochiltree felt it would have been sheer "madness for the Confederate troops to remain in New Mexico."[7] Ochiltree also swore that he was with Sibley when the Stapleton Ranch had been seized and that nothing of personal use had been taken by the general. In fact, when Ochiltree had left for Richmond General Sibley had only four dollars in his possession, two dollars of which the captain had borrowed.

Lieutenant Dwyer, like Ochiltree, argued that the general was not drunk but only ill at Fort Thorn and Valverde. Dwyer did not deny "that the camps were filled with the rumor that General Sibley was drunk," but at no time during the entire campaign did Sibley "use liquor to such an extent as to intoxicate him and render him unfit for duty."[8] Dwyer too recalled Sibley's visits to the hospital at Doña Ana and Sibley's twice a day visits to the Valverde wounded. Dwyer argued that it had been more humane to leave the sick and wounded

[5] Thurmond's charges could not be found. The specifics are taken from Sibley's defense. For the sacking of the Stapleton Ranch see: Peticolas, 23 February 1862, p. 52.

[6] Tom P. Ochiltree to My Dear General, 28 November 1862, L.R., A.G.O., R.G. 109.

[7] Ibid.

[8] Memorandum Statement by Jos. E. Dwyer, n.d., L.R., A.G.O., R.G. 109.

where they could be taken by the Federals to the hospital at Socorro than to try to take them through the mountains. With reference to the charge of cowardice, Dwyer wrote that Sibley had been in the saddle at Valverde from daybreak until 1:30 P.M. when he had been forced to retire because of his "feeble health." Dwyer argued further that his commander, owing to lack of provisions, had no alternative but to order the evacuation. Furthermore, to Dwyer "the march through those mountain passes and the difficulties the army of New Mexico overcame were certainly equal to a victory."[9]

The testimony of Brownrigg and Magoffin, who wrote a seven-page joint statement in Sibley's defense, was similar to that of Ochiltree and Dwyer. They had been with Sibley continuously during the campaign and argued that he was sick, not drunk, at Fort Thorn and Valverde. Stating that he was drunk at Albuquerque was "untrue and atrocious" and an "unmitigated lie." With reference to the other charges, Brownrigg and Magoffin stated they had been with Sibley under fire at Valverde and had seen no evidence of cowardice. Although the Rebel retreat certainly had not resembled a "dress parade," it, nevertheless, was a success, they argued.[10]

The most moving, frank, and convincing defense of Sibley came from Captain Robards. Robards had no doubt that to the "casual observer unacquainted with the habits and temperament of General Sibley, it might appear that he occasionally drank too much." Sibley, nevertheless, "like most of the old army officers," was convivial but always had complete control of himself. Robards swore flatly that Sibley was a "high toned gentleman" who "detests and loaths a drunkard."[11] At Valverde Sibley had pneumonia and was not drunk as Thurmond had charged. To Robards the other charges were equally absurd.

The testimony of Sibley's five defenders shows amazing similarities. They, like Sibley, had had ample time prior to the Richmond visit to rehearse their stories. Their futures in the Confederate military were tied closely to that of their commander. They certainly were some of the general's most loyal supporters and undoubtedly were chosen for this reason.

[9] Ibid.

[10] R.T. Brownrigg and Samuel Magoffin, Jr. to General, 27 November 1862, L.R., A.G.O., R.G. 109.

[11] W.L. Robards to Jefferson Davis, 8 December 1862, L.R., A.G.O., R.G. 109.

While in Richmond Sibley was able to confer with President Davis. From the few sketchy details of the meeting, it is possible to ascertain that the two men talked frankly and that Davis was not overly concerned about the charges against Sibley, still continuing to have faith in his General of the West. The two also talked at some length about the political and military situation in Louisiana with the president impressing upon the general "the importance of immediate and active operations" in the Bayou State.[12]

It was perhaps to Sibley's advantage that his future was decided largely by President Jefferson Davis rather than by the newly appointed Secretary of War, James A. Seddon, with whom Sibley was not familiar. Davis had always liked Sibley, a West Pointer and Mexican War veteran, and from the beginning had professed faith in the outcome of the New Mexico campaign. Even the failure of the campaign did not dim the president's faith in Sibley. With the papers in the case being shuffled back and forth between the secretary of war and the president, Davis finally decided to dismiss the charges, writing that the papers in the case had not been properly preferred and had reached the adjutant general's office "informally."[13] Shortly thereafter Sibley was ordered to resume command of his brigade at New Iberia, Louisiana.

Sibley's reputation in the Lone Star State was further damaged when the Texas House of Representatives and Senate passed resolutions calling for an investigation into his conduct of the New Mexico Campaign and the resulting charges.[14]

There is little doubt that a proper and thorough investigation of the charges in the case might have ended Sibley's career in the Confederate Army. Sibley's familiarity with Richmond politics, his friendship with the president, as well as the convincing defense by members of his staff no doubt saved him. Even in a careful, painstaking

[12] H.H. Sibley to T.H. Holmes, 25 December 1862, *O.R.*, I, XV: 910.

[13] Miscellaneous Document, n.d., L.R., A.G.O., R.G. 109.

[14] James M. Day, ed. *House Journal of the Ninth Legislature, First Called Session of the State of Texas* (Austin, 1963), 209; James M. Day, ed. *Senate Journal of the Ninth Legislature, First Called Session of the State of Texas* (Austin, 1963), 153. Although the resolution was adopted by both houses of the Texas Legislature, an investigation was never concluded, possibly as a result of Richmond's decision to drop the charges. The investigation may well have been pushed by P.A. Thurmond a relative to Captain Thurmond who represented Goliad, Refugio, and San Patricio Counties in the House of Representatives.

investigation Colonel Steele and Captain Thurmond would have been hard-pressed to prove many of their accusations.

At the same time General Sibley was preparing to defend himself from Thurmond's charges, another closely related dispute erupted in Texas and Richmond. From the beginning of the Confederate invasion of New Mexico, Sibley and John Robert Baylor had been at odds. Sibley, as commander of the Army of New Mexico, and Baylor, colonel and self-proclaimed governor of Arizona, were both egotistical, overly confident, fiercely independent, and envious of one another's position. Although Sibley had incorporated Baylor's Second Texas Mounted Rifles into the Army of New Mexico, he had no intention of superseding Baylor's authority as governor of Arizona. Nevertheless, Baylor's pride was hurt, for it was he, not Sibley, who had led the Confederate thrust into the Mesilla Valley and it was he, a Texan, in whom many in the Army of New Mexico had great faith. The nature of the two men and their respective military and political positions inevitably led to mistrust and a running feud.

The origins of the Sibley-Baylor confrontation can be traced to the arrival of the Army of New Mexico in the Mesilla Valley when Mescalero Apache ran off one hundred valuable horses and mules. Baylor, with 150 men, pursued the Indians across the international boundary deep into the Sierra Madre Mountains of Chihuahua to the remote mining village of Carretas. Although the Indians attempted to surrender, Baylor ordered their annihilation, and only a few escaped the Carretas Massacre.

Baylor's wrath was further aroused when another band of Indians, reported to number some 120, attacked a patrol in the Mesilla Valley escorting two wagons of rifles and medical supplies. The Apache not only carried off between fifty and seventy-five rifles but also set fire to the wagons and medicines. One soldier wrote that the mountains were "full of Indians and we dread them worse then we do the Lincolnites."[15]

When Baylor heard that a band of Apache had been talking to Thomas Helm, captain of a Confederate company which was guarding the mines at Pinos Altos, he issued an extermination order: "You will therefore use all means to persuade the Apaches or any tribe to come in for the purposes of making peace, and when you get them

---

[15] Austin *Texas State Gazette*, 15 February 1862.

together kill all the grown Indians. Buy whiskey and such other goods as may be necessary for the Indians and I will order vouchers to cover the amount expended. Leave nothing undone to insure success, and have sufficient number of men around to allow no Indians to escape."[16] This infamous order would cause Baylor and Sibley much trauma in the future.

Although he never gave up hopes of conquering the West for the Confederacy, Baylor was so envious of Sibley's position and so intolerant of Sibley's heavy drinking that he resigned as governor of Arizona and as colonel in the Confederate Army.[17] In fact Baylor's letter of resignation had been written to Richmond three days before he issued his controversial extermination order to Captain Helm. Baylor had hoped to go to the Confederate capital to obtain permission to raise a regiment of his own.

General Sibley learned of Baylor's extermination order upon his return to Fort Bliss in May 1862 after the evacuation of the territory. Although Sibley had spent much of his life at military posts on the frontier and had had frequent contact with Indians, he never learned to hate the native Americans as Baylor did. In fact, from the time of his youth at Grand Ecore when Caddo chiefs had strolled the spacious grounds of his grandfather's plantation and later at Miami Grammar School when he had shared the classroom with Indian children from Louisiana, he had held the natives in respect. Sibley viewed Baylor's policy toward the hostile Indians in New Mexico and Arizona as one of intense ruthlessness, deserving the severest censure.

Sibley associated Baylor with that faction of his army which had instigated the charges against him. Shocked by Baylor's extermination order and disliking Baylor personally, either the general or one of his aides, probably Ochiltree, sent a copy of Baylor's infamous order to the War Department in Richmond which responded with instant shock and indignation.

The Confederate Government had only recently negotiated trea-

[16] John R. Baylor to Thomas Helm, 20 March 1862, O.R., I, L: 942.

[17] John R. Baylor to H.H. Sibley, 17 March 1862, C.M.S.R. of John R. Baylor. R.G. 109. President Jefferson Davis later restored Baylor to his previous rank of colonel. Also of interest is: John to Emy, 12 January 1862, John R. Baylor Papers, University of Texas Archives. Also, Thompson, pp. 77–79. Baylor's problems in the Mesilla Valley had been complicated by his shooting to death the editor of the *Mesilla Times*, Robert Kelley. Also, *San Antonio Weekly Herald*, 4, 11 January 1862.

ties with the Five Civilized Tribes, and if news of Baylor's attempts at exterminating Apache reached the Indian Territory, it would no doubt have far-reaching repercussions. Secretary of War George Randolph was so shocked that he had a copy of Baylor's order returned to Sibley for verification. When it was returned as a "true and full copy," Randolph sent it on to President Davis. Randolph's agitation and displeasure were perhaps best reflected in his clerk's diary: "Now it will go to the President—and we shall see what will follow. He cannot sanction such a perfidious crime."[18]

Not long after the extermination order reached Richmond, either Sibley or Ochiltree gave a copy of the order to Robert W. Loughery, editor of the Marshall *Texas State Republican*, who demanded that Baylor be punished.[19] Shortly thereafter the Houston *Tri-Weekly Telegraph* also published the order along with a comment by Ochiltree. Baylor, hearing of the furor his order had created, furiously blamed Ochiltree and Sibley for the controversy. Baylor, blind with rage and prejudice, in a lengthy and sarcastic letter to the Houston newspaper, bluntly stated: "I issued it, and meant precisely what I said; and if I am so fortunate as to return to Arizona, I intend to get rid of the Indians in any way I can."[20]

Baylor's loathing of the Apache was matched only by his hatred of Sibley. Referring to Sibley as the "hero of the waggon [sic] train at the battle of Val Verde," Baylor spent more time in a venomous personal attack on Sibley than in defending his Indian policy. In reference to his plan to lure the Indians into Pinos Altos before killing them, Baylor wrote: "General Sibley needs no information: it is enough for him to know that there was to be a quantity of whiskey used in the enterprise to shock and horrify him. I could not have been guilty of a greater crime in the estimation of the 'hero' than to waste whiskey in killing Indians."[21] Elsewhere in the lengthy letter Baylor made yet another biting reference to Sibley's heavy drinking: "General Sibley

[18] John B. Jones, *A Rebel War Clerk's Diary*, Earl Schenck Miers, ed. (New York, 1961), 109.

[19] Houston *Tri-Weekly Telegraph*, 17 October 1862. The 27 September 1862, Marshall *Texas State Republican* has been lost, but it is possible to ascertain Loughery's remarks by reading Baylor's reply.

[20] Ibid. A clipping of this issue of the Houston *Tri-Weekly Telegram*, 17 October 1862, can also be found in Letters Received, Secretary of War, R.G. 109.

[21] Ibid.

no doubt, would never resort to such means of ridding the country of such pests, but if the Indians could by any means be converted into whiskey, I have no doubt he would drink the whole Apache nation in a week."[22]

Baylor's denunciation of Sibley went beyond the charge of drunkenness to include cowardice. During the Battle of Valverde, Baylor asserted, Sibley had been "doubled up in his ambulance in the centre of the wagons a mile from the battleground and with a hospital flag hoisted over him." There were not thirty men in Sibley's entire brigade that would serve under him if they had a chance, Baylor asserted. Sibley was an "infamous coward" who was detested as "mean and worthless," not only by his men, but by the people of Texas, in every highway and street, every village and city, from the Red River to the Rio Grande. "I venture the assertion that there never was a man in this state so universally detested and abhorred as General Sibley," Baylor concluded.[23] Loughery, in his Marshall *Texas State Republican*, attempted to defend Sibley by stating bluntly that Baylor was morally corrupt and infused with poison and that his letter should "be justly regarded as unworthy."[24]

Sibley did not respond to Baylor's bitter denunciation, and the feud did not go beyond the Marshall and Houston newspapers. The controversy, however, did much to discredit both men, especially Sibley. In such a quarrel there could be no winners, only losers.

Richmond would have the last word in the Sibley-Baylor feud. When President Davis received a copy of Baylor's letter to the Houston *Tri-Weekly Telegraph*, he decided to take action. "It is an avowal of an infamous crime" he wrote and proceeded to instruct Secretary of War Randolph to order General John Bankhead Magruder, commanding the Trans-Mississippi, to revoke Baylor's commission in the Confederate Army.[25] Furthermore, Magruder was to order Baylor to write a full report to the president explaining the barbaric order. Baylor did write a lengthy report to Magruder, who was so impressed that he attempted to keep Baylor as governor of Arizona and commander of a new regiment that Baylor had recruited. In his attempts at getting

[22] Ibid.
[23] Ibid.
[24] Marshall *Texas Republican*, 8 November 1862.
[25] Jefferson Davis to Secretary of War, 29 March, 1863, *O.R.*, I, XV: 919; George Randolph to H.L. Clay, 7 November 1862, *O.R.*, I, XV: 857.

Baylor reinstated, Magruder asserted that the Apache were "not better than wild beasts and totally unworthy of sympathy."[26] Richmond turned a deaf ear. Events of a greater nature were soon to occupy the attentions of Sibley, Baylor, Davis, and Magruder.

Prior to his visit to Richmond to defend himself against the Thurmond charges, General Sibley had moved the headquarters of the Sibley Brigade to Marshall, deep in the piney woods of east Texas, where he, along with his family, moved into the Adkins House on September 9, 1862.[27]

Throughout the fall of 1862 there had been a great deal of confusion in Richmond, the Trans-Mississippi, and in Texas as to exactly what to do with the Sibley Brigade. The Secretary of War had at first decided to send the brigade to New Iberia, Louisiana, there to be placed under the command of General Richard Taylor, son of the late President Zachary Taylor, who was preparing to defend southern Louisiana from a Union force that was expected to push northward up the Mississippi and Red Rivers from New Orleans. Prior to ordering the reassembling of his troops and a march to Louisiana, Sibley had sent a letter to General Paul O. Hebert, commanding the Department of Texas, to determine if "the state of Texas was in imminent peril of invasion."[28] Less than three weeks later, one month after the bloody Battle of Antietam, orders arrived directing the brigade to report to Richmond with as little delay as possible. To expedite the transfer the brigade was to leave its horses and arms in Texas and be remounted and armed once it arrived in Virginia.[29]

The decision to send the brigade to Virginia was revoked when an even more desperate plea for reinforcements came from General John C. Pemberton who was attempting to defend Vicksburg from a large Federal force under General Ulysses S. Grant, who was moving against the strategic Southern bastion from the north.[30] General Sibley learned of the decision to send his brigade to Vicksburg rather than Rich-

[26] John R. Baylor to John B. Magruder, 29 December 1862, O.R., I, XV: 914-918; J. Bankhead Magruder to H.L. Clay, 6 February 1863, O.R., IV: 918.

[27] Marshall Texas Republican, 13 September 1862; Dallas Herald, 20 September 1862.

[28] H.H. Sibley to George W. Randolph, 1 October 1862, O.R., I, XV: 819.

[29] S.S. Anderson to P.O. Hebert, 18 October, 1862, O.R., I, XV: 832; S.S. Anderson to G.M. Bryan, 18 October 1862, O.R., I, XV: 833; Th. H. Homes endorsement on latter document.

[30] Th. H. Holmes to J.C. Pemberton, 25 November 1862, O.R., I, XXII: 898.

mond while at Mobile, Alabama, on his way to Richmond to answer the Thurmond charges.[31]

When General Pemberton at Vicksburg learned that the only reinforcements he would receive from the west was Sibley's brigade, he disgustedly wrote President Davis that Sibley would help Vicksburg "but little."[32] President Davis, who did not want the brigade sent to Vicksburg anyway, responded to Pemberton by stating that he was "disappointed by a renewed attempt to withdraw Sibley's brigade from the special service for which it was designed."[33] Finally on November 29, 1862, after a considerable amount of confusion as to what to do with the brigade, General Cooper decided to send the troops to Louisiana to join General Taylor where they had originally been ordered two months previously.[34]

The transfer of the brigade to Louisiana was delayed when it was ordered to assist in the recapture of Galveston on January 1, 1863. The gallantry of the brigade at Galveston proved to be their proudest moment. Some of the brigade even served on board ship during the battle, earning the title of "horsemarines." Soon after the Battle of Galveston, the brigade received orders to take up the line of march for Louisiana but was delayed by the lack of transportation and the poor condition of the brigade's horses and mules. Further delays were caused by heavy winter rains that turned many of the roads in east Texas into a quagmire. From Houston on January 31, 1863, Colonel Reily wrote Sibley that it would "be a hard and difficult task to report the brigade at New Iberia." Contrary to what Baylor and Thurmond had been writing, Reily, one of Sibley's most loyal supporters, informed the general that there was not an "officer or man in the brigade that does not feel proud of having fought under your immediate command and we separate with sorrow from a hero who had learned [sic] us how to conquer both on land and water."[35]

Sibley was able to leave the capital during the second week of December 1862. With a Federal Army in possession of western Tennessee, he was forced to take a southern route through the Carolinas, Georgia, Alabama, and on to Jackson, Mississippi, where he received

[31] S. Cooper to the President, 29 November 1862, O.R., I, XVII, I: 768.

[32] J.S. Pemberton to Jefferson Davis, 28 November 1862, O.R., I, XVII: 767.

[33] Jefferson Davis to S. Cooper, 28 November 1862, O.R., I, XVII: 767.

[34] S. Cooper to J.C. Pemberton, 29 November 1862, O.R., I, XXII, I: 899.

[35] James Reily to H.H. Sibley, 31 January 1863, O.R., I, XV: 970.

the first news that his brigade had been ordered to Galveston. From Jackson he went on to Vicksburg where high on the bluffs overlooking the Mississippi, he met with West Point classmate Pemberton. Crossing the Mississippi into Louisiana, he reached Opelousas on Christmas Day, 1862.

In Opelousas, Louisiana's Confederate capital since the fall of Baton Rouge, Sibley met with the governor of Louisiana, Thomas O. Moore, and several members of the state legislature. The general quickly learned that south central Louisiana was in terrible condition: "This part of the State of Louisiana, by far the richest in the Confederacy, is in a lamentably defenseless condition," Sibley wrote General Holmes, commanding the Trans-Mississippi.[36] Many of the citizens had lost faith in the Confederate government and were "fleeing from every quarter in every direction." "This country is absolutely destitute, I fear of both men and material," Sibley continued. Sibley went on to New Iberia where he spent several days reconnoitering the roads streams and general topography of the land. He was especially interested in the area around the valuable salt works at Avery Island. Evidently, President Davis had impressed upon him the urgency of protecting the large salt mine while Sibley was in Richmond. The protection of the mine was critical, the Union occupation of New Orleans and the Federal blockade having cut the flow of salt into the South. In fact the protection of the mine was one of the reasons Davis had wanted the brigade sent to Louisiana. Salt, which was used to preserve meat and to season foods, was something the South could not do without.

If Union intelligence can be believed, General Sibley did not hesitate in taking to the field of battle upon his arrival in Louisiana. Only a week after arriving in Opelousas, with his brigade still in Texas, Sibley was reported at the head of a Rebel column at Indian Village on the west bank of the Mississippi, southeast of Opelousas. The general successfully forced the evacuation of the village of Plaquemines before being driven out three weeks later.[37]

Two and a half months after his arrival in Louisiana his old brigade reached New Iberia from Texas. The general had not seen his army in more than five months and the reunion was a memorable one. As

---

[36] H.H. Sibley to T.H. Holmes, 25 December 1862, O.R., I, XV: 910–11.
[37] James H. Bogart to General Grover, 4 January 1863, O.R., I, XV: 197.

Richmond had directed, the brigade was placed under the command of General Richard Taylor who was preparing to defend the Bayou Teche region against a Federal Army under General Nathaniel Banks, Union commander of the Department of the Gulf.

General Taylor found Sibley's army so lacking in arms that it took the entire Confederate arsenal at New Iberia to equip the brigade properly. The men of the brigade were nevertheless, "hardy and many of the officers brave and zealous," Taylor felt.

An English officer, James Arthur Lyon Fremantle, traveling through the region at the time, talked with a regiment of the brigade and found the men to be "dressed in every variety of costume, and armed with every variety of weapon. About sixty had Enfield rifles: the remainder carried shotguns, carbines, or long rifles of a peculiar and antiquated manufacture. None had swords or bayonets—all had six-shooters and bowie knives."[38]

The brigade was also appallingly lacking in discipline, perhaps a serious reflection on Sibley's lack of leadership during the New Mexico Campaign. Distinctions of rank in the brigade were unknown. According to Taylor, "officers and men addressed each other as Tom, Dick, or Harry, and had no more conception of military gradations than of the celestial hierarchy of the poets."[39] When the brigade had arrived from Texas, Taylor had ridden out to inspect one of the regiments. Upon approaching the Texan camp, he found everything strangely quiet, evidence of good discipline, he thought. Drawing nearer, he found the colonel of the regiment seated on the ground beneath a huge oak tree absorbed in a game of monte as his men huddled around. When Taylor declined to join in the game, the colonel of the regiment seemed displeased. He became further angered when he was forced to abandon his game to converse with General Taylor. Taylor's encounter with the Sibley Brigade tends to support the hypothesis that the South lost the war partly as a result of the fierce in-

[38] James Arthur Lyon Fremantle, *The Fremantle Diary*, Walter Lord, ed. (London, 1956), 58.

[39] Richard Taylor, *Destruction and Reconstruction*, Richard B. Harwell, ed. (New York, 1955), 150. Taylor's memoirs are thought by many to be the best written memoirs of any Civil War general. See: Jon L. Wakelyn, *Biographical Dictionary* of the Confederacy (Westport, 1977), 407. General Taylor's encounter with the Sibley Brigade appears to be a classic example of David Donald's assertion that the Confederacy was stymied by too much democracy. David Donald, "Died of Democracy," *Why the North Won the Civil War*, David Donald, ed. (Baton Rouge, 1969), 77–90.

dividualism of the Southern fighting man as well as an overemphasis on democracy in the military hierarchy.

General Bank's Bayou Teche Campaign to capture southern Louisiana, a prelude to moving up the Red River for an advance against east Texas, began haphazardly in March 1863. By early April as many as eighteen thousand Union infantry, cavalry, and artillery had been concentrated in the Berwick Bay area along with piles of provisions. From here Federal gunboats were sent up the Atchafalaya River, Grand Lake, and into Bayou Teche.

Earlier, on February 4, 1863, General Sibley had written the commander of Port Hudson, General Frank Gardner, from his temporary headquarters at Rosedale, that one of his officers near the mouth of the Red River had spotted the Union gunboat-ram, the *Queen of the West*, which was thought to be proceeding up the Red River. The *Queen*, which had previously run by the Confederate guns at Vicksburg, was equipped with twelve 12-pounder guns. Sibley immediately sent out a company of cavalry accompanied by a battery of artillery to try to capture the *Queen*.[40] General Taylor, hearing this intelligence report, rode south and assisted in the capture of the ram.

The biggest prize came less than two weeks later when the Union gunboat *Diana*, while making a reconnaissance of Grand Lake, steamed up the Atchafalaya by mistake to where the Sibley Brigade waited in camp. Sibley's cavalry at first was content to dash alongside the boat. This proved fatal when the *Diana's* guns riddled the horsemen, killing several of the Texans and forcing the remainder to take refuge in a nearby woods.

The Valverde battery, the captured guns from New Mexico, was able to open a deadly fire on the *Diana* which lasted for over three hours. Disabled, the *Diana* became a death trap. The gunboat was riddled from stem to stern as "hunks of flesh and spots of slippery blood and gore soon littered the decks." A white flag of surrender was welcomed by the Texans. Thirty Federals had been killed in the carnage and 120 men and officers captured; the *Diana*, with its five valuable heavy guns, was hurriedly repaired and put into action by the Con-

---

[40] H.H. Sibley to Frank Gardner, 4 February 1863, *The Official Records of the Union and Confederate Navies in The War of the Rebellion* (Washington, 1889), I, XXIV: 225. This set of records will hereafter be referred to as *O.R.N.* The same letter can be found in *O.R.*, I, XXIV: 339.

federates.[41] After the disaster in New Mexico, the capture of the *Diana*, as well as the victory at Galveston, did much to rejuvenate the morale of the Sibley Brigade.

Originally, Taylor expressed confidence that Sibley would have few problems "whipping all the raw Yankees" on Bayou Teche. If Banks attacked in force, possibly in two columns, Sibley was to concentrate his forces "in a central position and strike a heavy blow" on the nearest Federals. In fact, Taylor was so confident that he felt it was only a matter of time before Sibley, with his "fine artillery and superior cavalry," would be able to "clear out our side of the river."[42]

Sibley disagreed with Taylor on how to defend the Acadian bayou country. Sibley was convinced that it was impossible to fortify and successfully defend the Bayou Teche south of New Iberia. A Confederate defense should be made at New Iberia, he argued, where it would be impossible to outflank the outnumbered Confederates. Here Bayou Teche could easily be blocked by sunken boats. Sibley was overruled by both Taylor and public opinion. General Taylor, who felt Sibley was in "feeble health," was determined to stop the Union advance at a spot on the Teche between the villages of Pattersonville and Centerville.

Here at what was called Fort Bisland, simple breastworks were thrown up across a narrow neck of dry land that extended on both sides of the bayou. On the extreme Rebel right and left, large cypress swamps and canebreaks, overlooked by redoubts, secured the Rebel flanks. On either side of the bayou were fields of knee-high sugar cane. The entire Confederate line of over three thousand men stretched for a mile on both sides of the bayou. Sibley was placed in command of the west bank where fifteen hundred men were strung out from the bayou to the cypress swamp. On Sibley's extreme right Colonel Green's Fifth Texas Regiment and Colonel Edwin Waller's Battalion, both dismounted, held the line. On their left was the Valverde Battery and in the center a regiment of Louisiana infantry. On Sibley's extreme left, two batteries of artillery including a 24-pounder seige

[41] John D. Winters, *The Civil War in Louisiana* (Baton Rouge, 1963), 222; Morris Raphael, *The Battle in the Bayou Country* (Detroit, 1975), 77–85; *Dallas Herald*, 15 April 1863.

[42] R. Taylor to H.H. Sibley, 2 March 1863, Henry Hopkins Sibley Letters, New York Historical Society, New York, New York.

gun, commanded the bayou and the wagon road along the west bank.[43] The captured gunboat *Diana* with a crew from the Valverde Battery was placed in the center of the bayou to anchor the center of the Rebel line. The scene was set for the decisive Battle of Bisland.

Taylor, upon hearing that a large Federal force was preparing to land on the west bank of Grand Lake to his rear, decided to seize the initiative by ordering Sibley to make a general attack against Bank's left at daybreak on April 13. Taylor was convinced that such a move could drive the Federals back and throw the Union Army into confusion thus forcing Banks to withdraw the army in the Rebel rear. Sibley, despite Taylor's order, decided such a plan was impractical due to lack of time and did not respond. Taylor returned to the west bank at daybreak only to find that Sibley had refused to put the plan into action, and had never had any intentions of doing so. Taylor was furious. Disgusted with Sibley's inactivity during the battle, Taylor argued that had the desired attack been made, it "would have accomplished the most favorable results."[44]

As daylight crept across the bayou country and a heavy fog lifted, Taylor found Banks' entire army advancing against his lines. On the west bank Union Generals Godfrey Weitzel and Halbert E. Paine sent more than four thousand men against Sibley's line. Two regiments of New Yorkers who were attempting to turn the Rebel right were forced into a thick canebreak by a heavy cannonade. Twice the New Yorkers attempted to turn the Confederate right but were driven off by Green's Fifth Regiment and Waller's Battalion reinforced by the Louisiana Regiment, all covered by the artillery. At three o'clock in the afternoon Sibley was able to make an advance by his right against the weakened Federal left.[45] With the famous Rebel yell the Confederates plunged into the cypress swamp and canebreak, but owing to the denseness of the vegetation and the impenetrable swampland, the enemy, in most instances, could not even be seen. All day the two

[43] Winters, p. 225; Raphael, p. 94; Charles Spurlin, ed. *West of the Mississippi with Waller's 13th Texas Cavalry Battalion, C.S.A.* (Hillsboro, 1971).

[44] Report of Richard Taylor, 26 April 1863, *O.R.*, I, XV: 389. For a history of the Valverde Battery see: P.N. Broune, "Captain T.D. Nettles and the Valverde Battery," *Texana,* 2 (No.1), 1–23. For the battles of Bisland and Irish Bend see: Jack Rudolph, "Battles in the Bayous," *Civil War Times Illustrated,* 23 (January, 1985), 12–21.

[45] Ibid., p. 390.

forces skirmished back and forth on the west bank without either side able to seize the initiative.

Banks, hoping that his movement in the Rebel rear would force Taylor to evacuate Bisland, had been content during the day simply to hold the Confederates in position. As dusk fell, Banks withdrew his army all along the line and went into bivouac. In the Rebel camp Taylor received disastrous news. Colonel Reily, who had been acting as Taylor's reserve but had been rushed to the rear upon hearing of the successful Union landing on the shore of Grand Lake, brought word that the Federals had repulsed his counterattack and controlled the only road by which Taylor could evacuate Bisland. Taylor, outnumbered twelve thousand to four thousand with impending disaster about to engulf his army, had no alternative but to order a general retreat, attack the army in his rear, and drive through to the safety of New Iberia, twenty-five miles up Bayou Teche. Without waiting for daylight, Taylor commenced his retreat.

At three o'clock on the morning of April 14, just as the Confederates' rear guard prepared to move out, Banks discovered Taylor's plan. At daybreak when the aroused Federals stormed the Bisland breastworks, no Rebels were in sight. Green, acting as Taylor's rear guard, was able to hold Bank's advance in check "with great coolness and steadiness."[46] In the final Federal charge Colonel Reily was wounded and died on the field. His death must have been a serious blow to Sibley. Reily, a loyal supporter, had been an integral part of the New Mexico Campaign as he carried Confederate hopes into Sonora and Chihuahua.

In the retreat from Bisland Sibley was placed in charge of a long train of wagons carrying the army's entire quartermaster, commissary, medical, and ordnance stores. Still furious at Sibley for his refusal to attack the enemy at Bisland on the morning of the 13th, Taylor insultingly placed General Alfred Mouton, a junior officer, over Sibley.

As the wagon train moved up Bayou Teche, Sibley, without notifying Taylor, sent one of his staff officers to Green who was commanding the rear guard, ordering him to fall back as quickly as possible to Franklin. It was critical that the enemy not gain control of the road leading up the bayou. Green not only fell back to Franklin but taking for granted that all the Confederates had passed ahead of

---

[46] Ibid., p. 392.

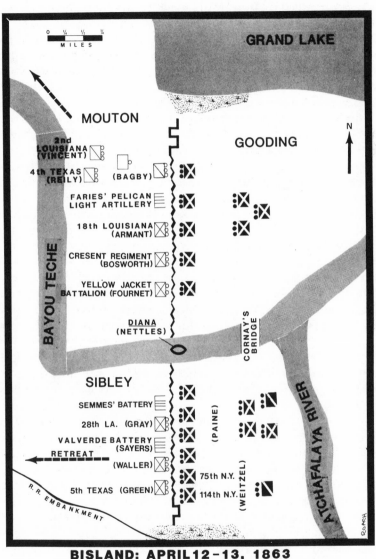

BISLAND: APRIL 12–13, 1863

him, set fire to the bridge over Bayou Yokely.[47] Unknown to Green or Sibley was the fact that General Mouton, who had been holding the Confederate rear during the Battle of Bisland in what came to be called the Battle of Irish Bend, had not yet retreated. In fact, when Mouton did retreat over Bayou Yokely, the bridge was on fire and barely passable.

General Taylor was especially concerned about the fate of the men on the *Diana* on Bayou Teche. His fears were fully realized when it was learned that the crew had been captured. Sibley's lack of awareness about the disposition of the Confederate Army almost turned a defeat into a total disaster. Furthermore, Taylor was furious that Sibley, instead of supervising the preparation for the retreat as he had been ordered, had gone to bed instead.

At Franklin, Taylor decided to fire all the steamboats that had been used for transportation on the lower Teche to prevent them from falling into the hands of the enemy. Taylor issued orders for Sibley to place the sick and wounded in wagons, carts, carriages, and ambulances at Franklin for safe transit northward since Union gunboats were already in control of the bayou above the town. Instead Sibley disregarded Taylor's orders, and devised a plan of his own by which the sick and wounded as well as the Federal prisoners would be passed through the Federal line on the steamer *Cornie* flying a hospital flag. To Taylor the plan, undertaken by the Chief Surgeon of the Confederate Army under direct orders from Sibley, was so stupid that it was "unheard of."[48] The *Cornie* and all on board easily fell into the enemy's hands.

Sibley's blundering did not end here. Upon leaving Franklin, Taylor sent Sibley in person to march at the head of the retreating Confederates, to prevent straggling and disorderly conduct and to select a bivouac site for the night. Late in the afternoon, Taylor, who rode at the rear of the column, was shocked to see Confederates confused and "straggling without order over the whole line of march."[49] They were even scattered for miles over the adjacent countryside. In fact a number of Rebels, especially from Sibley's Brigade, simply walked off and began to make their way back to Texas.

Taylor was further miffed and baffled when he discovered that Sib-

[47] Ibid.; Taylor, p. 130.
[48] Ibid., p. 393.
[49] Ibid.

ley was not with his troops. The general could not even be found. It was later learned that during the retreat Sibley somehow had taken a different road from that of his men. Taylor immediately dispatched a note ordering prompt obedience to his orders. When Sibley failed to reply, Taylor was forced in person to select the campsite and collect as many stragglers as possible. Later in the evening Sibley rode into camp and reported to Taylor. Sibley told Taylor that he was sick and asked permission to go on the line of retreat in advance of the column.[50] Totally disgusted, but with little alternative, Taylor acquiesced.

The decisive rout of the Confederates in the Battle of Bisland lost the bayou Acadian country once and for all for the Confederacy. The defeat also allowed Banks to capture the state capital at Opelousas, forcing the state government to retreat to Shreveport. Furthermore, the defeat enabled Union forces to plunder the lower Red River.

Within months more disastrous news arrived from the east. The strategic Mississippi River bastion of Port Hudson had fallen on July 9, only five days after the even more disheartening fall of Vicksburg on July 4. On the Red River the Confederate retreat did not stop until Taylor reached Natchitoches, 160 miles upriver.

There seems little doubt as Taylor concluded at the time, that the strikingly poor leadership of Brigadier General Henry Hopkins Sibley contributed markedly to the Confederate defeat at Bisland. Within a short forty-eight-hour period Sibley had made four tactical errors.

Historically, the general's ineptness during the Battle of Bisland appears amazingly similar to his performance during the battle of Valverde some fourteen months before. Sibley undoubtedly was seriously ill, but his unexplainable behavior during the retreat hints at inebriation.

Ironically, Sibley's decision to burn the bridge over Yokely Bayou west of Franklin, which appeared to be such a blunder at the time, may conceivably have helped to save Taylor's army. Thirty-six years later, Taylor in his brilliant memoirs, *Destruction and Reconstruction*, wrote that the Federals "stopped just short of the prize. Thirty minutes would have given them the wood bridge, closing the trap on my force."[51] General Sibley's actions, which drew Taylor's wrath in

[50] Ibid.
[51] Taylor, p. 129.

his official report of April 23, had largely been forgotten when Taylor sat down to write his classic *Destruction and Reconstruction*. Regardless, Sibley's abilities as a leader had reached a new low. For all practical purposes General Sibley's career in the Confederate States Army was at an end. Shortly after the battle Taylor preferred charges and ordered him court-martialed.

General Sibley was charged with disobedience of orders by not attacking the enemy as ordered on the morning of the 13th at Bisland; allowing the *Cornie* carrying sick and wounded Confederates as well as Federal prisoners to be captured; and for not taking command of the retreating column from Franklin as ordered. Furthermore, he was charged with unofficerlike conduct by sending orders on the 14th to Green to fall back to Franklin without so informing General Taylor and of neglecting properly to supervise the retreat from Bisland.[52]

In the confusion of moving the Department of the Trans-Mississippi to Shreveport, the court-martial was delayed for over three months. During this time Sibley remained with his brigade, although not in command, as it retreated up the Teche before Banks. At Opelousas, Taylor's army was divided, the infantry continuing north up the Red River past Alexandria which fell on May 7, 1862, and the cavalry moving westward to the Sabine River to forage. The general was not present as his army, now christened the "Green Brigade" for its new commander, countermarched to participate in the successful assault on the weakened Union garrison at Brashear City, Banks having turned east to assist in the successful Union siege of Port Hudson.[53] The brigade next moved eastward to assault Donaldsonville and after a Union counterattack retreated up the Teche again, acting as Taylor's rear guard.

Finally on July 21, 1863, by Special Orders No. 91, signed by the new commander of the Trans-Mississippi, General E. Kirby Smith, a court-martial was convened at Shreveport on the morning of August 15. From the beginning it had been difficult to assemble enough officers for the trial. Senior on the court-martial panel and acting as president was forty-one-year-old Major General John G. Walker, a veteran of Antietam. Next came Brigadier General John S. Roane; then

---

[52] General Orders No. 47, 25 September 1863, L.R., Trans-Mississippi Department, Confederate War Department, R.G. 109. The same document may be found in *O.R.*, I, XV: 1093–95.

[53] Noel, pp. 81–2.

Brigadier General Thomas Green, recently promoted and needing no introduction to the accused; Colonel Hiram Randall of the 28th Texas Cavalry; Colonel W.G. Vincent of the Second Louisiana Cavalry; Colonel R.H. Hubbard, 22nd Texas Infantry; Colonel Henry Gray, 28th Louisiana Cavalry; and finally Captain C.S. West, assistant adjutant general of the District of Louisiana.[54]

After what appears to have been a capable defense by the accused and after several hours of deliberation, Sibley was found not guilty of all charges and specifications. Surprisingly, the court found that in the first specification of the first charge Sibley was ordered censured for not showing promptness in attacking the enemy at Bisland. But in a technicality the court found that owing to a number of unavoidable circumstances he had not deliberately disobeyed orders.[55]

Under the second specification of the first charge, the court found that the prosecution had proven its charge against Sibley. Although Sibley was responsible for allowing the steamer *Cornie* to be captured by the Federals, the court felt this could not have been prevented and therefore attached "no criminality" to Sibley's actions.[56]

With respect to the third specification in which Sibley was charged with failing to take charge of the retreating column as ordered, the court refused "to acquit the accused [sic] of having done all that he should have done" but felt this arose "from a misconception of the orders of his superior."[57] The court did not explain its ruling of not guilty in the second charge of unofficer-like conduct.

Following the court-martial General Sibley became a general without a command as he remained at the headquarters of the Trans-Mississippi. With Rebel ranks growing thinner almost weekly no positions were available for a cavalry commander in either the District of Arkansas or Louisiana. He could not return to his old brigade, for it remained, at least for the time, under command of General Taylor, and Sibley was not welcome at Taylor's headquarters. Finally on November 23, 1863, General E. Kirby Smith wrote the commander of the District of Texas, J.B. Magruder, to see if a place could be found for

[54] Special Orders No. 47, 25 September 1863, L.R., Trans-Mississippi Department, Confederate War Department, R.G. 109.

[55] General Orders No. 47, 25 September 1863, L.R., Trans-Mississippi Department, Confederate War Department, R.G. 109.

[56] Ibid.

[57] Ibid.

Sibley there.[58] When General Smith received a negative reply, he decided early in 1864 to send Sibley to Richmond, hoping the adjutant general there might find a place for him in the East.

For the third time Sibley was on his way to the Confederate capitol, and with the passage of time the conditions under which he traveled east had become increasingly painful. Always the eternal optimist, the general was hoping that a command in the East might yet yield the glory that had eluded him in the deserts of New Mexico and the swamps of Louisiana. Arriving in Richmond during the second week of February 1864, and with little money, he immediately reported to the quartermaster general's office where he asked for $600 in funds which he alleged were transportation expenses from Shreveport to Richmond.[59]

The half-starved Richmond that Henry saw in 1864 was very different from the city that he had seen in 1861 and even that of 1862. The capital was showing evidence of weakening and cracking. Inflation was rampant. Uncertainty and queasiness were everywhere. The wounded, their wounds half bandaged, littered the city's streets. The Confederate Congress had just adjourned after endless quarrels with President Davis. William Tecumseh Sherman was preparing to move into Mississippi and Georgia. Ulysses S. Grant, soon to command the Armies of the United States, would, within months, unleash a massive all-out drive against Richmond. Only days after Sibley arrived in town, a Federal Cavalry force under Colonel Ulrich Dahlgren raided within a few miles of Richmond throwing a scare into an insecure populace. Out west Federal gunboats were steaming for Alexandria as Banks continued to push hard up the Red River.

On February 25 Sibley reported to General Cooper and asked for assignment to a brigade of cavalry then defending Richmond. Cooper seemed baffled at why Smith had ordered Sibley to Richmond in the first place. Evidently the adjutant general was not familiar with Sibley's actions during the Battle of Bisland and the resulting court-martial. It is also evident that Sibley did not volunteer such information.[60]

[58] H.P. Pratt to J.B. Magruder, 23 November 1863, L.R., District of Texas, R.G. 109. List of brigadier generals in the Trans-Mississippi Department, 15 December 1863, L.R., A.G.O., R.G. 109.

[59] Voucher of H.H. Sibley, 13 February 1864, Unfiled Papers Belonging in Confederate Compiled Service Records, R.G. 109.

[60] H.H. Sibley to S. Cooper, 25 February 1864, C.M.S.R. of H.H. Sibley, R.G. 109.

Cooper at first had ideas of sending Sibley to the Department of East Tennessee where General James Longstreet, Robert E. Lee's "Old War Horse," had recently asked for the assignment of a cavalry commander. Longstreet, however, passed Sibley's request on to General Braxton Bragg who had been called to Richmond to become military advisor to the president. Bragg seemed as puzzled as Cooper as to what Sibley was doing in Richmond and, in placing Sibley's request for a command before the president, wrote that Smith had "no right to order General Sibley from his command."[61] Bragg was evidently less familiar with Sibley's problems in the Trans-Mississippi than Adjutant General Cooper.

After more than six weeks in Richmond, it was finally decided by the Confederate hierarchy to send Sibley back to the Trans-Mississippi where the general would await further orders.[62]

In late March, Sibley and his aide-de-camp, Lieutenant A. Flournoy, left Richmond. With the fortunes of the Confederate States of America waning weekly, travel back to the Trans-Mississippi was becoming more precarious and uncertain. Sibley first went south through the Carolinas to Atlanta, Georgia, and to Mobile, Alabama. There he learned that it would be impossible to reach the Trans-Mississippi Headquarters at Shreveport by normal route across the Mississippi. Sibley learned that Federal forces were in control of the entire river. With the fall of Vicksburg and Port Hudson, Union forces had successfully severed the forty thousand men of the Confederate Trans-Mississippi from the main body of the Confederacy. From out west, word came that Banks had pushed up the Red River to Sibley's home town of Natchitoches.

After consulting with Confederate military authorities and several old friends Sibley decided to try to reach the Trans-Mississippi by a different route.[63] He would steam across the Gulf of Mexico through an ever-tightening Union blockade, to Havana, Cuba, then westward some one thousand miles to Matamoros, Mexico, where he would make his way overland into Texas and eventually to Louisiana. To reach Shreveport, about three hundred miles from Mobile, Sibley would therefore be traveling some twenty-four hundred miles. A pre-

---

[61] Endorsements on H.H. Sibley to S. Cooper, 25 February 1864, C.M.S.R. of H.H. Sibley, R.G. 109.

[62] Special Orders No. 67, 21 March 1864, C.M.S.R. of H.H. Sibley, R.G. 109.

[63] H.H. Sibley to C.J. Helm, 20 April 1864, C.M.S.R. of H.H. Sibley, R.G. 109.

posterous plan, full of uncertainties, the journey would take weeks if not months to complete. But then without a command, Sibley had plenty of time.

Sailing from Mobile, the general and his aide reached Havana during the third week of April 1864. He was unable to obtain passage to Mexico for several weeks. Stranded, Sibley quickly ran out of money and ran up debts of over two hundred dollars. He had no alternative but to plead with the Confederate agent in Havana, Major Charles Helm, for funds. Sibley told Helm that it was absolutely essential that he have five hundred dollars to pay his debts in Havana and to enable him and his aide to continue on to Mexico. Helm found the incident embarrassing: "I had no alternative, as a Brigadier General of the Confederate Army could not be permitted to have his bills here unpaid, or beg his way, and gave him the money," the Confederate agent wrote Richmond.[64]

After Helm advanced Sibley five hundred dollars in gold to pay his debts, Sibley was able to obtain passage on the steamer *Inary* to Matamoros. Authorities in Richmond felt Sibley had no authority to go to Havana in the first place, but by the time they got around to formally disapproving, the brigadier general had already steamed for Mexico. At Bagdad, Mexico, at the mouth of the Rio Grande, Sibley found a sizeable Union Army in control of the lower Texas Rio Grande Valley. To get back into the Confederacy, he was forced to travel by horseback two hundred miles up the south bank of the river to Laredo where he was able to cross into Texas. From Laredo, Sibley rode north through the brush country to San Antonio and overland through the piney woods of east Texas to Confederate Headquarters at Shreveport. It was a long and exhausting journey for a forty-eight-year-old general in bad health.

Arriving in Shreveport, Sibley learned that the Confederates had repulsed Bank's Red River Campaign. Taylor had routed Banks in the Battle of Sabine Cross Road, near Mansfield, Louisiana, and although thrown back the next day in a bloody counterattack at Pleasant Hill, he had forced Banks to retreat. In both engagements Sibley's old brigade had performed with considerable dignity.[65] While pursuing Banks downriver, Sibley learned that General Tom Green had been decap-

---

[64] Ch. J. Helm to Thos. L. Bayne, 25 April 1864, C.M.S.R. of H.H. Sibley, R.G. 109.

[65] Ludwell H. Johnson, *Red River Campaign, Politics and Cotton in the Civil War* (Baltimore, 1958), 132–50.

itated on April 12, 1864, while leading an attack on Union gunboats at Blair's Landing. Eighteen days later his old regimental commander, William Scurry, the hero of Glorieta, wounded while leading a cavalry charge at Jenkins' Ferry had bled to death after refusing to be taken to the rear.

Despite over two years of optimism, the walls of the Confederacy were cracking. General Ulysses S. Grant had placed Robert E. Lee's Army of Northern Virginia on the defensive at Petersburg and throughout the winter of 1864–1865 continued to pound the besieged and outnumbered Rebels. An equally devastating blow came in September 1864 when William T. Sherman took Atlanta, one of the South's strategic transportation and communication centers.

Sibley sensed the impending doom that was about to descend on the Confederacy. In July 1864 Charlotte and daughter Helen Margaret and son Sidney Johnston left Louisiana for Brooklyn. "It will afford me pleasure to pass Mrs. Sibley, daughter, and son through my lines on their way North," Union General Frederick Steele wrote the Confederate commander of the Trans-Mississippi, General E. Kirby Smith.[66]

In the Trans-Mississippi the clock was also approaching midnight. During these troubled days Sibley remained at Confederate Headquarters in Shreveport. Even after Lee's surrender at Appomattox Court House on April 9, 1865, the armies in the Trans-Mississippi held out until June 2, when E. Kirby Smith capitulated. Six days later Sibley signed his parole papers at Shreveport.[67] Ironically for Sibley, the Rebels in the Trans-Mississippi surrendered to Major-General E.R.S. Canby, his comrade from the western frontier and adversary from the Civil War in New Mexico.

Sibley remained in Shreveport for at least another month. On July 2 he complained to Union authorities that someone had stolen his horse, described as a bay fourteen hands high with a slit ear, from a hitching post in town. Canby, never known for his vindictiveness, ordered a thorough search of the Union camp. It is not known whether Sibley and Canby met face to face. If so, their conversation would certainly have been historic.

Late in July 1865 Sibley left Shreveport for New Orleans, riding

[66] Frederick Steele to E. Kirby Smith, 2 July 1864, *O.R.*, II, VII: 438.
[67] Parole No. 505, 8 June 1865, C.M.S.R. of H.H. Sibley, R.G. 109. Sibley listed New Orleans as his residence on his parole papers.

south along the Red River, past the dilapidated remains of the Sibley Plantation at Grand Ecore, past his childhood home and his father's grave at Natchitoches, then on to Alexandria and finally down the Mississippi to New Orleans, where he arrived during the first week of August.[68]

For forty-nine-year-old Brigadier General Henry Hopkins Sibley, ex-general of the defeated Confederate States of America, there was one last moment of fresh air before the turning of the tide. Reconstruction had come to Louisiana and the Old South.

---

[68] *Daily Picayune,* 9 August 1865; *Daily Southern Star,* 24 September 1865.

Chapter XII

In The Land of
The Ancient Pharaohs

After the Battle of Bisland a soldier in the Sibley Brigade attempted General Sibley's Civil War epitaph when he wrote: "In bidding General Sibley an adieu, we do so under the full conviction that we have parted with a highminded, noble, valorous, and gifted officer, endowed with a principle too lofty and honorable to design to any acts calculated to wrong anyone, let him be whom he may."[1]

It is difficult to determine at what point in his military career alcohol began seriously to affect Sibley's leadership capabilities. For most of his life he had lived in the territory west of the Appalachians where it was common to rely on whiskey for relaxation, amusement, and medicine. Nowhere in the west was alcohol consumed more readily than on the isolated frontier outposts where Sibley had spent much of his life. Here temperance influences were weak.[2] Here, also, Sibley could "be whom he may" and appeared happiest.

[1] Noel, p. 78.

[2] Allen M. Winkler, "Drinking on the American Frontier," *Quarterly Journal of Studies of Alcohol,* 29 (1968) 414. A recent study of the use of liquor in the nineteenth

There is some evidence that Sibley began to drink heavily during the Mexican War. His inebriety appears to have continued during his two years on the Texas Frontier. On remote posts whiskey was used to cope with the hostile environment and to help soldiers relieve the sense of isolation. They could often supplement their rations with purchases from the post sutler or whiskey peddlers.

Percival Lowe, one of Sibley's Boston recruits, wrote that the soldiers on the frontier "learned to quench thirst, subdue hunger, and otherwise obliterate their misery with whiskey."[3] Environmental influences here were strong and probably contributed to Sibley's energetic indulgence. So common was the use of whiskey on frontier military posts that it became an expected part of all social intercourse, and one could not refuse a drink without being offensive.

One question which remains unanswered was did Sibley become alcoholic because of his heavy drinking to ease pain or did the drinking cause the illness? Certainly the above mentioned social conditions could have made either possible. The only known professional diagnosis of his illness was that of Dr. Edward N. Covey, medical director of the Army of New Mexico, who, prior to the Battle of Valverde, reported Sibley's ailment to be colic. If Dr. Covey's examination is accurate, it is probable that Sibley would have had renal colic, an ailment of the kidneys which would have caused severe pain not only in the kidneys but also in the abdomen, genitals, and legs. Symptoms included nausea, vomiting, perspiration, and frequent urination.[4] Taking into consideration that his father had succumbed to a "kidney ailment," it is possible that Henry had inherited some form of degenerate kidney disorder. No doubt he would have used whiskey to ease such pain as it was very common in nineteenth century America to use alcoholic beverages to suppress such sensations.[5] This was especially true of whiskey and wine, and the few

---

century indicates that Americans drank more alcoholic beverages than at any time in our history. W.J. Rorabaugh, *The Alcoholic Republic: An American Tradition* (New York, 1979).

[3] Lowe, p. 122.

[4] Benjamin F. Miller and Claire Brackman Keane, *Encyclopedia and Dictionary of Medicine* (Philadelphia, 1972), 217. Two members of the general's staff, however, reported him to have had pneumonia.

[5] Mark Keller, "Other Effects of Alcohol," *Drinking and Intoxication*, Raymond G. McCarthy, ed. (New Haven, 1964), 16.

sketchy records that remain relative to Sibley's heavy drinking indicate that he preferred champagne.

There is some evidence that Sibley had learned how much to drink and when to stop before becoming totally incapacitated. He appears to have developed early in his career the skill of holding his liquor and was therefore not drunk to the eye, something he was unable to do by the Civil War.

The effect of alcohol on Sibley's leadership capabilities was most evident during the Civil War and later in Egypt. Alcohol, however, may have caused the shouting match he had with his commander, Colonel Edwin Sumner, at the cavalry barracks outside México City during the Mexican War. During this incident in México and later in his quarrel with Colonel Cooke in Utah, Sibley appears to have been free in speech and less cautious of his conduct than he might otherwise have been. Such actions appear to be indicative of regressive behavior which is often alcohol-related. Alcohol undoubtedly caused his court-martial in the wilds of Utah in 1856. It was during the New Mexico Campaign at Valverde, but especially later at the Battle of Bisland in Louisiana, that liquor appears to have affected Sibley's most basic capabilities including remembering, thinking, reasoning, and problem solving. At Bisland, certainly more so than at any other time, he at least temporarily lost control of his actions.

Another possible source of Sibley's heavy drinking, besides his illness, may have come from the anxiety he experienced from attempting to attain ambitious goals such as those he aspired to in the New Mexico Campaign.[6] Setting himself a difficult target and the resulting disappointment may have made him susceptible to anxieties. Undoubtedly such anxieties would have been experienced by a captain preparing to lead his dragoons into battle during the Mexican War in 1847, a brigadier-general in command of a brigade of Texans prior to the Battle of Valverde in 1862, the same brigadier commanding some sixteen hundred men in battle at Bisland one year later, or a general of artillery planning the Mediterranean defenses of Egypt in the early 1870s. Not only the fear of failure but also the fear of combat and possible death would have been lessened by alcohol.

Sibley's dependency on alcohol when under stress is best illustrated by an 1858 visit to Washington when he was called into the

---

[6] Rorabaugh, p. 174.

office of the treasury auditor to explain several earlier discrepancies in his recruiting accounts. Henry remembered how "a drink of brandy-and-water from a secret store revived my depressed spirits, and gave me courage to face the music."[7]

Early in 1882, Henry wrote an article for Frank Leslie's *Popular Monthly*, in which he described the nightmarish hallucinations of the chronic alcoholic. There is little doubt that he was writing about himself. It also seems certain that Henry's sensory distortions are indicative of someone exhibiting traits of a paranoid personality. His sense of inadequacy and fear of failure had manifested into severe feelings of persecution and depression. To Henry, "drunkenness, like the night, with slow and noiseless footsteps, comes creeping everywhere." He continued: "Insidious and without warning the day merges into night through the hazy twilight into the deep gloom of midnight with its phantoms and weird reflections, so drunkenness merges from tippling to dram-drinking, from dram-drinking to the morning appetizer, from this to stealing one's own liquor, and finally to any and every excuse to rise in the night and take a drop just to quiet the frightened nerves."[8]

"Toward morning," Henry wrote, "specks flit across the retina; the mind becomes confused and bewildered; insects of larger growth dart across the vision, swarming and buzzing about the head in countless myriads. The excited fancy pictures frightfully droll figures, grinning and gesticulating around his bedside. Some garment hanging on a chair is transfigured into an assassin about to assault him with a huge knife, whilst another aims a gun at him. Processions of departed kindred and friends pass and repass mournfully before him, ill, terror stricken, he hops from his bed and seeks the sheltering arms of vacuity."[9] Although Henry possessed many misconceptions about alcoholism, such as believing that addiction to alcohol was hereditary, his writings are amazingly frank and indicative of someone who had experienced much of the trauma of the alcoholic.

Henry Hopkins Sibley was not the only general, North or South, to have a weakness for the bottle. Probably the most famous boozer of the era was Sibley's Mexican War drinking partner General Ulysses

---

[7] [Sibley], "Military History of a Double-Barreled Shotgun," p. 443.

[8] [Henry H. Sibley], "A Curious Plan of Reformation," *Popular Monthly*, (17 December 1881), pp. 11–12.

[9] Ibid.

S. Grant who was reported to have been drinking both at Shiloh and during the siege of Vicksburg. In fact, Grant had resigned from the Army in 1854 to avoid a court-martial for inebriation and other charges.

General Joe Hooker, who commanded the Army of the Potomac at Chancellorsville, had his share of charges hurled at him for drunkenness. Union General James Totten was said always to have gone into battle with a canteen full of brandy on his hip thus acquiring the nickname, "Bottle-nosed Totten." General Totten was eventually dismissed from the army for his excessive drinking. Probably the worst behavior of a general in battle because of alcohol, even worse than Sibley at the Battle of Bisland, was that of Union General James Hewitt Ledlie, who commanded an assault division at the Battle of the Crater during the siege of Petersburg in July 1864. After the attack Ledlie was found totally drunk in a bombproof some four hundred yards behind the line.[10] Other Union generals who were reported to have been drunk at one time, either in bivouac or battle, included Generals Phil Sheridan and Judson Kilpatrick.

Generals in gray who were overly fond of liquor included John Magruder, Tom Rosser, George B. Crittenden, Earl Van Dorn, John B. Villepigue, John C. Breckinridge, Nathan G. Evans, Theophilus Hunter Holmes, and Louis T. Wigfall. Next to Sibley the Confederate general who had the worst reputation for overindulgence was Benjamin F. Cheatham, who according to his commander, Braxton Bragg, was so drunk during the Battle of Murfreesboro that a staff officer had to hold him on his horse.[11]

There was one basic difference between most of the generals who drank and Sibley. Few were habitually drunk like Sibley, and even those who were addicted to the bottle were not affected in the way Sibley was. Rather than diminish their efficiency during times of crises, alcohol, especially in the case of Grant and others, acted as a stimulant whereas in the case of Sibley, alcohol was consumed in such quantities that the liquor acted as a depressant thus seriously diminishing his ability to command.

At the end of the war in 1865, Sibley did not remain long in New

---

[10] Harold B. Simpson, "Booze in Battle and Bivouac During the Late Unpleasantness," a paper delivered before the Houston Civil War Round Table, September 1973, p. 7.

[11] Ibid., p. 9.

Orleans as he had originally hoped to do when he signed his parole papers in Shreveport. Unlike many Southerners who had joined the Rebel Army at the beginning of hostilities, Sibley had no home to return to. In fact he had no land, no wealth and in August 1865, no visible means of support. His only hope was a vague inheritance claim to a small piece of land in western Louisiana near Natchitoches. By a proclamation issued by Abraham Lincoln in March 1864, he could not vote or hold political office since he had held the rank of colonel or above in the Rebel Army. Furthermore, he had resigned from the United States Army to assist the rebellion. In late 1865 he applied for clemency directly to President Andrew Johnson, but like other Confederates in his predicament this was not approved until 1867. Although royalties from the wide-scale use of the Sibley tent during the war amounted to over $100,000, the government refused any compensation because of his disloyalty.[12]

From New Orleans in late 1865 Sibley went north to Brooklyn to join Charlotte and the children who in 1864 had gone to live with her aging father and two unmarried sisters. While in Brooklyn, Henry worried much about finding employment. In December of 1866 he spoke with Joseph E. Johnston about the possibilities of obtaining a lucrative government contract to construct telegraph lines in either Texas or California for $1,000 a mile. Later, after Johnston had moved to Selma, Alabama, Henry continued to communicate with Johnston who had become president of the National Express and Transportation Company, but the proposed scheme fell through largely because of the lack of financial backing.[13] All attempts at finding employment failed, and Henry remained with his family in New York where he at least had a place to live.

In New York the Sibley's only son, Sidney Johnston, age fifteen, remained with his mother and father, but Helen had married John Gregory Stokes, a bespectacled lawyer who had fought as a Confederate colonel and who had gone on to become an editor of the Montgomery, Alabama, *Journal* during the early years of Reconstruction. Three children were born of the marriage: Henry Lee, named af-

[12] Report No. 344, "Estate of Henry H. Sibley," 69th Congress, 1st Session, 11 March 1926, Library of Congress.

[13] J. E. Johnston to My Dear General, December 1866, Henry Hopkins Sibley Papers, New York Historical Society; Gilbert E. Govan and James W. Livingood, *A Different Valor: The Story of General Joseph E. Johnston, C.S.A.* (Indianapolis, 1956), 378–79.

ter his grandfather, in 1866; Elmore Kendall in 1870; and Flora McDonald in 1871; all in Montgomery. Sometime late in 1872 or early 1873 the Stokes family left Alabama and moved to New York where John worked as an attorney and wrote for the *New York Sun.* Certainly Helen's desire to be with her father and mother was a motivational factor in the Stoke's move to the North.[14]

Due to the lack of any surviving personal correspondence, little is known of Sibley's life in Brooklyn at this time. His views concerning Reconstruction, however, were outlined in a rare 1868 letter addressed to a friend in the South. The friend had written asking the General for his views on the political predicament of the South. With typical frankness, Henry blamed much of the political turmoil on the Northern Democrats who were exploiting the hatred and resentment of the Southern Democrats. For the South, Henry saw further divisiveness and conceivable disaster in the possible election of Governor Horatio Seymour of New York, the Democratic candidate for president in the 1868 general election. Consequently, continued conflict would result in the complete annihilation of the South with Carpetbaggers and Scalawags reaping the benefits. "We are a conquered peoples," Henry wrote, and used an interesting analogy to describe the political dilemma of the conquered South. "Like the bear tied to the tail of a cart he pulled back until his neck was sore. Very sensibly, the bear concluded that it was the best policy to follow the cart, not only that but to get into the cart."[15] As Henry saw it, there was little choice for the South. "Quit the concern—go with the cart and rejoice in the election of Grant."

It was while Sibley was in Brooklyn in 1869 that an opportunity of a lifetime came his way. In a rare stroke of good luck he was contacted by an adventurer named Thaddeus Mott, agent for the Khedive of Egypt. Mott told Sibley that he was seeking Civil War veterans to help in reorganizing the Egyptian military and was hoping Henry was interested. Mott had served as a colonel in the United States Army and at one time had fought against Sibley in Louisiana. Mott had first contacted an old friend, General William Tecumseh Sherman, who

---

[14] Miscellaneous notes in possession of Margaret Belcher, La Marque, Texas. These documents will hereafter be referred to as Belcher-Sibley Papers.

[15] Henry H. Sibley to My Dear Sir, 20 October 1868, Henry Sibley Papers.

in turn suggested Sibley and several other Civil War officers, both
North and South, as possible recruits for the Egyptian military.[16]

Mott told Sibley confidentially that the real objective of reorganizing the Egyptian Army would be to prepare for the time when the
khedive felt his country would be able to make a break from the tyrannical and oppressive rule of the Turks.[17]

Anticipating a promising future in the Egyptian Army, Henry completed a formal contract with Mott on December 17, 1869. Henry
agreed to serve five years in the Egyptian Army with the khedive re-
serving the right to retain his services for another five years. Sibley
waived all his rights as a citizen of the United States and agreed to
abide by the orders of the Egyptian Minister of War. In no way would
he be "controlled by orders or proclamations of the United States
Government."[18] In return, however, he would not be obliged to bear
arms against the United States.

If he became ill during the time of his service, he would have the
option of returning to the United States, receiving travel expenses and
two months severance pay. He could be dismissed at anytime for any
reason but would be given six months pay. If Egypt were to go to war,
he would receive one-fifth more than his regular pay, which would
be that of a brigadier general of infantry in the United States Army.
Mott agreed that Henry would also receive a horse, rations and be furnished quarters. If he were to die of natural causes during the period
of his service, Charlotte would receive a year's salary. If he was killed
in battle or die of his wounds, Charlotte and the children would receive a sizeable pension.[19]

To Sibley, Mott was a savior straight from Heaven. Mott offered
Sibley not only a generalship in the Egyptian Army but also a chance
for vindication. With a black cloud of disrepute hanging over his military reputation, there was a driving psychological compulsion to ac-
complish on the banks of the Nile what he had been shamefully unable to do on the Rio Grande and in the bayous of Louisiana.

Not only would Sibley be made a general by Ismail, Khedive of

---

[16] William B. Hesseltine and Hazel C. Wolf, *The Blue and the Gray on the Nile* (Chicago 1961), 19; Pierre Crabites, *Americans in the Egyptian Army* (London, 1938), 8.

[17] Charles Chaille-Long, *My Life in Four Continents*, (London, 1912), I: 17.

[18] Contract, Thaddeus Mott and Henry H. Sibley, 17 December 1869, Henry Sibley
Papers.

[19] Ibid.

Egypt, under whose authority Mott was acting, but he would also be compensated for all transportation costs between New York and Cairo. Sibley was one of Mott's first recruits. The other was William Wing Loring, Sibley's old friend from the Mexican War, the Utah Expedition, and the New Mexico frontier. The one-armed Loring, who bragged that he had been under fire more than any other living man, had a controversial Civil War career hanging over his head much like Sibley and was anxious to prove himself in Egypt. Jobless like Sibley, he had drifted to New York where Mott found him in 1869.

With a shining chance for exoneration, for adventure, for money, and always the romantic dreamer, Sibley said good-bye to his wife and family in Brooklyn late in 1869 and accompanied by Loring and Mott steamed for the ancient land of the pharaohs.

The three-week trip from New York to Cairo took the adventurers first across the rough and dark North Atlantic to Liverpool, England, on a Cunard liner where they caught the train which sped them across the English midlands to London's Charing Cross station. Here they changed trains for the short ride to Dover on the English Channel. From Dover they crossed the channel by steamer and went on to Paris by train. Aided by Sibley's ability to speak fluent French, the warriors probably remained in Paris long enough to take in some of the historic sights. From Paris they traveled by train again, this time through the snowy Alps to sunny Italy. From Rome they went on to the port of Brindisi on the Adriatic where a steamer waited for the four-day trip down the Greek peninsula past the Peloponnesus and the island of Crete into the eastern Mediterranean and Alexandria at the mouth of the Nile.[20]

Alexandria, the historic city founded by Alexander the Great, defended by Caesar, and taken by Napoleon, must have appeared to Sibley, as it did to later arrivals from the South, much like New Orleans. Highly cosmopolitan, the center of commerce and custom of the eastern Mediterranean, Alexandria was a city where a profusion of languages was heard. Ancient stone docks, much like the levees of Louisiana, jutted into the blue Mediterranean. Cotton bales and sacks of rice were piled high near the water's edge. Blacks, stripped to the waist, loaded cargo on ships bearing the flags of many nations. Riders

[20] Chaille-Long, p. 17; Hesseltine and Wolf, p. 43: Crabites, p. 49. Others went directly from Paris to Marseilles and then to Alexandria.

whipped donkeys and camels through the narrow streets and crowded bazaars. Hundreds of hungry, decrepit-looking beggars pleaded for alms. Dark-skinned fellahin, the ever-present Egyptian peasantry, incessantly screeched and yelled at one another. Noise and turmoil echoed from the small boxlike shops which lined the crowded streets. Flies were thick, and the smell was sickening. To the adventurers from America, Egypt was strangely unlike any other country in the world. As Loring would later write, the Americans were "in the midst of a race totally different . . . in customs, color, dress, and religion."[21]

From Alexandria the travelers sped inland and southward by train across the rich crescent-shaped delta toward Cairo. A warm January wind was blowing and for mile upon mile an enormous agricultural panorama stretched to the horizon in all directions. The plains were golden with rich harvests of wheat, barley, lentils, and dotted with elegant villas, surrounded by roses as well as lebbek and acacia trees. Over fields of green clover roamed camels, donkeys, and horses. Occasionally a snow-white ibis could be seen perched on the back of a water buffalo, which was usually mired to its belly in the rich delta mud. Here and there vast swarms of insects darted about the backs of the huge horned beasts.

At Kafr-el-Zaiat, the half-way station, the train came to a screeching halt. Here Sibley and Loring were given a few minutes for refreshments. Everywhere were the fellahin, male and female, young and old, toiling with bent backs and sun-blistered bodies. Many young women scurried about, their faces mysteriously concealed by the Islamic veil so alien to the westerners. On the women's heads were neatly balanced huge wicker baskets filled with oranges, bananas, and dates. As the trip continued southward toward Cairo, an occasional nomadic Bedouin clad in his white Roman-like toga or a dark skinned Soudanese could be seen from the train window.

As the train neared Cairo the outline of the majestic and ancient pyramids of Giza came into sight on the horizon. Far to the east the arid summits of the mountains of the Sinai Peninsula appeared through the desert haze. Much closer yet was the broad and mighty Nile, glistening like a silver ribbon against the yellow hills that rose above its historic banks.

[21] W. W. Loring, *A Confederate Soldier in Egypt* (New York, 1884), 7; Hesseltine and Wolf, p. 44. A lengthy front page interview with Loring appeared in the *New York Herald* on 8 September 1882, and is reprinted in Wessels, pp. 101–20.

Arriving at Cairo on the east bank of the Nile, about 130 miles inland, Sibley and Loring gazed at one of the great cities of the Near East: majestic Cairo and its four hundred mosques and minarets "glittering in the eternal sun."[22] From the train station they were taken through the crowded and winding streets in a carriage preceded by a barefooted groom.

Cairo's streets were much like those of Alexandria. People were everywhere. The sheer bulk of humanity at times seemed to close in and engulf the Americans. There were old men on horses, women and children on donkeys, vendors of fruits and various wares, decrepit beggars and the pathetic poor, and here and there an elegantly decorated carriage, indicative of the city's aristocracy. Somehow, above the smell of human sweat, the sweet aroma of roses drifted through the warm air. In the distance were the muffled sounds of gala musicians. Farther yet, barely discernable, echoed the muezzin's shrieks from the minarets calling the Islamic faithful to prayer. At the New Hotel, a comfortable lodging place, the Americans arrived to sip juleps with Europeans on a large veranda which overlooked acres of beautiful gardens.

There was time to see the ancient sights of Egypt. Visiting the ruins only eight miles outside of Cairo, especially the pyramids, was one of Sibley's great pleasures. Besides the Great Pyramid there was the mystifying Sphinx with the body of a lion and the head of a pharaoh. There were the Pyramid of Cheops and the tunnel of the Sacred Bulls. The Boulac Museum with its vast collection of artifacts was a must for the Americans as it was for any western traveler.

For entertainment there was the grand Cairo Opera House where the music of Verdi wafted into the warm Egyptian nights and where the khedive could frequently be seen with his family. There was also the richly decorated French theatre which, like the opera house, was only a few months old, having been constructed to celebrate the opening of the Suez Canal. Sibley and Loring were given free tickets to both the theatre and the opera by the khedive who asked only that the Americans always appear in full-dress uniform. Sibley visited the huge mosque of Gama-el-Azur which loomed over the city's narrow streets and impressive skyline.

[22] Loring, p. 87; Leonard Scott, "Alexandria and Cairo; Notes of Travel in Egypt," *Popular Monthly*, (February 1877), III: 86–93.

Not long after their arrival in Cairo, they met with Khedive Ismail at which time Sibley was appointed Inspector-General of Artillery and Loring Inspector-General of the Army. In the elaborate ceremony the two were presented with medals and gifts of ivory. For Sibley there was also a silk mantel embroidered with gold thread.[23] The khedive also made them Lewan Pashas, a position which commanded respect in Egyptian society. It was the high point of Sibley's Egyptian experience and one of the most memorable of his life. The khedive's gifts would long remain family treasures.

Ismail, who had been educated in Paris, spoke to the Americans in French thanking them for their response to his invitation. Sibley, who was fluent in French, had the advantage over Loring whose French was unreliable despite his West Point education. They had been chosen, the khedive said, because they had experience in the Civil War and because the United States, unlike European imperialists, had no selfish aims to pursue in Egypt. The khedive warned the Americans to expect jealousy from the native officers but asked them to be tolerant and indulgent. They were to be part of a vast modernization plan for Egypt that included the building of railroads, bridges, telegraphs, roads, military fortifications, irrigation works, as well as gardens and palaces.

The khedive was attempting to do in Egypt what Peter the Great had done in Russia a century and a half before. As Mott had confided to Sibley in New York, however, it became evident that the real aim of modernization was the revitalization of the Egyptian military, which the khedive hoped would eventually free Egypt from Turkish tyranny.

It was a time of extraordinary prosperity for Egypt. The American Civil War had sent cotton spinners from western Europe scurrying to Egypt clamoring for the precious white fiber to feed their hungry textile mills, and Sibley had arrived in Egypt only a few months after the elaborate festivities that opened the Suez Canal.

Sibley passed several weeks learning court etiquette, and taking instructions on how to make the salaam. Next came elaborate state functions in the Abdeen Palace where the khedive loved to display his elegantly dressed American mercenaries. Pashas and ministers

---

[23] Miscellaneous Notes, Belcher-Sibley Papers. Studies of Khedive Ismail include: Edward Diley, *The Story of the Khediviate* (London, 1902) and Gaston Zananiri, *Le Khedive Ismail et L'Egypte* (Alexandria, 1923).

also extended invitations to the Americans to attend a vast range of social affairs. At such gatherings the Americans always appeared in full regalia. Sibley's uniform, which resembled that of a Presbyterian parson, consisted of a blue coat with gold epaulettes, gold chevrons on the arms and gold aiguillettes. His trousers were an outlandish reddish-red with a bright yellow stripe down the legs. All was topped by a shining red fez with a long black tassel. He was a sight to behold, even in the Near East.

Despite their Christian bias against Islam, the Americans attended several religious festivities. They were quietly intolerant, however, of the polygamy which abounded in the khedive's extensive harem, and expressed disgust toward the eunuchs who crowded the courts.

On December 24, 1870, the Americans were invited by the khedive to attend the annual reception known as the Beiram feast which traditionally commenced the day after the close of the Ramadan fast. They were greeted by the khedive's mother and were said to have made a "fine display."[24] All were served coffee sherbets.

At other times Pashas Sibley and Loring were guests at royal weddings. On one such occasion at the khedive's Geezeerah Palace, the Americans mingled among five thousand guests. For a hard drinker like Sibley such occasions must have been frustrating despite his fondness for pomp and pageantry. Like the other Americans he was ethnocentric toward a culture and religion so alien to his own, especially one that rigidly insisted on a total abstinence from liquor.

Most of Loring and Sibley's activities centered around the huge Citadel, a vast fortress in Cairo that served as headquarters of the Egyptian Army. One of their first official tasks was the inspection of the country's meager coastal defenses which stretched from Alexandria in the west to Damietta and Port Said in the east. They found the sixty thousand man Egyptian Army to be well trained and disciplined but the few forts to be in a dilapidated condition. With Egypt's navy non-existent and inadequate defenses at the mouth of the Nile and the Suez Canal, the khedive's chances of waging a successful war were nil. In fact, Egypt was almost defenseless. The Americans con-

---

[24] Consular Dispatches, January 1871, American Consulate, Cairo Egypt, Records of the Department of State, Record Group 84, The National Archives, Washington, D.C. General studies of Egypt during this period include: J.C.B. Richmond, *Egypt, 1798–1952: Her Advance Towards a Modern Identity* (New York, 1977) and P.G. Elgood, *The Transit of Egypt* (New York, 1969).

vinced the khedive of the necessity for massive fortifications along the Mediterranean coast. Moving their headquarters from the Citadel to a small rundown palace in Alexandria, Sibley and Loring set out to supervise the construction of badly needed fortifications.[25]

While in Alexandria, Sibley and Loring found time to meet new arrivals from America. Among the first to arrive in April 1870 were Colonel Charles Chaille-Long, an adventurer who had served in the Union Army and who would later write a book on his Egyptian experiences; Colonel Beverly Kennon, an officer of considerable distinction who had served in the Confederate Navy; and a mysterious Major Cameron, who had once served the Confederacy as a chaplain but ended the war as a combat officer.

Sibley greeted the newcomers at the landing pier and ushered them to the fashionable Hotel d'Oriente where they were introduced to Shihin Pasha, the Minister of War, who promised to take the Americans to Cairo in his private railway car.[26] Sibley and Loring volunteered to show the newcomers the historic attractions of what had once been the scientific and literary center of the ancient world. Here were the ruins of the ancient fort and lighthouse of Pharos, the fort of Kom-el-Nadourah, the Palace of Ras-el-Tin, the city's macabre catacombs, and the picturesque mosque of Gama-bin-Bir-Darek with its fabeled 1,001 columns. There was also Pompey's Pillar which had been erected in honor of the Emperor Diocletian, and the beautiful rose granite obelisks which Cleopatra had brought from Heliopolis and placed on the Temple of Caesar.

Not long after his arrival in Africa, Sibley was instrumental in persuading the khedive to admit into the Egyptian service his son, Sidney Johnston, who at age twenty-two was the youngest American to serve the khedive. A lieutenant, he was also lowest in rank. During the Civil War, when he was twelve, while his father was serving under General Taylor in the bayou country, Sidney had worked at the Confederate arsenal in Shreveport. In 1863 he joined the army as a courier in the Trans-Mississippi serving "with great credit to himself."[27] Sibley's son's presence in Egypt helped to relieve the boredom and loneliness of an assignment five thousand miles from home.

[25] Hesseltine and Wolf, p. 67. Loring, in 450 pages of his *A Confederate Soldier in Egypt*, surprisingly does not mention Sibley a single time.

[26] Chaille-Long, p. 22

[27] *New York Herald*, 22 September 1871.

Young Sibley would later recall many of his Egyptian experiences with his general-father. Once while General Sibley was inspecting the coastal defenses near Aboukir Bay, the scene of Lord Nelson's crushing defeat of the French Navy in the Battle of the Nile in 1798, he observed several fishermen casting their nets into the bay and upon hauling in their catch noticed that one man had retrieved a heavy metal object. Upon inspection, it was found that the object was an ancient navy pistol in an excellent state of preservation despite numerous barnacles that made it appear twice its normal size. Believing the weapon to have been used in Nelson's great victory, Henry presented the fishermen with sufficient baksheesh to acquire the weapon, had it cleaned, and presented to the Minister of War, who placed the weapon in a museum near Cairo.[28]

Sibley heard from his old friend from the frontier—Lafayette McLaws. McLaws hoped that Sibley would use his influence with Loring and the Egyptian authorities to obtain the appointment of Thomas W. Cumming of Augusta, Georgia, who had served in the Confederate Army as a major. Cumming, "a uncommon, daring and gallant soldier" according to McLaws, was not "a soldier of fortune but seeks adventure for its own sake." In writing to Sibley, McLaws fondly recalled their friendship during the Navajo campaign of 1860 and "of our first camp in the canyon leading from Fort Defiance."[29] Bragging of their valor at Valverde, Glorieta, and Peralta and expressing a desire to "traverse those sandy regions where strode the great Napoleon," veterans of the Army of New Mexico also wrote the General hoping to find employment in the Egyptian Army.[30]

While Sibley was in Egypt two distinguished visitors arrived from America. The first, who came in 1871, was former Secretary of State William H. Seward. The khedive provided Seward with a special train from Alexandria to Cairo where he was royally entertained at the Abdeen Palace, and furnished Seward with a steamer for a lengthy excursion up the Nile. Sibley visited with Seward in Cairo at which time Seward expressed satisfaction that Henry was so honorably employed by a foreign government.

In the winter of 1872 General William T. Sherman arrived in Egypt. Sherman, who had suggested Sibley's recruitment in the first place,

[28] [Sidney J. Sibley], "Egyptian Reminiscences," n.d., Henry Sibley Papers.
[29] Lafayette McLaws to H.H. Sibley, 11 December 1871, Belcher-Sibley Papers.
[30] John Buchanan to H.H. Sibley, 22 April 1870, Henry Sibley Papers.

was now commander-in-chief of the United States Army. He was accompanied by Fred Grant, the son of President Ulysses Grant. At an
elaborate reception given in Cairo by the khedive, Sibley greeted the
Union war hero and thanked him for his kindness. While in the city
Sherman visited the city's museums, the pyramids, and called on
members of the Egyptian royalty.[31]

By mid-1870 numerous other adventurous Americans had arrived
in Egypt to assist in the khedive's grandiose plans. They were the
vanguard of some fifty officers who had fought on both sides during
the war who would eventually arrive in Egypt.

Of all the arrivals, the most important to Sibley was Charles Pomeroy Stone, a Union general who became chief of staff in Cairo. Stone,
who had become a scapegoat of the Ball's Bluff fiasco during the Civil
War, had come to Egypt in search of redemption, and like Sibley and
Loring he was hoping somehow to remove the cloud of doubt which
still hung over his career as a result of having spent several months
in a New York prison. Five of the newcomers were assigned to Sibley's and Loring's staff at Alexandria. They included Chaille-Long,
who had been in Egypt for several months; Allen Vanderbilt, a one-
time brevet major of Federal volunteers; James M. Morgan, who had
served at the Confederate States Naval Academy; Alexander W. Reynolds, a Confederate brigadier general and 1838 West Point classmate of Sibley; and his son Frank A. Reynolds, who had been a lieutenant colonel in the Confederate Army.

The coast became a beehive of military activity. Charles C. Graves
was made responsible for the establishment of lighthouses stretching from the Gulf of Suez in the east to the Gulf of Aden in the west.
Torpedo training was being taught at Rosetta, and plans were for-
mulated for the establishment of a submarine school. Elaborate sur-
veys of the Mediterranean and Red Sea coasts were well underway by
late 1871. General Stone even had ideas of constructing a military
railroad connecting Alexandria, Rosetta, Damietta, and Port Said.[32]

[31] For Seward's Egyptian visit see: Glyndon G. Van Deusen, *William Henry Seward*
(New York, 1967), 180, and Frederic Bancroft, *The Life of William H. Seward,*
(Gloucester, 1967), I: 523. For Sherman see: James M. Merrill, *William Tecumseh
Sherman* (Chicago, 1971), 345, and Lloyd Lewis, *Sherman, Fighting Prophet* (New York,
1958), 613.

[32] Frederick J. Cox, "The American Naval Mission in Egypt," *Journal of Modern History,* 26 (1954), 174–76.

Three other Americans, all ex-Confederates, also worked close with Sibley and Loring at Alexandria. They included Kennon, whose valuable experiences in the Confederate Navy helped Sibley and Loring in planning the coastal defenses; William W. Dunlap, a Confederate colonel who was to supervise the Artillery School at Damietta; and Walter H. Jenifer, a Confederate colonel who was to serve as Inspector of Cavalry at Alexandria.

In the planning and construction of Egypt's coastal and river fortifications, Sibley appears to have been subordinate to Loring although both held the rank of general. Sibley spent a great deal of time at Rosetta at the mouth of one of the Nile's branches, about thirty-five miles east of Alexandria where he acted as chief foreman and supervisor of construction.[33]

Rosetta, known to the Arabs as Raschid, was a crumbling, run-down garrison town, housing as many as ten thousand soldiers. Years before when the bustling Nile had brought an abundance of commerce to the city, Rosetta had threatened to rival Alexandria as Egypt's leading port, but the river had become clogged with silt, and the once-booming city was slowly dying. Its streets now echoed only to the sound of soldier's boots and the shrieks of a colony of lepers who begged for alms in the dirty bazaars. To the east lay the green carpet of the fertile delta; far to the west the scorching Libyan desert; and to the north the narrow shore line of the Mediterranean and the foaming surf at the mouth of the broad Nile.

Together, Sibley and Loring with the help of Kennon set out to plan and construct elaborate coastal fortifications. At the western end of the Bay of Alexandria, they constructed a huge fortress sturdy enough to withstand any bombardment. Hundreds of fellahin conscripts, laboring under the burning African sun, built the defenses. The fellahin toiled to dig gun emplacements and drag stones for miles across the burning desert sand, laboring much as their ancestors had done three thousand years before.

Sibley was especially interested in the plight of the peasants as they sweated in the terrible heat and humidity of the coast. The poor fellah, with nothing but a rag around his loins, presented a wretched image as he sweated without pay on the canals and public works

---

[33] Ibid., p. 69; Wessel, p. 78. It was of course near Rosetta that one of Napoleon's soldiers some seventy-one years earlier had discovered the stone that helped to unlock the fourteen hundred year-old mystery of Egyptian writing.

throughout the country. The poverty of the peasantry left such a mark on Sibley that he would later devote a considerable amount of effort lecturing on the subject.

The forts, each mounting a single high-powered gun designed to overlook the blue waters of the Mediterranean, were to stretch thirty-five miles along the coast from Alexandria in the west to Rosetta in the east. One unique design feature of the forts was that they were to be sunk in the sand to seem invisible. Machinery was devised to raise the gun to a firing position and then ingeniously return it safely to beneath the surface of the earth. Kennon was largely responsible for the design of the forts, which featured a conical hood over the guns for protection, but Sibley, always priding himself on his inventive inclinations, supervised and assisted in the project.[34] The first fort was completed at Ras-el-tin guarding the harbor of Alexandria. So impressive was the fort that both Egyptians and Americans came to the coast to admire it.

The khedive, his treasury dwindling as a result of the costly construction, was forced to end the building of the fortifications in 1873. Interesting, however, is the fact that the Sibley-Kennon designed fort at Ras-el-tin was all that survived the British bombardment of Alexandria eleven years later.

In Alexandria a feud between the former Confederate officers Loring, Campbell, and Alexander W. Reynolds, and Consul General George H. Butler erupted in July 1872. The feud, in which Sibley appears to have been a bystander, had its origins in the fact that Butler was the nephew of Benjamin "Beast" Butler, the Union general who had occupied New Orleans during the war and had become so widely despised in the South. George H. Butler wrote his congressman uncle, Benjamin Butler, and Secretary of State Hamilton Fish complaining that the Confederates had shot at him and on more than one occasion had attempted to kill him. The feud, which eventually reached the halls of Congress in Washington, was not stopped until Butler fled Alexandria, and the consulate, under new direction, was moved to Cairo.

There is evidence that Sibley, Loring, Rhett, Mott and Kennon joined in a conspiracy to secure Stone's removal as chief of staff in Cairo. Another American, James M. Morgan, later wrote that Gen-

[34] Ibid., p. 71.

eral Stone "handled the whole crowd as though they were so many naughty children; and before he got through with them they were tame enough to eat out of his hand and beg for his influence when they wanted any favors from the khedive."[35] Stone, despite Sibley and Loring's early influence with the khedive, was a born manipulator of men and the only American who had unlimited access to the khedive.

Problems of a more serious nature developed between Sibley and Major Cameron. Ever since his arrival in Egypt with Chaille-Long and Kennon, Cameron's actions had become more and more bizarre, to the point that it became evident to Sibley that he was suffering from acute paranoia. Somehow Cameron had become convinced that Sibley and others had formed a plot to murder him. On one occasion, after having challenged Colonel Kennon to a duel, Cameron spent the night before the arranged spectacle shooting up the hotel in Alexandria where he was staying, believing every shadow to be that of his imagined adversary. On another occasion Cameron had to be forceably subdued after attempting to poison Colonel Chaille-Long.[36] With little alternative, Sibley assisted in having his fellow Confederate arrested and his contract annulled by the minister of war. The following day Sibley watched while Cameron was placed on board a ship bound for England. He was not heard from again.

Sibley had been one of the first Americans to arrive in Egypt, and he was also one of the first to leave. As expected it was Sibley's chronic alcoholism, which appears to have worsened considerably since his ineptitude at the Battle of Bisland in 1863, that was his undoing. Shortly after arriving in Alexandria to begin work on the coastal fortifications, Sibley rented a plush apartment in the European quarter of the city from an English merchant named Andrew Victor Philip. In November 1871 Philip sued Sibley asserting that Sibley had not only completely wrecked the apartment but consumed the owner's eleborate stock of alcoholic beverages.[37] If Philip's accusations toward Sibley bear any remnants of accuracy, it is a sad reflection of how severe Sibley's alcoholism had become and how miserable his personal life must have been as a result. According to Philip, Sibley had

[35] James Morris Morgan, *Recollections of a Rebel Reefer* (Boston, 1917), 300.

[36] Chaille-Long, pp. 37–38.

[37] George H. Butler to Hamilton Fish, n.d., Consular Dispatches, R.G. 84; Hesseltine and Wolf, p. 117.

broken the front door to the apartment, stained and damaged two mattresses, damaged and broken the furniture in the apartment, smashed three champagne glasses, six tumblers, and one wine jug, besides breaking or losing all of the owner's silverware and china. Sibley had also consumed sixteen bottles of Dudesheur, fifteen bottles of Houcheumer, fourteen of Scharlachberger, eleven of Port, and three pints of ale, besides losing several of the landlord's books and a love letter.[38] Philip had sent Sibley a bill for the damages to the apartment and the lost items as well as the missing beverages, all to no avail.

While in Alexandria, Sibley had also gained the confidence of another Englishman, David Robertson, a bookseller and trader. Robertson had not only sold Sibley a large amount of goods over a period of several months but had also loaned Sibley a considerable sum of money to pay other debts. Finally disgusted with Sibley's inability or unwillingness to pay his debts, Robertson sued. With interest added, Sibley owed the book seller £ 52.13.9.[39]

A local merchant in Alexandria also presented a bill to the courts claiming Sibley had not paid him for a long list of goods including custom-made shoes, gold epaulettes, a sword with a gold cord, postage stamps sold to Sibley from 1870 to 1873, teaspoons, newspapers, and a telegram to Cairo.

To complicate matters many of Sibley's creditors appealed directly to the American consul-general in Alexandria, George H. Butler, who forwarded the claims and accusations to Chief of Staff General Charles P. Stone, in Cairo. Undoubtedly the government's inability to pay Sibley's salary which one month came from the khedive's private purse and the next from the Alexandria Customhouse, complicated Sibley's Egyptian service. His alcoholism, as indicated by his debts and squalor in Alexandria, indicates beyond doubt how chronic his drinking had become. In the end it was his undoing.

It is not known what effect Sibley's habitual drunkenness had on his son, for Sidney evidently was not attached to his father's com-

[38] Andrew Victor Philip to James Lane, 20 November 1871, Miscellaneous and Semi-Official Letters Received, 1865–1873, American Consulate, Cairo, Egypt, Records of the Department of State, Record Group 84, The National Archives, Washington, D.C.

[39] David Robertson to James Lane, 20 November 1871, and David Robertson to Colonel Butler, both in Ibid.; Hesseltine and Wolf, pp. 113–14.

mand in Alexandria. Upon his return to America, Sidney became estranged from his parents.

Shortly after June 30, 1873, when Sibley was last listed as a brigadier general on the military rolls, the khedive, fed up with his drunken incompetence, dismissed him. The khedive's wrath toward the general was not total as Sibley received, besides his severance pay and travel expenses back to New York, a personal gift of 500 pounds from "his highness."[40] The dismissal was probably with the recommendation of General Stone who had found Sibley's behavior an embarrassment. The *New York Herald* announced on December 9, 1873, that Loring and Stone had been promoted to major general but Sibley "had been discharged on account of physical inability."[41]

General Sibley had gone to the banks of the Nile in search of vindication and personal redemption. He found neither. By 1872 most Americans realized that there was little future in the Egyptian military. For Sibley there was no future in America either, so he lingered in Egypt until his expulsion. For the historian, Sibley's Egyptian experience sheds additional light on his Civil War record and reinforces the concept of his failure as a military commander. As the steamer taking him home to America departed the land of the pharaohs, taps had at last been blown over his military career.

[40] Reynolds to H.H. Sibley, 30 September 1873, Henry Sibley Papers.
[41] *New York Herald*, 9 December 1873.

"From the 25th day of December, 1869, until November, 1873, I was out of the United States and in the employ of the Egyptian Government, having entered that service, though retaining my American citizenship, because of my poverty, and because I could get no employment in this country wherewith to support myself and family. I have been applying to several Congresses for relief and have never neglected or abandoned my claim against the Government for the use of my invention, known as the Sibley tent. My claim is a just one."

Affidavit of Henry H. Sibley, Fredericksburg, Virginia, January 25, 1886.

Chapter XIII

By the Banks of
the Rappahannock

Henry Hopkins Sibley returned to the United States from Egypt sometime late in 1873. He first went to Charlotte's ancestral home in Brooklyn, New York, but remained there for only a few months, going on to Fredericksburg, Virginia, where his daughter Helen was living. He spent the latter part of his life heavily reliant on his daughter.

Helen, who was described by a relative as "a petted only daughter" and not as "patient as a wife should be," had separated from her husband John Stokes because of his habitual gambling.[1] Despite her marital problems, Henry was proud of his socialite daughter, for Helen was not only well educated but was also said to have had a "beautiful voice," singing leading roles in French, German, and Italian operas in New York and Washington. While in Brooklyn, she had served as organist and soloist at Trinity Episcopal Cathedral, and had been a composer and a poet. While the Stokeses were residing in New York,

---

[1] Addie Stokes Mitchell to Margaret McKee, 24 June 1935, Belcher-Sibley Papers.

they also, for some unexplained reason, possibly their marital problems, had established a home in Fredericksburg sometime prior to 1874. When Stokes died unexpectedly from appendicitis at the age of forty-four on May 4, 1877, Helen moved permanently to Virginia.

It was perhaps appropriate that the old general should spend the latter part of his life in Fredericksburg, a place almost synonymous with the fury that was the Civil War. Fredericksburg's strategic location, on the right back of the Rappahannock, mid-way between Washington and Richmond, had turned the entire area into a vast battlefield during the war where over one hundred thousand soldiers had fallen in a destruction of human life, the like of which the world had never seen: first at Fredericksburg in December, 1862, Chancellorsville in May, 1863, and then in the carnage of the Wilderness and Spotsylvania in 1864.

The rich historical heritage of the town was predominately antebellum. On William Street, not far from the Sibley home on South Princess Anne Street, a large stone could still be seen where slaves had once been sold to prosperous tobacco planters. A few blocks away were shell-damaged and bombed out buildings, remnants of the fiery violence that had helped to destroy the institution of slavery.[2]

To Sibley, Fredericksburg was much like his childhood home of Natchitoches. At the lower end of town, near the Sibley home, steamers up to two hundred feet in length, docked to unload their cargoes for the town's merchants.

Fredericksburg remembered the youth of George Washington who had grown to manhood only a few miles away on the north bank of the Rappahannock. It was there that the celebrated Cherry Tree and Silver Dollar incidents allegedly occurred.

If the post Civil War years were lean ones for Fredericksburg and the South, they were even more meager for Henry Hopkins Sibley. In 1874 Henry found himself in the same bad economic predicament as he had been at the end of the Civil War. Briefly after his return from Egypt, he gave lectures on the conditions of the Egyptian peasants,

[2] Histories of Fredericksburg include: Silvanus Jackson Quinn, *A History of the City of Fredericksburg, Virginia* (Richmond, 1908); Robert Reid Howison, *Fredericksburg, Past, Present and Future* (Fredericksburg, 1880); and Alvin Thomas Embrey, *History of Fredericksburg, Virginia* (Richmond, 1937).

the fellahin, but what little money he had made was quickly spent.[3] Unable to find work of any kind, not even in the field of engineering for which he had been trained at West Point, he had to live from the little money Helen inherited from her husband's savings. So desperate was Henry for employment that in September 1878 he advertised in the local newspaper his willingness to teach French to "a limited number of pupils, young misses, young men, and adults."[4] Commenting on his advertisement, the Fredericksburg *Virginia Star* remarked that Sibley was a gentleman of culture and refinement and well qualified to teach French.

Much of the latter part of his life was spent in futile and frustrating legalistic and political endeavors to obtain royalties from his invention of the Sibley tent. This badly needed income had abruptly ended when he joined the Confederacy in 1861. Undoubtedly the payment of over $100,000 by the government to Major William W. Burns, to whom Sibley had given one-half interest in the tent, motivated him to seek monetary relief. The basic difference between the two was that Burns had remained loyal to the Union in 1861; Sibley had not. In the lengthy litigation which his son-in-law John Stokes had helped to instigate prior to 1877, Sibley argued that he had signed a loyalty oath, had been pardoned by President Andrew Johnson on August 16, 1868, was therefore a citizen of the United States, and was due the same rights and privileges as anyone else. Accordingly, the government owed him $101,242 and fifty cents for tents manufactured for the government, some 47,541 of which had been used by the Union Army in the Civil War. Congress passed a bill requiring that in such cases army officers would have had to remain loyal to the Federal Government and not "aided or abetted the rebellion."[5]

Sibley had been given hope when, in the Armstrong v. United States

---

[3] Daniel Ruggles, "Obituary of H.H. Sibley," *1887 Annual Returns of the Association of Graduates* (West Point, 1887), 22; Margaret McKee, Miscellaneous Notes, Belcher-Sibley Papers.

[4] Fredericksburg *Virginia Star*, 21 September 1878.

[5] Hearings Before the Subcommittee of the Committee on War Claims of the House of Representatives, Seventieth Congress, First Session, "A Bill for the Relief of the Legal Representatives of the Estate of Henry H. Sibley, Deceased," 8 February 1928, U.S. Government Printing Office, Washington, D.C., pp. 1–32; Carrol H. Quenzel, "General Henry Hopkins Sibley: Military Inventor," *Virginia Magazine of History and Biography*, 64 (1955), 175.

case in 1871, the Supreme Court ruled that individuals like Sibley, despite their disloyalty during the Civil War, had the right to sue in the Court of Claims. Numerous bills were introduced in the Congress by Virginia politicians for Sibley's financial relief. Although at least two were favorably reported out of committee, one of which passed the Senate in 1886, none was ever enacted. Evidently the argument prevailed that Sibley had helped to make war against the government, thus increasing the number of tents manufactured. To the lawmakers it seemed illogical, if not downright stupid, to allow a man to profit from his own wrongdoing.

Sibley's inability to collect royalties for his tent, however, did not stymie his inclinations toward military invention. His decision to do so was partly out of financial desperation due to his inability to find a job. His first project, which is certainly indicative of his innovative brilliance, was a farsighted "improvement in projectiles for ordnance."[6]

On December 18, 1873, after several months of tedious letter writing and paperwork, which included the retention of attorneys and the completion of several sketches, Henry made application for a patent. His invention consisted of an ingeniously designed artillery shell in which compressed cotton, felt, or other fabric was used to force a shell casing. The cloth, which would be lubricated, would cleanse the barrel at every firing and so eliminate the current need for swabbing after each firing. Furthermore, the compressed cotton or other fabric was designed to fit tightly into the barrel of the artillery piece, thus adding stability, preventing windage, and thus achieving greater accuracy and distance. In some ways the improved projectile anticipated developments later used in modern heavy naval ordnance. Henry had evidently observed sufficient ordnance during the Civil War and in Egypt to know many of the problems facing the artillery and what needed to be done in the way of improvement.

Four months after submitting his application, Henry received notice from the Patent Office that he had been granted a patent, numbered 148,330 and dated March 10, 1874.[7] Any effort to induce the military to take a serious look at his improved projectile went for naught, as the army refused to even experiment with the weapon. He

[6] H.H. Sibley, "Specifications Forming Part of Letter Patent No. 148,330, 10 March 1874," Patent Office Records, N.A., R.G. 241.
[7] Ibid.

was not dismayed, however, and continued to work on his invention. For six years he labored at improving the original projectile. Much like the first, his second "improved projectile" was for use in large artillery pieces and would improve velocity, flatten trajectory, increase range and penetration, decrease windage, improve accuracy, and have less of an effect on fouling the bore and groove of the gun. Once again he hired two patent attorneys from Washington who helped to obtain the necessary sketches and make the application. Finally after submitting a twenty dollar fee and making several modifications at the suggestion of the Patent Office, he was granted a patent numbered 225,650 on March 16, 1880.[8] Sadly, however, the army still was not interested.

Henry also worked on a raft-like device by "means of which any person may sustain himself in the water for any length of time, and swim, or float at his pleasure without danger of drowning."[9] The gadget, Henry thought, could be used by troops crossing a river. An advantage of the float was that a soldier could place his rifle on it while crossing a stream or river, all the time firing at the enemy. By modifying it with a metallic keel and compartment to hold a supply of water, the device could also be used as a life preserver at sea in times of distress. Life could thus be sustained for several days.

Another invention was an aquatic mail and treasure preserver. Actually an air-tight, water-tight metallic float shaped like a whale boat, the object was constructed to float upright in the most violent storms. It could be furnished with "three or more compartments with circular hatchways on which the hatches were fastened and locked, thus securing the mail and treasure deposit therein."[10] A small derrick could be built on the float from which an attached bell would ring when hit by a wave, thus attracting the attention of passing ships especially at night.

Other inventions included a rocking chair, a movable bake oven designed for use by troops in the field, and a modification of the Sibley tent for hospitals, camp meetings, and circuses.[11] When the cen-

[8] H.H. Sibley, "Specifications Forming Part of Letter Patent No. 225,650, 16 March 1880," Patent Office Records, N.A., R.G. 241.

[9] Last Will and Testament of H.H. Sibley, Will Book I, Circuit Court of Fredericksburg, Virginia, 10 February 1886.

[10] Ibid.

[11] Ibid.

sus enumerator came to South Princess Ann Street in 1880, Henry proudly listed his occupation as inventor.[12]

A few days before Christmas, 1880, token financial assistance arrived in the form of a Christmas gift from a surprising distant relative, Henry Hastings Sibley, late Brevet Major General in the Union Army and first governor of the state of Minnesota, who sent his distant relative $25. Henry Hastings had first met Henry Hopkins when the latter was stationed either in Baltimore or New York on recruiting duty at which time Henry Hastings was then serving in Congress as representative from the Minnesota Territory. The governor had first heard of Henry's financial misfortunes and ill health from General William Tecumseh Sherman.[13]

Desperate for any kind of financial assistance, Henry submitted, in a period of three years, twelve articles to the New York publishing magnate Frank Leslie. The articles were published in two of Leslie's thirteen periodicals—*Popular Monthly* and *Chimney Corner*. For his literary efforts, Henry received anywhere from thirty dollars for a lengthy article in *Popular Monthly* to a meager five dollars for a short piece in the weekly *Chimney Corner*. The articles dealt with a variety of subjects although most were in some way related to his life in the Second Dragoons. Conspicuously absent was any recollection of his adventures in either the Confederate or Egyptian Armies. Only one article carried a by-line; two others indicated they were written by "An Old Army Officer."[14]

In one composition entitled, "A Curious Plan of Reformation," which was published in the *Popular Monthly*, Henry described in amazingly vivid and frank terms his nightmarish hallucinations which resulted from his chronic alcoholism. Three of his articles are indicative of his long held respect and admiration for the American Indian. One piece, "A Tragic Story of the Indian Sense of Disgrace," recalled the death of Koweaka, the Wichita Chief, on the Clear Fort of the Brazos in Texas in 1853. The entire episode was a sad and tragic event that had played deeply on his conscience for over three decades. Another well-written article, which included not only some of the latest scholarship on the subject but his own astute observations,

---

[12] Census of Fredericksburg, Spottsylvania County, Virginia, 8 June 1880, National Archives.

[13] H.H. Sibley to Gen'l H.H. Sibley, 13 December 1880, Henry Sibley Papers.

[14] For a complete listing of the articles, see the bibliography.

dealt with the Pueblo Indians of the Territory of New Mexico, especially the Zuni. An article entitled "Indian Gambling," centered around his recollections of a Caddo-Choctaw game of lacrosse he had witnessed as a child in Natchitoches in 1825. Three articles were based on his Mexican War experiences: "How We Took Alvarado," "Scott in Mexico," and "Ascending the Popocatepetl."

One piece, "Recollections of Cadet Life," centered around what Henry could remember of his life as a cadet at West Point. In retrospection he recalled not only the harsher aspects of his academy education but the more humorous moments as well. One article, "Recollections of the School for Verdants," contained several humorous reminiscences of his Louisiana childhood. Two other articles, "Military History of a Double Barreled Shotgun" and "Moveable Homes and Tent Life," related various episodes of his life as a Second Dragoon. The latter article, which presented many of his favorable conclusions toward the Sibley tent, indicates a thorough understanding of world geography and history.

Generally speaking, Henry's articles were interesting and scholarly. Furthermore, they are representative of someone with a remarkable and extensive vocabulary and superior intelligence. The latter becomes especially evident when one considers the psychological restraints and difficulties under which the frequently ill, sixty-five old writer labored. All offer a rare, although slight, glimpse into a world not revealed in his voluminous official correspondence.

Henry received $150 from Leslie for his twelve articles. It wasn't much money, even in the 1880s, considering the length of the pieces and the effort expounded.[15] Nevertheless, the money was badly needed in the Sibley household and was welcomed with considerable glee.

Although the old general spent the last decade of his life in poverty and obscurity, there were a few important friends who helped him through these difficult times. One was the gallant Daniel Ruggles, an ex-Confederate general who had served early in the war in Virginia, fought bravely at Shiloh, but like Sibley, had run into controversy and ended the war without a command. Much earlier Ruggles and Sibley had served together in Mexico and on the Texas frontier. The two had much in common. Ruggles was a recognized inventor, experimenting with rainmaking, working on the principles of the telephone, and

[15] Miscellaneous notation, n.d., Henry Sibley Papers.

patenting the first propellor ever used on a steamboat.[16] Prior to the
Civil War Ruggles had also invented an instrument whereby an elec-
tric bell on a ship would ring when the ship approached a rock or dangerous point of land where a similar device had been placed. Ruggles,
who was superintendent of schools in Fredericksburg, would later remember his friend Sibley as "a genial companion, of brilliant con-
versational powers [and] of a liberal disposition."[17]

Another Civil War general and native of Fredericksburg who helped
and sympathized with Henry was Carter Littlepage Stevenson. General Stevenson, a West Point classmate of Sibley's with whom Henry
had served on the Texas frontier, was a veteran of Vicksburg, Chat-
tanooga, and Chickamauga.

As his life began to fade, Sibley turned to religion for therapy and
solace. Although born and raised a Presbyterian in Natchitoches, he
had converted to Catholicism early in life. In Fredericksburg, largely
because of the influence of his wife and daughter, he began to attend
St. George's Episcopal Church which was only a few minutes walk
from the Sibley home. R.J. McBryde, St. George's dashing and amiable young minister, was able to convince Henry that the Catholic
Church was dogmatically shallow and that he should convert to
Episcopalianism.

On April 12, 1878, Henry was confirmed as an Episcopalian beneath St. George's towering spire, and from that moment on he became one of Fredericksburg's most devout churchgoers, spending
more and more of his time in prayer. According to his grandson, Henry
Lee Stokes, the old general felt that religion "should have an uplift-
ing, soul satisfying power which touches one's inner-being and in turn
is radiated to others."[18] His growing interest in religion may have also
resulted from the deterioration of his health.

Many years later the grandson remembered his grandfather as "a
kind, but stern, upright man with a determination to stick by what
he though to be right."[19] Psychologically, Henry Lee became a sur-

[16] John T. Goolrich, *Historic Fredericksburg: The Story of an Old Town* (Richmond,
1922), 109; Ezra J. Warner, *Generals in Gray* (Baton Rouge, 1978), 266.

[17] Ruggles, p. 22.

[18] Margaret McKee, Miscellaneous Notes, n.d., Belcher-Sibley Papers. For the history of St. George's see: Carrol H. Quenzel, *The History and Background of St. George's
Episcopal Church* (Richmond, 1951).

[19] Ibid.

rogate son to the old general, especially following Sibley's return from Egypt when Sidney Johnston Sibley had settled at San Antonio, Uvalde, Montell, and finally San Angelo where he worked on the *San Angelo Enterprise*. Sidney Johnston would be referred to by Henry Lee as a "wander-lust type," having little if any communication with his mother and father in the East. Residents of San Angelo remembered him as "under average height" and of "slight physique." He was said to have had a "personal magnetism" that made it "impossible for anyone to bear unkind feelings toward him." Sidney Johnston was admired in San Angelo as a "versatile genius" and an "elocutionist of high order" who possessed "mental faculties extraordinarily numerous."[20]

The grandson patiently listened to stories of the Mexican War, sagas of Indian encounters on the western frontier, the valor and righteousness that was the Civil War, and life along the Nile in far-off Egypt. Henry Lee, who in 1880 was fourteen, four years older than his brother Elmore and six years older than his only sister Flora, was especially fond of his grandfather, even sharing his bed with the general. In return the general bequeathed to his grandson all the military souvenirs which he had collected through the years while serving in three armies on two continents. These included his prized Civil War sword, an elegantly engraved pistol which had been given him by the citizens of New Orleans, medals, mementos, and an ebony cross from Egypt.

The last few years of Sibley's life were particularly painful. The family, including his daughter and her three children, subsisted on Helen's earnings as a music teacher. Henry's illness with colic had become acutely worse in Egypt and had continued to worsen upon his return to the United States. So bad was his condition that by 1883 he had virtually become an invalid, suffering so intensely that severe dizziness made him unable to stand for long periods of time. Lacking control of either his bowels or kidneys, he was forced to wear a large thick diaper, causing him considerable embarrassment. The excruciating pain which he suffered during the last few years of his life caused incessant heavy drinking. It was said that the old general always kept an ample supply of whiskey readily available. In his des-

[20] Miscellaneous Notes, n.d., Belcher-Sibley Papers. Sidney Johnston died at San Angelo, Texas, 10 January 1902; *San Angelo Standard*, 11 January 1902; L. Boyd Finch to Jerry D. Thompson, 9 September 1983.

peration he also had Henry Lee collect from the Virginia countryside various species of herbs which he chewed in an attempt to relieve the intense pain. Henry's friend, General Ruggles, recalled later that Henry returned from Egypt with "broken health" and that he "lingered several years a distressed invalid."[21]

Finally on February 10, 1886, the old soldier, feeling that the end was in sight, made his last will and testament. Hoping that his financial predicament, which had caused him much embarrassment, would be alleviated by a just and fair settlement of his royalty claims either in the Congress or in the courts, Henry asked that his debts "be paid to the uttermost penny."[22] From his long-anticipated royalties, Henry hoped to give Charlotte's two unmarried sisters, Mercie and Theresa Kendall, with whom Margaret and Henry had lived after the Civil War and who were still living in Brooklyn, a thousand dollars jointly. To his brother-in-law, Robert Sevier, in Richmond, Missouri, Henry planned to give $250 and claims to a small piece of land near Natchitoches in western Louisiana. To his close friend and confidant, Reverend R.J. McBryde, then living in Lexington, Virginia, he left $250. To his loyal and ever-loving grandson, Henry Lee, he allotted another $250.

To his only son in Texas, whom Henry had evidently never stopped loving and with whom he had shared a never-to-be-forgotten experience in Egypt, he willed his inventions which he felt were all practical and could easily be made lucrative. To secure patents on those inventions, not yet licensed, Henry gave his son $1,000 of the hoped-for money. To his wife and daughter, the two individuals who had stood by him to the end and whom he loved the most, he gave the remainder of the sum.[23]

The end finally came at five o'clock in the morning of August 23, 1886. After so many years of poignant suffering, his death was almost a blessing. His poverty and obscurity had somehow come to shadow his Civil War exploits, and only the two local newspapers, the *Fredericksburg Star* and the *Free Lance*, bothered to note his passing.[24]

Late in the afternoon of the following day, a sizeable crowd gath-

[21] Ibid.; Ruggles, p. 22.
[22] Sibley Will.
[23] Ibid.
[24] Fredericksburg *Free Lance*, 24 August 1886; *Fredericksburg Star*, 25 August 1886. The date of his death is erroneously inscribed on his tombstone as 22 August 1886.

ered beneath the tall steeple of St. George's to pay tribute to the old warrior. A few ex-Confederates met in Veterans' Hall, a wing of the local courthouse, to give homage. Several followed his remains from St. George's, the seven blocks down William Street, to the City Cemetery where he was laid to rest in the Stevenson Family plot. Two Confederate veteran groups, the Maury Camp and Fredericksburg Grays, fired a salute over his grave. The old warrior had fought his last battle.

Had his New Mexico Campaign succeeded, the entire history of the Southern Confederacy might have been radically altered. But all that was history in 1886. He was seventy years old. His grave would remain unmarked for another seventy.

Bibliography

PRIMARY SOURCES

Manuscripts and Archival Collections

Adjutant General's Records. Texas State Archives, Austin, Texas.

Application Papers of Cadets. Records of the Adjutant General's Office. Record Group 94. The National Archives, Washington, D.C.

Banta, William and Caldwell, John Wesley. "Fifty Years in Texas." Archives, University of Texas, Austin, Texas.

Barret, Mason. Papers. Special Collections, Howard-Tilton Library, Tulane University, New Orleans, Louisiana.

Battalion Orders. Archives, United States Military Academy. West Point, New York.

Baylor, John R. Papers. Archives, Louisiana State University, Baton Rouge, Louisiana.

Baylor, John R. Letters. Archives, University of Texas, Austin, Texas.

Burns, W.W. "History of My Connection with [the] Sibley Tent." Quartermaster General's Office. Record Group 92. The National Archives, Washington, D.C.

Census of Fredericksburg, Spotsylvania County, Virginia. The National Archives, Washington, D.C.

Clark, Edward. Papers. Texas State Archives, Austin, Texas.

Compiled Military Service Record of Alfred S. Thurmond. Records of the Confederate Adjutant General's Office. Record Group 109. The National Archives, Washington, D.C.

Compiled Military Service Record of Henry Hopkins Sibley. Records of the Confederate Adjutant General's Office. Record Group 109. The National Archives, Washington, D.C.

Consular Dispatches. Cairo, Egypt. Records of the Department of State. Record Group 84, The National Archives, Washington, D.C.

Court Martial Records in the Case of H.H. Sibley. Judge Advocate General's Office. Record Group 153. The National Archives, Washington, D.C.

DeShields Papers. Daughters of the Republic of Texas Library, San Antonio, Texas.

Estate of Henry H. Sibley. Report No. 344, 69th Congress, 1st Session, 11 March 1926. Library of Congress.

"Hearings of Subcommittee No. 2 of the Committee on War Claims on House Report 8749, A Bill for the Relief of the Legal Representatives of the Estate of Henry H. Sibley, Deceased." Documents Division, The Library of Congress, Washington, D.C.

Howell, Randolph. Diary and Letters. Archives, University of Texas, Austin, Texas.

Johnston, Josiah Stoddard. Papers. Pennsylvania Historical Society, Philadelphia, Pennsylvania.

Letters Received. Army of Occupation in Mexico. Records of the Adjutant General's Office. Record Group 94. The National Archives, Washington, D.C.

Letters Received. Confederate Adjutant General's Office. Record Group 109. The National Archives, Washington, D.C.

Letters Received. Consolidated Correspondence File on the Sibley Tent. Quartermaster General's Office. Record Group 92. The National Archives, Washington, D.C.

Letters Received. Department of New Mexico. Records of the Adjutant General's Office. Record Group 393. The National Archives, Washington, D.C.

Letters Received. District of Santa Fe. Records of the Adjutant General's Office. Record Group 393. The National Archives, Washington, D.C.

Letters Received. District of Texas. Records of the Confederate War Department. Record Group 109. The National Archives, Washington, D.C.

Letters Received. Records of the Adjutant General's Office. Record Group 94. The National Archives, Washington, D.C.

Letters Received. Second Dragoons. Records of the Adjutant General's Office. Record Group 94. The National Archives, Washington, D.C.

Letters Received. Trans-Mississippi Department. Records of the Confederate War Department. Record Group 109. The National Archives, Washington, D.C.

Letters Sent. Department of the West. Records of the Adjutant General's Office. Record Group 94. The National Archives, Washington, D.C.

Letters Sent. Volume V. Recruiting Service. Record Group 94. The National Archives, Washington, D.C.

Letters Sent. Second Dragoons. Record of the Adjutant General's Office. Record Group 94. The National Archives, Washington, D.C.

McRae, John. Letters. Southern Historical Collection, Archives, University of North Carolina, Chapel Hill, North Carolina.

Merrick, M.W. "Notes and Sketches of Campaigns in New Mexico, Arizona, Texas, Louisiana, and Arkansas by a Participant, Dr. M.W. Merrick, from Feb. 16, 1861, to May 26, 1865, Actual Service in the Field." Daughters of the Republic of Texas Library, The Alamo, San Antonio, Texas.

Mexican War Widows' Service Pension Records. Records of the War Department. The National Archives, Washington, D.C.

Office of Indian Affairs. Archives, University of Texas, Austin, Texas.

Peticolas, Alfred B. Diary. George W. Baylor, Jr., Tucson, Arizona.

Post Orders. Fort Union. Records of the Adjutant General's Office. Record Group 391. The National Archives, Washington, D.C.

Post Orders. Volumes VI and VII. Archives, United States Military Academy. West Point, New York.

Post Returns. Fernando de Taos. Records of the Adjutant General's Office. Record Group 393. The National Archives. Washington, D.C.

Post Returns. Fort Belknap. Records of the Adjutant General's Office. Record Group 94. The National Archives, Washington, D.C.

Post Returns. Fort Croghan. Records of the Adjutant General's Office. Record Group 94. The National Archives, Washington, D.C.

Post Returns. Fort Graham. Records of the Adjutant General's Office. Record Group 393. The National Archives, Washington, D.C.

Post Returns. Fort Jesup. Records of the Adjutant General's Office. Record Group 94. The National Archives, Washington, D.C.

Post Returns. Fort Phantom Hill. Records of the Adjutant General's Office, Record Group 94. The National Archives, Washington, D.C.

Post Returns. Fort Union. Records of the Adjutant General's Office, Record Group 94. The National Archives, Washington, D.C.

Post Returns. Fort Washita. Records of the Adjutant General's Office. Record Group 94. The National Archives, Washington, D.C.

Register of Graduates. Archives, United States Military Academy. West Point, New York.

Register of Letters Received, 1851–1857. Volume II. Department of Texas. Records of the Adjutant General's Office. Record Group 94. The National Archives, Washington, D.C.

Regimental Returns of the Second Dragoons. Records of the Adjutant General's Office. Record Group 391. The National Archives, Washington, D.C.

Register of Letters Received. Department of Utah. Records of the Adjutant General's Office. Record Group 391. The National Archives, Washington, D.C.

Register of Letters Sent. Department of Utah. Records of the Adjutant General's Office. Record Group 391. The National Archives, Washington, D.C.

Sibley, George Champlin. Papers. Missouri Historical Society, St. Louis, Missouri.

Sibley, Henry Hopkins. Commission. Lewis Leigh, Jr., Fairfax, Virginia.

Sibley, H.H. "Last Will and Testament." Will Book I, Circuit Court of Fredericksburg, Virginia.

Sibley, Henry Hopkins. Miscellaneous Notes and Data. Margaret Belcher, La Marque, Texas.

———. Letters. New York Historical Society, New York, New York.

———. Miscellaneous Documents. Henry Sibley, Adams' Basin, New York.

———. Specifications Forming Part of Letter Patent No. 225,650: March 16, 1880, Patent Office Records. Record Group 241. The National Archives, Washington, D.C.

Succession Records in the Case of Samuel Hopkins Sibley. Natchitoches Parish Courthouse, Natchitoches, Louisiana.

Wright, W.C. "Reminiscences of H.C. Wright of Austin." Archives, University of Texas, Austin, Texas.

Books

Adams, F.G., ed. *Transactions of the Kansas State Historical Society, Embracing the Fifth and Sixth Biennial Reports, 1886–1888, Together with Copies of Official Papers During a Portion of the Administration of Governor Wilson Shannon, 1856, and the Executive Minutes of Governor John W. Geary During His Administration, Be-*

ginning September 9, 1856, and Ending March 10, 1857. Topeka: Kansas Publishing House, 1890.

Alberts, Don E., ed. *Rebels on the Rio Grande: The Civil War Journal of A.B. Peticolas.* Albuquerque: University of New Mexico Press, 1984.

Ardoin, Robert Bruce L., comp. *Louisiana Census Records: Iberville, Natchitoches, Pointe Coupee, and Rapides Parishes, 1810 and 1820.* Vol. II. Baltimore: Genealogical Publishing Co., 1972.

Bancroft, Hubert H. *History of Arizona and New Mexico, 1530–1888.* San Francisco: The History Company, 1889.

Day, James M., ed. *House Journal of the Ninth Legislature, First Called Session of the State of Texas.* Austin: Texas State Library, 1963.

———. ed. *Senate Journal of the Ninth Legislature, First Called Session of the State of Texas.* Austin: Texas State Library, 1963.

Evans, Clement A., ed. *Confederate Military History.* 12 Vols. Atlanta: Confederate Publishing Company, 1899.

Farmer, James E. *My Life with the Army in the West.* Ed. Dale F. Giese. Santa Fe: Stagecoach Press, 1967.

Ford, John Salmon. *Rip Ford's Texas.* Ed. Stephen B. Oates. Austin: University of Texas Press, 1963.

Fremantle, James Arthur Lyon. *The Fremantle Diary.* Ed. Walter Lord, London: Andre Deutsch, 1956.

Gove, Jesse A. *The Utah Expedition, 1857–1858: Letters of Captain Jesse A. Gove.* Ed. Otis G. Hammond, New Hampshire Historical Society, 1928.

Grant, U.S. *Personal Memoirs of U.S. Grant.* Vol. I. New York: Charles L. Webster, 1885.

Hafer, Leroy R. and Ann W., eds. *The Utah Expedition, 1857–1858: A Documentary Account of the United States Military Movement Under Colonel Albert Sidney Johnston and the Resistance by Brigham Young and the Mormon Nauvoo Legion.* Glendale: Arthur H. Clark Company, 1958.

Hammond, George P., ed. *Campaigns in the West, 1856–1861: The Journal and Letters of Colonel John Van Deusen Du Bois.* Tucson: Arizona Pioneers Historical Society, 1949.

Heartsill, W.W. *Fourteen Hundred and 91 Days in the Confederate Army.* Marshall: W.W. Heartsill, 1876.

Hollister, Ovando J. *Boldly They Rode.* Lakewood: The Golden Press, 1949.

Improved Conical Tent, Invented and Patented by Maj. H.H. Sibley, U.S. Army. Baltimore: Sherwood and Company, 1860.

Jones, John B. *A Rebel War Clerk's Diary.* Ed. Earl Schenck Miers. New York: A.S. Barnes and Company, 1961.

Loring, W.W. *A Confederate Soldier in Egypt.* New York: Dodd, Mead and Company, 1884.

Lowe, Percival G. *Five Years a Dragoon and Other Adventures on the Great Plains.* Norman: University of Oklahoma Press, 1965.

Morgan, James Morris. *Recollections of a Rebel Reefer.* Boston: Houghton Mifflin Company, 1917.

Mumey, Nolie., ed. *Bloody Trails Along the Rio Grande: A Day by Day Diary of Alonzo Ferdinand Ickis.* Denver: The Old West Publishing Company, 1958.

Noel, Theophilus. *A Campaign From Santa Fe to the Mississippi, Being a History of the Old Sibley Brigade.* Martin Hardwick Hall and Edwin Adams Davis, eds. Houston: Stagecoach Press, 1961.

———. *Autobiography.* Chicago: By the Author, 1904.

Official Records of the Union and Confederate Navies in the War of the Rebellion. 30 Volumes. Washington: U.S. Government Printing Office, 1894–1922.

Rodenbough, Theodore F. *From Everglade to Canon with the Second Dragoons.* New York: D. Van Nostrand, 1875.

Sibley, George Champlin. *The Road to Santa Fe, The Journal and Diaries of George Champlin Sibley.* Ed. Kate L. Gregg. Albuquerque: University of New Mexico Press, 1952.

Sibley, John. *An Account of Louisiana, 1803.* Boston: Directors of the Old South, n.d.

———. *A Report from Natchitoches in 1807.* Intro. Annie Heloise Abel. New York: Museum of the American Indian, Heye Foundation, 1922.

Sterne, Adolphus. *Hurrah for Texas.* Ed. Archie P. McDonald. Waco: Texian Press, 1969.

Taylor, Richard. *Destruction and Reconstruction.* Ed. Richard B. Harwell. New York: Longmans, Green and Company, 1955.

War of the Rebellion: A Compilation of the Official Records of the Union and Confederate Armies. 128 Volumes. Washington: U.S. Government Printing Office, 1880–1901.

Whitford, William Clarke. *Colorado Volunteers in the Civil War: The New Mexico Campaign in 1862.* Denver: The State Historical and Natural History Society, 1906.

Wright, Marcus J., comp. *Texas in the War, 1861–1865.* Ed. Harold B. Simpson. Hillsboro: Hill Junior College Press, 1965.

Articles

Anderson, Latham. "Canby's Service in the New Mexican Campaign," *Battles and Leaders of the Civil War.* Vol. II, New York: Castle Books, 1956.

Bell, J.M. "The Campaign of New Mexico, 1862," *War Papers Read Before the Commandry of the State of Wisconsin, Military Order of the Loyal Legion of the United States.* Vol. I. Milwaukee: Burdick, Armitage and Allen, 1891.

Bloom, Landsing B., ed. "Confederate Reminiscences of 1862," *New Mexico Historical Review,* 5 (July 1930).

Collins, Thomas Benton. "A Texan's Account of the Battle of Valverde," *Panhandle Plains Historical Review,* 37 (1964).

Cooper, Samuel. "Report of Colonel Samuel Cooper, Assistant Adjutant General of the United States, of an Inspection Trip from Fort Graham to the Indian Villages on the Upper Brazos Made in June, 1851," *Southwestern Historical Quarterly,* 42 (April 1937).

Cox, C.C. "Reminiscences," *Quarterly of the Texas State Historical Association,* 6 (1902–1903).

Crimmins, M.L., contr. "The Battle of Val Verde," *New Mexico Historical Review,* 7 (October 1932).

Garrett, Julia Kathryn., ed. "Dr. John Sibley and the Louisiana–Texas Frontier, 1803–1814," *Southwestern Historical Quarterly*, 45 and 48 (January 1942, July 1943, and April 1949).

Gracy, David B., II, ed. "New Mexico Campaign Letters of Frank Starr, 1861–1862," *Texas Military History*, 4 (1964).

Hall, Martin Hardwich., ed. "An Appraisal of the 1862 New Mexico Campaign: A Confederate Officer's Letter to Nacogdoches," *New Mexico Historical Review*, 51 (October 1976).

———., ed. "The Journal of Ebenezer Hanna," *Password*, 3 (January, 1958).

Hass, Oscar, trans. "The Diary of Julius Giesecke, 1861–1862," *Military History of Texas*, 3 (Winter, 1963).

Merchant, S.W. "Fighting With Sibley in New Mexico," *Hunter's Magazine*, 1 (November, 1910).

Pettis, George H. "The Confederate Invasion of New Mexico and Arizona," *Battles and Leaders of the Civil War*. Vol. II. New York: Yoseloff and Company, 1956.

Ruggles, Daniel. "Obituary of H.H. Sibley," *1887 Annual Returns of the Association of Graduates*. West Point: United States Military Academy, 1887.

[Sibley, Henry H.], "Ascending the Popocatepetl," *Frank Leslie's Chimney Corner*, (25 June 1881).

———. "A Curious Plan of Reformation," *Popular Monthly*, (17 December 1881).

———. "How We Took Alvarado," *Frank Leslie's Chimney Corner*, (2 July 1881).

———. "Indian Gambling," *Frank Leslie's Chimney Corner*, (11 February 1882).

———. "Military History of a Double-Barreled Shotgun," *Popular Monthly*, (17 May 1883).

———. "Moveable Homes, and Tent Life," *Popular Monthly*, (26 August 1881).

———. "The Pueblo Indians of New Mexico," *Popular Monthly*, (29 September 1883).

———. "Recollections of Cadet Life Forty Years Ago," *Popular Monthly*, (17 June 1881).

———. "Recollections of the School for Verdants," *Popular Monthly*, (15 August 1884).

———. "Scott in Mexico," *Frank Leslie's Chimney Corner*, (16 July 1881).

———. "Thoughts on Smoking," *Popular Monthly*, (27 April 1883).

———. "A Tragic Story of the Indian Sense of Disgrace," *Frank Leslie's Chimney Corner*, (15 February 1882).

Smith, William Henry. "With Sibley in New Mexico: The Journal of William Henry Smith," *West Texas Historical Association Year Book*, Contr. Walter A. Faulkner, XXVII.

Stowers, Robert E. and Ellis, John M., eds. "Charles A. Scott's Diary of the Utah Expedition, 1857–1861," *Utah Historical Quarterly*, 28 (1960).

Teel, T.T. "Sibley's New Mexican Campaign: Its Objects and the Causes of its Failure," *Battles and Leaders of the Civil War*. Vol. II. New York: Yoseloff and Company, 1956.

Tracy, Albert. "Journal of Albert Tracy," *Utah State Historical Quarterly*, (January-October, 1945).

Newspapers

Austin *Texas State Gazette*, 2, 16 October 1852; 16 April, 3 September 1853; 22 April, 4, 6 May 1854; 10 August, 7, 14, 21, 28 September, 12, 19, 26 October, 2, 9, 16 November, 7, 14, 21 December 1861; 16 February, 22 March, 5 April, 3, 17 May, 7 June 1862.

Clarksville *Northern Standard,* 21 February 1852; 16 April, 11 June, 17 September 1853; 21 October 1861.

Dallas Herald, 3 July, 7, 21 August 1861; 15 January, 10 May, 20 September, 22 November 1862; 15, 29 April, 27 May 1863; 3 September 1864; 14 August 1884.

Fredericksburg *Free Lance,* 18, 30 May, 24 August 1886.

Fredericksburg Star, 25 August 1886.

Fredericksburg *Virginia Star,* 21 September 1878.

Houston *Tri-Weekly Telegraph,* 30 December 1861; 29 March, 7 April, 12, 21, 22, 28 May, 6, 12, 18, 27 June, 2, 7, 21 July, 18, 27 August, 5 September, 8, 17 October 1862.

Marshall *Texas Republican,* 13 September, 8 November, 1862.

Mesilla Times, 13 August, 3, 10 October 1861; 8, 15 January 1862.

Mexico City *American Star,* 12, 16 April, 19 May 1848.

New Orleans *Daily Picayune,* 2, 15, 16 July, 2 August, 20 October 1861; 27 March 1862; 9 August 1865.

New Orleans *Daily Southern Star,* 24 September 1865.

New Orleans *Tagliche Deutsche Zeitung,* 8 January 1862.

New York Herald, 22 September 1871; 9 December 1873; 8 September 1882.

Pueblo *American Star,* 15 July 1847.

San Antonio *Daily Ledger and Texan,* 13 August 1861.

San Antonio Weekly Herald, 26 October, 3 November, 14 December 1861; 4, 11 January, 22 March 1862.

Santa Fe *Weekly Gazette,* 10 November 1860; 26 April, 3 May 1862.

SECONDARY SOURCES

Books

Adams, Ephraim Douglass. *Great Britain and the American Civil War.* New York: Russell and Russell, 1958.

Ambrose, Stephen E. *Duty, Honor, Country: A History of West Point.* Baltimore: Johns Hopkins University Press, 1966.

Arrington, Leonard J. *Brigham Young: American Moses.* Champaign: University of Illinois Press, 1986.

Bailey, Paul. *Holy Smoke, A Dissertation on the Utah War.* Los Angeles: Westernlore Books, 1978.

Bauer, K. Jack. *The Mexican War: 1846–1848.* New York: Macmillan Company, 1974.

Bill, Alfred Hoyt, *The Beleagured City: Richmond, 1861–1865.* New York: Alfred A. Knopf, 1946.

Boatner, Mark M. *The Civil War Dictionary.* New York: David McKay Company, 1969.

Brownlee, Richard S. *Grey Ghosts of the Confederacy, Guerilla Warfare in the West, 1861–1865.* Baton Rouge: Louisiana State University Press, 1958.

Buker, George E. *Swamp Sailors.* Gainesville: University of Florida Press, 1975.

Callahan, James M. *The Diplomatic History of the Southern Confederacy.* Baltimore: Johns Hopkins Press, 1901.

Cash, Wilbur J. *The Mind of the South*. New York: Vintage Books, 1941.

Colton, Ray C. *The Civil War in the Western Territories*. Norman: University of Oklahoma Press, 1959.

Crabites, Pierre. *Americans in the Egyptian Army*. London: George Routledge and Sons, 1938.

Dabney, Virginuis. *Richmond, the Story of a City*. New York: Doubleday and Company, 1976.

Dicey, Edward. *The Story of the Khediviate*. London: Rivingtons, 1902.

Dick, Everett, *The Dixie Frontier*. New York: Capricorn Books, 1964.

Dornbusch, C.E., comp. *Military Bibliography of the Civil War*. Vol. II. New York: New York Public Library, 1967.

Eaton, Clement. *Jefferson Davis*. New York: The Free Press, 1977.

Elgood, P.G. *The Transit of Egypt*. New York: Russell and Russell, 1969.

Eliot Ellsworth, Jr. *West Point in the Confederacy*. New York: G.A. Baker and Co., 1941.

Embrey, Alvin Thomas. *History of Fredericksburg, Virginia*. Richmond: Old Dominion Press, 1937.

Emmett, Chris. *Fort Union and the Winning of the Southwest*. Norman: University of Oklahoma Press, 1965.

Faulk, Odie. *General Tom Green, Fightin' Texan*. Waco: Texian Press, 1963.

Fehrenbach, T.R. *Comanches: The Destruction of a People*. New York: Alfred A. Knopf, 1974.

Foote, Shelby. *The Civil War: A Narrative, Fort Sumner to Perryville*. New York: Random House, 1958.

Franklin, John Hope. *The Militant South*. Cambridge: Harvard University Press, 1956.

Frazer, Robert W. *Forts of the West*. Norman: University of Oklahoma Press, 1972.

Freeman, Douglas Southall. *R.E. Lee: A Biography*. Vol. I. New York: Charles Scribner's Sons, 1962.

Furman, Erna. *A Child's Parent Dies, Studies in Childhood Bereavement*. New Haven: Yale University Press, 1974.

Furniss, Norman F. *The Mormon Conflict, 1850–1859*. New Haven: Yale University Press, 1960.

Gallaway, B.P. (ed.). *The Dark Corner of the Confederacy*. Dubuque: Kendall-Hunt Publishing Company, 1972.

Ganaway, Loomis M. *New Mexico and the Sectional Controversy, 1846–1861*. Albuquerque: University of New Mexico Press, 1944.

Geise, William Royston. *The Confederate Military Forces in the Trans-Mississippi West, 1861–1865: A Study in Command*. Austin: University of Texas Press, 1974.

Goff, Richard D. *Confederate Supply*. Durham: Duke University Press, 1969.

Goolrich, John T. *Historic Fredericksburg: The Story of an Old Town*. Richmond: Whitlet and Shepperson, 1922.

Grinstead, Marion C. *Life and Death of a Frontier Fort: Fort Craig, New Mexico, 1854–1885*. Socorro: Socorro County Historical Society, 1973.

Hall, Martin H. *Sibley's New Mexico Campaign*. Austin: University of Texas Press, 1960.

——— *The Confederate Army of New Mexico*. Austin: Presidial Press, 1978.

Harris, Gertrude. *A Tale of Men Who Knew Not Fear*. San Antonio: Alamo Printing Company, 1935.

Hart, Herbert H. *Old Forts of the Northwest*. New York: Bonanza Books, 1963.

———. *Old Forts of the Southwest*. New York: Bonanza Books, 1964.

Havinghurst, Walter. *The Miami Years: 1809–1969*. New York: G.P. Putnam's Sons, 1958.

Heitman, Francis B. *Historical Register and Dictionary of the United States Army*. Vol. I. Urbana: University of Illinois Press, 1965.

Henderson, Harry M. *Texas in the Confederacy*. San Antonio: The Naylor Company, 1955.

Hesseltine, William B., and Wolfe, Hazel C. *The Blue and Gray on the Nile*. Chicago: University of Chicago Press, 1961.

Heyman, Max L. *Prudent Soldier: A Biography of Major-General E.R.S. Canby*. Glendale: Arthur H. Clark Company, 1859.

Hirshson, Stanley P. *The Lion of the Lord: A Biography of Brigham Young*. New York: Alfred A. Knopf, 1969.

Hollon, Eugene W. *Beyond the Cross Timbers: The Travels of Randolph B. Marcy, 1812–1887*. Norman: University of Oklahoma Press, 1955.

Howison, Robert Reid. *Fredericksburg, Past, Present, and Future*. Fredericksburg: R.B. Merchant, 1880.

Hughes, W.J. *Rebellious Ranger: Rip Ford and the Old Southwest*. Norman: University of Oklahoma Press, 1964.

Hunt, Aurora. *The Army of the Pacific*. Glendale: The Arthur H. Clark Company, 1951.

Johnson, Ludwell H. *Red River Campaign, Politics and Cotton in the Civil War*. Baltimore: Johns Hopkins Press, 1958.

Jones, Charles T. *George Champlin Sibley: The Prairie Puritan*. Independence: Jackson County Historical Society, 1970.

Karnes, Thomas L. *William Gilpin, Western Nationalist*. Austin: University of Texas Press, 1970.

Keleher, William A. *Turmoil in New Mexico*. Santa Fe: Rydal Press, 1952.

Kerby, Robert Lee. *The Confederate Invasion of New Mexico and Arizona, 1861–1862*. Los Angeles: Westernlore Press, 1958.

———. *Kirby Smith's Confederacy: The Trans-Mississippi South, 1863–1865*. New York: Columbia University Press, 1972.

Krick, Robert K. (comp.). *Roster of the Confederate Dead in the Fredericksburg Confederate Cemetery*. Fredericksburg, 1974.

Langley, Harold D., *To Utah With the Dragoons*. Salt Lake City: University of Utah Press, 1974.

Lewis, Oscar. *The War in the Far West, 1861–1862*. Garden City: Doubleday and Company, 1961.

Long, E.B. *The Civil War Day by Day*. Garden City: Doubleday and Company, 1971.

Lonn, Ella. *Salt as a Factor in the Confederacy*. New York: 1933.

McNitt, Frank. *Navajo Wars*. Albuquerque: University of New Mexico Press, 1972.

McWhiney, Grady and Jamieson, Perry D. *Attack and Die: Civil War Military Tactics and the Southern Heritage*. University, Alabama: University of Alabama Press, 1982.

Mahon, John K. *History of the Second Seminole War*. Gainesville: University of Florida Press, 1967.

Mayhall, Mildred P. *Indian Wars of Texas*. Waco: Texian Press, 1965.

Military Operations of the Civil War: A Guide-Index to the Official Records of the Union and Confederate Armies, 1861–1865, Trans-Mississippi and Pacific Coast Theatre of Operations. Washington: National Archives and Records Service, 1980.

Miller, Benjamin F., and Keane, Claire Brachman. *Encyclopedia and Dictionary of Medicine*. Philadelphia: W.B. Saunders Co., 1972.

Miller, Darlis A. *The California Column in New Mexico*. Albuquerque: University of New Mexico Press, 1982.

Morrison, James L. Jr. *The Best School in the World: West Point—The Pre-Civil War Years, 1833–1866*. Kent: Kent State University Press, 1986.

Nardini, Louis Raphael. *My Historic Natchitoches, Louisiana and Its Environment*. Natchitoches: Nardini Publishing Co., 1963.

———. *No Man's Land*. New Orleans: Pelican Publishing Company, 1961.

Neighbours, Kenneth F. *Indian Exodus: Texas Indian Affairs, 1835–1859*. Nortex Publications, 1973.

———. *Robert Simpson Neighbors*. Waco: Texian Press, 1975.

Nevins, Allan. et al. *Civil War Books, A Critical Bibliography*. Vol. I. Baton Rouge: Louisiana State University Press, 1967.

Nichols, James L. *The Confederate Quartermaster in the Trans-Mississippi*. Austin: University of Texas Press, 1964.

Oates, Stephen B. *Confederate Cavalry West of the River*. Austin: University of Texas Press, 1961.

Owsley, Frank Lawrence. *King Cotton Diplomacy*. Chicago: University of Chicago Press, 1959.

———. *To Purge This Land With Blood*. New York: Harper and Row, 1970.

Prucha, Francis Paul. *The Sword of the Republic*. Toronto: Macmillan Company, 1969.

Quenzel, Carrol H. *The History and Background of St. George's Episcopal Church*. Richmond: Hermitage Press, 1951.

Quinn, Silvanus Jackson. *A History of the City of Fredericksburg, Virginia*. Richmond: Hermitage Press, 1908.

Ramsdell, Charles W. *Behind the Lines of the Southern Confederacy*. Baton Rouge: Louisiana State University Press, 1944.

Ramsdell, Charles. *San Antonio: A Historical and Pictorial Guide*. Austin: University of Texas Press, 1959.

Raphael, Morris. *The Battle in the Bayou Country*. Detroit: Harlo Press, 1975.

Rawley, James A. *Race and Politics: "Bleeding Kansas" and the Coming of the Civil War*. New York: J.B. Lippincott Company, 1969.

Rhodes, James Ford. *History of the United States From the Compromise of 1850*. Ed. Allan Nevins. Chicago: University of Chicago Press, 1956.

Richardson, Rupert Norval. *The Frontier of Northwest Texas, 1846–1876*, Glendale: Arthur H. Clark Company, 1963.

Richmond, J.C.B. *Egypt, 1798–1952: Her Advance Toward a Modern Identity*. New York: Columbia University Press, 1977.

Roland, Charles P. *Albert Sidney Johnston: Soldier of Three Republics.* Austin: University of Texas Press, 1964.

Roller, David C., and Twyman, Robert W., eds. *The Encyclopedia of Southern History.* Baton Rouge: Louisiana State University Press, 1979.

Rorabaugh, W.J. *The Alcoholic Republic: An American Tradition.* New York: Oxford University Press, 1970.

Sibley, James Scarborough. *The Sibley Family in America 1629–1972.* Honolulu: By the Author, 1972.

Simmons, Marc. *The Little Lion of the Southwest.* Chicago: Swallow Press, 1973.

———. *Albuquerque: A Narrative History.* Albuquerque: University of New Mexico Press, 1982.

Simpson, James H. *Navajo Expedition.* Ed. Frank McNitt. Norman: University of Oklahoma Press, 1964.

Smith, Justin H. *The War With Mexico.* Vol. I. Gloucester: Peter Smith, 1963.

Spurlin, Charles (ed.). *West of the Mississippi with Waller's 13th Texas Cavalry Battalion, C.S.A.* Hillsboro: Hill Junior College Press, 1971.

Stafford, G.M.G. *The Wells Family of Louisiana and Allied Families.* Alexandria: Claitor's Publishing Division, 1976.

Stanley, Francis Louis Crochiola. *The Civil War in the New Mexico Territory.* Denver: The World Press, 1960.

Strickland, Rex W. *Six Who Came to El Paso, Pioneers of the 1840's.* El Paso: Texas Western Press, 1963.

Thompson, Jerry D. *Colonel John Robert Baylor: Texas Indian Fighter and Confederate Soldier.* Hillsboro: Hill Junior College Press, 1971.

Twitchell, R.E. *Leading Facts of New Mexican History.* Vol. II. Cedar Rapids: The Torch Press, 1911.

Utley, Robert M. *Frontiersmen in Blue: The United States Army and the Indian, 1848–1865.* New York: The Macmillan Company, 1967.

Villard, Oswald Garrison. *John Brown: A Biography Fifty Years After.* Gloucester: Peter Smith Publishing Company, 1965.

Wakelyn, Jon L. *Biographical Dictionary of the Confederacy.* Westport: Greenwood Press, 1977.

Walker, J.G. and Shepherd, O.L. *Navajo Reconnaissance.* Ed. L.R. Bailey. Los Angeles: Westernlore Press, 1964.

Warner, Ezra F. *Generals in Gray: Lives of the Confederate Commanders.* Baton Rouge: Louisiana State University Press, 1970.

———. *Generals in Blue: Lives of the Union Commanders.* Baton Rouge: Louisiana State University Press, 1972.

Webb, Walter Prescott and Carroll, H. Bailey, eds. *The Handbook of Texas.* Austin: Texas State Historical Association, 1952.

Weigley, Russell F. *History of the United States Army.* New York: The Macmillan Company, 1967.

Wessels, William L. *Born to be a Soldier.* Fort Worth: Texas Christian University Press, 1971.

Winther, Oscar Osburn. *A Classified Bibliography of the Periodical Literature of the Trans-Mississippi West, 1811–1957.* Bloomington: Indiana University Press, 1964.

———. and Orman, Richard A. Van. *A Classified Bibliography of the Periodical Literature of the Trans-Mississippi West, A Supplement (1957–67)*. Bloomington: Indiana University Press, 1970.

Winters, John D. *The Civil War in Louisiana*. Baton Rouge: Louisiana State University Press, 1963.

Young, Otis E. *The West of Philip St. George Cooke, 1809–1895*. Glendale: Arthur H. Clark Company, 1955.

Zananiri, Gaston. *Le Khedive Ismail et L'Egypte*. Alexandria: Moloco, 1923.

Articles

Alberts, Don E. "The Battle of Peralta," *New Mexico Historical Review*, 58 (October, 1983).

Archambeau, Ernest R., Jr. "The New Mexico Campaign of 1861–1862," *Panhandle-Plains Historical Review*, 37 (1964).

Blackburn, Forest R. "Army Families in Frontier Forts," *Military Review*, 59 (1969).

Boyd, Le Roy. "Thunder on the Rio Grande, the Great Adventure of Sibley's Confederates for the Conquest of New Mexico and Colorado," *Colorado Magazine*, 24 (July 1947).

Broune, P.N. "Captian T.D. Nettles and the Valverde Battery," *Texana*, 2 (No. 1).

Cox, Frederick J. "The American Naval Mission in Egypt," *Journal of Modern History*, 26 (1954).

Donnell, F.S. "The Confederate Territory of Arizona from Official Sources," *New Mexico Historical Review*, 17 (April 1942).

Dunn, Milton. "History of Natchitoches," *Louisiana Historical Quarterly*, 3 (January 1920).

Faulk, Odie B. "Confederate Hero at Val Verde," *New Mexico Historical Review*, 38 (1963).

Finch, L. Boyd, "Arizona's Governors Without Portfolio: A Wonderfully Diverse Lot," *The Journal of Arizona History*, 26 (Spring 1985).

———. "Surprise at Brashear City: Sherod Hunter's Sugar Cooler Cavalry," *Louisiana History*, 25 (Fall 1984).

———. "Sherod Hunter and the Confederates in Arizona," *The Journal of Arizona History*, 10 (Fall 1982).

Ganaway, Loomis Morton. "New Mexico and the Sectional Controversy," *New Mexico Historical Review*, 18 (April, July, October 1943).

Hall, Martin Hardwick. "Colonel James Reily's Diplomatic Missions to Chihuahua and Sonora," *New Mexico Historical Review*, 31 (July 1956).

———. "Colorado Volunteers Save New Mexico for the Union," *Mid-America*, 38 (October 1956).

———. "The Formation of Sibley's Brigade and the March to New Mexico," *Southwestern Historical Quarterly*, 59 (January 1958).

———. "The Skirmish at Picacho," *Civil War History*, 4 (March 1959).

———. "The Skirmish at Mesilla," *Arizona and the West*, 1 (Winter, 1958).

———. "The Baylor-Kelley Fight: A Civil War Incident in Old Mesilla," *Password*, 5 (July 1960).

————. "Albert Sidney Johnston's First Confederate Command," *McNeese Review*, 13 (1962).

————. "The Mesilla Times: A Journal of Confederate Arizona," *Arizona and the West*, 5 (Winter, 1963).

————. "Native Mexican Relations in Confederate Arizona, 1861–1862," *The Journal of Arizona History*, 8 (Autumn, 1967).

————. "Negroes with Confederate Troops in West Texas and New Mexico," *Password*, 13 (Spring, 1968).

————. "Planter vs. Frontiersman: Conflict in Confederate Indian Policy." *Essays on the American Civil War*. Austin: University of Texas Press, 1968.

————. "Captain Thomas J. Mastin's Arizona Guards, C.S.A.," *New Mexico Historical Review*, 49 (April 1974).

Hatcher, John H. "Fort Phantom Hill," *Texas Military History*, 3 (1965).

Hayes, A.A. "The New Mexican Campaign of 1862," *Magazine of American History*, 15 (February 1886).

Hunsaker, William J. "Lansford W. Hastings' Project for the Invasion and Conquest of Arizona and New Mexico for the Southern Confederacy," *Arizona Historical Review*, 4 (2), (1931–32).

Jarrell, John. "Sibley and the Confederate Dream," *New Mexico Magazine*, 54 (August 1976).

Keller, Mark. "Other Effects of Alcohol," *Drinking and Intoxication*. Ed. Raymond G. McCarthy. New Haven: College and University Press, 1964.

McCoy, Raymond. "Confederate Cannon," *New Mexico Magazine*, 31 (September 1953).

————. "The Battle of Glorieta Pass," *United Daughters of the Confederacy Magazine*, 15 (February 1952).

McLeary, J.H. "History of Green's Brigade," *A Comprehensive History of Texas*, Vol. II, Ed. Dudley G. Wooten, Dallas: Scarff: 1898.

Meyer, Sandra L. "Fort Graham: Listening Post on the Texas Frontier," *West Texas Historical Association Year Book*, 59 (1983).

Miller, Darlis A. "Hispanos and the Civil War in New Mexico: A Reconsideration," *New Mexico Historical Review*, 54 (April 1979).

————. "Military Supply in Civil War New Mexico," *Military History of Texas and the Southwest*, 16 (1983).

Molen, Dayle H. "Decision at La Glorieta Pass," *Montana, the Magazine of Western History*, 13 (1962).

Neeley, James Lee. "The Desert Dream of the South: An Introductory Discussion of the Civil War Campaign in New Mexico and Arizona," *The Smoke Signal*, 4 (Fall 1961).

Neighbours, Kenneth F. "Fort Belknap," *Frontier Forts of Texas*. Waco: Texian Press, 1966.

Oates, Stephen B. "Supply for the Confederate Cavalry in the Trans-Mississippi," *Military Affairs*, 25 (1961).

Oder, Broech N. "The New Mexico Campaign, 1862," *Civil War Times Illustrated*, 17 (August 1978).

Perrine, David P. "The Battle of Valverde, New Mexico Territory, February 21, 1861," *Civil War Battles in the West*. Manhattan: Sunflower Press, 1981.

Quenzel, Carrol H. "General Henry Hopkins Sibley: Military Inventor," *Virginia Magazine of History and Biography*, 44 (1956).

Rister, C.C. "The Border Post of Phantom Hill," *The West Texas Historical Association Year Book*, (October 1938).

Rudolph, Jack. "Battles in the Bayous," *Civil War Times Illustrated*, 23 (January 1985).

Santee, J.F. "The Battle of La Glorieta Pass," *New Mexico Historical Review*, 6 (January 1931).

Steere, Edward. "Rio Grande Campaign Logistics," *Military Review*, (November 1953).

Smith, Duane Allen. "The Confederate Cause in the Colorado Territory, 1861–1865," *Civil War History*, 7 (1961).

Smith, Robert E. "Henry Hopkins Sibley," *Ten More Texans in Gray*. W.C. Nunn ed. Hillsboro: Hill Junior College Press, 1980.

Tafel, Anthony. "Heiter vs. Sibley," *North South Trader*, (March 1975).

Thompson, Jerry. "Mexican-Americans in the Civil War: The Battle of Valverde," *Texana*, 10 (No. 1, 1972).

———. "Henry Hopkins Sibley: "Military Inventor on the Texas Frontier," *Military History of Texas and the Southwest*, 10 (No. 4, 1972).

———. "Henry Hopkins Sibley and the Mexican War," *Texana*, 11 (No. 4, 1973).

———. "Henry Hopkins Sibley: Confederate General of the West," *Confederate Historical Institute Journal*, I (No. 3, 1980).

———. "From Valverde to Bisland: A Brief History of the Sibley Brigade," *Confederate History Symposium*. Hillsboro: Hill College Press, 1982.

———. "The Vulture Over the Carrion: Captain James 'Paddy' Graydon and the Civil War in the Southwest," *Journal of Arizona History*, 24 (Winter 1983).

Waldrip, William I. "New Mexico During the Civil War," *New Mexico Historical Review*, 28 (July 1953).

Walker, Charles S., Jr. "Confederate Government in Doña Ana County," *New Mexico Historical Review*, 6 (July 1931).

———. "Causes of the Confederate Invasion of New Mexico," *New Mexico Historical Review*, 8 (April 1933).

Waller, J.L. "The Civil War in the El Paso Area," *West Texas Historical Association Year Book*, 22 (October 1946).

Watford, W.H. "Confederate Western Ambitions," *Southwestern Historical Quarterly*, 44 (October 1940).

———. "The Far-Western Wing of the Rebellion," *California Historical Society Quarterly*, 34 (June 1955).

Whittington, G.P. "Dr. John Sibley of Natchitoches, 1757–1837," *Louisiana Historical Quarterly*, 10 (October 1927).

Windham, William T. "The Problem of Supply in the Trans-Mississippi Confederacy," *The Journal of Southern History*, 27 (May 1961).

Winkler, Allan M. "Drinking on the American Frontier," *Quarterly Journal of Studies of Alcohol*, 29 (1968).

Wyllys, Rufus K. "Arizona and the Civil War," *Arizona Highways*, 27 (1951).

Zinn, Howard, "William Homes McGuffey," *Encyclopedia of American Biography*, John A. Garraty, ed. New York: Harper and Row, 1974.

Unpublished Material

Gamble, Richard Dalzell, "Garrison Life at Frontier Military Posts, 1830–1869." Ph.D. Dissertation, University of Oklahoma, 1956.

Griess, Thomas E. "Dennis Hart Mahan: West Point Professor and Advocate of Military Professionalism, 1830–1871." Ph.D. Dissertation, Duke University , 1968.

Hastings, Virginia M. "A History of Arizona During the Civil War, 1861-1865." M.A. Thesis, University of Arizona, 1943.

Hostetter, John D. "The Second Dragoons and American Expansion: 1836–1861." M.A. Thesis, Florida State University, 1961.

Rogan, Francis Edward. "Military History of New Mexico Territory During the Civil War." Ph.D. Dissertation, University of Utah, 1961.

Simpson, Harold B. "Booze in Battle and Bivouac During the Late Unpleasantness." Houston Civil War Round Table, September 1973.

Winton, George Peterson, Jr. "Ante-Bellum Military Instruction of West Point Officers, and its Influence Upon Confederate Military Organization and Operations." Ph.D. Dissertation, University of South Carolina, 1972.

Interviews

Belcher, Margaret, La Marque, Texas. 17 September 1975; 21 February 1977.

Cabello, Sara A. Psychotherapist. Laredo, Texas, Interview, 3 September 1980.

Hughes, Richard, Psychologist. Laredo, Texas. Interview, 4 September 1980.

Correspondence

Finch, L. Boyd. Tucson, Arizona. Letter: 9 September 1983.

Hall, Martin H. Professor of History, University of Texas at Arlington. Various letters; September, 1972–October, 1978.

Persyn, Mary G. Assistant Social Sciences Librarian, Miami University, Oxford, Ohio. Letter; 17 December 1971.

Rapp. Kenneth W. Assistant Archivist, United States Military Academy, West Point, New York. Letter; 21 October 1971.

Sibley, Sylvan. Purchasing Agent. Northwest Louisiana State University. Various Letters; July 1975–October 1978.

Index